On agriculture, with a recension of the text and an English translation by Harrison Boyd Ash - Primary Source Edition

Columella, Lucius Junius Moderatus

LUCIUS JUNIUS MODERATUS COLUMELLA

ON AGRICULTURE

I

LUCIUS JUNIUS MODERATUS COLUMELLA

ON AGRICULTURE

IN THREE VOLUMES

I

RES RUSTICA I–IV

WITH A RECENSION OF THE TEXT AND AN ENGLISH TRANSLATION BY

HARRISON BOYD ASH, Ph.D.
ASSOCIATE PROFESSOR OF LATIN, UNIVERSITY OF PENNSYLVANIA

CAMBRIDGE, MASSACHUSETTS
HARVARD UNIVERSITY PRESS
LONDON
WILLIAM HEINEMANN LTD
MCMLX

First printed 1941
Reprinted 1948, 1960

Printed in Great Britain

CONTENTS

CONTENTS

THE ORIGINAL PREFACE TO VOL. I

The text here translated, for Books I–II, VI–VII, X–XI, and *De Arboribus*, is based on that of Lundström, with some changes in orthography, punctuation, and capitalization to conform more nearly to English and American usage. For the remaining six books the translator has attempted to construct a reasonably comparable text by the collation of five important manuscripts with the latest printed edition, that of Schneider (1794).

The translator is greatly indebted to the Faculty Research Fund of the University of Pennsylvania for a grant which made it possible for him to examine a number of Columella manuscripts abroad and to purchase photostatic copies of the four major codices. Grateful acknowledgment is made of the permission of the Trustees of the Pierpont Morgan Library to include the readings of the Morgan manuscript of Columella. The thanks of the writer are due also to his colleague Axel Johan Uppvall, Professor of Scandinavian Languages at the University of Pennsylvania, for the translation of numerous Swedish works.

A full index to this work of Columella will be supplied at the end of the third volume when issued.

Harrison Boyd Ash.

University of Pennsylvania
April 10, 1940

PREFATORY NOTE

Owing to the death of Dr. Harrison Boyd Ash of the University of Pennsylvania shortly after the publication of the first volume (Books I–IV) of the *De Re Rustica* of Columella, the Editors entrusted me with the remainder of the work.

There has been no complete modern edition of the text since J. G. Schneider's (Leipzig 1794), but the principles laid down by Dr. Ash appear to me to be entirely satisfactory. He describes them as follows: "The text and manuscript readings of the present edition, for Books I–II, VI–VII, X–XI and the *De Arboribus*, rest substantially on the work of Lundström. For Books III–V, VIII–IX and XII, the translator has attempted to construct a critical text in some approximation to that of Lundström by the collation of four major manuscripts with the text of Schneider." It was natural to conclude from these words that a text constructed by Dr. Ash would be available for the rest of the work, but no traces of the existence of such a text have been found in America. It has, therefore, been necessary to undertake the construction of a new text, and I have tried to conform as far as possible with Dr. Ash's system, using Lundström's edition for those books which he has edited and attempting a new text for Books V, VIII, IX and XII. For this purpose I have been fortunate, through the good offices of Professor L. A. Post, in obtaining from America photostats of the four most

important MSS. (see p. xx of Vol. I), which fall into two classes, (*a*) the two 9th–10th century MSS. and (*b*) the two best of the 15th-century MSS. The photostats, which were used by Dr Ash for his collation of Books III and IV, were purchased with a grant provided by the Faculty Research Fund of the University of Pennsylvania. The only point in which my text of these books differs from that of Dr. Ash is that I have not had an opportunity, which Dr. Ash had, of comparing my text with that of the MS. known as *Morganensis* 138, formerly *Hamiltonensis* 184 in the Pierpont Morgan Library in New York.

For some unexplained reason the text of Book V, especially Chapter VIII to the end, is in a worse condition than in any other part of the work, and there is the further complication that, from Chapter X to the end, the text, though slightly longer, is closely identical with that of *De Arboribus*, Chapter XVIII to the end. It seems certain that the *De Arboribus* is part of an earlier and shorter treatise which was afterwards superseded by the *De Re Rustica.* It is a question how far the text of these similar chapters in the *De Rustica* and the *De Arboribus* should be corrected from one another. There are numerous places in which the text of Book V is deficient or careless, and these can be corrected from the *De Arboribus*, but it also appears that the author made a good many verbal changes as well as inserting new matter. I have, therefore, refrained from making the two slightly different versions correspond exactly and have kept the MS. reading in both treatises where it makes sense—very often the same sense in slightly different

words—but the fact that there are these two versions has necessitated a larger *apparatus criticus* in these chapters of Book V than for any other part of the work.

I have to thank His Grace the Duke of Devonshire for lending me [M. C. Curtius], *L. Junius Moderatus Columella on Husbandry in Twelve Books and his Book concerning Trees* (London 1745) (a very rare work) from the Chatsworth Library, and Mademoiselle Hélène Rousseau for obtaining for me in Paris a copy of M. Nisard, *Les Agronomes Latins* (Paris, 1844), for which I had been searching for many months.

EDWARD S. FORSTER.

Upon the death of Professor Forster, the Editors of this Library entrusted to me the responsibility of completing the unfinished project. In the circumstances this assignment naturally extended to the making of a thorough examination of every aspect of the work. The photostats mentioned by my predecessor in the above lines were in due time returned to America and were fully utilized in the process of examination and study. In the checking between these manuscripts, as well as in the verification of references to important earlier editions of Columella, very substantial assistance was furnished to me by my wife, which I desire gratefully to acknowledge here. It is to be hoped that the process of restudying and reviewing has resulted in an improved product. It is always a serious thing to find yourself differing with another person on matters of a scholarly nature; to handle such materials when left

by the hand of one who is no longer able to speak in defence of his interpretation imposes many a delicate task. Naturally there are numerous passages in the text of Columella, and also in the English version, which I would have handled somewhat differently from the manner in which they were treated by my predecessor if I had been free to shape things *de novo*. However, this statement applies rather to materials involving the factors of taste and judgment than to those where the essential thought was an issue.

The reader might be reminded of the Bibliography prepared by the late Professor Ash and included in Vol. I of this Library. The works pertaining to Columella that are there cited were obviously made use of by Professor Forster, as they were also utilized by me.

EDWARD H. HEFFNER.

INTRODUCTION[1]

Life and Works of Columella

Our knowledge of the personal history of Lucius Junius Moderatus Columella, and of the dates of his writings, has been derived almost entirely by conjecture from those incidental references which he makes, at various places in his works, to himself and his contemporaries.[2] From these sources we learn that he was a native of Gades (Cadiz),[3] a Roman *municipium* of the province of Baetica in southern Spain; and although the date of his birth is unknown, it is obvious that he was born near the beginning of the first century of our era.

Columella defines his period loosely by his mention of Marcus Varro (*circa* 116–27 B.C.) as a contemporary of his grandfather.[4] His time is more clearly indicated in a reference to Seneca[5] as living in his day; so, too, he speaks of Cornelius Celsus[6] (*fl.* 1st cent. A.D.) as a contemporary. He also quotes as

[1] Taken in part from H. B. Ash, *L. Iuni Moderati Columellae Rei Rusticae Liber Decimus: De Cultu Hortorum*, Philadelphia, 1930.

[2] Biographers have added but little to the facts first deduced by Filippo Beroaldo (1453–1505), *In Libros XIII Columellae Annotationes*, and printed in several of the early editions. *Cf.* Barbaret, *De Columellae Vita et Scriptis* (Nancy, 1887), p. 9.

[3] VIII. 16. 9; X. 185. [4] I *Praef.* 15 [5] III. 3. 3.

[6] I. 1. 14; III. 1. 8; III. 2. 31; III. 17. 4; IV. 1. 1. Celsus is thought by Cichorius (*Röm. Stud.*, 1922, pp. 411–417) to have written his agricultural treatise A.D. 25–26.

authorities of his time several others of whom we have definite knowledge, as Trebellius,[1] Graecinus,[2] Julius Atticus,[3] Volusius,[4] and Gallio.[5] From these and other references [6] it is clear that Columella was living during the time of Lucius Annaeus Seneca (*circa* 4 B.C.–A.D. 65) and Pliny the Elder (23–79), by whom he is quoted, and that he was of about the same age as the former and several years older than the latter. We have reason to believe, from the conclusion of Book XII,[7] that his work was completed when he was well advanced in years.[8]

[1] V. 1. 2. M. Trebellius, *legatus* of Vitellius (Tac. *Ann.* VI. 41. 1), was governor of Syria A.D. 36.

[2] I. 1. 14; IV. 3. 6. Julius Graecinus was put to death under Caligula (Tac. *Agr.* 4) in 39 or 40.

[3] IV. 1. 1; IV. 8. 1. Nothing more is known of Julius Atticus than is found in Columella's scattered references to him as a contemporary of Celsus. Reitzenstein (*De Scriptorum Rei Rusticae Libris Deperditis*, p. 27) concludes from this evidence that he was somewhat older than Celsus and that he wrote in the time of Tiberius.

[4] I. 7. 3. The Lucius Volusius mentioned by Pliny (*N.H.* VII. 49), who died A.D. 56 at the age of ninety-three; *cf.* Tac. *Ann.* XIII. 30, XIV. 56.

[5] IX. 16. 2. Gallio, brother of the younger Seneca, died A.D. 65.

[6] Collected by Reitzenstein *op. cit.*, pp. 52f. [7] XII. 59. 5.

[8] Reitzenstein (*op. cit.*, p. 31; *cf.* Becher, *op. cit.*, p. 11) inclines to the view that the works of Columella appeared in the year 64, and certainly not before 61, basing his argument on the late date of Seneca's ownership of the Nomentan farm (III. 3. 3), which, as Pliny writes (*N.H.* XIV. 45, 49) in A.D. 77, was bought by Remmius Palaemon *in hisce viginti annis* and sold to Seneca within ten years. Haussner (*Die handschriftliche Ueberlieferung des . . . Columella*, p. 7), carrying the question further, places the date of Seneca's purchase in 62 or 63, the composition of Columella's third book between that date and the year of Seneca's death (65), and the publication of the whole work after 65.

The parents of Columella are named nowhere in his works, but he speaks often and with the greatest respect of an uncle, Marcus Columella,[1] an expert farmer of the Baetic province, in whose company much of his youth appears to have been spent. The Pythagorean philosopher, Moderatus of Gades, mentioned by Plutarch,[2] may have been a relative.

It is likewise uncertain at what time Columella left his native Spain to take up residence in the neighbourhood of Rome. But here, *in hoc Latio et Saturnia terra*,[3] he seems to have spent the greater part of his life, owning at various times farms at Carseoli, Ardea, and Albanum, in Latium,[4] and a farm which he called *Ceretanum*,[5] located perhaps at Caere in Etruria. We have evidence [6] that he visited Syria and Cilicia at some period in his life; and from an inscription [7]

L. IVNIO L. F. GAL.

MODERATO

COLVMELLAE

TRIB. MIL. LEG. VI. FERRATAE

found at Tarentum we may assume that he was then in military service, since his native town of Gades

[1] II. 15. 4; VII. 2. 4; XII. 21. 4; XII. 40. 2; XII. 43. 5; *et al.*

[2] *Quaest.* VIII. 7. 1.

[3] I. *Praef.* 20.

[4] III. 9. 2.

[5] III. 3. 3. *Cf.* Wilhelm Becher, "Das Caeretanum des L. Iunius Moderatus Columella," *Philologisch-historische Beitrage*, Kurt Wachsmuth (1897), pp. 186–191.

[6] II. 10. 18. Perhaps in A.D. 36, under Trebellius; *cf.* Cichorius, *op. cit.*, pp. 417–422.

[7] *C.I.L.* IX. 235 (= Dessau 2923).

belonged to the *tribus Galeria*, which furnished troops for the *LEGIO VI FERRATA*, stationed at that time in Syria.[1] From this inscription it is generally believed that Columella died and was buried at Tarentum.

Columella is known to us by the twelve books of his *Res Rustica* and the book *De Arboribus*. Cassiodorus,[2] however, mentions sixteen books of his authorship, a number thought by some [3] to have been due to an error of transcription, but defended by others,[4] who hold the opinion that the larger work is an expansion of an earlier manual of three or four books on the same subject, of which only the second,[5] *De Arboribus*, has survived. This view is supported by the fact that the book on trees deals with the same subjects that are discussed at greater length in Books III–V of the *Res Rustica*. The *De Arboribus* appears in the manuscripts and first printed editions as the third book of the whole work, so that the book now properly marked as the third stands in the

[1] The legion was stationed in Syria in A.D. 23 and remained there during the rule of Tiberius; *cf.* H. M. D. Parker, *The Roman Legions* (Oxford, 1928), pp. 119, 129, 267.

[2] *Div. Lect.* 28, sed Columella xvi libris per diversas agriculturae species eloquens ac facundus illabitur, disertis potius quam imperitis accommodus, ut operis eius studiosi non solum communi fructu, sed etiam gratissimis epulis expleantur.

[3] *Cf.* Becher, *De Col. Vit. et Scr.*, p. 58; M. L. W. Laistner in *Am. Jour. Phil.* LIX. 116.

[4] *Cf.* Gesner, *Script. Rei Rust.*, Introd., p. 9; Haussner, *op. cit.*, p. 7; Becher, *op. cit.*, p. 29.

[5] That one book preceded is evident from *De. Arb.* 1. 1, Quoniam de cultu agrorum abunde primo volumine praecepisse videmur, non intempestiva erit arborum virgultorumque cura.

earliest editions as the fourth, and so on.[1] Mention is made of a work *Adversus Astrologos*[2] and to a treatise proposed, but possibly not written, on the religious ceremonies connected with agriculture.[3]

The *Res Rustica*, addressed to a certain Publius Silvinus,[4] is the most comprehensive and systematic of all treatises of Roman writers on agricultural affairs. The first book contains general directions regarding the choice of land, the water supply, the arrangement of farm buildings, and the distribution of various tasks among the farm staff. The second deals with agriculture proper, the ploughing and enrichment of the soil, and the care of various crops. The third, fourth, and fifth books are devoted to the cultivation, grafting, and pruning of fruit trees and shrubs, the vine, and the olive. The sixth contains instructions for selecting, breeding, and rearing cattle, horses, and mules, together with a discourse on veterinary medicine. The seventh continues the subject with reference to smaller domestic animals, sheep, goats, swine, and dogs. The eighth has to do with the management of poultry and fish-ponds. The ninth treats similarly of bees. The tenth, an experiment in hexameters to satisfy the request of Gallio and of Silvinus for "a taste of

[1] That the book on trees does not belong to the larger work is evident from the fact that it is not addressed to Silvinus, as are the other twelve, and from statements in later books of the *Res Rustica* giving an exact accounting of the number of books preceding, *e.g.* X. *Praef.* 1; VIII. 1. 1; XI. 1. 2; XII. 13. 1. Iucundus, editor of the first Aldine edition (1514), was the first to set the misplaced *De Arboribus* at the end, as a thirteenth book, and all later editors have followed his example.

[2] XI. 1. 31. [3] II. 21. 5–6.

[4] Known only from Columella's numerous references to him, but obviously a countryman and a neighbour of the author.

metrical composition,"[1] deals with gardening, as a sort of supplement to Vergil's fourth *Georgic*. It is evident from a statement in the preface to the whole work,[2] as well as from the conclusion of Book IX[3] and the Preface of Book X,[4] that the tenth book was intended to complete the work; but at the still insistent urgings of Silvinus[5] there was added an eleventh book containing a discussion of the duties of a farm overseer, a *Calendarium Rusticum*, in which the times and seasons for various kinds of farm labour are fixed in connection with the risings and settings of the stars, and a long chapter on gardening to supplement the treatise in verse. The twelfth book, written for the overseer's wife and defining her special duties, contains recipes for the manufacture of various kinds of wine and for the pickling and preserving of vegetables and fruits. That the twelve books were sent to Silvinus one by one as they were completed, and that they have been transmitted to us in the order written, is indicated by the fact that their opening or closing lines usually contain some reference to comments on the book just preceding or to the subject matter of the book that is to follow.

The *De Arboribus*, thought to have been addressed to Eprius Marcellus,[6] deals with the cultivation and

[1] XI. 1. 2; *cf.* IX. 16. 2; X. *Praef.* 1, 3.
[2] I. *Praef.* 25–28. [3] IX. 16. 2. [4] X. *Praef.* 1.
[5] XI. 1. 2.
[6] This supposition has resulted from a colophon in the manuscripts, found after a long table of contents following Bk. XI (XII): *Praeter hos duodecim libros singularis eius liber ad Eprium Marcellum.* Eprius Marcellus was appointed to a vacant praetorship in 49 A.D., which expired at the end of a few days or hours (Tac. *Ann.* XII. 4). He later became an informer under Nero.

propagation of the vine, the olive, and various trees; and, while its subject matter is treated more fully in the *Res Rustica*, the work is still of considerable interest and value in that it throws some light on the larger and later work, especially on the corrupt manuscript text of the fifth book.

The works of Columella, though comparatively neglected since the eighteenth century, have held an important place in their special field. The author is cited by his contemporary Pliny among authorities for his work on natural history.[1] The veterinarian Pelagonius, who wrote before the time of Vegetius (fourth century), often quotes verbatim precepts from Columella's sixth book;[2] so often Eumelus, a Greek writer on the veterinary art.[3] Vegetius praises his *facultas dicendi*.[4] He is much quoted in the fourth-century *De Re Rustica* of Palladius,[5] who seems also to have been inspired by Columella's metrical *De Cultu Hortorum* to write his last book, *De Insitione*, in verse. Cassiodorus[6] of the sixth century mentions him as one of the outstanding writers on agriculture, as also does Isidore[7] in the seventh century. The *Hortulus* of Walafrid Strabo (*circa* 809–849), in 443 hexameters, may owe something to Columella's

[1] *E.g.*, Pliny, *N.H.* VIII. 153; XV. 17–19, 66; XVII. 51–52, 137, 162; XVIII. 70, 303; XIX. 68.

[2] Ihm lists seventeen parallel passages in the index of his Teubner edition of Pelagonius, *Artis Veterinariae quae exstant*, p. 241.

[3] Ihm, *op. cit.*, p. 7.

[4] Vegetius, *Ars Veterinaria*, *Praef.* 2.

[5] Becher (*op. cit.*, p. 55) finds twenty-five such citations.

[6] *Div. Lect.* 28; see page xii, note 2, above.

[7] *Orig.* XVII. 1. 1, *Columella, insignis orator, qui totum corpus disciplinae eiusdem complexus est.*

versified treatise on gardening.[1] He is praised in the sixteenth century in an epigram of Theodore Beza;[2] and in the next century Milton, in his short treatise *On Education*, would have the students of his ideal school devote their thoughts, "after evening repast till bed-time," first to the Scriptures and next to "the authors of agriculture, Cato, Varro, and Columella, for the matter is easy; and if the language is difficult, so much the better." "Here," he adds, "will be an occasion of inciting and enabling them hereafter to improve the tillage of their country, to recover bad soil," etc.

Manuscripts and Editions

The manuscripts of Columella fall into two groups. Oldest and best are:

Cod. Sangermanensis Petropolitanus 207, now *Cl. L. F. v. N.* 1 (= *S*), fol. 138, 9th cent., in the State Library at Leningrad. Written apparently at Corbie, and taken with a large collection of Corbie manuscripts to the Abbey of St. Germain des Prés in Paris during the first half of the seventeenth century. Removed, with many other valuable manuscripts, during the French Revolution by the Russian envoy Dubrowsky to the Imperial Library in Petrograd.

Cod. Ambrosianus L 85 *sup.* (= *A*), fol. 252, 9th–10th

[1] *Cf.* V. Lundström, "Walahfrid Strabus och Columella," *Eranos* XXX. 124–127; M. Manitius in *Philologus* XLVIII. 566.

[2]
Orphea mirata est Rhodope sua fata canentem,
Si modo Vergilii carmina pondus habent.
Tu vero, Iuni, silvestris rura canendo
Post te ipsas urbes in tua rura trahis.
O superi, quales habuit tunc Roma Quirites,
Quum tam iucundum cerneret agricolam.

cents., in the Ambrosian Library in Milan. Written in the German Insular hand, probably at Fulda. Closely related to *S*.

Added to these are some twenty fifteenth-century manuscripts, known collectively as *R*, all related and thought to be descended, directly or indirectly, from an ancient manuscript found by Poggio Bracciolini (1380–1459) and taken by him to Italy. Outstanding members of this fifteenth-century family are:

Cod. Laurentianus plut. 53.32 (= *a*), fol. 172, in the Laurentian Library at Florence.

Cod. Brerensis Mediolanus A.D. XV. 4 (= *b*), folia not numbered, in the Brera Library, Milan.

Cod. Caesenas Malatestianus plut. 24.2 (= *c*), fol. 218, in the Malatesta Library at Cesena. Contains the agricultural works of Cato, Columella, and Varro.

Cod. Laurentianus Conv. Suppr. 285 (= *d*), in the Laurentian Library.

Less important are: *Vallicellianus* E 39 (= *g*); *Laurentianus* plut. 53.24 (= *k*); *Lipsiensis Bibl. Comm.* rep. I f. 13 (= *l*); *Venetus Marcianus* 462 (= *m*), which often agrees with *b*; *Laurentianus* plut. 53.27 (= *p*); *Laurentianus* plut. 91.6 inf. (= *q*), often agreeing with *c*; *Vaticanus* lat. 1525 (= *r*); *Laurentianus-Strozzianus* 69 (= *s*); *Bononiensis* 2523 (= *t*); *Urbino-Vaticanus* 260 (= *u*); *Vaticanus* lat. 1526 (= *v*); *Vaticanus* lat. 1524 (= *w*); *Vaticanus* lat. 1527 (= *y*); *Parisinus* lat 6830 A (= *ä*); *Parisinus* lat. 6830 B (= *ö*); *Parisinus* lat. 6830 C (= *ü*); *Mosquensis Demidovianus* (= *μ*), now lost.[1]

[1] The *Codex Mosquensis*, seen by Matthaei in the library of the Demidoffs in Moscow, was destroyed by fire in 1812. Its readings are preserved in C. F. Matthaei, *Lectiones Mosquenses*, Vol. I, Leipzig, 1779.

All the manuscripts listed above were known and used by Lundström in his editions of *Res Rustica*, Books I–II, VI–VII, X–XI, and *De Arboribus*, and their readings are given in his *apparatus criticus*.[1] Those to which he and others have attached greatest importance,[2] especially *S*, *A*, *a*, *b*, *c*, *d*, were collated by him or by his associates, Langlet and Stroemberg, with particular care. His readings of less important codices are given with correspondingly less fullness. More than half of the total number of manuscripts were evaluated and collated by Häussner for his edition of Book X, *De Cultu Hortorum*.[3] The present translator has examined a number of the best manuscripts in their respective libraries, and has collated *S*, *A*, *a*, *c* with Schneider's text for Books III–V, VIII–IX, and XII. In addition he has compared with the texts and apparatuses of Lundström and of Schneider the readings of *Morganensis* 138, olim *Hamiltonensis* 184 (= *M*), a beautiful piece of Roman writing signed and dated by Henriettus Rufinus de Murialdo in the year 1469 and now in possession of The Pierpont Morgan Library, New York City.

That the two oldest manuscripts, *S* and *A*, are derived from the same archetype is generally agreed It is more difficult, however, to determine the re-

[1] See p. xx, n. 1. The recent edition of Books VI–VII includes readings of ten additional MSS. of the *R* family, and of three MSS. of the 11th and 14th centuries containing excerpts from these books.

[2] Lundström rates *a*, *b*, *c*, *d*, *m*, *q*, *s* as best of the fifteenth-century class. *Cf.* his "Ein Columella-Excerptor aus dem 15. Jahrhundert," *Skrifter utgifna af Humanistiska Vetenskapssamfundet i Upsala* (Upsala, 1894), III 6 11; and *L. Iuni Moderati Columellae opera quae exstant*, fasc. 1 (Upsala, 1897), *Praef.* viii–x.

[3] See p. xxi, n. 1.

lationship of *R*, the fifteenth-century group, to *S* and *A*. Van Buren [1] thinks the *R* family to be descended from *A*, to which they often bear close resemblance when *S* and *A* differ. The most recent and thorough treatment of the manuscript tradition is that of Sobel,[2] whose ingenious and carefully constructed stemma [3] shows, through a series of lost archetypes, the descent of representative members of the *R* class from a common ancestor (Sobel's *β*); the relationship of *A* to *R* through a better line of descent from the same early ancestor; the descent of *S* and *A* from a common archetype, *S* inheriting the better readings through an intermediary copy of mixed parentage; and the descent of them all from an ultimate archetype (Sobel's ω) written after the fifth century. The vexed question as to how and when the *De Arboribus* became inserted in the *Res Rustica* is likewise discussed by Sobel.[4]

Columella's works were edited many times in the century following the introduction of printing, usually in company with Cato, Varro, and Palladius.[5] The *editio princeps*, edited by George Merula, was printed at Venice by Nicolas Jenson, in a collection of *Rei Rusticae Scriptores*, in the year 1472. This was

[1] A. W. Van Buren, "The Text of Columella," *Suppl. Papers of the Am. Sch. of Class. Stud. in Rome*, Vol. I, pp. 189–190.

[2] Ragnar Sobel, *Studia Columelliana Palaeographica et Critica*, Goteborg, 1928.

[3] *Op. cit.*, p. 15.

[4] *Op. cit.*, pp. 15–21. *Cf.* J. Trotsky, "Studien zur Ueberlieferungsgeschichte Columellas," *Raccolta . . . Ramorino* (Pubblicazioni della Università Cattolica del Sacro Cuore, Vol. VII, Milano), p. 449f

[5] Only the most important editions are here named. For a full account of the early editions, see Schneider's *Rei Rusticae Scriptores*, Vol. II. 2, pp. 5–15, and Vol. IV. 1, pp. 73–80.

followed by the Bruschian edition, published at Reggio in 1482. The edition of the Veronese architect, Iucundus, came from the press of Aldus Manutius at Venice in 1514. This, the first Aldine edition, showed a wider acquaintance with the manuscripts, and restored the twelve books of the *Res Rustica* to their proper numerical order. A second Aldine edition, of no additional importance, appeared in 1533. The most noteworthy annotated editions of the complete works are found in the *Scriptores Rei Rusticae Veteres Latini* of J. M. Gesner, printed at Leipzig in 1735, reprinted by Ernesti in 1773 with the readings of the Sangermanensis Ms.; and in the *Scriptores Rei Rusticae Veteres Latini* of J. G. Schneider, which appeared at Leipzig during the years 1794–1796. The edition of Schneider takes account of all earlier works and is still the most valuable complete edition that we possess. No modern critical edition of the entire work of Columella has been produced, although the eminent Swedish scholar, Vilhelm Lundström, has made a notable start in that direction with the publication of seven of the thirteen books.[1] The poem on gardening (Book X) has been included in a few annotated editions of *Poetae Latini Minores*, of which Wernsdorf's (1794), reproduced with few changes in Lemaire's recension (*Bibliotheca Classica Latina*, Vol. VII, Paris, 1826), is the best. In more recent times the tenth book, with text and critical apparatus only, has been edited separately by

[1] V. Lundström, *L. Iuni Moderati Columellae opera quae exstant*: fasc 1 (*De Arboribus*), Upsala, 1897; fasc. 6 (Bk. X), Upsala, 1902; fasc. 7 (Bk. XI), Upsala, 1906; fasc. 2 (Bks. I–II), Göteborg, 1917; fasc. 4 (Bks VI–VII), Göteborg, 1940.

Häussner,[1] by Lundström, and by Postgate,[2] whose critical apparatus is an abridgement of the manuscript variants published by Häussner and Lundström. Modern contributors to Columelliana, many of them pupils of Lundström, include in addition to those above mentioned the names of M. Ahle, P. Kottman, W. Koller, R. Pomoell, J. Svennung, T. Kleberg, G. Nystrom, F. Prix, H. Linde, N. Dahllöf, E. Weiss, C. Brakman, E. Stettner, G. Helmreich, P. G. Krauss, and Lizzie B. Marshall.

The text and manuscript readings of the present volume rest, for Books I–II, substantially on the work of Lundström. For Books III–IV, the translator has attempted to construct a critical text in some approximation to that of Lundström by the collation of four major manuscripts with the text of Schneider. He has also added throughout important conjectures and divergences of reading of other editors and commentators, together with the variants of the Morgan Ms. Major departures from the respective texts of Lundström and of Schneider are noted. The sigla of Lundström are preserved.

[1] J. Haussner, *Die handschriftliche Ueberlieferung des L. Junius Moderatus Columella, mit einer kritischen Ausgabe des X. Buches*, Karlsruhe, 1889.

[2] J. P. Postgate, *Corpus Poetarum Latinorum*, London, 1905, Vol. II, pp. 206–209.

BIBLIOGRAPHY

Principal Editions

Editio princeps. Venetiis apud Nicolaum Jensonum, 1472.

Editio secunda. Regii, opera et impensis Bartholomaei Bruschii, 1482.

Iucundi Veronensis editio *De Re Rustica*, Venetiis apud Aldum, 1514.

Gesner, J. M., *Scriptores Rei Rusticae Veteres Latini*, Leipzig, 1735.

Schneider, J. G., *Scriptores Rei Rusticae Veteres Latini*, Vol. II, Leipzig, 1794.

Lundström, V., *L. Iuni Moderati Columellae opera quae exstant*: fasc. 1 (*De Arb.*), Upsala, 1897; fasc. 6 (Bk. X), Upsala, 1902; fasc. 7 (Bk. XI), Upsala, 1906; fasc. 2 (Bks. I–II), Göteborg, 1917; fasc. 4 (Bks. VI–VII), Göteborg, 1940.

Manuscripts and Text

Ahle, M., *Sprachliche und kritische Untersuchungen zu Columella* (Diss. Würzburg), Munich, 1915.

Brakman, C., "Ad Columellae librum decimum," *Mnemosyne*, LX. 107–112.

Häussner, J., *Die handschriftliche Ueberlieferung des L. Junius Moderatus Columella, mit einer kritischen Ausgabe des X. Buches*, Karlsruhe, 1889.

Kleberg, T., "Några textkritiska anmärkninger till Columellas nionde bok," *Eranos*, XXXV. 22–31.

Langlet, V., " Ad Columellae Codicem Sangermanensem qui vocatur," *Eranos*, I. 86–94.
Linde, H., *Studier till Columellas nionde bok* (Diss.), Göteborg, 1936.
Lundström, V., " Ein Columella-Excerptor aus dem 15. Jahrhundert," *Skrifter utgifna af Humanistiska Vetenskapssamfundet i Upsala*, III. 6, Upsala, 1894.
Lundström, V., " Emendationes in Columellam," *Eranos*, I. 38–47, 86–94, 169–180; II. 49–59; IV. 181–186; VII. 73–77.
Lundström, V., " De nyaste textkritiska bidragen till Columellas tionde bok," *Eranos*, VI. 66—71.
Pomoell, R., *Textkritiska Studier till Columellas femte bok* (Diss.), Göteborg, 1931.
Postgate, J. P., " The Moscow Manuscript of Columella," *Classical Review*, XVII. 47.
Schmitt, J. C., " De Codice Sangermanensi," *Festschrift für Ludw. Urlichs*, Würzburg, 1880, 139–162.
Sobel, Ragnar, *Studia Columelliana Palaeographica et Critica* (Diss.), Göteborg, 1928.
Svennung, J., " De Columella per Palladium emendato," *Eranos*, XXVI. 145–208.
Trotzky, J., " Studien zur Ueberlieferungsgeschichte Columellas," *Raccolta di Scritti in onore di Felice Ramorino*, Pubblicazioni della Università Cattolica del Sacro Cuore (Milan), VII. 449f.
Trotzky, J., " Kritische Beiträge zum 5. Buch von Columellas *De Re Rustica*," *Mélanges Tolstoi*, 46–51, Leningrad Academy of Science, 1928.
Van Buren, A. W., " The Text of Columella," *Supplementary Papers of the American School of Classical Studies in Rome*, I. 157–190.

BIBLIOGRAPHY

Translations

Curtius, M. C., *L. Iunius Moderatus Columella of Husbandry in Twelve Books and His Book Concerning Trees*, London, 1745.

DuBois, Louis, *L'économie rurale de Columelle*, Bibliothèque Latine-Française, Vol. III, Paris, 1844–1845.

Löffler, Karl, *L. Junius Moderatus Columella De Re Rustica*, übersetzt durch Heinrich Oesterreicher, Abt von Schussenried. A late 15th cent. translation of some early edition, published in *Bibliothek des litterarischen Verein in Stuttgart*, Vols. CCLXIII–CCLXIV, Tübingen, 1914.

Nisard, M., *Les agronomes latins, Caton, Varron, Columelle, Palladius*, Paris, 1844.

Tinajero, Vicente, *Los doce libros de agricultura de Lucio Junio Moderato Columella*, 2 vols., Madrid, 1880.

Miscellaneous

Barbaret, V., *De Columellae Vita et Scriptis*, Nancy, 1887.

Becher, Wilhelm, *De L. Iuni Moderati Columellae Vita et Scriptis* Leipzig, 1897.

Billiard, Raymond, *La vigne dans l'antiquité*, Lyons, 1913.

Billiard, Raymond, *L'agriculture dans l'antiquité d'après les Géorgiques de Virgile*, Paris. 1928.

Brehaut, Ernest, *Cato the Censor on Farming*, New York, 1933.

Carl, G., *Die Agrarlehre Columellas in soziologischer Betrachtung* (Diss.), Heidelberg, 1925.

Cichorius, Conrad, "Zur Biographie Columellas," *Römische Studien*, 417–422, Leipzig–Berlin, 1922.

Dahllöf, N., *Tempora och modi hos Columella* (Diss.), Göteborg, 1931.

Daubeny, Charles, *Lectures on Roman Husbandry*, Oxford, 1857.

Dickson, Adam, *The Husbandry of the Ancients*, Edinburgh, 1788.

Frank, Tenney, *An Economic Survey of Ancient Rome*, Vol. V, Baltimore, 1940.

Heitland, W. E., *Agricola*: A Study of Agriculture and Rustic Life in the Graeco-Roman World from the Point of View of Labour, Cambridge, 1921.

Hooper, W. D., and H. B. Ash, *Cato and Varro De Re Rustica* (Loeb Classical Library), London, and Cambridge, Mass., 1934.

Klek, J., and L. Armbruster, *Columella und Plinius, Die Bienenkunde der Römer*, Freiburg, 1921.

Koller, W., *Die Tierheilkunde nach Columella* (Diss.), Munich, 1925.

Kottman, P., *De Elocutione L. Junii Moderati Columellae*, Rottweil, 1903.

Krauss, P. G., *Die Quellen des Columella*, Münnerstadt, 1907.

Lundström, V., "Småplock ur Columellas sprak," *Eranos*, XIII. 196–203; XIV. 90–96; XV. 201–207; XVI. 186–190; XVII. 147–150; XXVI. 31–33.

Marshall, Lizzie B., *L'horticulture antique et le poème de Columelle*, Paris, 1918.

Nystrom, G., *Variatio Sermonis hos Columella* (Diss.), Göteborg, 1926.

Orth, F., *Der Feldbau der Römer*, Frankfurt, 1900.

Reitzenstein, R., *De Scriptorum Rei Rusticae Libris Deperditis* (Diss.), Berlin, 1884.

BIBLIOGRAPHY

Schroeter, W., *De Columella Vergilii Imitatore*, Jena, 1882.

Semple, Ellen C., "Ancient Mediterranean Agriculture," *Agricultural History*, II (1928). 61–98, 129–156.

Storr-Best, Lloyd, *Varro on Farming* (Bohn Library), London, 1912.

Stettner, E., *De L. Iunio Moderato Columella Vergilii Imitatore*, Triest, 1894.

Weiss, E., *De Columella et Varrone Rerum Rusticarum Scriptoribus*, Breslau, 1911.

The titles of many useful reference works on general agriculture, viticulture, animal husbandry, veterinary medicine, botany, etc, are omitted altogether or mentioned only in the notes.

SIGLA

S = Cod. Sangermanensis Petropolitanus 207, now Cl. L. F. v. N. 1 (9th cent.).
A = Cod. Ambrosianus L 85 sup. (9th–10th cents.).
R = all or the consensus of 15th cent. MSS.
  a = Cod. Laurentianus plut. 53. 32.
  c = Cod. Caesenas Malatestianus plut. 24. 2.
  M = Morganensis 138, formerly Hamiltonensis 184.
vett. edd. = the two earliest editions.
  ed. pr. = editio princeps (Jensoniana), Venice, 1472.
  Brusch. = editio secunda (Bruschiana), Reggio, 1482.
Ald. = the first Aldine edition, Venice, 1514.
Gesn. = J. M. Gesner, *Script. Rei Rust.*, Leipzig, 1735.
Schn. = J. G. Schneider, *Script. Rei Rust.*, Leipzig, 1794.
Lundström = V. Lundström, *L. Iun. Mod. Colum. Lib. I–II, VI–VII, X–XI, De Arb.*, Upsala-Göteborg, 1897–1940.

For a full list of manuscripts and early editions, see under Manuscripts and Editions in the Introduction.

LUCIUS JUNIUS MODERATUS COLUMELLA

ON AGRICULTURE

L. IUNI MODERATI COLUMELLAE

REI RUSTICAE

LIBER I

PRAEFATIO

Saepenumero civitatis nostrae principes audio culpantes modo agrorum infecunditatem, modo caeli per multa iam tempora noxiam frugibus intemperiem; quosdam etiam praedictas querimonias velut ratione certa mitigantes, quod existiment ubertate nimia prioris aevi defatigatum et effetum[1] solum nequire pristina benignitate praebere mortalibus alimenta.
2 Quas ego causas, P.[2] Silvine, procul a veritate abesse certum habeo, quod neque fas est existimare rerum[3] Naturam, quam primus ille mundi genitor perpetua fecunditate donavit, quasi quodam morbo sterilitate adfectam; neque prudentis est credere Tellurem, quae divinam et aeternam iuventam sortita com-

[1] effectum *R.* [2] *om. R.* [3] humi *R.*

---

[a] An Epicurean theory; *cf.*, *e.g.*, Lucretius, II. 1150–1174. Columella holds to the Aristotelian theory.

LUCIUS JUNIUS MODERATUS COLUMELLA

ON AGRICULTURE

BOOK I

PREFACE

Again and again I hear leading men of our state condemning now the unfruitfulness of the soil, now the inclemency of the climate for some seasons past, as harmful to crops; and some I hear reconciling the aforesaid complaints, as if on well-founded reasoning, on the ground that, in their opinion, the soil was worn out and exhausted by the over-production of earlier days and can no longer furnish sustenance to mortals with its old-time benevolence.[a] Such 2
reasons, Publius Silvinus,[b] I am convinced are far from the truth; for it is a sin to suppose that Nature, endowed with perennial fertility by the creator of the universe, is affected with barrenness as though with some disease; and it is unbecoming to a man of good judgment to believe that Earth, to whose lot was assigned a divine and everlasting youth, and who is called the common mother

[b] See Introduction p. xiii.

munis omnium parens dicta sit, quia et cuncta peperit semper et deinceps paritura sit, velut hominem
3 consenuisse. Nec post haec reor violentia[1] caeli nobis ista, sed nostro potius accidere vitio, qui rem rusticam pessimo cuique servorum velut carnifici noxae dedimus, quam maiorum nostrorum optimus quisque et optime tractaverat.[2]

Atque ego satis mirari non possum, quid ita dicendi cupidi seligant oratorem, cuius imitentur eloquentiam; mensurarum et numerorum modum rimantes placitae disciplinae consectentur magistrum; vocis et cantus modulatorem nec minus corporis gesticulatorem scrupulosissime requirant saltationis ac musicae
4 rationis studiosi; iam qui aedificare velint, fabros et architectos advocent; qui navigia mari concredere, gubernandi peritos; qui bella moliri, armorum et militiae gnaros; et ne singula persequar, ei studio, quod quis agere velit, consultissimum rectorem adhibeat; denique animi sibi quisque formatorem praeceptoremque virtutis e coetu sapientium arcessat: sola res rustica, quae sine dubitatione proxima et quasi consanguinea sapientiae est, tam discenti-
5 bus egeat quam magistris. Adhuc enim scholas rhetorum et, ut dixi, geometrarum musicorumque

[1] violentia *SA*, *Lundström*: intemperantia *R*, *plerique edd.*
[2] tractaverit *R*, *plerique edd.*

---

[a] *Cf.* Lucretius, V. 826–827, *sed quia finem aliquam pariendi debet habere, destitit ut mulier spatio defessa vetusto.*

[b] So Pliny (*N.H.* XVIII. 19–21), who attributes the former plenty to cultivation of the soil by the hands of generals, consuls, tribunes, and senators.

of all things—because she has always brought forth all things and is destined to bring them forth continuously—has grown old in mortal fashion.[a] And, 3
furthermore, I do not believe that such misfortunes come upon us as a result of the fury of the elements, but rather because of our own fault; for the matter of husbandry, which all the best of our ancestors had treated with the best of care, we have delivered over to all the worst of our slaves, as if to a hangman for punishment.[b]

As for me, I cannot cease to wonder why those who wish to become speakers are so careful in the choosing of an orator whose eloquence they may imitate; those who investigate the science of surveying and mathematics emulate a master of the art of their choice; those who devote themselves to the study of dancing and music are most scrupulous in their search for one to teach modulation of the speaking and singing voice, and no less for an instructor in graceful movement of the body; even 4
those who wish to build call in joiners and master-builders; those who would entrust ships to the sea send for skilful pilots; those who make preparations for war call for men practised in arms and in campaigning; and, not to go through the list one by one, for any study which one wishes to pursue he employs the most expert director; in short, everyone summons from the company of the wise a man to mould his intellect and instruct him in the precepts of virtue; but agriculture alone, which is without doubt most closely related and, as it were, own sister to wisdom, is as destitute of learners as of teachers. For 5
that there are to this day schools for rhetoricians and, as I have said, for mathematicians and musicians,

vel, quod magis mirandum est, contemptissimorum vitiorum officinas, gulosius condiendi cibos et luxuriosius fercula [1] struendi, capitumque et capillorum concinnatores non solum esse audivi, sed et ipse vidi: agricolationis neque doctores, qui se profite-
6 rentur,[2] neque discipulos cognovi. Cum etiam si praedictarum artium professoribus civitas egeret, tamen, sicut apud priscos florere posset res publica [3] —nam sine ludicris artibus atque etiam sine causidicis olim satis felices fuerunt [4] futuraeque sunt urbes; at sine agri cultoribus nec consistere mortales nec ali posse manifestum est.

7 Quo magis prodigio [5] simile est, quod accidit, ut res corporibus nostris vitaeque utilitati maxime conveniens minimam [6] usque in hoc tempus consummationem haberet idque sperneretur genus amplificandi relinquendique [7] patrimonii, quod omni crimine caret. Nam cetera diversa et quasi repugnantia dissident a iustitia, nisi aequius existimamus cepisse praedam ex militia, quae nobis nihil sine
8 sanguine et cladibus alienis adfert. An bellum perosis [8] maris et negotiationis alea [9] sit optabilior, ut rupto naturae foedere terrestre animal homo ventorum et maris obiectus irae fluctibus pendeat [10]

[1] fericula *S, Lundström.*
[2] profitentur *M.*
[3] res prima *SA*[1].
[4] fuere *R, plerique edd.*
[5] prodigio *codd., Lundström*: prodigii *vulgo.*
[6] minime *Schn. cum Pontedera.*
[7] retinendique *R, Ald., Gesn.*
[8] perosis *vulgo*: per obsessa *Lundström (cum codicibus, ut videtur).* An . . . optabilior *om. M.*
[9] alia *SAa.*
[10] fluctibus pendeat *Lundström (cum duobus codd. dett.)*: fluctibus tendere *SA*: se fluctibus pendeat *a*: fluctibus

or, what is more to be wondered at, training-schools for the most contemptible vices—the seasoning of food to promote gluttony and the more extravagant serving of courses, and dressers of the head and hair—I have not only heard but have even seen with my own eyes; but of agriculture I know neither self-professed teachers nor pupils. For even if the 6
state were destitute of professors of the aforementioned arts, still the commonwealth could prosper just as in the times of the ancients—for without the theatrical profession and even without case-pleaders [a] cities were once happy enough, and will again be so; yet without tillers of the soil it is obvious that mankind can neither subsist nor be fed.

For this reason, what has come to pass is the more 7
amazing—that the art of the highest importance to our physical welfare and the needs of life should have made, even up to our own time, the least progress; and that this method of enlarging and passing on an inheritance, entirely free from guilt, should be looked upon with scorn. For other methods, diverse and in conflict as it were, are at odds with justice; unless we think it more equitable to have acquired spoils by the soldier's method, which profits us nothing without bloodshed and disaster to others. Or, to those who detest war, 8
can the hazard of the sea and of trade be more desirable, that man, a terrestrial being, violating the law of nature and exposing himself to the wrath of wind and sea, should hang on the waves and always

[a] In a contemptuous sense, as commonly in the use of *causidicus* (*e.g.* Quintilian, XII. 1. 25).

---

tenderet (alias *in abbr. suprascr.*) pendeat *M* : se fluctibus audeat credere *c*, *cett. edd.*

semperque ritu volucrum longinqui litoris peregrinus
ignotum pererret orbem? An faeneratio probabilior
9 sit, etiam his invisa quibus succurrere videtur? Sed
ne caninum[1] quidem, sicut dixere veteres, studium
praestantius locupletissimum quemque adlatrandi et
contra innocentes ac pro nocentibus neglectum a
maioribus, a nobis etiam concessum intra moenia
et in ipso foro latrocinium. An honestius duxerim[2]
mercenarii salutatoris mendacissimum aucupium
circumvolitantis limina potentiorum somnumque
regis sui rumoribus augurantis? Neque enim ro-
ganti, quid agatur intus, respondere servi dignantur.
10 An putem fortunatius a catenato repulsum ianitore
saepe nocte sera foribus ingratis adiacere miserri-
moque famulatu per dedecus fascium decus et
imperium, profuso tamen patrimonio, mercari?
Nam nec gratuita servitute, sed donis rependitur
honor.

Quae si et ipsa et eorum similia bonis fugienda
sunt, superest, ut dixi, unum genus liberale et
ingenuum rei familiaris augendae, quod ex agri-
11 colatione contingit. Cuius praecepta si vel temere
ab indoctis, dum tamen agrorum possessoribus,
antiquo more administrarentur, minus iacturae
paterentur res rusticae; nam industria dominorum

[1] nec animum *S*. [2] dixerim *R nonnulli*.

---

[a] The expression is attributed by Sallust (*Hist. Fr.* 2. 37 Dietsch) to Appius Claudius, censor in 312 B.C., and refers, of course, to the profession of the snarling *causidici*; *cf* also Quint. XII. 9. 9. Lactantius (*Div. Inst.* VI. 18. 26) accuses even Cicero of *canina eloquentia*.

[b] *I.e.* at the *salutatio* or early morning call.

[c] The bundles of rods carried by attendants of high officials as symbols of authority.

wander over an unknown world in the manner of birds, a stranger on a distant shore? Or is usury more commendable, a thing detested even by those whom it appears to aid? But certainly no more 9
admirable is the "canine pursuit,"[a] as the ancients called it, of barking at every man of outstanding wealth, and the practice of legal banditry against the innocent and in defence of the guilty—a fraud despised by our ancestors, but even allowed by us within the city and in the very forum. Or should I regard as more honourable the hypocritical fawning of the man who frequents the levees, for a price, and hovers about the thresholds of the mighty,[b] divining the sleeping hours of his lord by hearsay? For the servants do not deign to reply to his questions as to what is going on indoors. Or am I to think it a 10
greater gift of fortune for a man, rebuffed by a door-keeper in chains, to loiter about those ungrateful doors, often until late at night, and by the most demeaning servility to purchase at the price of dishonour the honour and power of the *fasces*,[c] though with the dissipation of his own inheritance? For it is not with voluntary servitude, but with bribes, that preferments are bought.

If good men are to shun these pursuits and their kind, there remains, as I have said, one method of increasing one's substance that befits a man who is a gentleman and free-born, and this is found in agriculture. If the precepts of this science were 11
put in practice in the old-fashioned way, even in imprudent fashion by those without previous instruction (provided, however, that they were owners of the land), the business of husbandry would sustain smaller loss; for the diligence that goes with pro-

cum ignorantiae detrimentis multa pensaret, nec quorum commodum ageretur, tota vita vellent imprudentes negotii sui conspici eoque discendi
12 cupidiores agricolationem pernoscerent. Nunc et ipsi praedia nostra colere dedignamur et nullius momenti ducimus peritissimum quemque vilicum facere vel, si nescium, certe vigoris experrecti, quo celerius, quod ignoret,[1] addiscat. Sed sive fundum locuples mercatus est, e turba pedisequorum lecticariorumque defectissimum annis et viribus in agrum relegat, cum istud opus non solum scientiam, sed et viridem aetatem cum robore corporis ad labores sufferendos desideret; sive mediarum facultatum[2] dominus, ex mercenariis[3] aliquem iam recusantem cotidianum illud tributum, quia vectigali[4] esse non possit,[5] ignarum rei, cui praefuturus est, magistrum fieri iubet.

13 Quae cum animadvertam, saepe mecum retractans ac recogitans, quam turpi consensu deserta exoleverit disciplina ruris, vereor ne flagitiosa et quodam modo pudenda ingenuis aut inhonesta sit.[6] Verum cum complurimis[7] monumentis scriptorum admonear apud antiquos nostros fuisse gloriae curam rustica-

[1] ignorat *S*, *Schn.*

[2] facultatium *SA*, *Lundström.*

[3] mercennariis *vel* mercenariis *R* : mercedariis *SA*.

[4] quia vectigali *S*, *Lundström* · q vectigali *A* : qui (*vel* q) vectigalis *R*, *et vulgo* : quia (qui) . . . possit *incl. Gesn. et Schn. veluti glossam.*

[5] posset *SA*, *Lundström.*

prietorship would compensate in large measure the losses occasioned by lack of knowledge; and men whose interests were at stake would not wish to appear forever ignorant of their own affairs, and for that reason more zealous to learn, they would gain a thorough knowledge of husbandry. As it is, we 12
think it beneath us to till our lands with our own hands, and we consider it of no importance to appoint as an overseer a man of very great experience or at least, if he is inexperienced, one who is wide-awake and active, that he may learn more quickly what he does not know. But if a rich man purchases a farm, out of his throng of footmen and litter-bearers he sends off to the fields the one most bankrupt in years and strength, whereas such work requires, not only knowledge, but the age of vigour and physical strength as well, to endure its hardships; or, if the owner is of moderate means, out of the number of his hands for hire he orders someone who now refuses him the daily tribute money, since the man cannot be a source of income, to be made a foreman, though he may know nothing of the work which he is to superintend.

When I observe these things, reviewing in my mind 13
and reflecting upon the shameful unanimity with which rural discipline has been abandoned and passed out of use, I am fearful lest it may be disgraceful and, in a sense, degrading or dishonourable to men of free birth. But when I am reminded by the records of many writers that it was a matter of pride with our forefathers to give their attention

---

[6] pudenda, aut inhonesta videatur ingenuis *vulgo*.
[7] pluribus, *Gesn.*, *Schn.*

tionis, ex qua Quinctius Cincinnatus, obsessi consulis et exercitus liberator, ab aratro vocatus ad dictaturam venerit ac rursus fascibus depositis, quos festinantius victor reddiderat quam sumpserat imperator, ad eosdem iuvencos et quattuor iugerum avitum
14 herediolum redierit, itemque C. Fabricius et Curius Dentatus, alter Pyrrho finibus Italiae pulso, domitis alter Sabinis, accepta, quae viritim dividebantur, captivi agri septem iugera non minus industrie coluerit, quam fortiter armis quaesierat; et ne singulos intempestive nunc persequar, cum tot alios Romani generis intuear memorabiles duces hoc semper duplici studio floruisse vel defendendi vel colendi patrios quaesitosve fines, intellego luxuriae et deliciis nostris pristinum morem virilemque vitam
15 displicuisse. Omnes enim, sicut M. Varro iam temporibus avorum conquestus est, patres familiae falce et aratro relictis intra murum correpsimus et in circis potius ac theatris quam in segetibus ac vinetis[1] manus movemus; attonitique miramur gestus effeminatorum, quod a natura sexum viris

[1] *sic codices recentiores et fere omnes ex Varrone, R.R. II. Praef.* 3: vineis *SA, Lundström.*

---

[a] According to tradition, Cincinnatus was called from the plough to the dictatorship in 458 B.C., to save the Roman army besieged by the Aequians on Mt. Algidus. He delivered the consul Minucius and his army, resigned the dictatorship, and returned to his little farm after holding the office only sixteen days. *Cf.* Livy, III. 26–29.

[b] One *iugerum* = about three-fifths of an acre.

[c] Consul in 282 and 278 B.C., his noble conduct toward Pyrrhus, king of Epirus, led to the evacuation of Italy by that king.

to farming, from which pursuit came Quinctius Cincinnatus,[a] summoned from the plough to the dictatorship to be the deliverer of a beleaguered consul and his army, and then, again laying down the power which he relinquished after victory more hastily than he had assumed it for command, to return to the same bullocks and his small ancestral inheritance of four *iugera*;[b] from which pursuit 14
came also Gaius Fabricius[c] and Curius Dentatus,[d] the one after his rout of Pyrrhus from the confines of Italy, the other after his conquest of the Sabines, tilling the captured land which they had received in the distribution of seven *iugera* to a man, with an energy not inferior to the bravery in arms with which they had gained it; and, not unseasonably to run through individual cases at this time, when I observe that so many other renowned captains of Roman stock were invariably distinguished in this twofold pursuit of either defending or tilling their ancestral or acquired estates, I understand that yesterday's morals and strenuous manner of living are out of tune with our present extravagance and devotion to pleasure. For, even as Marcus Varro[e] 15
complained in the days of our grandfathers, all of us who are heads of families have quit the sickle and the plough and have crept within the city-walls; and we ply our hands[f] in the circuses and theatres rather than in the grainfields and vineyards; and we gaze in astonished admiration at the posturings of effeminate males, because they counterfeit by

[d] Consul in 290 and 275 B.C. Famous for his frugality and his conquests over the Samnites, Sabines, Lucanians, and Pyrrhus, he retired to his farm, refusing all share in the booty.

[e] Varro, *R.R.* II. *Praef.* 3.

[f] That is, in applauding the performers.

denegatum muliebri motu mentiantur decipiantque
16 oculos spectantium. Mox deinde, ut apti veniamus ad ganeas, cotidianam cruditatem Laconicis[1] excoquimus et exusto sudore sitim quaerimus noctesque libidinibus et ebrietatibus, dies ludo vel somno consumimus, ac nosmet ipsos ducimus fortunatos, quod "nec orientem solem videmus[2] nec occiden-
17 tem." Itaque istam vitam socordem persequitur valetudo. Nam sic iuvenum corpora fluxa et resoluta sunt, ut nihil mors mutatura videatur.

At mehercules vera illa Romuli proles assiduis venatibus nec minus agrestibus operibus exercitata firmissimis praevaluit corporibus ac militiam belli, cum res postulavit, facile sustinuit durata pacis laboribus semperque rusticam plebem praeposuit urbanae. Ut enim qui in villis[3] intra consaepta morarentur, quam qui foris terram molirentur, ignaviores habitos, sic eos, qui sub umbra civitatis intra moenia desides cunctarentur, quam qui rura colerent administrarentve opera colonorum,[4] seg-
18 niores visos. Nundinarum etiam conventus mani-

[1] laconicis *R plerique, edd.*: lactucis *A*, *Lundström*: lacticis *S*.

[2] videmus *SA*, *Gesn.*: vidimus *alii* (viderunt *Cato apud Sen. Epist.* 122. 2).

[3] qui in villis *R plerique*: quae inutilis *SA*: vilis in utiles qui *M*.

[4] administrarentve opera colonorum *om. SA*, *vett. edd.*

[a] The *Laconicum*, or sweat-chamber, was so called because thought to have been first used by the Laconians; though

their womanish motions a sex which nature has denied to men, and deceive the eyes of the spectators. And presently, then, that we may come to our 16 gluttonous feasts in proper fettle, we steam out our daily indigestion in sweat-baths,[a] and by drying out the moisture of our bodies we arouse a thirst; we spend our nights in licentiousness and drunkenness, our days in gaming or in sleeping, and account ourselves blessed by fortune in that "we behold neither the rising of the sun nor its setting."[b] The 17 consequence is that ill health attends so slothful a manner of living; for the bodies of our young men are so flabby and enervated that death seems likely to make no change in them.

But, by heaven, that true stock of Romulus, practised in constant hunting and no less in toiling in the fields, was distinguished by the greatest physical strength and, hardened by the labours of peace, easily endured the hardships of war when occasion demanded, and always esteemed the common people of the country more highly than those of the city. For as those who kept within the confines of the country houses[c] were accounted more slothful than those who tilled the ground outside, so those who spent their time idly within the walls, in the shelter of the city, were looked upon as more sluggish than those who tilled the fields or supervised the labours of the tillers. It is evident, too, that their 18

Herodotus (IV. 75) speaks of it as well known throughout Greece, and not peculiar to the Spartans. For a description of this chamber, see Vitruvius, *De Arch.* V. 10. 5, VII. 10. 2.

[b] Cato *ap.* Sen. *Epist.* 122. 2.

[c] *I.e.* those members of the *familia rustica* whose duties kept them indoors or close to the farm buildings.

festum est propterea usurpatos, ut nonis tantummodo diebus urbanae res agerentur, reliquis administrarentur rusticae. Illis enim temporibus, ut ante iam diximus, proceres civitatis in agris morabantur et, cum consilium publicum desiderabatur, a villis arcessebantur[1] in senatum; ex quo, qui eos
19 evocabant, viatores nominati sunt. Isque mos dum servatus est, perseverantissimo colendorum agrorum studio veteres illi Sabini Quirites atavique Romani, quamquam inter ferrum et ignes hosticisque[2] incursionibus vastatas fruges largius[3] tamen condidere quam nos, quibus diuturna permittente pace prolatare licuit rem rusticam.

20 Itaque in "hoc Latio et Saturnia terra," ubi di fructus[4] agrorum progeniem suam docuerant, ibi nunc ad hastam locamus, ut nobis ex transmarinis provinciis advehatur frumentum, ne fame laboremus, et vindemias condimus ex insulis Cycladibus ac regionibus Baeticis Gallicisque. Nec mirum, cum sit publice concepta et confirmata iam vulgaris existimatio rem rusticam sordidum opus et id esse negotium quod nullius[5] egeat magisterio praeceptove.
21 At ego, cum aut magnitudinem totius rei quasi

[1] arcessiebantur *S, Lundström*: arcessabantur *A*.
[2] hosticis *SA*.
[3] parcius *SA*.
[4] cultus *R*.
[5] nullis *S*: nullo *R*.

---

[a] The *nundinae* (ninth day, according to the Roman method of reckoning) at the end of the eight-day week, was a day of rest from agricultural labour, set aside for buying and selling and attention to public and religious affairs in the city; *cf.* Varro, *R. R.* II. *Praef.* 1; Paul. ex Fest. 176 L; Macrob. *Sat.* I. 16. 34.

[b] *Cf.* Cicero, *De Sen.* 16. 56.

[c] The authorship of this phrase is attributed to Ennius; *cf.* V. Lundström, "Nya Enniusfragment," *Eranos*, XV. 1–3, and Warmington, *Remains of Old Latin*, II. frag. 26 (L.C.L.).

market-day[a] gatherings were employed for this purpose—that city affairs might be transacted on every ninth day only and country affairs on the other days. For in those times, as we have previously remarked, the leading men of the state used to pass their time in the fields and were summoned from their farms to the senate when advice on matters of state was wanted; as a result of which those who summoned them were called *viatores*[b] or "road-men."
And so long as this custom was preserved, with a 19
most persevering enthusiasm for tilling their lands, those old Sabine *Quirites* and our Roman forefathers, even though exposed to fire and sword, and despite the devastation of their crops by hostile forays, still laid by a greater store of crops than do we, who, with the sufferance of long-continued peace, might have extended the practice of agriculture.

So, then, in "this Latium and Saturnian land,"[c] 20
where the gods had taught their offspring of the fruits of the fields, we let contracts at auction[d] for the importation of grain from our provinces beyond the sea, that we may not suffer hunger; and we lay up our stores of wine from the Cyclades Islands and from the districts of Baetica[e] and Gaul. Nor is it to be wondered at, seeing that the common notion is now generally entertained and established that farming is a mean employment and a business which has no need of direction or of precept. But 21
for my part, when I review the magnitude of the

[d] Lit. "at the spear." A spear was stuck in the ground at the place where an auction was held, originally as a sign of the sale of plunder taken in battle.

[e] A district of southern Spain, modern Andalusia. Here Columella was born, in the town of Gades (Cadiz).

quandam vastitatem corporis aut partium eius velut singulorum membrorum subtilitatem dispicio,[1] vereor, ne supremus ante me dies occupet [2] quam universam disciplinam ruris possim cognoscere.

22 Nam qui se in hac scientia perfectum volet profiteri, sit oportet rerum naturae sagacissimus, declinationum mundi non ignarus, ut exploratum habeat quid cuique plagae conveniat, quid repugnet. Siderum ortus et occasus memoria repetat, ne imbribus ventisque imminentibus opera incohet laboremque
23 frustretur. Caeli et anni praesentis mores intueatur, neque enim semper eundem velut ex praescripto habitum gerunt, nec omnibus annis eodem vultu venit aestas aut hiems, nec pluvium semper est ver aut umidus autumnus; [3] quae praenoscere sine lumine animi et sine exquisitissimis disciplinis non quemquam posse crediderim. Iam ipsa terrae varietas et cuiusque soli habitus quid nobis neget,
24 quid promittat, paucorum est discernere. Contemplatio vero cunctarum in ea disciplina partium quoto [4] cuique contingit,[5] ut et segetum arationumque perciperet usum et varias dissimillimasque terrarum species pernosceret—quarum non nullae colore, non nullae qualitate fallunt, atque in aliis regionibus nigra terra, quam pullam vocant, ut in Campania, est laudabilis, in his [6] pinguis lubrica [7]

[1] subtilitatem dispicio (dispitio *S*) *SA*, *Lundström*: numerum recenseo *R*, *alii*.

[2] excipiat *M*.

[3] umidum autumnum *Lundström*, *cum SA et R plerisque ut vid.*

[4] quoto *Madvig*, "*forsitan recte*" *dicit Lundström*: quanto *SA*, *Schn.*, *Lundström* quando *Gesn.*, *cum Ald.*, *sed* quanto *vel* quoto *maluit*: quid *R*.

[5] contingit *SA et R plerique, et edd. ante Schn.*: contingerit *M*: contigit *duo codd. dett.*, *Schn.*, *Lundström.*

entire subject, like the immensity of some great body, or the minuteness of its several parts, as so many separate members, I am afraid that my last day may overtake me before I can comprehend the entire subject of rural discipline.

22 For one who would profess to be a master of this science must have a shrewd insight into the works of nature; he must not be ignorant of the variations of latitude, that he may have ascertained what is suitable to every region and what is incompatible. He should tell over in his mind the rising and setting of the stars, that he may not begin his operations when rains and winds are threatening, and so bring his toils to naught. He must observe the behaviour 23 of the current weather and season, for they do not always wear the same habit as if according to a fixed rule; summer and winter do not come every year with the same countenance; the spring is not always rainy or the autumn moist. These matters I cannot believe that any man can know beforehand without the light of intelligence and without the most accurate instruction. Indeed, it is granted to few to discern what the very diversity of land and the nature of each soil may deny us, or what they may promise us. Of how many, in fact, is it the lot to 24 survey all parts of this science, so as thoroughly to understand the practice of cropping and ploughing and to have an accurate knowledge of the varied and very unlike types of soil (of which some deceive us by their colour, some by their texture; in some lands the black soil which they call *pulla*, as in Campania, is commended; in others a fat, glutinous soil answers

---

[6] his *SA*, *Lundström*: aliis *R*, *et vulgo*.
[7] lubrica *SAR*, *Lundström*: rubrica *alii*.

melius respondet, quibusdam sicut in Africa Numidiaque[1] putres harenae fecunditate vel robustissimum solum vincunt, in Asia Mysiaque densa et
25 glutinosa terra maxime exuberat—atque in his
ipsis haberet cognitum, quid recusaret collis, quid
campestris positio, quid cultus, quid silvestris ager,
quid umidus et graminosus, quid siccus et spur-
cus, rationem quoque dispiceret et in arboribus
vineisque, quarum infinita sunt genera, conserendis
ac tuendis et in pecoribus parandis conservandisque,
quoniam et hanc adscivimus quasi agri culturae
partem, cum separata sit ab agricolatione pastoralis
26 scientia? Nec ea tamen simplex, quippe aliud
exigit equinum atque aliud bubulum armentum,
aliud pecus ovillum, et in eo ipso dissimilem rationem
postulat Tarentinum atque hirtum; aliud caprinum,
et id ipsum aliter curatur mutilum et raripilum,
aliter cornutum et saetosum, quale est in Cilicia.
Porculatoris vero et subulci diversa professio, diversae pastiones, nec eundem glabrae sues densaeque
caeli statum nec eandem educationem cultumve
27 quaerunt. Et ut a pecoribus recedam, quorum in
parte avium cohortalium et apium cura posita est,
quis tanti studii fuit, ut super ista, quae enumera-
vimus, tot nosset[2] species insitionum, tot putatio-
num, tot pomorum holerumque cultus exerceret, tot

[1] Numidiaque *Lundström*: numidia *codd., et plerique edd.*: Numidiae *Schn.*

[2] nosceret *R.*

---

[a] In Asia Minor, south of the Propontis (Sea of Marmara); now a part of Turkey.

[b] On the sheep of Tarentum (in southern Italy) see VII. 4, and Palladius, XII (*November*) 13. 5. Sheep of this breed were covered with skins to protect their fine wool; *cf.* Varro, *R.R.* II. 2. 18, and Horace, *Od.* II. 6. 10.

better; in some countries, as in Africa and Numidia, a crumbling, sandy soil surpasses in fertility even the strongest land; while in Asia and Mysia [a] a stiff and viscous soil is especially productive)? Of how 25
many is it the lot to have an understanding in the matter of these soils, as to what crop a hillside will refuse to yield, what a level situation, what a cultivated land, what a wooded land, what a land that is moist and grassy or dry and blasted; to discern also the method of planting and tending trees and vineyards, of which there are endless varieties; and of acquiring and keeping cattle, since we have admitted this as a part of agriculture, though the herdsman's art is distinct from husbandry? And yet even 26
this is not of one pattern; for a stud of horses requires one kind of management; a herd of cattle another; a flock of sheep still another, and of these the Tarentine breed [b] demands a different method from the coarse-wooled; a still different treatment is required by the goat kind, and of these the hornless and thin-haired are cared for in one way, the horned and shaggy-haired, as in Cilicia,[c] in another way. Moreover, the business of the swine-breeder and swineherd is different, their method of feeding is different; nor do light-coated and heavy-coated swine require the same climate, rearing, and care. And, 27
to take my leave of cattle, as a part of which the care of farmyard poultry and bees is reckoned, who has extended his studies so far as to be acquainted, in addition to the points which I have enumerated, with the many methods of grafting and pruning? to put in practice the cultivation of the many fruits and vegetables? to devote his attention to the many

[c] In the south-eastern part of Asia Minor.

generibus ficorum sicut rosariis impenderet curam, cum a plerisque etiam maiora neglegantur,[1] quamquam et ista iam non minima vectigalia multis esse
28 coeperint?[2] Nam prata et salicta, genistaeque et harundines, quamvis tenuem nihilo minus aliquam desiderant industriam.

Post hanc tam multarum tamque multiplicum rerum praedicationem non me praeterit, si, quem desideramus agricolam quemque describemus,[3] exegero a participibus agrestium operum, tardatum iri[4] studia discentium, qui tam variae tamque vastae scientiae desperatione conterriti nolent[5] experiri,
29 quod se consequi posse diffident. Verum tamen, quod in Oratore iam M. Tullius rectissime dixit, par est eos, qui generi humano res utilissimas conquirere et perpensas exploratasque memoriae tradere concupierint, cuncta temptare.[6] Nec si vel illa praestantis ingenii vis vel inclitarum artium defecerit instrumentum, confestim debemus ad otium et inertiam devolvi, sed quod sapienter speraverimus,[7] perseveranter consectari. Summum enim columen[8] adfectantes satis honeste vel in secundo fastigio
30 conspiciemur. An[9] Latiae Musae non solos adytis suis[10] Accium et Vergilium recepere, sed eorum et

[1] negligantur *R plerique, edd. ante Lundström.*
[2] coeperunt *R aliquot, edd. ante Lundström.*
[3] describemus *codd., vett. edd., Lundström*: describimus *vulgo.*
[4] tardatum iri *omnes post Ald.*: tardat ut rei *SA et R plerique*: tardi ab rei studio discedent *M.*
[5] nolent *M, edd.*: nollent *SA et R plerique.*
[6] tentare *R plerique, edd. ante Lundström.*
[7] *sic codd., Lundström*: speravimus *vulgo*.
[8] culmen *AR, edd. ante Lundström.*
[9] Nam *Schneider ex Cic. Orat.* 1.
[10] *om. S.*

varieties of figs as well as to rose-gardens, when even greater things are neglected by most people even though they have now begun to be, for many farmers, not the least part of their revenue? For 28
meadows and willow-thickets, broom-plants and reeds, though they require little attention, still require some.

After this announcement of subjects so many and so varied, it does not escape me that, if I demand, of those who are concerned with farm-work, the farmer whom we seek and shall describe, the enthusiasm of the learners will be cooled; for, being disheartened by the hopelessness of mastering so varied and so vast a science, they will not wish to try what they distrust their ability to attain. Nevertheless, as Marcus 29
Tullius has very properly said in his *Orator*,[a] it is right that those who have an earnest desire to investigate subjects of the greatest utility for the human race, and to transmit to posterity their carefully weighed findings, should try everything. And if the force of an outstanding genius or the equipment of celebrated arts is wanting, we should not immediately relapse into idleness and sloth, but rather that which we have wisely hoped for we should steadfastly pursue. For if only we aim at the topmost peak, it will be honour enough for us to be seen even on the second summit. Have not the 30
Muses of Latium admitted to their sanctuaries, not Accius[b] and Vergil alone, but also assigned seats

[a] Columella expresses the sense, though not the exact wording, of Cicero, *Orat.* 1–2.

[b] A tragic poet of the second century B.C., highly rated by Quintilian (X. 1 97). His works survive only in fragments. See Warmington, *Remains of Old Latin*, II, L C.L.

proximis et procul a secundis sacras concessere sedes? Nec Brutum aut Caelium Pollionemve cum Messala et Calvo[1] deterruere ab eloquentiae studio fulmina illa Ciceronis. Nam neque ipse Cicero territus cesserat tonantibus Demostheni Platonique, nec parens eloquentiae deus ille Maeonius vastissimis fluminibus facundiae suae posteritatis studia re-
31 stinxerat. Ac ne minoris quidem famae opifices per tot iam saecula videmus laborem suum destituisse, qui Protogenen Apellenque cum Parrhasio mirati sunt, nec pulchritudine Iovis Olympii Minervaeque Phidiacae sequentis aetatis attonitos piguit experiri Bryaxin, Lysippum, Praxitelen, Polyclitum, quid efficere aut quousque progredi possent. Sed in omni genere scientiae et summis admiratio veneratio-
32 que et inferioribus merita laus contigit. Accedit huc, quod illi, quem nos perfectum esse volumus agricolam, si quidem artis consummatae non sit, nec[2] in universa rerum natura sagacitatem Democriti vel Pythagorae fuerit consecutus, et in motibus astrorum ventorumque Metonis providentiam vel Eudoxi et in pecoris cultu doctrinam Chironis ac

[1] Catulo *R nonnulli, Ald., Gesn.*: Catullo *R pauci.*

[2] *sic vulgo*: consummatae sit et *Lundström cum vett. edd. et codd. ut videtur* (*praeter* consummataest *S*).

---

[a] *Cf.* Cicero, *Ad Fam.* IX. 21. 1.

[b] Five famous Roman orators, younger contemporaries of Cicero.

[c] Homer.

[d] Three celebrated Greek painters of the fourth century B.C.

[e] *I.e.* the chryselephantine statue of Zeus at Olympia and of Athena in the Parthenon.

[f] Bryaxis, Lysippus and Praxiteles (all of the fourth cent. B.C.) and Polyclitus (fifth cent. B.C.) were, like Phidias who overtopped them, distinguished Greek statuaries.

of honour to those next to them and to those far from second rank? The far-famed fulminations of Cicero[a] did not deter from the pursuit of eloquence Brutus or Caelius, Pollio or Messala or Calvus;[b] for Cicero himself had not yielded in fright to the thunderings of Demosthenes and Plato, and the father of eloquence, that divine Maeonian,[c] with the mighty floods of his rhetoric had not quenched the zeal of those who came after him. And we observe that 31
even artists of lesser fame, who through these many generations have been admirers of Protogenes and Apelles and Parrhasius,[d] have not ceased from their own labours; and, though stunned by the beauty of Phidias' Olympian Jove and of his Minerva,[e] men of the succeeding age, Bryaxis, Lysippus, Praxiteles, and Polyclitus,[f] were not reluctant to try what they could do or how far they could advance. But in every branch of knowledge the highest have attained to admiration and reverence, and those of lesser worth have received their meed of praise. Added to this 32
is that in the case of the man whom we wish to be a finished husbandman, even though he be not a man of consummate skill, though he may not have attained to the sagacity of a Democritus or a Pythagoras[g] in the nature of the universe, and the foreknowledge of Meton or Eudoxus[h] in the movements of the stars and the winds, the learning of Chiron[i] and Melampus[j]

[g] Democritus (fifth cent. B.C.) and Pythagoras (sixth cent. B.C.), early Greek philosophers

[h] Two Greek astronomers of the fifth and fourth centuries B.C.

[i] According to Greek mythology Chiron was a Centaur, half-man and half-horse, learned in many arts and the tutor of many mythological heroes.

[j] A famous seer and physician of Greek mythology.

Melampodis, et in agrorum solique molitione Triptolemi aut Aristaei prudentiam, multum tamen profecerit si usu Tremelios Sasernasque et Stolones
33 nostros aequaverit. Potest enim nec subtilissima nec rursus, quod aiunt, pingui Minerva res agrestis administrari. Nam illud procul vero est, quod plerique crediderunt, facillimam esse nec ullius acuminis rusticationem. De cuius universitate nihil attinet plura nunc disserere, quoniam [1] quidem cunctae partes eius destinatis aliquot voluminibus explicandae sunt, quas ordine suo tunc demum persequar, cum praefatus fuero quae reor ad universam disciplinam maxime pertinere.

I. Qui studium agricolationi dederit, antiquissima sciat haec sibi advocanda: prudentiam rei, facultatem impendendi, voluntatem agendi. Nam is demum cultissimum rus habebit, ut ait Tremelius, qui et colere sciet et poterit et volet. Neque enim scire aut velle cuiquam satis fuerit sine sumptibus, quos
2 exigunt opera; nec rursus faciendi aut impendendi

[1] quoniam *Lundström*: quoniam (*in abbr.*) *vel* quom *vel* cum *codd.*: quandoquidem *vulgo.*

---

[a] A mythical character, said to have been the founder of agriculture and the inventor of the plough (Servius on Vergil, *Georg.* I. 163).

[b] Son of Apollo and the nymph Cyrenê, said to have taught mankind the management of bees and cattle and the cultivation of the olive.

[c] Writers on husbandry, often cited by Varro and Columella: *i.e.* Cn. Tremelius Scrofa (*cf.* Varro, *R.R.* I. 2. 9–10, II. 4); the

in the care of cattle and the prudent wisdom of Triptolemus [a] or Aristaeus [b] in the tilling of the fields and the soil, still he will have made great progress if he has equalled in practice our own Tremeliuses and Sasernas and Stolos.[c] For agriculture 33 can be conducted without the greatest mental acuteness, but not on the other hand, "by the fat-witted,[d]" to use a frequent expression. For far from the truth is the belief, held by many, that the business of husbandry is extremely easy and requires no mental keenness. There is no occasion for further discussion of the subject as a whole at this point, inasmuch as its several divisions are to be set forth in the several Books assigned to them, which I shall carry through, each in its own order, but only after I have said by way of preface what I judge to be especially pertinent to the science in general.

I. One who devotes himself to agriculture should understand that he must call to his assistance these most fundamental resources: knowledge of the subject, means for defraying the expenses, and the will to do the work. For in the end, as Tremelius remarks, he will have the best-tilled lands who has the knowledge, the wherewithal, and the will to cultivate them. For the knowledge and willingness will not suffice anyone without the means which the tasks require; on the other hand, the will to 2

two Sasernas, father and son (I. 1. 12; Varro I. 2. 22); and C. Licinius Stolo (I. 3. 11; Varro I. 2. 9).

[d] Lit. "fat Minerva." *Cf.* Cicero, *De Amic.* 5. 19, *pingui Minerva;* Horace, *Serm.* II. 2. 3, *rusticus . . . crassaque Minerva.*

voluntas profuerit sine arte, quia caput est in omni negotio nosse quid agendum sit, maximeque in agri cultura, in qua voluntas facultasque citra scientiam saepe magnam dominis adferunt iacturam, cum imprudenter facta opera frustrantur impensas.
3 Itaque diligens pater familiae, cui cordi est ex agri cultu certam sequi rationem rei familiaris augendae, maxime curabit ut et[1] aetatis suae prudentissimos agricolas de quaque re consulat et commentarios antiquorum sedulo scrutetur atque aestimet, quid eorum quisque senserit, quid praeceperit, an universa, quae maiores prodiderunt, huius temporis
4 culturae respondeant an aliqua dissonent. Multos enim iam[2] memorabiles auctores comperi persuasum habere longo aevi situ qualitatem caeli statumque mutari, eorumque consultissimum astrologiae professorem Hipparchum prodidisse tempus fore, quo cardines mundi loco moverentur, idque etiam non spernendus auctor rei rusticae Saserna videtur
5 adcredidisse. Nam eo libro, quem de agri cultura scriptum reliquit, mutatum caeli situm sic colligit, quod quae regiones antea propter hiemis adsiduam violentiam nullam stirpem vitis aut oleae depositam custodire potuerint, nunc mitigato iam[3] et intepescente pristino frigore largissimis olivitatibus

[1] *om. R plerique, edd. praeter Lundström.*
[2] tam *SAa, Lundström.* [3] iam *om. A.*

[a] A famous Greek astronomer and mathematician, the inventor of trigonometry, who lived in the second century B.C.

do or the ability to make the outlay will be of no use without knowledge of the art, since the main thing in every enterprise is to know what has to be done —and especially so in agriculture, where willingness and means, without knowledge, frequently bring great loss to owners when work which has been done in ignorance brings to naught the expense incurred. Accordingly, an attentive head of a household, whose 3
heart is set on pursuing a sure method of increasing his fortune from the tillage of his land, will take especial pains to consult on every point the most experienced farmers of his own time; he should study zealously the manuals of the ancients, gauging the opinions and teachings of each of them, to see whether the records handed down by his forefathers are suited in their entirety to the husbandry of his day or are out of keeping in some respects. For 4
I have found that many authorities now worthy of remembrance were convinced that with the long wasting of the ages, weather and climate undergo a change; and that among them the most learned professional astronomer, Hipparchus,[a] has put it on record that the time will come when the celestial poles will change position, a statement to which Saserna, no mean authority on husbandry, seems to have given credence. For in that book on 5
agriculture which he has left behind he concludes that the position of the heavens has changed from this evidence: that regions which formerly, because of the unremitting severity of winter, could not safeguard any shoot of the vine or the olive planted in them, now that the earlier coldness has abated and the weather is becoming more clement, produce olive harvests and the vintages of Bacchus in the

Liberique vindemiis exuberent. Sed haec sive
falsa seu [1] vera ratio est, litteris astrologiae conceda-
6 tur. Cetera non dissimulanda erunt agrorum cultori
praecepta rusticationis, quae cum plurima tradiderint
Poeni ex Africa scriptores, multa tamen ab his falso
prodita coarguunt nostri coloni, sicut Tremelius, qui
querens id ipsum tamen excusat, quod Italiae et
Africae solum caelumque diversae naturae nequeat
eosdem proventus habere. Quaecumque sunt [2]
autem, quae [3] propter disciplina [4] ruris nostrorum
temporum cum priscis discrepat, non deterrere
debent a lectione discentem. Nam multo plura
reperiuntur [5] apud veteres, quae nobis probanda sint,
quam quae repudianda.

7 Magna porro et Graecorum turba est de rusticis
rebus praecipiens, cuius princeps celeberrimus vates
non minimum professioni nostrae contulit Hesiodus
Boeotius. Magis deinde eam iuvere fontibus orti
sapientiae Democritus Abderites, Socraticus Xenophon, Tarentinus Archytas, Peripatetici magister ac
8 discipulus Aristoteles cum Theophrasto. Siculi quoque non mediocri cura negotium istud prosecuti
sunt Hieron et Epicharmus, cuius [6] discipulus
Philometor et Attalus. Athenae vero scriptorum
frequentiam pepererunt, e qua [7] probatissimi auctores

[1] sive *R*. [2] sunt *om. Schn.* [3] quae *om. S, Schn.*
[4] disciplina *Ursinus* (*teste Schn.*), *Lundström cum Cod. Laurent.* 53. 27 : disciplinam *SAR, plerique edd.*
[5] repperiuntur *SAa, Lundström.*
[6] cuius *add. Lundström* : *om. SAR.*
[7] e qua *Lundström* : eaquae *SA* : aeque *vel* eque *R* : e queis *vulgo.*

---

[a] One of the earliest Greek poets, said by Pliny (XVIII. 201) to have been the first writer of agricultural precepts.

greatest abundance. But whether this theory be true or false, we must leave it to the writings on astronomy. Other precepts of husbandry are not to 6
be concealed from the tiller of the soil; and while Punic writers from Africa have handed them down in large numbers, yet many of them are assailed as erroneous by our farmers, as, for example, by Tremelius, who, though he brings this very charge, provides the excuse that the soil and the climate of Italy and of Africa, being of a different nature, cannot produce the same results. But whatever the causes by reason of which the agricultural practice of our times is at variance with the ancient principles, they should not discourage the learner from reading them; for in the works of the ancients far more is found to merit our approval than our rejection.

There is, furthermore, a great throng of Greeks who 7
give instruction on husbandry; and the first of them, that most renowned poet, Hesiod [a] of Boeotia, has contributed in no small degree to our art. It was then further assisted by men who have come from the well-spring of philosophy—Democritus of Abdera, Xenophon the follower of Socrates, Archytas of Tarentum, and the two Peripatetics, master and pupil, Aristotle and Theophrastus. Sicilians, too, 8
have pursued that occupation with no ordinary zeal, Hieron and Epicharmus, whose pupil was even Attalus Philometor.[b] Athens assuredly has been the mother of a host of writers, of whom our most out-

His surviving works include *Works and Days*, a collection of agricultural and moral teachings.

[b] For a discussion of the names and defence of the text, *cf.* V. Lundstrom, "Litteraturhistoriska Bidrag, etc. 2 Epicharmos och Attalos Philometor," *Eranos*, XV. 165–171.

Chaereas, Aristandros, Amphilochus, Euphronius, Chrestus[1]—Euphronius[2] non, ut multi putant, Amphipolites, qui et ipse laudabilis habetur agricola,
9 sed indigena soli Attici. Insulae quoque curam istam celebraverunt, ut testis est Rhodius Epigenes, Chius Agathocles, Evagon et Anaxipolis Thasii. Unius quoque de septem Biantis illius populares Menander et Diodorus in primis sibi vindicaverunt agricolationis prudentiam. Nec his cessere Milesii Bacchius et Mnaseas,[3] Antigonus Cymaeus, Pergamenus Apollonius, Dion Colophonius, Hegesias
10 Maronites. Nam quidem Diophanes Bithynius Uticensem totum Dionysium, Poeni Magonis interpretem, per multa diffusum volumina sex epitomis circumscripsit. Et alii tamen obscuriores, quorum patrias non accepimus, aliquod stipendium nostro studio contulerunt. Hi sunt Androtion, Aeschrion, Aristomenes, Athenagoras, Crates, Dadis,[4] Dionysius,
11 Euphyton, Euphorion. Nec minore fide pro virili parte tributum nobis intulerunt Lysimachus et Eubulus, Menestratus, et Plentiphanes,[5] Persis et
12 Theophilus. Et ut agricolationem Romana tandem civitate donemus (nam adhuc istis auctoribus Graecae

[1] Chaerestaeus *Varro, R.R.* I. 1. 8.

[2] Euphronius *Lundström praeeuntibus Reitzensteinio, Ursino, Pontedera*: euphrontis *SAR*: Euphronis *vulgo*.

[3] Mnasias *S, Lundström*: manassias *A*: manasseas *R*.

[4] dadis *vel* eladis *vel* cladis *R*: dandis *SA*.

[5] et Plentiphanes *Lundström*: Pleutiphanes *vulgo*: euantiphanes (et *om.*) *SA*: *alii alia in R*.

standing authorities are Chaereas, Aristandrus, Amphilochus, Euphronius, and Chrestus—Euphronius being not, as many believe, the Euphronius of Amphipolis (who is himself regarded as a praiseworthy farmer), but a native of Attica. The islands, too, 9
have honoured the study, as witness Epigenes of Rhodes, Agathocles of Chios, and Evagon and Anaxipolis of Thasos. Menander and Diodorus also, fellow-countrymen of the renowned Bias, one of the Seven,[a] were among the first to lay claim to a knowledge of agriculture. Not inferior to these are Bacchius and Mnaseas of Miletus, Antigonus of Cymê, Apollonius of Pergamus, Dion of Colophon, and Hegesias of Maronea. As a matter of fact, 10
Diophanes of Bithynia epitomized in six abridged volumes the entire work of Dionysius of Utica, who translated in many prolix volumes the treatise of the Carthaginian Mago.[b] Other writers, too, though of lesser fame, whose countries we have not learned, have made some contribution to our study. Such are Androtion, Aeschrion, Aristomenes, Athenagoras, Crates, Dadis, Dionysius, Euphyton, and Euphorion. And with no less 11
fidelity have Lysimachus and Eubulus, Menestratus and Plentiphanes, Persis and Theophilus, to the best of their ability, brought us their tribute. And that 12
we may endow Agriculture at last with Roman citizenship (for it has belonged thus far to writers

[a] The Seven Sages of Greece, all belonging to the period from 620 to 550 B.C. The names are variously given, but those usually mentioned are: Cleobulus, Periander, Pittacus, Bias, Thales, Chilon, and Solon.

[b] *Cf.* Varro, *R.R.* I. 1. 10; and see V Lundström, "Magostudien," *Eranos*, II. 60–67: J. P. Mahaffy, "The Work of Mago on Agriculture," *Hermathena*, VII. 29–35.

gentis fuit) iam nunc M. Catonem Censorium illum memoremus, qui eam latine loqui primus instituit, post hunc duos Sasernas, patrem et filium,[1] qui eam diligentius erudiverunt, ac deinde Scrofam Tremelium, qui etiam eloquentem reddidit, et M. Terentium qui expolivit, mox Vergilium,[2] qui carminum [3] quoque
13 potentem fecit. Nec postremo quasi paedagogi eius meminisse dedignemur Iuli Hygini, verum tamen ut Carthaginiensem Magonem rusticationis parentem maxime veneremur; nam huius octo et viginti memorabilia illa volumina ex senatus consulto in
14 Latinum sermonem conversa sunt. Non minorem tamen laudem meruerunt nostrorum temporum viri Cornelius Celsus et Iulius Atticus, quippe Cornelius totum corpus disciplinae quinque libris complexus est, hic de una specie culturae pertinentis ad vitis singularem librum edidit. Cuius velut discipulus duo volumina similium praeceptorum de vineis Iulius Graecinus composita facetius et eruditius posteritati tradenda curavit.

15 Hos igitur, P. Silvine, priusquam cum agricolatione

[1] filium et patrem *SA*. [2] virgilium *R*. [3] carmine *R*.

---

[a] Regarded by Pliny (*N.H.* XVII. 199) as the most ancient and most distinguished husbandmen after Cato.

[b] A contemporary of Varro and one of the speakers in Varro's agricultural treatise.

[c] Marcus Terentius Varro.

[d] A slave whose duty it was to guard his master's children, escort them to school, and perhaps give some elementary instruction at home.

[e] Freedman and librarian of Augustus, and a writer of great versatility. Two works, dealing with mythology and astronomy, survive under his name.

of the Greek race), let us now recall that illustrious Marcus Cato the Censor, who first taught her to speak in Latin; after him the two Sasernas,[a] father and son, who continued her education with greater care; then Tremelius Scrofa,[b] who gave her eloquence, and Marcus Terentius,[c] who added refinement; and presently Vergil, who gave her the power of song as well. And finally, let us not disdain to mention 13
her *paedagogus*,[d] so to speak, Julius Hyginus,[e] though still paying greatest reverence to the Carthaginian Mago as the father of husbandry, inasmuch as his twenty-eight memorable volumes were translated into the Latin tongue by senatorial decree. No less honour, however, is due to men of our own 14
time, Cornelius Celsus[f] and Julius Atticus;[g] for Cornelius has embraced the whole substance of the subject in five books, while the latter has published just one book on one kind of agriculture, that concerned with vines. And his pupil, as it were, Julius Graecinus,[h] has taken care that two volumes of similar instructions on vineyards, composed in a more elegant and learned style, should be handed down to posterity.[i]

These, then, Publius Silvinus, are the men whom 15

[f] An encyclopaedic writer, who flourished in the time of Tiberius; called the "Roman Hippocrates" for his great learning in medicine. Eight books of his medical writings have come down to us (in L.C.L., 3 vols., by W. Spencer).

[g] Known from this passage as a contemporary of Columella, by whom he is often quoted.

[h] Father of Julius Agricola, the father-in-law of Tacitus.

[i] Our meagre knowledge of the lives and works of agricultural writers (Varro excepted) between the time of Cato and that of Columella is summed up by R. Reitzenstein in his dissertation, *De Scriptorum Rei Rusticae Libris Deperditis* (Berlin, 1884).

contrahas, advocato in consilium, nec tamen sic mente dispositus velut summam totius rei sententiis eorum consecuturus, quippe[1] eiusmodi scriptorum monumenta magis instruunt quam faciunt artificem.
16 Usus et experientia dominantur in artibus, neque est ulla disciplina, in qua non peccando discatur.[2] Nam ubi quid perperam administratum cessit[3] improspere, vitatur quod fefellerat, illuminatque rectam
17 viam docentis magisterium. Quare nostra praecepta non consummare scientiam, sed adiuvare promittunt. Nec statim quisquam compos agricolationis erit his perlectis rationibus, nisi et obire eas voluerit et per facultates potuerit. Ideoque haec velut adminicula studiosis promittimus, non profutura per se sola, sed cum aliis.

18 Ac ne ista quidem praesidia, ut diximus, non adsiduus labor et experientia vilici, non facultates ac voluntas impendendi tantum pollent quantum vel una praesentia domini; quae nisi frequens operibus intervenerit, ut in exercitu cum abest imperator, cuncta cessant officia. Maximeque reor hoc significantem[4] Poenum Magonem suorum scriptorum primordium talibus auspicatum sententiis: "Qui agrum paravit domum vendat, ne malit urbanum quam rusticum larem colere; cui magis cordi fuerit

[1] quia *R plerique*. [2] discitur *S*.
[3] cesserit *R aliquot*. [4] significante *S*.

[a] *Cf.* the maxim of Cato, 4, *frons occipitio prior est;* Pliny, *N.H.* XVIII. 31 *frontemque domini plus prodesse quam occipitium;* and Palladius, I. 6. 1, *praesentia domini provectus est agri.*

you are to call into consultation before you make any contract with agriculture, yet not with any thought that you will attain perfection in the whole subject through their maxims; for the treatises of such writers instruct rather than create the craftsman. It is practice and experience that hold 16
supremacy in the crafts, and there is no branch of learning in which one is not taught by his own mistakes. For when a venture turns out unsuccessfully through wrong management, one avoids the mistake that he had made, and the instructions of a teacher cast a light upon the right course. Hence 17
these precepts of ours promise, not to bring the science to perfection, but to lend a helping hand. And no man will immediately become a master of agriculture by the reading of these doctrines, unless he has the will and the resources to put them into practice. We set them forth, therefore, in the nature of supports to those who wish to learn, not intended to be beneficial by themselves alone, but in conjunction with other requirements.

And, as I have stated, not even those aids, nor 18
the constant toil and experience of the farm overseer, nor the means and the willingness to spend money, avail as much as the mere presence of the master;[a] for if his presence does not frequently attend the work, all business comes to a standstill, just as in an army when the commander is absent. And I believe that Mago the Carthaginian was pointing this out most particularly when he began his writings with such sentiments as these: "One who has bought land should sell his town house, so that he will have no desire to worship the household gods of the city rather than those of the country; the man who takes

urbanum domicilium, rustico praedio non erit opus."
19 Quod ego praeceptum, si posset his temporibus observari, non immutarem. Nunc quoniam [1] plerosque nostrum civilis ambitio saepe evocat ac saepius detinet evocatos, sequitur ut suburbanum praedium commodissimum esse putem, quo vel [2] occupato cotidianus excursus facile post negotia fori contingat.[3]
20 Nam qui longinqua, ne dicam transmarina rura mercantur, velut heredibus patrimonio suo et,[4] quod gravius est, vivi cedunt servis suis, quoniam quidem et illi tam longa dominorum distantia corrumpuntur et corrupti [5] post flagitia, quae commiserunt, sub exspectatione successorum rapinis magis quam culturae [6] student.

II. Censeo igitur in propinquo agrum mercari, quo et frequenter dominus veniat et frequentius venturum se,[7] quam sit venturus, denuntiet. Sub hoc enim metu cum familia vilicus erit in officio. Quicquid vero dabitur occasionis, ruri moretur, quae non sit mora segnis nec umbratilis. Nam diligentem patrem familiae decet agri sui particulas omnis et omni tempore anni frequentius circumire, quo prudentius naturam [8] soli sive in frondibus et herbis sive iam maturis frugibus contempletur, nec ignoret quicquid
2 in eo recte fieri poterit. Nam illud vetus est Catonis agrum pessime mulcari,[9] cuius dominus quid in eo

[1] quom *vel* cum *R, ut saepe.* [2] ut *SA* : velut *R pauci.*
[3] contingant *S.* [4] vel *Schn. cum Gronovio.*
[5] corruptis *SA, et R plerique*
[6] culturis *R aliquot, Schn.*
[7] se venturum *ante Lundström.*
[8] natura *SA.*
[9] multari *R plerique, et vulgo* : mulctari *R pauci, vett. edd.*

[a] *Cf* Pliny, *N.H.* XVIII. 7.

greater delight in his city residence will have no need
of a country estate ".[a] This precept, if it could be 19
carried out in our times, I would not change. But
as things are, since political ambition often calls
most of us away, and even more often keeps us
away when called, I consequently rate it as most
advantageous to have an estate near town, which
even the busy man may easily visit every day after
his business in the forum is done. For men who 20
purchase lands at a distance, not to mention estates
across the seas, are making over their inheritances
to their slaves, as to their heirs and, worse yet,
while they themselves are still alive; for it is certain
that slaves are corrupted by reason of the great
remoteness of their masters and, being once corrupted
and in expectation of others to take their places after
the shameful acts which they have committed, they
are more intent on pillage than on farming.

II. I am of the opinion, therefore, that land should
be purchased nearby, so that the owner may visit
it often and announce that his visits will be more
frequent than he really intends them to be; for
under this apprehension both overseer and labourers
will be at their duties. But whenever the chance
offers, he should stay in the country; and his stay
should not be an idle one nor one spent in the shade.
For it behooves a careful householder to go around
every little bit of his land quite frequently and at
every season of the year, that he may the more
intelligently observe the nature of the soil, whether in
foliage and grass or in ripened crops, and that he may
not be ignorant of what may properly be done on it.
For it is an old saying of Cato that land is most 2
grievously maltreated when its master does not direct

faciendum sit non docet, sed audit vilicum. Quapropter vel a maioribus traditum possidenti vel empturo fundum praecipua cura sit scire, quod maxime regionis genus probetur, ut vel careat
3 inutili vel mercetur laudabilem. Quod si voto fortuna subscribit,[1] agrum habebimus salubri caelo, uberi glaeba, parte campestri, parte alia collibus vel ad orientem vel ad meridiem molliter devexis; terrenisque aliis [2] atque aliis silvestribus et asperis, nec procul a mari vel navigabili flumine, quo deportari fructus et per quod merces invehi possint. Campus in prata et arva salictaque et harundineta digestus
4 aedificio subiaceat. Colles alii vacui arboribus, ut solis segetibus serviant; quae tamen modice siccis ac pinguibus campis melius quam praecipitibus locis proveniunt, ideoque etiam celsiores agri frumentarii planitias habere et quam mollissime devexi ac simillimi debent esse campestri positioni. Alii deinde colles olivetis vineisque [3] et earum futuris pedamentis vestiantur, materiam lapidemque, si necessitas aedificandi coegerit, nec minus pecudibus pascua praebere possint, tum rivos decurrentes in prata et hortos et salicta villaeque aquas salientes
5 demittant. Nec absint greges armentorum ceterorumque quadrupedum [4] culta et dumeta pascentium.

[1] subriserit *vel* surriserit *R plerique*: subscripserit *vulgo.*
[2] aliis cultis (*deest codd.*) *Gesn.*: aliis ac cultis *Schn.*
[3] vinetisque *R, plerique edd.*
[4] quadripedum *SAa, Lundström.*

[a] Not found in Cato as now extant; but *cf.* the sentiment of Cato, 2, and especially 5. 2, where the overseer is enjoined not to consider himself wiser than his master. Pliny (*N.H.* XVIII. 36), after citing the instructions of Cato as to the qualifications for an overseer, considers it sufficient to add

what is to be done thereon but listens to his overseer.[a] Therefore, let it be the chief concern of one who owns a farm inherited from his ancestors, or of one who intends to buy a place, to know what kind of ground is most approved, so that he may either be rid of one that is unprofitable or purchase one that is to be commended. But if fortune attends our prayer, 3
we shall have a farm in a healthful climate, with fertile soil, partly level, partly hills with a gentle eastern or southern slope; with some parts of the land cultivated, and other parts wooded and rough; not far from the sea or a navigable stream, by which its products may be carried off and supplies brought in. The level ground, divided into meadows, arable land, willow groves, and reed thickets, should be adjacent to the steading. Let some of the hills 4
be bare of trees, to serve for grain crops only; still these crops thrive better in moderately dry and fertile plains than in steep places, and for that reason even the higher grainfields should have some level sections and should be of as gentle a slope as possible and very much like flat land. Again, other hills should be clad with olive groves and vineyards, and with copses to supply props for the latter; they should be able to furnish wood and stone, if the need of building so requires, as well as grazing ground for herds; and then they should send down coursing rivulets into meadows, gardens, and willow plantations, and running water for the villa. And let 5
there be no lack of herds of cattle and of other four-footed kind to graze over the tilled land and the

that the overseer should possess an intelligence nearly equal to that of his master, though he should not himself be conscious of it.

Sed haec positio, quam desideramus, difficilis et rara paucis contingit; proxima est huic, quae plurima ex his habet; tolerabilis, quae non paucissima.

III. Porcius quidem Cato censebat inspiciendo agro [1] praecipue duo esse consideranda, salubritatem caeli et ubertatem loci; quorum si alterum deesset ac nihilo minus quis vellet incolere mente esse captum atque eum ad agnatos et gentiles deducendum.
2 Neminem enim sanum debere facere sumptus in cultura sterilis soli, nec rursus pestilenti quamvis feracissimo pinguique agro dominum ad fructus pervenire. Nam ubi sit cum Orco ratio ponenda, ibi non modo perceptionem fructuum, sed et vitam colonorum esse dubiam vel potius mortem quaestu
3 certiorem. Post haec duo principalia subiungebat illa non minus intuenda: viam, aquam, vicinum.[2] Multum conferre agris iter commodum: primum, quod est maximum, ipsam praesentiam domini, qui libentius commeaturus sit, si vexationem viae non reformidet; deinde ad invehenda et exportanda utensilia, quae res frugibus conditis auget pretium

[1] *sic Lundström cum S* (*m. pr.*) *et R nonnullis*: censebat in inspiciendo agro *S* (*m. alt.*) *A et R nonnulli*: censebat in emendo inspiciendo agro *cod. Lips. Bibl. Comm. I.f.* 13: c. i e. inspiciendoque a. *vulgo.*

[2] vicinam *R*: viam et aquam vicinam *vett. edd*: v. et a. et vicinum *vulgo.*

---

[a] The substance of these words is found in Cato I. 2–3; but the passage as a whole bears a closer resemblance to Varro, *R.R.* I. 2. 8.

[b] A legal expression. *Cf.* Varro, *loc. cit.*, *quorum si alterutrum decolat et nihilo minus quis vult colere, mente est captus adque agnatos et gentiles est deducendus.* Under the Laws of the Twelve Tables the *agnati* (blood relatives on the father's side)

thickets. But such a situation as we desire is hard to find and, being uncommon, it falls to the lot of few; the next best is one which possesses most of these qualities, and one is passable which lacks the fewest of them.

III. Porcius Cato, indeed, held the opinion that in the inspection of farm land two considerations were of chief importance—the wholesomeness of the climate, and the fruitfulness of the region;[a] and that if either of these were wanting and one had the desire none the less to live there, he had lost his senses and should be turned over to his legal guardians.[b] For no one in his right mind should go 2
to the expense of cultivating barren soil, and, on the other hand, in an unhealthful climate, no matter how fruitful and rich the soil, the owner cannot live to the harvest; for where the reckoning must be made with Orcus,[c] not only the harvesting of the crops but also the life of the husbandmen is uncertain, or rather death is more certain than gain. After these 3
two primary considerations he added, as deserving no less attention, the following: the road, the water, and the neighbourhood. A handy road contributes much to the worth of land: first and most important, the actual presence of the owner, who will come and go more cheerfully if he does not have to dread discomfort on the journey; and secondly its convenience for bringing in and carrying out the necessaries—a factor which increases the value of stored crops and lessens the expense of bringing

and *gentiles* (members of the same gens) were legal guardians in cases of lunacy; *cf.* Frag. *XII Tab. ap.* Cicero, *De Inv.* II. 50 (148), SI FVRIOSVS ESCIT AGNATVM GENTILIVMQVE IN EO PECVNIAQVE EIVS POTESTAS ESTO.

[c] *I.e.* with Death. *Cf.* Varro, *R.R.* I. 4. 3.

et minuit impensas rerum invectarum, quia minoris
4 adportentur eo, quo facili nisu perveniatur; nec non [1] nihil esse etiam parvo vehi, si conductis iumentis iter facias, quod magis expedit quam tueri propria; servos quoque, qui secuturi patrem familiae sint, non aegre iter pedibus ingredi. De bonitate aquae ita omnibus clarum est ut pluribus non sit disserendum.
5 Quis enim dubitet eam maxime probatam haberi, sine qua nemo nostrum vel prosperae vel adversae valetudinis vitam prorogat? De vicini commodo non est quidem certum, quia [2] non numquam mors aliaeque nobis eum [3] causae diversae [4] mutant. Et ideo quidam respuunt Catonis sententiam; qui tamen multum videntur errare. Nam quem ad modum sapientis est fortuitos casus magno animo sustinere, ita dementis est ipsum sibi malam facere fortunam, quod facit, qui nequam vicinum suis nummis parat, cum a primis cunabulis, si modo liberis parentibus est oriundus, audisse potuerit:

οὐδ' ἂν βοῦς ἀπόλοιτ' εἰ μὴ γείτων κακὸς εἴη.

6 Quod non solum de bove dicitur, sed [5] de omnibus partibus rei nostrae familiaris; adeo quidem ut multi praetulerint carere penatibus et propter iniuriam vicinorum sedes suas profugerint. Nisi

[1] non *om. Schn.*
[2] quia *S, Lundström* : qui *AR* : quem *edd. vulgo.*
[3] nobis eum *Lundström* : nobiscum *SAR, cett. edd.*
[4] diversae *om. SAa* : *inc. Schn.*
[5] sed etiam *R aliquot, et vulgo* : etiam *om. SA, Lundström.*

[a] Lundström justifies this interpretation of the unanimous reading *nec non nihil* of the Mss.; *cf.* "Småplock ur Columellas språk: 22. Tredubbel negation," *Eranos*, XV. 205.

things in, as they are transported at lower cost to a place which may be reached without great effort; and it means a great deal,[a] too, to get transportation 4 at low cost if you make the trip with hired draught-animals, which is more expedient than looking after your own; furthermore, that the slaves who are to accompany the master will not be reluctant to begin the journey on foot. As to the goodness of the water, the point is so apparent to everyone that it needs no further discussion; for who can doubt that water— 5 without which none of us, whether of sound or delicate health, can prolong his life—is most highly esteemed? As to the suitability of a neighbour, there is, as a matter of fact, no fixed rule, since death and various other circumstances sometimes change him in our eyes. It is for this reason that some people reject Cato's opinion, though they appear to be badly mistaken. For, as it is the part of a wise man to endure the blows of fortune with a stout heart, so it is the mark of a madman to create misfortunes for himself voluntarily; and this is what he does who spends his money in the purchase of a worthless neighbour, even though he might have heard, from his first days in the cradle, provided he comes of gentle stock, the Greek proverb:

> Not even an ox would be lost but for an evil neighbour.[b]

And this saying applies not only to the ox, but to all 6 parts of our estate; to such an extent, in fact, that many have preferred to forsake their household gods and have quit their homes because of the wrong-doing of their neighbours; unless we attribute it to

[b] Hesiod, *Works and Days*, 348.

aliter existimamus diversum orbem gentes universas petisse relicto patrio solo, Achaeos dico et Hiberos, Albanos quoque nec minus Siculos et, ut primordia nostra contingam, Pelasgos, Aborigines, Arcadas,
7 quam quia malos vicinos ferre non potuerant. Ac ne tantum de publicis calamitatibus loquar, privatos quoque memoria tradidit et in regionibus Graeciae et in hac ipsa Hesperia detestabiles fuisse vicinos, nisi Autolycus ille cuiquam potuit tolerabilis esse conterminus, aut Aventini montis incola Palatinis ullum gaudium finitimis [1] suis Cacus attulit. Malo enim praeteritorum quam praesentium meminisse, ne vicinum meum nominem, qui nec arborem [2] prolixiorem stare nostrae regionis nec inviolatum seminarium nec pedamenta [3] ad nexum vineae nec etiam pecudes neglegentius pasci sinit. Iure igitur, quantum mea fert opinio, M. Porcius talem pestem vitare censuit et in primis futurum agricolam praemonuit, ne sua sponte ad eam perveniret.

8 Nos ad cetera praecepta illud adicimus, quod sapiens unus de septem in perpetuum posteritati pronuntiavit, adhibendum modum mensuramque rebus, idque ut non solum aliud acturis, sed et agrum paraturis dictum intellegatur, ne maiorem,

[1] finitissimis *S*. [2] ne carbonẽ *SA*.
[3] pedamentum *vel* pedamenti *vel* pedamenti quicquam *R plerique, edd. ante Lundstrom.*

[a] The master-thief of Greek mythology, son of Hermes (Mercury) and maternal grandfather of Odysseus. Autolycus possessed the gift of making himself and his stolen property invisible or of changed appearance.

[b] A monster of Roman legend, who stole from Hercules the

some other motive than their inability to put up with bad neighbours that whole nations (I speak of the Achaeans and Hiberians, the Albanians, too, and the Sicilians as well; and, to touch upon our own beginnings, the Pelasgians, the Aborigines, and the Arcadians) abandoned their native soil and sought out a different part of the world. And not to speak 7
merely of disasters affecting communities at large, it is a matter of tradition that private individuals too, both in the countries of Greece and in our own Hesperia, have been abominable neighbours; unless anyone could have endured that infamous Autolycus [a] on an adjoining place, or unless Cacus,[b] a resident of the Aventine mount, brought joy to his neighbours on the Palatine! For I prefer to speak of men of past times rather than of the present, so as not to call by name a neighbour of my own who does not allow a tree of any great spread to stand on our common line; who does not let a seed-bed go unhurt, or stakes to support the vines; who does not even let the cattle graze undisturbed. Rightly, then, as far as my opinion goes, did Marcus Porcius advise the avoidance of such a nuisance and particularly warn the farmer-to-be not to come near it of his own free will.

To the other injunctions we add one which one of 8
the Seven Sages [c] delivered to posterity for all time: that measure and proportion be applied to all things, and that this be understood as spoken not only to those who are to embark on some other enterprise, but also to those who are to acquire land

cattle of Geryon. The story of Cacus is told at great length by Vergil, *Aen.* VIII. 193–267.

[c] See I. 1. 9, note.

quam ratio calculorum patitur, emere velint.[1] Nam huc pertinet praeclara nostri poetae sententia:

laudato ingentia rura,
Exiguum colito.

9 Quod vir eruditissimus, ut mea fert opinio, traditum vetus praeceptum numeris signavit, quippe acutissimam gentem Poenos dixisse convenit imbecilliorem agrum quam agricolam esse debere, quoniam, cum sit conluctandum cum eo, si fundus praevaleat, adlidi dominum. Nec dubium quin minus reddat laxus
10 ager non recte cultus quam angustus eximie. Ideoque post reges exactos Liciniana illa septena iugera, quae plebis[2] tribunus viritim diviserat, maiores quaestus antiquis rettulere,[3] quam nunc nobis praebent amplissima veterata. Tanta M'.[4] quidem Curius Dentatus, quem paulo ante rettulimus, prospero ductu parta victoria ob eximiam virtutem deferente populo praemii nomine quinquaginta soli iugera supra consularem triumphalemque fortunam putavit esse, repudiatoque publico munere populari
11 ac plebeia mensura contentus fuit. Mox etiam cum

[1] velint *Pontedera, Schneider, Lundström*: velit *SAR, et alii.*
[2] plebi *Schn.*
[3] retulere *SAR.*
[4] tanta M'. *Lundström, praeeunte Madvigio*: tanta *vel* tantam *codd. plerique.*

---

[a] Vergil, *Georg.* II. 412–413.
[b] *Cf.* Palladius I. 6. 8, *Fecundior est culta exiguitas quam magnitudo neglecta.*
[c] The first Roman agrarian law, made by Romulus, allotted to every citizen two *iugera* of land (Varro, *R.R.* I. 10. 12; *cf.* Pliny, *N.H.* XVIII. 7). For the seven *iugera*, *cf.* Varro,

—not to want to buy more than a regard for their reckonings allows. For this is the meaning of that famous maxim of our own poet:

Admire large farms, but yet a small one till.[a]

This precept, which a most learned man has expressed in verse, is, in my opinion, a heritage from antiquity, inasmuch as it is agreed that the Carthaginians, a very shrewd people, had the saying that the farm should be weaker than the farmer; for, as he must wrestle with it, if the land prove the stronger, the master is crushed. And there is no doubt that an extensive field, not properly cultivated, brings in a smaller return than a little one tilled with exceeding care.[b] For this reason those seven *iugera* of Licinius,[c] which the tribune of the plebs distributed to each man after the expulsion of the kings, rewarded the ancients with greater returns than our very extensive fallow-lands bestow upon us nowadays. So great an amount, in fact, did Manius Curius Dentatus, whom we mentioned a little above,[d] regard as a good fortune greater than that of one who had been consul and had received a triumph, when after the winning of a victory under his successful leadership, the people bestowed upon him, in token of reward for his unusual ability, fifty *iugera* of land; and, declining the generosity of the state, he was content with the portion allotted to his fellow-citizens and to the common people. Later on, even

(9 beside "This precept"; 10 beside "ing care."; 11 beside "citizens and")

I. 2. 9, who speaks of such a distribution of land as first made by the tribune Gaius Licinius 365 years after the expulsion of the kings; also Pliny, XVIII. 18. A like distribution by decree of the senate, after the conquest of Veii (396 B.C.), is recorded by Livy, V. 30.

[d] *Praef.* 14.

agrorum vastitatem victoriae nostrae et interneciones hostium fecissent, criminosum tamen senatori fuit supra quinquaginta iugera possedisse, suaque lege C. Licinius damnatus est, quod agri modum, quem in magistratu rogatione tribunicia promulgaverat, immodica possidendi libidine transcendisset, nec magis quia superbum videbatur tantum loci detinere quam quia flagitiosius,[1] quos hostis profugiendo desolasset agros, novo more civem Romanum supra vires
12 patrimonii possidendo deserere. Modus ergo, qui in omnibus rebus, etiam parandis agris habebitur.[2] Tantum enim obtinendum est, quanto est opus, ut emisse videamur quo potiremur,[3] non quo oneraremur ipsi atque aliis fruendum eriperemus more praepotentium, qui possident fines gentium, quos ne circumire quoque [4] valent, sed proculcandos pecudibus et vastandos ac populandos [5] feris derelinquunt aut occupatos nexu civium et ergastulis tenent. Modus autem erit sua cuique voluntas [6] facultasque.
13 Neque enim satis est, ut iam prius dixi, possidere [7] velle, si colere non possis.

[1] flagitiosum *R aliquot, et vulgo ante Lundström.*

[2] *sic SA, et R aliquot, Lundström* : adhibebitur *vel* adhibetur *alii.*

[3] poteremur *S, Lundström.*

[4] quoque *codd., vett. edd., Lundström* : equis quidem *vulgo.*

[5] ac populandos *om. SA.*

[6] *sic codd., vett. edd., Lundström* : cuique moderata voluntas *vulgo, sed* moderata *inc. Schn.*

[7] *om. SA.*

---

[a] Schneider alone reads *quingenta*, 500.

[b] The tribune Gaius Licinius Stolo, proposer of the Licinian Rogations (passed in 367 B.C.) which limited ownership of land to 500 *iugera*. *Cf.* Varro, *R.R.* I. 2. 9; Pliny, *N.H.* XVIII. 17.

[c] Under the old Roman law of debt the borrower bound himself, in default of payment, to work out the debt as a

though our victories and the annihilation of the enemy had desolated vast stretches of country, it was still a criminal matter for a senator to have more than fifty[a] *iugera* in his possession. And Gaius Licinius[b] was condemned under the terms of his own law when, with an unrestrained passion for ownership, he had exceeded the limit of landholdings which he had set up by legislation proposed when he was a tribune; and this not only because it was a mark of arrogance to occupy holdings of such extent, but quite as much for the reason that it seemed the more scandalous for a Roman citizen, by extending his ownership in unheard-of fashion beyond the sufficiency of his inheritance, to leave untilled those lands which the enemy by their flight had
abandoned. Therefore, as in all matters, so too in the 12
acquiring of land, moderation shall be exercised. For only so much is to be occupied as is needed, that we may appear to have purchased what we may keep under control, not to saddle ourselves with a burden and to deprive others of its use and enjoyment after the manner of men of enormous wealth who, possessing entire countries of which they cannot even make the rounds, either leave them to be trampled by cattle and wasted and ravaged by wild beasts, or keep them occupied by citizens enslaved for debt[c] and by chain-gangs. But every man's limit will be determined by his own desire
plus his means; for, as I have said before, the desire 13
for possession does not suffice if you lack the wherewithal for cultivation.

quasi slave (*nexus*) of his creditor. *Cf.* Varro, *L.L.* VII. 105, *Liber qui suas operas in servitutem pro pecunia quadam debebat, dum solveret, nexus vocatur, ut ab aere obaeratus.*

IV. Sequitur deinceps Caesonianum praeceptum, quo fertur usus etiam Cato Marcus, agrum esse revisendum saepius eum, quem velis mercari. Nam prima inspectione neque vitia neque virtutes abditas ostendit, quae mox retractantibus facilius apparent. Inspectionis quoque velut formula nobis a maioribus tradita est agri pinguis ac laeti, de cuius qualitate dicemus suo loco, cum de generibus terrae disseremus.
2 In universum tamen quasi testificandum atque saepius praedicandum habeo, quod primo iam Punico bello dux inclitissimus M.[1] Atilius Regulus dixisse memoratur: fundum sicuti ne fecundissimi quidem soli, cum sit insalubris, ita nec effeti, si[2] vel saluberrimus sit, parandum; quod Atilius aetatis suae agricolis maiore cum auctoritate censebat[3] peritus
3 usu, nam Pupiniae pestilentis simul et exilis agri cultorem fuisse eum loquuntur[4] historiae. Quapropter cum sit sapientis non ubique emere nec aut ubertatis inlecebris aut deliciarum concinnitate decipi, sic verum industrii patris familiae est, quicquid aut emerit aut acceperit, facere fructuosum atque utile, quoniam et gravioris caeli multa remedia priores tradiderunt, quibus mitigetur pestifera lues, et in exili terra cultoris prudentia ac diligentia

[1] *om. SA.*
[2] *om. SA.*
[3] censebat *R aliquot, Lundström*: veniebat *SAR vett. cdd.*: suadebat *Ald., Gesn., Schn.*
[4] locuntur *SA, Lundström.*

---

[a] Unknown. [b] *Cf.* Cato, I. 1. [c] II. 2.
[d] *Cf.* Pliny, *N.H.* XVIII. 27.
[e] A barren tract in Latium, near Tusculum; *cf* Varro, *R.R.* I. 9. 5. Valerius Maximus (IV. 4. 6) tells us that Regulus possessed seven *iugera* of land in this region.

IV. Next in order is the precept of Caesonius,[a] which Marcus Cato[b] also is said to have employed, that land which one intends to purchase should be visited again and again; for at the first examination it does not reveal the hidden qualities, bad or good, which are more readily apparent to those who go over it again soon afterwards. Our ancestors, too, have handed down to us what may be called a standard for the appraisal of rich and fertile land, of whose properties we shall speak in a fitting place, when we come to the discussion of types of soil.[c] I have, 2
however, a general rule which should be an attesting witness, so to speak, and should be proclaimed again and again; a rule which Marcus Atilius Regulus, a general of the greatest renown in the first Punic War, is reported to have laid down: that as a farm, even of the richest soil, is not to be purchased if it be unwholesome, just so we are not to buy a piece of worn-out land even though it be most wholesome.[d] This advice Atilius gave to the husbandmen of his day with the greater authority as coming from the knowledge of experience; for history relates that he was 3
once the tiller of a pestilential and lean piece of ground in Pupinia.[e] Wherefore, though it may be the part of a wise man not to buy anywhere and everywhere and not to be beguiled by either the allurements of fruitful land or the charm of its beauty, it is just as truly the part of an industrious master to render fruitful and profitable any land that he has acquired by purchase or otherwise; for our predecessors have left to us many means of relief from a noxious climate, whereby pernicious plagues may be alleviated, and even on lean land the good sense and painstaking of the husbandman

4 maciem soli vincere potest. Haec autem consequemur,[1] si verissimo vati velut oraculo crediderimus dicenti:

> Ventos et proprium [2] caeli praediscere morem
> Cura sit ac patrios cultus [3] habitusque locorum
> Et quid quaeque ferat regio et quid quaeque recuset;

nec contenti tamen auctoritate vel priorum vel praesentium colonorum nostra promiserimus [4]
5 exempla novaque temptaverimus experimenta. Quod etsi per partes non numquam damnosum est, in summa tamen fit compendiosum, quia nullus ager sine profectu colitur, si multa temptando [5] possessor efficit, ut in id formetur, quod maxime praestare [6] possit. Ea res etiam feracissimos agros utiliores reddit. Itaque nusquam experimentorum varietas omittenda est, longeque etiam in pingui solo magis audendum, quoniam nec laborem nec sumptum
6 frustratur effectus. Sed quam [7] refert qualis fundus et quo modo colatur, tam villa qualiter aedificetur et quam utiliter disponatur. Multos enim deerrasse

[1] consequimur *SA*, *Lundström.*
[2] varium *codd. Verg.*
[3] cultusque *codd. Verg.*
[4] promiserimus (-is *A*) *SAR*, *Lundström* : praetermiserimus *M*, *et alii.*
[5] simul attentando *R plerique, vett. edd.*, *Ald.*, *Gesn.* : simul ac tentando *Schn.*
[6] praestari *SA et R pauci dett.*, *Lundström.*

can overcome the thinness of the soil. These 4
results we shall attain, moreover, if we pay heed, as to an oracle, to the truest of poets, who says:

> Be it our care to learn betimes the winds and moods of heaven,
> To learn the tillage of our sires and nature of the place,
> What fruits each district does produce and what it does refuse.[a]

And yet, not content with the authority of either former or present-day husbandmen, we must hand down our own experiences and set ourselves to experiments as yet untried. This practice, though 5
sometimes detrimental in part, nevertheless proves advantageous on the whole; because no field is tilled without profit if the owner, through much experimentation, causes it to be fitted for the use which it can best serve. Such management also increases the profit from the most fertile land. Accordingly, there should be no neglect, anywhere, of experimentation in many forms; and far greater daring should be shown on rich soil, because the return will not render the toil and expense a total loss. But as the nature of the farm and the method of 6
its cultivation is a matter of importance, even so is the construction of the farmstead and the convenience of its arrangement; for tradition has it that many have made mistakes, as is the case of two

[a] Vergil, *Georg.* I. 51–53.

[7] quam *Lundström cum R plerisque, ac deinceps* tam *cum codicibus omnibus ut videtur*: quoniam (*vel in abbr.*) *A et R nonnulli, edd. ante Gesn.*: cu *S*: cum (quum) . . . tum *Gesn., Schn., fortasse recte.*

memoria prodidit, sicut praestantissimos viros L. Lucullum et Q. Scaevolam, quorum alter maioris, alter minus amplas, quam postulavit modus agri, villas exstruxit, cum utrumque sit contra rem
7 familiarem. Diffusiora enim consaepta non solum pluris aedificamus, sed etiam impensis maioribus tuemur; at minora cum sunt, quam postulat fundus, dilabitur fructus. Nam et umidae res et siccae, quas terra progenerat, facile vitiantur, si aut non sunt aut propter angustias incommoda sunt tecta,
8 quibus inferantur. Pro portione etiam facultatum [1] quam optime pater familiae debet habitare, ut et libentius rus veniat et degat in eo iucundius. Utique vero, si etiam matrona comitabitur, cuius ut sexus ita animus est delicatior, amoenitate [2] aliqua demerenda erit, quo patientins moretur cum viro. Eleganter igitur aedificet agricola nec sit tamen aedificator, atque areae pedem tantum complectatur, quod ait Cato, quantum "ne villa fundum quaerat neve fundus villam." Cuius universum situm qualem oporteat esse, nunc explicabimus.

9 Quod incohatur [3] aedificium, sicut salubri regione ita saluberrima parte regionis debet constitui. Nam circumfusus aer corruptus plurimas adfert corporibus nostris causas offensarum. Sunt quaedam loca,

[1] facultatium *SA*, *Lundström*.
[2] delicatior. quamobrem amoenitate *Ald.*, *Gesn.*, *Schn.*
[3] incohatur *AaM* : inchoatur *S et R plerique*, *edd. omnes*.

---

[a] Consul in 74 B.C. Enriched by his campaigns against Mithridates, he became famous for his luxury and extravagance. He is said to have introduced the cherry (*cerasus*) into Italy from Cerasus in Pontus.

[b] A famous jurist, contemporary with Lucullus; *cf.* Pliny, *N.H.* XVIII. 32.

very eminent men, Lucius Lucullus [a] and Quintus Scaevola,[b] of whom the one put up too large a stand of buildings, the other not large enough to meet the requirements of his acreage; though either error is contrary to the interests of the owner. For 7
not only are we put to excessive expense in erecting buildings on too large a scale, but also we pay more for upkeep; on the other hand, when they are smaller than the farm requires, its products are wasted. For both the moist and the dry products which the earth produces are easily spoiled if there are no buildings into which they may be carried, or if such buildings are unsuitable because of their scantiness. Furthermore, the master should be 8
housed as well as possible in proportion to his means, so that he may more willingly visit the country and find more pleasure in staying there. And especially, if his wife also accompanies him, since her disposition, like her sex, is daintier, she must be humoured by amenities of some sort to make her stay more contentedly with her husband. The farmer, then, should build handsomely, but without letting building become his passion, and he should take in only so large a plot that, as Cato says, "the buildings may not seek for land, nor the land for buildings." [c] As to the qualities of a building site, I shall now speak in general terms.

As a building which is begun should be situated 9
in a healthful region, so too in the most healthful part of that region; for when the surrounding atmosphere is bad, it is a contributing factor to a host of physical ills. There are certain places, such

[c] Cato, 3. 1; *cf.* Varro, *R.R.* I 11. 1, and Pliny, *loc. cit.*

quae solstitiis minus concalescunt, sed frigoribus hiemis intolerabiliter horrent, sicut Thebas ferunt Boeotias; sunt quae tepent hieme, sed aestate saevissime candent, ut adfirmant Euboicam Chalcidem. Petatur igitur aer calore et frigore temperatus, qui fere medios obtinet [1] colles, quod neque depressus hieme pruinis torpet aut torret aestate vaporibus neque elatus in summa montium perexiguis ventorum motibus aut pluviis omni tempore anni saevit. Haec igitur est medii collis optima positio, loco tamen ipso paulum [2] intumescente, ne cum a vertice torrens imbribus conceptus adfluxerit, fundamenta convellat.

V. Sit autem vel intra villam vel extrinsecus inductus fons perennis, lignatio pabulumque vicinum. Si deerit fluens unda, putealis quaeratur in vicino, quae non sit haustus profundi, non amari saporis aut
2 salsi. Haec quoque si deficiet et spes artior aquae manantis coegerit, vastae cisternae hominibus piscinaeque pecori struantur; [3] quae tamen pluvialis aqua salubritati [4] corporis est accommodatissima, sed ea sic habetur eximia, si fictilibus tubis in contectam cisternam deducitur.[5] Huic proxima fluens aqua, quae [6] montibus oriunda per saxa praeceps devolvitur, ut est in Gaurano Campaniae; [7] tertia putealis

[1] optinet *SA*, *Lundström.*

[2] paululum A^2 *et R aliquot, edd. ante Lundström.*

[3] pecoribus instruantur *R plerique, Ald., Gesn., Schn.*

[4] quae . . . salubritati] *sic codd., vett. edd., Lundström*: colligendae aquae tandem pluviali, quae salubritati *Ald., Gesn., Schn.*

[5] deducatur *R plerique, edd. ante Lundström*: deducetur *M.*

[6] aqua, quae *Lundström*: aquae *vel* aque *vel* aqua e *codd., edd.*

as Thebes in Boeotia is said to be, which are comparatively free from heat in midsummer but become frightful and unbearable with the cold of winter; there are places which are mild in winter but glow with a most cruel heat in summer, as they say of Chalcis in Euboea. Let there be sought, then, 10
an atmosphere free from excesses of heat and cold; this is usually maintained halfway up a hill, because, not being in a hollow, it is not numbed with winter's frosts or baked with steaming heat in summer, and, not being perched on the top of a mountain, it is not fretted at every season of the year with every little breeze or rain. The best situation, then, is halfway up a slope, but on a little eminence, so that when a torrent formed by the rains at the summit pours around it the foundations will not be torn away.

V. Let there be, moreover, a never-failing spring either within the steading or brought in from outside; a wood-lot and pasture near by. If running water is wanting, make a search for a well close by, to be not too deep for hoisting the water, and not bitter or brackish in taste. If this too fails, and if 2
scanty hope of veins of water compels it, have large cisterns built for people and ponds for cattle; this rain-water is after all most suitable to the body's health, and is regarded as uncommonly good if it is conveyed through earthen pipes into a covered cistern. Next to this is flowing water which, having its source in the mountains, comes tumbling down over rocks as on Mount Gaurus in Campania. The

[7] ut . . . Campaniae *om. S, in marg. A.* Gaurano *Lundström, praeeunte Cluverio; ac sic maluerunt Gesn. et Schn.*: Guarceno *R, edd. vulgo.*

3 collina vel quae non infima valle reperitur; deterrima palustris, quae pigro lapsu repit; et [1] pestilens, quae in palude semper consistit. Hic idem tamen umor, quamvis nocentis naturae, temporibus hiemis edomitus imbribus mitescit; ex quo caelestis aqua maxime salubris intellegitur, quod etiam venenati liquoris eluit perniciem. Sed hanc potui proba-
4 tissimam diximus. Ceterum ad aestatum temperandos calores et amoenitatem locorum plurimum conferunt salientes rivi, quos, si conditio loci patietur, qualescumque, dum tamen [2] dulces, utique perducendos in villam censeo.

Sin summotus longius a collibus erit amnis et loci salubritas editiorque situs ripae permittet superponere villam praefluenti,[3] cavendum tamen erit, ut a tergo potius quam prae se flumen habeat et ut aedificii frons aversa sit ab infestis eius regionis ventis et amicissimis adversa; quoniam [4] plerique amnes aestate vaporatis, hieme frigidis nebulis caligant, quae nisi vi maiore inspirantium ventorum summoventur, pecudibus hominibusque conferunt
5 pestem. Optime autem salubribus, ut dixi, locis ad orientem vel ad meridiem, gravibus ad septentrionem villa convertitur. Eademque semper mare recte conspicit, cum pulsatur ac fluctu respergitur, num-

[1] repit, et *Lundström*: repet *SAR*: repit *vulgo.*
[2] dummodo (*vel* dumodo) *R, edd. ante Lundström.*
[3] profluenti *R plerique, edd. ante Lundström.*
[4] quom *vel* cum *R et multi edd., ut saepe.*

---

[a] *Cf.* Palladius, I. 17. 4, *nam caelestis aqua ad bibendum omnibus antefertur.* So by most authors rain-water was considered most wholesome.

[b] The common advice of all authorities.

third choice is well-water which is found on a hill-side or in a valley, if not in its lowest part. Worst 3
of all is swamp-water, which creeps along with sluggish flow; and water that always remains stagnant in a swamp is laden with death. But this same water, harmful though its nature is, is purified by the rains of the winter season and loses its virulence; from this fact water from the heavens is known to be most healthful, as it even washes away the pollution of poisonous water, and we have stated that this is most approved for drinking.[a] On 4
the other hand, bubbling brooks contribute greatly to the alleviation of summer heat and to the attractiveness of places; and, if local conditions will allow, I think that they, by all means, should be conducted into the villa, regardless of the quality of the water if only it is sweet.

But if the stream is far removed from the hills, and if the healthfulness of the region and the somewhat elevated position of its banks allow the placing of the villa above flowing water, care must still be taken that it have the stream at the rear rather than in front of it,[b] and that the front of the structure face away from the harmful winds peculiar to the region and towards those that are most friendly; for most streams reek with mists, hot in summer and cold in winter, and these, unless dispersed by the greater force of winds that blow upon them, are the cause of destruction to man and beast. It is best, moreover, as I have said, for a 5
villa to face the east or the south in healthful situations, the north in noxious. A villa is always properly placed when it overlooks the sea and receives the shock of the waves and is sprinkled with their spray;

quam ex ripa, sed haud paulum summota a litore.
6 Nam praestat a mari longo potius intervallo quam brevi refugisse, quia media sunt spatia gravioris halitus. Nec paludem quidem vicinam esse oportet aedificiis nec iunctam militarem viam, quod illa caloribus noxium virus eructat et infestis aculeis armata gignit animalia, quae in nos densissimis examinibus involant, tum etiam nantium serpentiumque pestes hiberna destitutas [1] uligine, caeno et fermentata colluvie venenatas [2] emittit, ex quibus saepe contrahuntur caeci morbi, quorum causas ne medici quidem perspicere queunt; sed et anni toto tempore situs atque umor instrumentum rusticum supellectilemque et inconditos conditosque fructus
7 corrumpit; haec autem praetereuntium viatorum populationibus et adsiduis devertentium hospitiis infestat rem familiarem. Propter quae censeo eius modi vitare incommoda villamque nec in via nec a via procul [3] editiore situ condere, sic ut frons eius
8 ad orientem aequinoctialem directa sit. Nam eius modi positio medium temperatumque libramentum ventorum hiemalium et aestivorum tenet, quantoque fuerit aedificii solum pronius orienti, tanto et aestate liberius capere perflatus et hiemis procellis minus infestari et matutino regelari ortu poterit, ut concreti rores liquescant, quoniam fere pestilens habetur,

[1] destituta *edd. ante Lundström.*

[2] vere natas *Schn.*

[3] nec a via procul *Lundström* : nec avia procul *R nonnulli dett.* : nec avia procul avie *c* : nec alia procul *SAR* : nec alio procul *vett. edd.* : nec pestilenti loco, sed procul et *Ald., Gesn., Schn.* : sed alio procul *Pontedera, probavit Schn.*

---

[a] *Cf.* Varro, *R.R.* I. 12. 1–2.

[b] *I e.* due east.

yet never on the shore but not a little distance removed from the edge of the water. For it is 6
better to move back a considerable distance from the sea rather than a short way, since the intermediate space is filled with a heavier air. And neither should there be any marsh-land near the buildings, and no military highway adjoining: for the former throws off a baneful stench in hot weather and breeds insects armed with annoying stings, which attack us in dense swarms; then too it sends forth plagues of swimming and crawling things deprived of their winter moisture and infected with poison by the mud and decaying filth, from which are often contracted mysterious diseases whose causes are even beyond the understanding of physicians;[a] and at every season of the year rust and dampness play havoc with farm implements and equipment, and with unstored and stored produce; the highway, more- 7
over, impairs an estate through the depredations of passing travellers and the constant entertainment of those who turn in for lodging. For these reasons my advice is to avoid disadvantages of this sort and to place the villa neither on a highway nor far from a highway, at a greater height, and to build it in such a way that it faces the point where the sun rises at the time of the equinox.[b] For a situation of 8
this kind maintains an even and steady balance between the winds of winter and those of summer; and the more the site of the building slopes toward the east the more freely can it catch the passing breezes in summer and the less be molested by the storms of winter, and it can be warmed by the morning sun so that the frosts will melt—since ground is regarded as well-nigh pestilential when it is in-

quod est remotum ac sinistrum soli et apricis flatibus; quibus si caret, nulla alia vis potest nocturnas pruinas et quodcumque rubiginis aut spurcitiae resedit siccare atque detergere. Haec autem cum hominibus adferunt perniciem, tum[1] et armentis et virentibus eorumque frugibus.[2]

9 Sed quisquis aedificare volet in declivibus areis, exstruere semper ab inferiore parte auspicetur, quia cum ex depressiore loco fuerint orsa fundamenta, non solum superficiem suam facile sustinebunt, sed et pro fultura et substructione fungentur adversus ea, quae mox, si forte villam prolatare libuerit, ad superiorem partem[3] applicabuntur, quippe ab imo praestructa valenter resistent contra ea, quae
10 postmodum superposita incumbant. At si summa pars clivi fundata propriam molem susceperit, quicquid ab inferiore mox apposueris, fissum erit rimosumque. Nam tum cum veteri adstruitur recens aedificium, quasi surgenti reluctans oneri cedit, et quod prius exstructum imminebit cedenti, paulatim degravatum pondere suo praeceps attrahetur. Igitur id structurae vitium, cum primum statim fundamenta iaciuntur, evitandum est.

VI. Modus autem membrorumque numerus aptetur universo consaepto et dividatur in tres partes, urbanam, rusticam, fructuariam. Urbana rursus

[1] tunc *SA*, *Lundström*.
[2] *fructibus R*, *Ald.*, *Gesn.*, *Schn.*
[3] ab superiore parte *S*, *Schn.*

[a] Containing the apartments of the landlord, and so called because built in the city style of architecture. On the whole matter of farm buildings compare especially Vitruvius, *De Architectura*, VI. 6; Varro, *R.R.* I. 11–13.

accessible and unfavourably situated with reference to the sun and the sun-warmed breezes; and if it is cut off from these, no other force can dry up or clear away the night frosts and any mould or dirt that has settled there. And these are destructive not only to men but to cattle and growing crops and their fruits as well.

But one who desires to erect a building on a 9
sloping site should always begin operations at the lower side; for when the foundations start from the less elevated point, they will not only easily support their own superstructure but will also serve as a buttress and underpinning for any additions which may later be made to the upper side, if it should prove desirable to enlarge the villa—for of course the previous structure below will offer strong support for any that may be built above and rest on it afterwards. On the contrary, if the foundation 10
at the upper side of the slope supports a load of its own, anything that you may later add below will be full of cracks and chinks; for when new construction is added to old, it draws away as if objecting to the growing burden, and the older structure will press upon it as it gives way until, gradually overpowered by its own weight, it will topple in ruins. Such a structural defect must therefore be avoided at the start when the foundations are first laid.

VI. The size of the villa and the number of its parts should be proportioned to the whole inclosure, and it should be divided into three groups: the *villa urbana* [a] or manor house, the *villa rustica* [b] or farmhouse, and the *villa fructuaria* or storehouse The

[b] Properly including quarters for the overseer, slaves, and livestock.

in hibernacula [1] et aestiva sic digeratur ut spectent
hiemalis temporis cubicula brumalem orientem,
2 cenationes aequinoctialem occidentem. Rursus
aestiva cubicula [2] spectent meridiem aequinoctialem,
sed cenationes eiusdem temporis prospectent hi-
bernum orientem. Balnearia occidenti aestivo advertantur, ut sint post meridiem et usque in vesperum
inlustria. Ambulationes meridiano aequinoctiali
subiectae sint, ut et [3] hieme plurimum solis et aestate
3 minimum recipiant. At in rustica parte magna et
alta culina ponetur,[4] ut et contignatio careat incendii
periculo et in ea commode familiares omni [5] tempore
anni morari queant. Optime solutis servis cellae
meridiem aequinoctialem spectantes fient; vinctis
quam saluberrimum subterraneum ergastulum plurimis, sitque id angustis [6] inlustratum fenestris atque
a terra sic editis, ne manu contingi possint.

4 Pecudibus stabula,[7] quae neque frigore neque
calore infestentur; domitis armentis duplicia bubilia [8]
sint hiberna atque aestiva; ceteris autem pecoribus.
quae intra villam esse convenit, ex parte tecta loca,
ex parte sub divo parietibus altis circumsaepta, ut
illic per hiemem, hic per aestatem sine violentia

[1] hiberna *R, et vulgo ante Lundström.*
[2] cubilia *R plerique.*
[3] et *om Gesn., Schn.*
[4] ponatur *ed. pr.*
[5] omnes *plerique codd., vett. edd.*
[6] plurimis idque angustis *Gesn., Schn.*
[7] fiant *ante* stabula *add. Ald.,* fient *Gesn., Schn.*
[8] bubula *SA, et R plerique, vett. edd.*

---

[a] South-east. [b] Due west. [c] Due south.
[d] South-east. [e] North-west.

manor house should be divided in turn into winter apartments and summer apartments, in such a way that the winter bedrooms may face the sunrise at the winter solstice,[a] and the winter dining-room face the sunset at the equinox.[b] The summer bed- 2
rooms, on the other hand, should look toward the midday sun at the time of the equinox,[c] but the dining-rooms of that season should look toward the rising sun of winter.[d] The baths should face the setting sun of summer,[e] that they may be lighted from midday up to evening The promenades should be exposed to the midday sun at the equinox, so as to receive both the maximum of sun in winter and the minimum in summer. But in the part devoted to 3
farm uses there will be placed a spacious and high kitchen, that the rafters may be free from the danger of fire, and that it may offer a convenient stopping-place for the slave household at every season of the year. It will be best that cubicles for unfettered slaves be built to admit the midday sun at the equinox; for those who are in chains there should be an underground prison, as wholesome as possible, receiving light through a number of narrow windows built so high from the ground that they cannot be reached with the hand.

For cattle there should be stables which will not 4
be troubled by either heat or cold; for animals broken to work, two sets of stalls—one for winter, another for summer; and for the other animals which it is proper to keep within the farmstead there should be places partly covered, partly open to the sky, and surrounded with high walls so that the animals may rest in the one place in winter, in the other in summer, without being attacked by wild

5 ferarum conquiescant. Sed ampla [1] stabula sic ordinentur, ne quis umor influere possit et ut quisque ibi conceptus fuerit quam celerrime dilabatur, ut nec fundamenta parietum corrumpantur nec ungulae
6 pecudum. Lata bubilia esse oportebit pedes decem vel minime novem, quae mensura et ad procumbendum pecori et iugario ad circumeundum laxa ministeria praebeat. Non altius edita esse praesaepia conveniet,[2] quam ut bos aut iumentum sine
7 incommodo stans [3] vesci possit. Vilico iuxta ianuam fiat habitatio, ut intrantium exeuntiumque conspectum habeat, procuratori supra ianuam ob easdem causas; et is tamen vilicum observet ex vicino, sitque utrique proximum horreum, quo conferatur omne rusticum instrumentum, et intra id ipsum clausus locus, quo ferramenta recondantur.

8 Bubulcis pastoribusque cellae ponantur iuxta sua pecora, ut ad eorum curam sit opportunus excursus. Omnes tamen quam proxime alter ab altero debent habitare, ne vilici diversas partes circumeuntis sedulitas distendatur et ut inter se diligentiae et neglegentiae cuiusque testes sint.

9 Pars autem fructuaria dividitur in cellam oleariam, torculariam, cellam vinariam, defrutariam, faenilia paleariaque et apothecas et horrea, ut ex iis, quae sunt in plano, custodiam recipiant umidarum rerum tamquam vini aut olei venalium; siccae autem [4] con-

[1] omnia *edd. ante Lundström.*
[2] convenit *R, Ald., Gesn., Schn.*
[3] status *SA, Lundström.*
[4] res *add. Ald., Gesn., Schn.*

[a] Palladius (I. 21) prescribes a stall eight feet wide and fifteen feet long for each pair of oxen. Vitruvius (VI. 6. 2)

beasts. But stables should be roomy and so 5
arranged that no moisture can flow in and that whatever is made there may run off very quickly, to
prevent the rotting of either the bases of the walls
or the hoofs of the cattle. Ox-stalls should be ten 6
feet wide, or nine at the least—a size which will allow
room for the animal to lie down and for the oxherd to
move around it in performing his duties.[a] The feed-
racks should not be too high for the ox or pack-animal
to feed from without inconvenience while standing.
Quarters should be provided for the overseer along- 7
side the entrance, so that he may have oversight
of all who come in and go out; and for the steward
over the entrance for the same reason, and also that
he may keep close watch on the overseer; and near
both of these there should be a storehouse in which
all farm gear may be collected, and within it a closet
for the storing of the iron implements.

Cells for the herdsmen and shepherds should be 8
adjacent to their respective charges, so that they
may conveniently run out to care for them. And yet
all should be quartered as close as possible to one
another, so that the diligence of the overseer may
not be overtaxed in making the rounds of the several
places, and also that they may be witnesses of one
another's industry and negligence.

As to the part devoted to the storage of produce, 9
it is divided into rooms for oil, for presses, for wine,
for the boiling down of must, lofts for hay and chaff,
storerooms, and granaries, that such of them as are
on the ground floor may take care of liquid products
for the market, such as oil and wine; while dry

gives dimensions of seven feet by ten (minimum) or fifteen (maximum).

gerantur tabulatis, ut frumenta, faenum, frondes,
10 paleae ceteraque pabula. Sed[1] granaria, ut dixi, scalis adeantur et modicis fenestellis aquilonibus inspirentur. Nam ea caeli positio maxime frigida et minime umida est, quae utraque perennitatem con-
11 ditis frumentis adferunt. Eadem ratio est in plano sitae vinariae cellae; quae summota procul esse debet a balineis,[2] furno, stercilino reliquisque immunditiis taetrum odorem spirantibus, nec minus a cisternis aquisve salientibus, quibus extrahitur umor, qui vinum corrumpit.

12 Neque me praeterit sedem frumentis optimam quibusdam videri horreum camara[3] contectum, cuius solum terrenum, priusquam consternatur, perfossum et amurca recenti non salsa madefactum velut Signi-
13 num opus pilis condensatur. Tum deinde cum exaruit, simili modo pavimenta testacea, quae pro aqua receperint amurcam mixtam calci et harenae, superternuntur et magna vi paviculis inculcantur atque expoliuntur; omnesque parietum et soli iuncturae testaceis pulvinis fibulantur, quoniam fere cum in his partibus aedificia rimas egerunt, cava praebent et latebras subterraneis animalibus. Sed et lacibus distinguuntur[4] granaria, ut separatim quaeque legu-
14 mina ponantur. Parietes oblinuntur amurca subacto luto, cui[5] pro paleis admixta sunt arida oleastri vel,

[1] pabulas et *SA*.
[2] ab alienis *SA*, *et R aliquot* : a balneis *R nonnulli*.
[3] camera *R*, *edd. ante Schn.*
[4] distinguntur *SA et R nonnulli*, *Lundström*.
[5] quoi *SA*, *Lundström*.

[a] A kind of flooring consisting of broken tiles, mixed with mortar, and beaten down with rammers. The name is derived from Signia (mod. Segni), a town of Latium, famous for its tiles

products, such as grain, hay, leaves, chaff, and other fodder, should be stored in lofts. But the 10
granaries, as I have said, should be reached by ladders and should receive ventilation through small openings on the north side; for that exposure is the coolest and the least humid, and both these considerations contribute to the preservation of stored grain. The same reason holds true in the placing 11
of the wine-room on the ground floor; and it should be far removed from the baths, oven, dunghill, and other filthy places which give off a foul odour, and no less so from cisterns and running water, from which is derived a moisture that spoils the wine.

And I am not unaware that some consider the 12
best place for storing grain to be a granary with a vaulted ceiling, its earthen floor, before it is covered over, dug up and soaked with fresh and unsalted lees of oil and packed down with rammers as is Signian work.[a] Then, after this has dried thoroughly, it is 13
overlaid in the same way with a pavement of tiles consisting of lime and sand mixed with oil lees instead of water, and these are beaten down with great force by rammers and are smoothed off; and all joints of walls and floor are bound together with a bolstering[b] of tile, for usually when buildings develop cracks in such places they afford holes and hiding-places for underground animals. But granaries are also divided into bins to permit the storage of every kind of legume by itself. The walls are coated with 14
a plastering of clay and oil lees, to which are added, in place of chaff, the dried leaves of the wild olive

[b] I.e., a raised border of the flooring, so called from its resemblance to a pillow or bolster (*pulvinus*).

si ea non sunt, oleae folia. Deinde [1] cum praedictum tectorium inaruit, rursus amurca respergitur, qua
15 siccata frumentum infertur. Ea res ab noxia curculionum et similium animalium commodissime videtur conditas fruges defendere, quae nisi diligenter repositae sint, celeriter ab iis consumuntur. Sed id genus horrei, quod scripsimus, nisi sicca positione villae quamvis granum robustissimum corrumpit situ; qui si nullus adsit, possit [2] etiam defossa frumenta servare, sicut transmarinis quibusdam provinciis, ubi puteorum in modum, quos apellant siros,
16 exhausta humus editos a se fructus recipit. Sed nos in nostris regionibus, quae redundant uligine, magis illam positionem pensilis horrei et hanc curam pavimentorum et parietum probamus, quoniam, ut rettuli, sic emunita sola et latera horreorum prohibent curculionem. Quod genus exitii cum incidit, multi opinantur arceri posse, si exesae fruges in horreo
17 ventilentur et quasi refrigerentur. Id autem falsissimum est; neque enim hoc facto expelluntur animalia, sed immiscentur totis acervis. Qui si maneant immoti, summis tantum partibus infestentur,[3] quoniam infra mensuram palmi non nascitur curculio; longeque praestat id solum, quod iam vitiatum est, quam totum periculo subicere. Nam

[1] dein *SA*, *Lundström*.
[2] possit *SAR*, *vett. edd.*: possis *Schn. in not.*, *Lundström*: possunt *vulgo*.
[3] infestantur *R*, *Ald.*, *Gesn.*, *Schn.*

---

[a] Varro (*R.R.* I. 57. 2) speaks of the use of pits (*siri*) in Cappadocia and Thrace, and of straw-bottomed wells (*putei*) in certain sections of Spain. Wheat, he says, has been known to keep in this way for as long as fifty years, and millet for more than a hundred; *cf.* Pliny, *N.H.* XVIII. 306. The

or, if these are wanting, of the olive. Then, when
the aforesaid plastering has dried, it is again sprinkled
over with oil lees: and when this has dried the grain
is brought in. This seems to be the most advan- 15
tageous method of protecting stored produce from
damage by weevils and like vermin, and if it is not
carefully laid away they quickly destroy it. But
the type of granary just described, unless it be in a
dry section of the steading, causes even the hardest
grain to spoil with mustiness; and if it were not
for this, it would be possible to keep grain even
buried underground, as in certain districts across
the sea [a] where the earth, dug out in the manner of
pits, which they call *siri*, takes back to itself the
fruits which it has produced. But we, living in 16
regions which abound in moisture, approve rather
the granary that stands on supports above the ground
and the attention to pavements and walls as just
mentioned, because, as I have said, the floors and
sides of storerooms so protected keep out the weevil.
Many think that when this kind of pest appears it can
be checked if the damaged grain is winnowed in the
bin and cooled off, as it were. But this is a most 17
mistaken notion; for the insects are not driven off
by so doing, but are mixed through the whole mass.
If left undisturbed, only the upper surface would be
attacked, as the weevil breeds no more than a
palm's breadth below;[b] and it is far better to en-
danger only the part already infested than to subject
the whole amount to risk. For it is easy, when

use of the trench "silo"—a word derived ultimately from *sirus*—is well known, of course, to modern farmers

[b] Similar statements are made by Varro (*loc. cit.*), Pliny (XVIII. 302), and Palladius (I. 19. 3), who cites Columella.

cum exiget usus,[1] facile est eo sublato, quod vitiatum erit, integro inferiore uti. Sed haec, etsi extrinsecus, non tamen intempestive videor hoc loco rettulisse.

18 Torcularia praecipue cellaeque oleariae calidae esse debent, quia commodius omnis liquor vapore solvitur ac frigoribus magnis conficitur;[2] oleum, quod minus provenit, si congelatur, fracescit.[3] Sed ut calore naturali est opus, qui contingit[4] positione caeli et declinatione, ita non est opus ignibus aut flammis, quoniam fumo et fuligine sapor olei corrumpitur. Propter quod torcular debet a meridiana parte inlustrari, ne necesse habeamus ignes lucernamque adhibere, cum premetur[5] olea.

19 Cortinale, ubi defrutum fiat, nec angustum nec obscurum sit, ut sine incommodo minister, qui sapam decoquet, versari possit. Fumarium quoque, quo materia, si non sit iam pridem caesa, festinato siccetur, in parte rusticae villae fieri potest iunctum rusticis balneis. Nam eas quoque refert esse, in quibus

20 familia, sed tamen[6] feriis, lavetur; neque enim corporis robori convenit frequens usus earum. Apothecae recte superponentur his locis, unde plerumque fumus exoritur, quoniam vina celerius vetustescunt, quae fumo quodam genere[7] praecoquem maturitatem trahunt. Propter quod et aliud tabulatum

[1] usus *om. SA, vett. edd.*

[2] magis (*R plerique*) constringitur *M, et Ald., Gesn., Schn. ex Pallad. I.* 20.

[3] fracescit *scripsi cum Schn. ad loc., Corrigenda et Addenda* : fracesset *SAR, vett. edd.* : fracescet *Ald., Gesn.* : fracessit *Lundström.*

[4] contigit *SA, et R aliquot.*

[5] premitur *S, Schn.*

[6] tantum *Cod. Laurent.* 53. 24, *plerique edd. ante Lundström.*

[7] fumi (*M*) quodam tenore *Ald., Gesn., Schn.*

occasion demands it, to remove the damaged portion and use the sound grain underneath. But these latter remarks, though brought in extraneously, I nevertheless seem to have introduced not unseasonably at this point.

The press-rooms especially and the store-rooms for oil [a] should be warm, because every liquid is thinned with heat and thickened by great cold; and if oil freezes, which seldom happens, it becomes rancid. But as it is natural heat that is wanted, arising from the climate and the exposure, there is no need of fire or flame, as the taste of oil is spoiled by smoke and soot. For this reason the pressing-room should be lighted from the southern side, so that we may not find it necessary to employ fires and lamps when the olives are being pressed. 18

The cauldron-room, in which boiled wine is made, should be neither narrow nor dark, so that the attendant who is boiling down the must may move around without inconvenience. The smoke-room, too, in which timber not long cut may be seasoned quickly can be built in a section of the rural establishment adjoining the baths for the countryfolk; for it is important also that there be such places in which the household may bathe—but only on holidays; for the frequent use of baths is not conducive to physical vigour. Storerooms for wine will be situated to advantage over these places from which smoke is usually rising, for wines age more rapidly when they are brought to an early maturity by a certain kind of smoke. For this reason there should be another loft to which they may be removed, to keep 19 20

[a] *Cf.* Vitruvius, VI. 6. 3; Palladius, I. 20.

esse debebit, quo amoveantur, ne rursus nimia suffumatione [1] medicata sint.

Quod ad villae [2] situm partiumque eius disposi-
21 tionem, satis dictum est. Circa villam deinceps haec esse oportebit: furnum et pistrinum, quantum futurus numerus colonorum postulaverit; piscinas minime duas, alteram, quae anseribus pecoribusque serviat, alteram, in qua lupinum, ulmi [3] vimina et virgas atque alia quae sunt usibus nostris apta, maceremus. Stercilina quoque duo sint, unum, quod nova purgamenta recipiat et in annum conservet, alterum, ex quo vetera vehantur, sed utrumque more piscinarum devexum leni clivo et exstructum pavi-
22 mentatumque [4] solo, ne umorem tramittant. Plurimum enim refert non adsiccato suco [5] fimum vires continere et assiduo macerari liquore, ut, si qua interiecta sint stramentis aut paleis spinarum vel graminum semina, intereant nec in agrum exportata segetes herbidas reddant. Ideoque periti rustici, quicquid ovibus stabulisque conversum progesserunt, superpositis virgis tegunt nec arescere [6] solis incursu patiuntur vel [7] exuri.

23 Area, si competit, ita constituenda est, ut vel a domino vel certe a procuratore despici possit, eaque

[1] sic *SAac, rell. edd., Lundström*: sufitione *vel* sufficione *R aliquot, Ald., Gesn. Schn.*

[2] villae pertinet situm *Ursinus, Gesn., Schn.*: villae situm pertinet *M*.

[3] ulmi *om. SA, plerique edd. ante Lundström.*

[4] pavimentatumque *scripsit Lundström*: pavim̄tuque *S*: pavimentumque *AR*: pavitumque *Laurentianus* 53. 24, *Lipsiensis I.f.*13: pavimentum que solo ne *rell. edd.* pavitumque solum habeat ne *Ald., Gesn., Schn.*

[5] suco *om. SA*.

[6] arescere ventis sinunt, aut solis *Ald., Gesn., Schn.*

them from becoming tainted, on the other hand, by too much smoking.

As for the situation of the villa and the arrangement of its several parts, enough has been said. It 21
will be necessary, next, that the villa have the following near it: an oven and a gristmill, of such size as may be required by the number of hands that are to be employed; at least two ponds, one to serve for geese and cattle, the other in which we may soak lupines, elm-withes, twigs, and other things which are adapted to our needs.[a] There should also be two manure-pits, one to receive the fresh dung and keep it for a year, and a second from which the old is hauled; but both of them should be built shelving with a gentle slope, in the manner of fish-ponds, and built up and packed hard with earth so as not to let the moisture drain away. For it is most important 22
that manure shall retain its strength with no drying out of its moisture and that it be soaked constantly with liquids, so that any seeds of bramble or grass that are mixed in the straw or chaff shall decay, and not be carried out to the field to fill the crops with weeds. And it is for this reason that experienced farmers, when they carry out any refuse from folds and stables, throw over it a covering of brush and do not allow it to dry out or be burned by the beating of the sun.

The threshing-floor is to be so placed, if possible, 23
that it can be viewed from above by the master, or at least by the farm-manager. Such a floor is best

[a] *Cf.* Varro, *R.R.* I. 13. 3; Palladius, I. 31.

---

[7] vel *add. Lundström.*

optima est silice constrata, quod et celeriter frumenta deteruntur, non cedente solo pulsibus ungularum tribularumque, et eadem eventilata mundiora sunt lapillisque carent et glaebulis, quas per trituram fere
21 terrena remittit area. Huic autem nubilar[1] applicari debet maximeque in Italia propter inconstantiam caeli, quo conlata semitrita frumenta protegantur, si subitaneus imber incesserit. Nam in transmarinis quibusdam regionibus, ubi aestas pluvia caret, supervacuum est. Pomaria quoque et hortos oportet saepto circumdari et esse in propinquo atque in ea parte, qua possit omnis stercorata colluvies cohortis[2] balneariorumque et oleis expressa amurcae sanies influere. Nam quoque eius modi laetatur alimentis et holus et arbor.

VII. His omnibus ita vel acceptis vel compositis, praecipua cura domini requiritur cum in ceteris rebus tum maxime in hominibus. Atque hi vel coloni vel servi sunt soluti aut vincti. Comiter agat cum colonis facilemque se praebeat, et avarius opus exigat quam pensiones, quoniam et minus id offendit et tamen in universum magis prodest. Nam ubi sedulo colitur ager, plerumque compendium, numquam, nisi si caeli maior vis aut praedonis incessit, detrimentum adfert, eoque remissionem colonus petere non audet.
2 Sed nec dominus in unaquaque re, cui[3] colonum obligaverit, tenax esse iuris sui debet, sicut in diebus

[1] nubilar *SA*, *Lundström* : nubilarium *R*, *plerique edd.*
[2] cohortis *R*, *vett. edd.* : chortes *SA* : chortis *Lundström* : cortis *Ald.*, *Gesn* , *Schn.*
[3] cui *R*, *Ald.*, *Gesn.*, *Lundström* : cum *SA*, *cett. edd.*

[a] Described by Varro, *R.R.* I. 52. 1 , *cf. L.L.* V. 21.
[b] *Cf.* Varro, *R.R.* I. 13. 5, where *nubilar* (*nubilarium*) is derived from *nubilare* (to be cloudy, *i.e.* to threaten rain).

when paved with hard stone, for the reason that the grain is threshed out quickly, since the ground does not give under the beating of hoofs and threshing-sledges,[a] and the winnowed grain is cleaner and is free from small stones and clods which a dirt floor nearly always casts up during the threshing. Adjoining this there should be a shed [b] (and especi- 24
ally in Italy, because of the changeableness of the weather), in which the half-threshed grain may be stacked under cover if a sudden shower comes up. In certain districts across the sea, where there is no rain in summer, this is unnecessary. The orchards, too, and the gardens should be fenced all around and should lie close by, in a place to which there may flow all manure-laden sewage from barnyard and baths, and the watery lees squeezed from olives; for both vegetables and trees thrive on nutriment of this sort too.

VII. After all these arrangements have been acquired or contrived, especial care is demanded of the master not only in other matters, but most of all in the matter of the persons in his service; and these are either tenant-farmers or slaves, whether unfettered or in chains. He should be civil in dealing with his tenants, should show himself affable, and should be more exacting in the matter of work than of payments, as this gives less offence yet is generally speaking, more profitable. For when land is carefully tilled it usually brings a profit, and never a loss, except when it is assailed by unusually severe weather or by robbers; and for that reason the tenant does not venture to ask for reduction of his rent. But the master should not be insistent on 2
his rights in every particular to which he has bound his tenant, such as the exact day for payment, or

pecuniarum vel[1] lignis et ceteris parvis accessionibus exigendis, quarum cura maiorem molestiam quam impensam rusticis adfert; nec sane est vindicandum nobis quicquid licet, nam summum ius antiqui summam putabant crucem. Nec rursus in totum remittendum, quoniam "vel optima nomina non apellando fieri mala" faenerator Alfius dixisse
3 verissime fertur. Sed et ipse nostra memoria veterem consularem virumque opulentissimum P. Volusium adseverantem audivi felicissimum fundum esse, qui colonos indigenas haberet et tamquam in paterna possessione natos iam inde a cunabulis longa familiaritate retineret. Ita certe mea fert opinio rem malam esse frequentem locationem fundi, peiorem tamen urbanum colonum, qui per familiam
4 mavult agrum quam per se colere. Saserna dicebat ab eius modi homine fere pro mercede litem reddi, propter quod operam dandam esse ut et rusticos et eosdem assiduos colonos retineamus, cum aut nobismet ipsis non licuerit aut per domesticos colere non expedierit; quod tamen non evenit nisi in his regionibus quae gravitate caeli solique sterilitate
5 vastantur. Ceterum cum mediocris adest et salubritas et terrae bonitas, numquam non ex agro plus sua cuique cura reddidit quam coloni, numquam non

[1] vel *Lundström*: ut *codd.*, *cett. edd.*

---

[a] *Cf.* Terence, *Heaut.* 796, *ius summum saepe summast malitia.* The proverb is given by Cicero (*De Off.* I. 33), *summum ius summa iniuria*, with the comment that it was worn threadbare.

[b] In the *Fasti Romani Consulares* the name of Q. Volusius Saturninus appears under the year 807 A.U.C. (= A.D. 55).

the matter of demanding firewood and other trifling
services in addition, attention to which causes
country-folk more trouble than expense; in fact, we
should not lay claim to all that the law allows, for
the ancients regarded the extreme of the law as the
extreme of oppression.[a] On the other hand, we
must not neglect our claims altogether; for, as Alfius
the usurer is reported to have said, and with entire
truth, "Good debts become bad ones if they are
not called". Furthermore, I myself remember 3
having heard Publius Volusius,[b] an old man who had
been consul and was very wealthy, declare that
estate most fortunate which had as tenants natives
of the place, and held them, by reason of long
association, even from the cradle, as if born on their
own father's property. So I am decidedly of the
opinion that repeated letting of a place is a bad
thing, but that a worse thing is the farmer who
lives in town and prefers to till the land through
his slaves rather than by his own hand. Saserna 4
used to say that from a man of this sort the return
was usually a lawsuit instead of revenue, and that for
this reason we should take pains to keep with us
tenants who are country-bred and at the same time
diligent farmers, when we are not at liberty to till
the land ourselves or when it is not feasible to
cultivate it with our own servants; though this does
not happen except in districts which are desolated
by the severity of the climate and the barrenness
of the soil. But when the climate is moderately 5
healthful and the soil moderately good, a man's
personal supervision never fails to yield a larger
return from his land than does that of a tenant
—never than that of even an overseer, unless the

etiam vilici, nisi si maxima vel neglegentia servi vel rapacitas intervenit. Quae utraque peccata plerumque vitio domini vel committi vel foveri nihil dubium est, cum liceat aut cavere ne talis praeficiatur negotio,
6 aut iam praepositus ut summoveatur curare. In longinquis tamen fundis, in quos non est facilis excursus patris familiae, cum omne genus agri tolerabilius sit sub liberis colonis quam sub vilicis servis habere, tum praecipue frumentarium, quem et minime, sicut vineas aut arbustum, colonus evertere potest et maxime vexant servi, qui boves elocant eosdemque et cetera pecora male pascunt nec industrie terram vertunt longeque plus imputant seminis iacti, quam quod severint, sed nec quod terrae mandaverunt sic adiuvant, ut recte[1] proveniat, idque cum in aream contulerunt, per trituram cotidie
7 minuunt vel fraude vel neglegentia. Nam et ipsi diripiunt et ab aliis furibus non custodiunt, sed nec conditum cum fide rationibus inferunt. Ita fit, ut et actor et familia peccent et ager saepius infametur. Quare talis generis praedium, si, ut dixi, domini praesentia cariturum est, censeo locandum.

VIII. Proxima est cura de servis, cui quemque officio praeponere conveniat quosque et qualibus operibus destinare. Igitur praemoneo ne vilicum ex eo genere servorum, qui corpore placuerunt,

[1] adiuvantur haec te *A*: adiuvantur nec te *a*: adiuvantur ut recte *R*.

greatest carelessness or greed on the part of the slave stands in the way. There is no doubt that both these offences are either committed or fostered through the fault of the master, inasmuch as he has the authority to prevent such a person from being placed in charge of his affairs, or to see to it that he is removed if so placed. On far distant estates, how- 6
ever, which it is not easy for the owner to visit, it is better for every kind of land to be under free farmers than under slave overseers, but this is particularly true of grain land. To such land a tenant farmer can do no great harm, as he can to plantations of vines and trees, while slaves do it tremendous damage: they let out oxen for hire, and keep them and other animals poorly fed; they do not plough the ground carefully, and they charge up the sowing of far more seed than they have actually sown; what they have committed to the earth they do not so foster that it will make the proper growth; and when they have brought it to the threshing-floor, every day during the threshing they lessen the amount either by trickery or by carelessness. For 7
they themselves steal it and do not guard against the thieving of others, and even when it is stored away they do not enter it honestly in their accounts. The result is that both manager and hands are offenders, and that the land pretty often gets a bad name. Therefore my opinion is that an estate of this sort should be leased if, as I have said, it cannot have the presence of the owner.

VIII. The next point is with regard to slaves—over what duty it is proper to place each and to what sort of tasks to assign them. So my advice at the start is not to appoint an overseer from that sort of slaves

instituamus, ne ex eo quidem ordine, qui urbanas ac
2 delicatas artes exercuerit. Socors et somniculosum genus id mancipiorum,[1] otiis, campo, circo, theatris, aleae, popinae, lupanaribus consuetum, numquam non easdem ineptias somniat; quas cum in agri culturam transtulit, non tantum in ipso servo quantum in universa re detrimenti dominus capit. Eligendus est rusticis operibus ab infante duratus et inspectus experimentis. Si tamen is non erit, de iis praeficiatur qui servitutem laboriosam toleraverunt;
3 iamque is[2] transcenderit aetatem primae iuventae nec dum senectutis attigerit, illa ne et auctoritatem detrahat ad imperium, quoniam maiores dedignentur parere adulescentulo, haec ne laboriosissimo succumbat operi. Mediae igitur sit aetatis et firmi roboris, peritus rerum rusticarum aut certe maximae curae, quo celerius addiscat. Nam non est nostri negotii
4 alterum imperare et alterum docere; neque enim recte opus exigere valet, qui quid aut qualiter faciendum sit ab subiecto discit. Potest etiam inlitteratus, dum modo tenacissimae memoriae, rem satis commode administrare. Eius modi vilicum Cornelius Celsus ait, saepius nummos domino quam librum adferre, quia nescius litterarum vel ipse minus possit

[1] mancupiorum *SA*, *Lundström.*

[2] iamque is *plerique edd., sed* isque qui iam *maluit Schn. in not* : iamque iis *S* : Iamque his A^1 : iamque qui *ad, vett. edd.* : iam qui A^2R.

---

[a] *Cf* XI. 1. 7.

who are physically attractive, and certainly not from that class which has busied itself with the voluptuous occupations of the city. This lazy and sleepy- 2
headed class of servants, accustomed to idling, to the Campus, the Circus, and the theatres, to gambling, to cookshops, to bawdy-houses, never ceases to dream of these follies; and when they carry them over into their farming, the master suffers not so much loss in the slave himself as in his whole estate. A man should be chosen who has been hardened by farm work from his infancy, one who has been tested by experience.[a] If, however, such a person is not available, let one be put in charge out of the number of those who have slaved patiently at hard labour; and he should already have passed beyond the time of 3
young manhood but not yet have arrived at that of old age, that youth may not lessen his authority to command, seeing that older men think it beneath them to take orders from a mere stripling, and that old age may not break down under the heaviest labour. He should be, then, of middle age and of strong physique, skilled in farm operations or at least very painstaking, so that he may learn the more readily; for it is not in keeping with this business of ours for one man to give orders and another to give instructions, nor can a man properly 4
exact work when he is being tutored by an underling as to what is to be done and in what way. Even an illiterate person, if only he have a retentive mind, can manage affairs well enough. Cornelius Celsus says that an overseer of this sort brings money to his master oftener than he does his book, because, not knowing his letters, he is either less able to falsify accounts or is afraid to do so through a second

rationes confingere vel per alium propter conscien-
5 tiam fraudis timeat.[1]

Sed qualicumque vilico contubernalis mulier adsig-
nanda est, quae et [2] contineat eum et in quibusdam
rebus tamen adiuvet; eidemque actori praecipiendum est, ne convictum cum domestico multoque
minus cum extero habeat. Non numquam tamen
eum, quem assidue sedulum et fortem in operibus
administrandis cognoverit, honoris causa mensae
suae die festo dignetur adhibere. Sacrificia, nisi ex
6 praecepto domini, ne fecerit. Haruspices sagasque,
quae utraque genera vana superstitione rudes animos
ad impensas ac deinceps ad flagitia compellunt,
ne admiserit, neque urbem neque ullas nundinas
noverit, nisi emendae vendendaeve pertinentis ad se
7 rei causa. Vilicus enim, quod ait Cato, ambulator
esse non debet; nec egredi terminos, nisi ut addiscat
aliquam culturam, et hoc si ita in vicino est, ut
remeare [3] possit. Semitas novosque limites in agro
fieri ne patiatur, neve hospitem, nisi amicum fami-
liaremque domini necessarium, receperit.

8 Ut ab his arcendus, ita exhortandus est ad instru-
mentorum [4] ferramentorumque curam, ut duplicia,
quam numerus servorum exigit, refecta et reposita
custodiat, ne quid a vicino petendum sit; quia plus
in operis servorum quam in pretio rerum eius modi
9 consumitur. Cultam vestitamque familiam magis

[1] timere *R*, *edd. ante Gesn.*
[2] *om. SA, et R aliquot.*
[3] remanere *SA*, *et R pauci*: re manere *Lundström.*
[4] instrumenti *M*, *vett. edd.*, *Schn.*

---

[a] *Cf.* Varro, *R R.* I. 17. 5.
[b] This precept and many of those that follow are repeated nearly word for word in XI. 1. 19–28.

party because that would make another aware of the
deception.

But be the overseer what he may, he should be 5
given a woman companion to keep him within
bounds [a] and yet in certain matters to be a help to
him; and this same overseer should be warned not
to become intimate with a member of the household,
and much less with an outsider, yet at times he may
consider it fitting, as a mark of distinction, to invite to
his table on a holiday one whom he has found to be
constantly busy and vigorous in the performance
of his tasks.[b] He shall offer no sacrifice except by
direction of the master. Soothsayers and witches, 6
two sets of people who incite ignorant minds through
false superstition to spending and then to shameful
practices, he must not admit to the place. He
must have no acquaintance with the city or with the
weekly market, except to make purchases and sales
in connection with his duties. For, as Cato says,[c] 7
an overseer should not be a gadabout; and he should
not go out of bounds except to learn something new
about farming, and that only if the place is so near
that he can come back. He must allow no foot-paths
or new crosscuts to be made in the farm; and he
shall entertain no guest except a close friend or kinsman of his master.

As he must be restrained from these practices, so 8
must he be urged to take care of the equipment and
the iron tools, and to keep in repair and stored away
twice as many as the number of slaves requires, so
that there will be no need of borrowing from a
neighbour; for the loss in slave labour exceeds the
cost of articles of this sort. In the care and clothing 9

[c] Cato, 5. 2.

utiliter quam delicate habeat munitamque diligenter a vento, frigore pluviaque, quae cuncta prohibentur pellibus manicatis, centonibus confectis vel sagis cucullis. Id si fiat, nullus dies tam intolerabilis est,
10 quo non sub divo moliri aliquid possit. Nec tantum operis agrestis sit artifex, sed et animi, quantum servile patitur ingenium, virtutibus instructus, ut neque remisse neque crudeliter imperet semperque aliquos ex melioribus foveat, parcat tamen etiam minus bonis, ita ut potius timeant eius severitatem, quam crudelitatem detestentur. Id contingere poterit, si maluerit custodire subiectos, ne peccent, quam neglegentia sua committere, ut puniat delinquentes.
11 Nulla est autem maior vel nequissimi hominis custodia quam operis exactio, ut iusta reddantur, ut vilicus semper se repraesentet. Sic enim et magistri singulorum officiorum sedulo munia sua exsequuntur,[1] et ceteri post fatigationem [2] operis quieti ac somno potius quam deliciis operam dabunt.

12 Iam illa vetera, sed optimi moris, quae nunc exoleverunt, utinam possint obtineri: ne conservo ministro quoquam, nisi in re domini, utatur; ne cibum nisi in conspectu familiae capiat neve alium quam

[1] exsequantur *SA*: exequantur *vett. edd.*: exequentur *Ald.*, *Gesn.*, *Schn.*

[2] defatigationem *Gesn.*, *Schn.*

of the slave household he should have an eye to usefulness rather than appearance, taking care to keep them fortified against wind, cold, and rain, all of which are warded off with long-sleeved leather tunics, garments of patchwork, or hooded cloaks. If this be done, no weather is so unbearable but that some work may be done in the open. He should be not 10
only skilled in the tasks of husbandry, but should also be endowed, as far as the servile disposition allows, with such qualities of feeling that he may exercise authority without laxness and without cruelty, and always humour some of the better hands, at the same time being forbearing even with those of lesser worth, so that they may rather fear his sternness than detest his cruelty. This he can accomplish if he will choose rather to guard his subordinates from wrongdoing than to bring upon himself, through his own negligence, the necessity of punishing offenders. There is, moreover, no 11
better way of keeping watch over even the most worthless of men than the strict enforcement of labour, the requirement that the proper tasks be performed and that the overseer be present at all times; for in that case the foremen in charge of the several operations are zealous in carrying out their duties, and the others, after their fatiguing toil, will turn their attention to rest and sleep rather than to dissipation.

Would that those well-known precepts, old but 12
excellent in morality, which have now passed out of use, might be held to to-day: That an overseer shall not employ the services of a fellow-slave except on the master's business; that he shall partake of no food except in sight of the household, nor of other

qui ceteris praebetur. Sic enim curabit ut et panis
diligenter confiat[1] et reliqua salubriter apparentur.
Ne extra fines nisi a se missum progredi sinat, sed
nec ipse mittat, nisi magna necessitate cogente.
13 Neve negotietur sibi pecuniamque domini aut animalibus aut rebus aliis promercalibus occupet; haec
enim negotiatio curam vilici avocat nec umquam
patietur eum cum rationibus domini paria facere,
sed ubi numeratio exigetur, rem pro nummis ostendit. In universum tamen hoc maxime obtinendum
ab eo est, nequid se putet scire quod nesciat, quae-
14 ratque semper addiscere quod ignorat. Nam cum
multum prodest perite quid facere, tum plus obest
perperam fecisse. Unum enim ac solum dominatur
in rusticatione, quicquid exigit ratio culturae, semel
facere, quippe cum emendatur vel imprudentia vel
neglegentia, iam res ipsa decoxit nec in tantum
postmodo exuberat, ut et se amissam restituat et
quaestum temporum praeteritorum resarciat.

15 In ceteris servis haec fere praecepta servanda sunt, quae me custodisse non paenitet, ut rusticos, qui modo non incommode se gessissent, saepius quam urbanos familiarius adloquerer, et cum hac[2] comitate domini levari perpetuum laborem eorum intel-

[1] conficiatur *vel* confitiatur *R nonnulli.*
[2] cum hac *Lundström, praeeunte Schn.*: hac *S*: hāc *A*: a *R*: enim *M*: cum *vett. edd.*

food than is provided for the rest; for in so doing he will see to it that the bread is carefully made and that other things are wholesomely prepared. He shall permit no one to pass beyond the boundaries unless sent by himself, and he shall send no one except there is great and pressing need. He shall carry on 13
no business on his own account, nor invest his master's funds in livestock and other goods for purchase and sale; for such trafficking will divert the attention of the overseer and will never allow him to balance his accounts with his master, but, when an accounting is demanded, he has goods to show instead of cash. But, generally speaking, this above all else is to be required of him—that he shall not think that he knows what he does not know, and that he shall always be eager to learn what he is ignorant of; for not only is it very helpful to do a thing skilfully, 14
but even more so is it hurtful to have done it incorrectly. For there is one and only one controlling principle in agriculture, namely, to do once and for all the thing which the method of cultivation requires; since when ignorance or carelessness has to be rectified, the matter at stake has already suffered impairment and never recovers thereafter to such an extent as to regain what it has lost and to restore the profit of time that has passed.

In the case of the other slaves, the following are, 15
in general, the precepts to be observed, and I do not regret having held to them myself: to talk rather familiarly with the country slaves, provided only that they have not conducted themselves unbecomingly, more frequently than I would with the town slaves; and when I perceived that their unending toil was lightened by such friendliness on the

legerem, nonnumquam etiam iocarer et plus ipsis iocari permitterem. Iam illud saepe facio, ut quasi cum peritioribus de aliquibus operibus novis deliberem et per hoc cognoscam cuiusque ingenium, quale quamque sit prudens. Tum etiam libentius eos id opus adgredi video, de quo secum deliberatum
16 et consilio ipsorum susceptum putant. Nam illa sollemnia sunt omnibus circumspectis,[1] ut ergastuli mancipia recognoscant,[2] ut explorent [3] an diligenter vincti sint, an ipsae sedes custodiae satis tutae munitaeque sint, num [4] vilicus aut alligaverit quempiam domino nesciente aut revinxerit. Nam utrumque maxime servare debet, ut et quem pater familiae tali poena multaverit, vilicus nisi eiusdem permissu compedibus non eximat et quem ipse sua sponte
17 vinxerit, antequam sciat dominus, non resolvat; tantoque curiosior inquisitio patris familiae debet esse pro tali genere servorum, ne aut in vestiariis aut in ceteris praebitis iniuriose tractentur, quanto et pluribus subiecti, ut vilicis, ut operum magistris, ut ergastulariis, magis obnoxii perpetiendis iniuriis, et rursus saevitia atque avaritia laesi magis timendi
18 sunt. Itaque diligens dominus cum et ab ipsis tum et ab solutis, quibus maior est fides, quaerit,[5] an ex

[1] circumseptis *SAa, vett. edd.*
[2] recognoscant *SAR*. recognoscam *Lundström.*
[3] explorent *SAR*: explorem *Lundström.*
[4] num *R, edd. vulgo*: numquam *SA*: num quem *Lundström.*
[5] quaerat *Ald., Gesn., Schn.*

part of the master, I would even jest with them at times and allow them also to jest more freely. Nowadays I make it a practice to call them into consultation on any new work, as if they were more experienced, and to discover by this means what sort of ability is possessed by each of them and how intelligent he is. Furthermore, I observe that they are more willing to set about a piece of work on which they think that their opinions have been asked and their advice followed. Again, it is the established custom 16
of all men of caution to inspect the inmates of the workhouse, to find out whether they are carefully chained, whether the places of confinement are quite safe and properly guarded, whether the overseer has put anyone in fetters or removed his shackles without the master's knowledge. For the overseer should be most observant of both points—not to release from shackles anyone whom the head of the house has subjected to that kind of punishment, except by his leave, and not to free one whom he himself has chained on his own initiative until the master knows the circumstances; and 17
the investigation of the householder should be the more painstaking in the interest of slaves of this sort, that they may not be treated unjustly in the matter of clothing or other allowances, inasmuch as, being liable to a greater number of people, such as overseers, taskmasters, and jailers, they are the more liable to unjust punishment, and again, when smarting under cruelty and greed, they are more to be feared. Accordingly, a careful master 18
inquires not only of them, but also of those who are not in bonds, as being more worthy of belief, whether they are receiving what is due to them under his in-

sua constitutione iusta percipiant, atque ipse panis potionisque probitatem[1] gustu suo explorat,[2] vestem, manicas pedumque tegumina recognoscit.[3] Saepe etiam querendi potestatem faciat de iis, qui aut crudeliter eos aut fraudulenter infestent. Nos quidem aliquando iuste dolentes tam vindicamus, quam animadvertimus in eos, qui seditionibus familiam concitant, qui calumniantur magistros suos; ac rursus praemio prosequimur[4] eos, qui strenue atque
19 industrie se gerunt. Feminis quoque fecundioribus, quarum in subole certus numerus honorari debet, otium, nonnumquam et libertatem dedimus, cum complures natos educassent. Nam cui tres erant filii, vacatio, cui plures,[5] libertas quoque contingebat.

Haec et[6] iustitia et cura patris familiae multum
20 confert augendo patrimonio. Sed et illa meminerit, cum e civitate remeaverit, deos penatis adorare; deinde, si tempestivum erit, confestim, si minus, postero die oculis perlustrare, omnes partes agri revisere atque aestimare num quid absentia sua de disciplina et custodia remiserit, num aliqua vitis, num arbor, num fruges absint; tum etiam pecus[7] et familiam recenseat fundique instrumentum et supellectilem. Quae cuncta si per plures annos facere instituerit, bene moratam disciplinam, cum senectus advenerit, obtinebit; nec erit ulla eius aetas annis ita confecta, ut spernatur a servis.

[1] bonitatem *R, Ald., Gesn., Schn.*
[2] exploret *R, Ald., Gesn., Schn.*
[3] recognoscat *R plerique, Ald., Gesn., Schn.*
[4] prosequamur *SA.*
[5] plus *SA, Lundström.*
[6] enim *Ald., Gesn.*
[7] pecudes *R.*

---

[a] *Cf.* Cato, 2.

structions; he also tests the quality of their food
and drink by tasting it himself, and examines their
clothing, their mittens, and their foot-covering. In
addition he should give them frequent opportunities
for making complaint against those persons who treat
them cruelly or dishonestly. In fact, I now and then
avenge those who have just cause for grievance, as
well as punish those who incite the slaves to revolt,
or who slander their taskmasters; and, on the other
hand, I reward those who conduct themselves with
energy and diligence. To women, too, who are un- 19
usually prolific, and who ought to be rewarded for
the bearing of a certain number of offspring, I have
granted exemption from work and sometimes even
freedom after they had reared many children.
For to a mother of three sons exemption from work
was granted; to a mother of more her freedom as
well.

Such justice and consideration on the part of the
master contributes greatly to the increase of his
estate. But he should also bear in mind, first to pay 20
his respects to the household gods as soon as he
returns from town;[a] then at once, if time permits,
if not, on the next day, to inspect his lands and re-
visit every part of them and judge whether his
absence has resulted in any relaxation of discipline
and watchfulness, whether any vine, any tree, or any
produce is missing; at the same time, too, he should
make a new count of stock, slaves, farm-equipment,
and furniture. If he has made it a practice to do all
this for many years, he will maintain a well-ordered
discipline when old age comes; and whatever his
age, he will never be so wasted with years as to be
despised by his slaves.

IX. Dicendum etiam est, quibus operibus quemque habitum corporis aut animi contribuendum putemus. Magistros pecoribus [1] oportet praeponere sedulos ac frugalissimos. Ea res utraque plus quam corporis statura roburque confert huic negotio, quoniam id ministerium custodiae diligentis et artis officium
2 est. Bubulco quamvis necessaria non tamen satis est indoles mentis, nisi eum vastitas vocis et habitus metuendum pecudibus efficit.[2] Sed temperet vires clementia, quoniam terribilior debet esse quam saevior, ut et obsequantur eius imperiis et diutius perennent boves, non confecti vexatione simul operum verberumque. Sed quae sint magistrorum
3 munia quaeque bubulcorum, suo loco repetam; nunc admonuisse satis est nihil in his, in illis plurimum referre vires et proceritatem. Nam longissimum quemque aratorem,[3] sicut dixi, faciemus, et propter id, quod paulo ante rettuli, et quod in re rustica nullo minus opere fatigatur prolixior, quia in arando stivae paene rectus innititur. Mediastinus qualiscumque status potest esse, dummodo perpetiendo labori sit
4 idoneus. Vineae non sic altos quemadmodum [4] latos et lacertosos viros exigunt, nam hic habitus fossuris et putationibus ceterisque earum culturis magis aptus. Minus in hoc officio quam in ceteris agrico-

[1] operibus *Gesn., Schn.*
[2] effecit *SA.*
[3] maiorem *SA, et R nonnulli.*
[4] quomodo *AaM.*

[a] The *bubulcus* was, in a restricted sense, as here and often, a ploughman (= *arator*) or ox-driver; in the wider sense, as just below and elsewhere, a herdsman in general charge of the cattle.

[b] See Bks. VII. 1–7 and VI. 1–26.

IX. Something should be said, too, as to what tasks we think each kind of body or mind should be assigned. As keepers of the flocks it is proper to place in charge men who are diligent and very thrifty. These two qualities are more important for this task than stature and strength of body, since this is a responsibility requiring unremitting watchfulness and skill. In the case of the ploughman,[a] intelligence, 2 though necessary, is still not sufficient unless bigness of voice and in bearing makes him formidable to the cattle. Yet he should temper his strength with gentleness, since he should be more terrifying than cruel, so that the oxen may obey his commands and at the same time last longer because they are not worn out with the hardship of the work combined with the torment of the lash. But what the duties of shepherds and herdsmen are, I shall treat again in their proper places;[b] for the present it is sufficient 3 to have called to mind that strength and height are of no importance in the one, but of the greatest importance in the other. For, as I have said, we shall make all the taller ones ploughmen, both for the reason I have just given and because in the work of the farm there is no task less tiring to a tall man; for in ploughing he stands almost erect and rests his weight on the plough-handle.[c] The common labourer may be of any height at all, if only he is capable of enduring hard work. Vineyards require not so much 4 tall men as those who are broad-shouldered and brawny, for this type is better suited to digging and pruning and other forms of viticulture. In this department husbandry is less exacting in the matter of

[c] Pliny (*N.H.* XVIII. 179) says that the ploughman does not steer a straight course unless he stoops to his work.

latio frugalitatem requirit, quia et in turba et sub
monitore vinitor opus facere debet ac plerumque
velocior animus est improborum hominum,[1] quem
desiderat huius operis conditio. Non solum enim
fortem, sed et acuminis strenui ministrum postulat,
ideoque vineta plurimum per alligatos excoluntur.
5 Nihil tamen eiusdem agilitatis homo frugi non melius
quam nequam faciet.

Hoc interposui, ne quis existimet in ea me opinione
versari, qua malim per noxios quam per innocentes
rura colere.[2] Sed et illud censeo, ne confundantur
opera familiae, sic ut omnes omnia exsequantur.
6 Nam id minime conducit agricolae, seu quia nemo
suum proprium aliquod esse opus credit, seu quia cum
enisus est, non suo sed communi officio proficit ideoque
labori multum se subtrahit; nec tamen viritim male-
factum deprehenditur, quod fit a multis. Propter
quod separandi sunt aratores a vinitoribus et vinitores
7 ab aratoribus[3] iique a[4] mediastinis. Classes etiam
non maiores quam denum hominum faciundae, quas
decurias appellaverunt antiqui et maxime probaverunt, quod is numeri modus in opere commodissime
custodiretur nec praeeuntis monitoris diligentiam
8 multitudo confunderet. Itaque si latior est ager, in
regiones diducendae[5] sunt eae classes dividundum-

[1] hominum *om. SA.* [2] coli *M.*

[3] *sic vulgo*: aratores (a *suprascr.* S^2) vinitoribus ab aratoribus *SA*: et vinitores ab aratoribus *inclusit Schn., monente Pontedera.*

[4] iique a] et qua *SA.*

[5] *sic* S^2 *et Schn. cum Gesn., not.*: deducendae S^1A, *Lundström cum edd. plerisque*: dividunde *R aliquot.*

honesty than in the others, for the reason that the
vine-dresser should do his work in company with others
and under supervision, and because the unruly are for
the most part possessed of quicker understanding,
which is what the nature of this work requires.
For it demands of the helper that he be not merely
strong but also quick-witted: and on this account
vineyards are commonly tended by slaves in fetters.
Still there is nothing that an honest man of equal 5
quickness will not do better than a rogue.

I have inserted this that no one may think me
obsessed of such a notion as to wish to till my land
with criminals rather than with honest men. But
this too I believe: that the duties of the slaves
should not be confused to the point where all take
a hand in every task. For this is by no means to 6
the advantage of the husbandman, either because
no one regards any particular task as his own or
because, when he does make an effort, he is
performing a service that is not his own but
common to all, and therefore shirks his work to a
great extent; and yet the fault cannot be fastened
upon any one man because many have a hand in it.
For this reason ploughmen must be distinguished
from vine-dressers, and vine-dressers from ploughmen, and both of these from men of all work.
Furthermore, squads should be formed, not to exceed 7
ten men each, which the ancients called *decuriae* and
approved of highly, because that limited number was
most conveniently guarded while at work, and the
size was not disconcerting to the person in charge as he
led the way. Therefore, if the field is of considerable 8
extent, such squads should be distributed over
sections of it and the work should be so apportioned

que ita opus, ut neque singuli binive sint, quoniam dispersi non facile custodiuntur; nec tamen supra decem, ne rursus, ubi nimia turba sit, id opus ad se pertinere singuli non existiment. Haec ordinatio non solum concitat aemulationem, sed et deprehendit ignavos; nam cum certamine opus excitetur, tum in cessantes animadversio iusta et sine querela videtur adhiberi.

9 Sed nimirum, dum quae maxime providenda sunt agricolae futuro praecipimus, de salubritate, de via, de vicino, de aqua, situ villae, fundi modo, colonorum et servorum generibus, officiorum operumque distributione tempestive per haec ad ipsum iam terrae cultum pervenimus, de quo pluribus libro insequente mox disseremus.

that men will not be by ones or twos, because they are not easily watched when scattered; and yet they should number not more than ten, lest, on the other hand, when the band is too large, each individual may think that the work does not concern him. This arrangement not only stimulates rivalry, but also it discloses the slothful; for, when a task is enlivened by competition, punishment inflicted on the laggards appears just and free from censure.

But surely, in pointing out to the farmer-to-be 9
those matters for which especial provision must be made—healthfulness, roads, neighbourhood, water, situation of the homestead, size of the farm, classes of tenants and slaves, and assignment of duties and tasks—we have now come properly, through these steps, to the actual tilling of the soil; of this we shall presently treat at greater length in the book that follows.

BOOK II

LIBER II

I. Quaeris ex me, P. Silvine, quod ego sine cunctatione non recuso docere, cur priore libro veterem[1] opinionem fere omnium, qui de cultu agrorum locuti sunt, a principio confestim reppulerim, falsamque sententiam repudiaverim censentium longo aevi situ longique iam temporis exercitatione fatigatam
2 et effetam humum consenuisse. Nec te ignoro cum et aliorum inlustrium scriptorum tum praecipue Tremeli auctoritatem revereri, qui, cum plurima rusticarum rerum praecepta simul eleganter et scite memoriae prodiderit, videlicet inlectus nimio favore priscorum de simili materia disserentium falso credidit parentem omnium terram, sicut muliebrem sexum aetate anili iam confectam, progenerandis esse fetibus inhabilem. Quod ipse quoque confiterer,
3 si in totum nullae fruges provenirent.[2] Nam et hominis tum demum declaratur sterile senium, non cum desinit mulier trigeminos aut geminos parere, sed cum omnino nullum conceptum edere valet. Itaque transactis iuventae temporibus, etiam si longe vita superest, partus tamen annis denegatus non resti-

[1] veterum *R*, *edd. ante Schn.*
[2] convenirent *SA*.

I. *Praef.* 1.

BOOK II

I. You ask me, Publius Silvinus, and I have no hesitation in informing you at once, why in the preceding book I immediately at the start[a] rejected the long-standing opinion of almost all who have discoursed on the subject of agriculture, and repudiated as mistaken the views of those who hold that the soil, wearied and exhausted by age-long wasting away and by cultivation now extending over a long period of time, has become barren. And I am not unaware 2
that you hold in reverence, not only the authority of other renowned writers, but particularly that of Tremelius, who, in handing down to posterity a very great number of agricultural precepts set forth with refinement as well as learning, being obviously misled through too great deference to the ancients who treat of a like subject, held the mistaken belief that the earth, the mother of all things, like womankind now worn out with old age, is incapable of bearing offspring. This fact I too should admit if no fruits whatever were being produced; for the old age of 3
a human being also is pronounced barren, not when a woman no longer gives birth to triplets and twins, but only when she is able to conceive and bring forth no offspring at all. Thus, after the period of youth is past, even though a long life still remains, still parturition is denied to years and is not re-

tuitur. At e contrario seu sponte seu quolibet casu derelicta[1] humus, cum est repetita cultu, magno
4 faenore cessatorum[2] colono respondet. Non ergo est exiguarum frugum causa terrae vetustas, si modo, cum semel invasit senectus, regressum non habet nec revirescere[3] aut repubescere potest; sed ne lassitudo quidem soli minuit agricolae fructum. Neque enim prudentis est adduci tamquam in hominibus nimiae corporis exercitationi[4] aut oneris alicuius ponderi,[5] sic cultibus et agitationibus agrorum
5 fatigationem succedere. Quid ergo est, inquis, quod adseverat Tremelius intacta et silvestria loca, cum primum ceperint[6] cultum, exuberare, mox deinde non ita respondere labori colonorum? Videt sine dubio quid eveniat, sed cur id accidat non pervidet. Neque enim idcirco rudis et modo ex silvestri habitu in arvum transducta fecundior haberi terra debet, quod sit requietior et iunior, sed quod multorum annorum frondibus et herbis, quas suapte natura progenerabat, velut saginata largioribus pabulis facilius edendis educandisque frugibus sufficit.
6 At cum perruptae rastris et aratris radices herbarum ferroque succisa nemora frondibus suis desierunt alere matrem, quaeque temporibus autumni frutectis

[1] destituta *R nonnulli deteriores, Ald., Gesn., Schn.*
[2] cessationis *M, Ald., Gesn., Schn.*
[3] reviviscere *R aliquot.*
[4] nimia . . . exercitatione *R nonnulli, Ald., Gesn.*
[5] ponderi *Schn., Lundström*: ponderis *SA¹a*: pondere *R plerique, edd. ante Schn.*
[6] ceperint *Lundström*: coeperint *SA et R aliquot, plerique edd.*; *deinde* cultu *Ald., Gesn.*

stored. But on the contrary, when the soil, whether abandoned deliberately or by chance, is cultivated anew, it repays the farmer with heavy interest for its periods of idleness.[a] The antiquity of the earth, 4
therefore, is not the reason for the scantiness of her fruits—if, I mean, when once old age sets in, it takes no backward step and has no power to grow vigorous and young again—but not even the weariness of the soil lessens its fruits for the farmer. For it is not like a man of intelligence to be persuaded that, as in the case of human beings exhaustion follows immoderate physical exertion or the bearing of some heavy burden, just so does it follow cultivation and activity on the part of the land. What then, you say, does 5
Tremelius mean by his assertion that virginal and wooded areas, when they are first cultivated, yield abundantly, but soon thereafter are not so responsive to the toil of those who work them? He observes, undoubtedly, what occurs, but does not understand thoroughly why it happens. For ground that is new and but recently taken out of its wooded state and brought under cultivation should not be regarded as more fruitful on this account, because it has lain fallow longer and is younger; but because, in the leaves and herbage of many years, which it has kept producing naturally, fattened, so to speak, with more plentiful nourishment, it more readily satisfies the requirements for bringing forth crops and supporting them. But when the roots of the plants, broken by 6
mattocks and ploughs, and when the trees, cut down by the axe, cease to nourish their mother with their foliage; when the leaves which fell from bushes and

[a] Lundström restores the reading of the best manuscripts, preferred also by Pontedera as *cessatorum* ⟨*temporum*⟩.

et arboribus delapsa folia superiaciebantur, mox conversa vomeribus et inferiori solo, quod plerumque est exilius, permixta atque absumpta sunt, sequitur, ut destituta pristinis alimentis macrescat humus.
7 Non igitur fatigatione, quemadmodum plurimi crediderunt, nec senio, sed nostra scilicet inertia minus benigne nobis arva respondent. Licet enim maiorem fructum percipere, si frequenti et tempestiva et modica stercoratione [1] terra refoveatur. De cuius cultu dicturos nos priori volumine polliciti iam nunc disseremus.

II. Callidissimi rusticarum rerum, Silvine, genera terreni tria esse dixerunt, campestre, collinum, montanum. Campum non aequissima situm planitie nec perlibrata, sed exigue prona, collem clementer et molliter adsurgentem, montem [2] sublimem et asperum, sed nemorosum et herbidum, maxime pro-
2 baverunt. His autem generibus singulis senae species contribuuntur, soli pinguis vel macri, soluti vel spissi, umidi vel sicci, quae qualitates inter se mixtae vicibus et alternatae plurimas efficiunt agrorum varietates. Eas enumerare non est artificis agricolae; neque enim artis officium est per species, quae sunt innumerabiles, evagari sed [3] ingredi per genera, quae possunt et cogitatione mentis et ambitu
3 verborum facile copulari. Recurrendum est igitur ad qualitatum [4] inter se dissidentium quasi quasdam

[1] sterceratione *SAa*, *Lundström.*
[2] montem non sublimem *Ald.*, *Gesn.*, *Schn.*
[3] et *SAa*, *vett. edd.*, *Lundström.*
[4] qualitatium *SA et R aliquot*, *Lundström.*

---

[a] *Cf.* Varro, *R.R.* I. 6. 2.
[b] *Cf.* Palladius, I. 5. 5.

trees in the autumn season and which were spread over her are presently turned under by the ploughshare and mixed with the subsoil, which is usually thinner, and are used up, the result is that the soil, being deprived of its old-time nourishment, grows lean. It is not, therefore, because of weariness, as 7
very many have believed, nor because of old age, but manifestly because of our own lack of energy that our cultivated lands yield us a less generous return. For we may reap greater harvests if the earth is quickened again by frequent, timely, and moderate manuring. As I promised in the preceding book to speak of its cultivation, I shall now begin the discussion.

II. Those who are most experienced in agricultural affairs have said, Silvinus, that there are three kinds of terrain—champaign, hilly, and mountainous.[a] Of champaign land they favoured especially that lying, not in a perfectly even and level plain, but in a somewhat sloping one; of hilly land, that with a gentle and gradual rise; of mountainous land, the high and rugged, but wooded and grassy.[b] Furthermore, 2
under each of these classes there fall six species of soil—fat or lean, loose or compact, moist or dry; and these qualities, in combination and in alternation with one another, produce a very great variety of soils. To enumerate them is not the mark of a skilled farmer; for it is not the business of any art to roam about over the species, which are countless, but to proceed through the classes, for these can readily be connected in the imagination and brought within the compass of words. We must have recourse, then, 3
to certain unions, as we may call them, between qualities which are at variance with each other—

coniunctiones, quas Graeci συζυγίας ἐναντιοτήτων,[1] nos "discordantium comparationes" tolerabiliter dixerimus. Atque etiam significandum est ex omnibus, quae terra progeneret, plura campo magis quam colle, plura pingui solo quam macro laetari.
4 De siccaneis et riguis non comperimus, utra numero vincant, quoniam utrimque paene infinita sunt,[2] quae siccis quaeque umidis locis gaudent; sed ex his nihil non melius resoluta humo quam densa provenit. Quod noster quoque Vergilius, cum et alias fecundi arvi laudes rettulisset, adiecit,

et cui putre solum namque hoc imitamur arando.

Neque enim aliud est colere quam resolvere et
5 fermentare terram; ideoque maximos quaestus ager praebet idem pinguis ac putris, quia cum plurimum reddat, minimum poscit, et quod postulat exiguo labore atque impensa conficitur. Praestantissimum igitur tale solum iure dicatur. Proximum deinde huic pinguiter densum, quod impensam
6 coloni laboremque magno fetu remuneratur. Tertia est ratio loci rigui, quia sine impensa fructum reddere potest. Hanc primam Cato esse dicebat, qui maxime reditum pratorum ceteris anteponebat; sed nos de
7 agitatione terrae nunc loquimur, non de situ. Nullum deterius habetur genus quam quod est pariter siccum et densum et macrum, quia cum difficulter

[1] *Graec. om., spat. relict. R plerique.*
[2] cum (*R*) utique p. i. sint (*R aliquot*) *Ald., Gesn.*

[a] Vergil, *Georg.* II. 204. [b] *Cf.* Cato, 9.

what the Greeks call συζυγίαι ἐναντιοτήτων, and which we may fairly render "the couplings of opposites." Furthermore, it must be pointed out that, of all things which the earth brings forth, more thrive better on a plain than on a hill, and more in fat land than in lean. As to dry ground and wet ground, 4 we have not ascertained which of these excels in number, since there are, in each case, almost limitless things which thrive in dry places, and the same in wet areas; but of this number there is nothing that does not grow better in loose soil than in dense. This, too, our own Vergil said when, after recounting the other good points of a fruitful field, he added:

> and one of crumbling soil; for this is what we rival when we plough.[a]

For cultivation is nothing else than the loosening and breaking up of the ground; and on this account a 5 field which is both rich and mellow yields the greatest returns, because in producing most it demands least, and what it does require is supplied with trifling labour and expense. Such a soil may therefore with justice be called the very best. Next in order to this is the combination of rich and dense, a soil which rewards the expense and toil of the husbandman with rich increase. Third in rank is a well-watered place, 6 because it can produce fruits without expense. Cato, who rated the yield of meadow lands far ahead of other returns, used to say that this kind of land was first;[b] but we are now speaking of land under cultivation, not of that left untilled. No kind is con- 7 sidered worse than that which is at the same time dry, stiff, and lean; for not only is it worked with

tractetur, tum ne tractatum quidem gratiam refert nec relictum pratis vel pascuis abunde sufficit. Itaque hic ager sive exercetur seu cessat, colono est paenitendus ac tamquam pestilens refugiendus. Nam ille mortem facit, hic taeterrimam comitem mortis famem, si tamen Graecis camenis habemus fidem clamitantibus:

λιμῷ δ' οἴκτιστον θανέειν.

8 Sed nunc potius uberioris soli meminerimus, cuius demonstranda est duplex tractatio, culti et silvestris. De silvestri regione in arvorum formam redigenda[1] prius dicemus, quoniam est antiquius facere agrum quam colere. Incultum igitur locum consideremus, siccus an umidus, nemorosus arboribus an lapidibus confragosus, iuncone sit et[2] gramine vestitus an[3]
9 filictis[4] aliisve frutectis impeditus. Si umidus erit, abundantia uliginis ante siccetur fossis. Earum duo genera cognovimus, caecarum et patentium. Spissis atque cretosis regionibus apertae relinquuntur; at ubi solutior humus est, aliquae fiunt patentes, quaedam etiam occaecantur, ita ut in ora[5] hiantium

[1] derigenda *S*: dirigenda *A et R aliquot, vett. edd.*
[2] *sic Lundström cum codd. plerisque ut videtur*: an *vel* de *R nonnulli, cett. edd.*
[3] *sic Lundström cum Laurentiano* 53. 27: ac *SAR, cett. edd.*
[4] filictis *R plerique, Ald., Gesn., Schn.*: felictis *SA, Lundström*: filicibus *vett. edd.*: salictis *R pauci.*

difficulty, but even when worked it makes no recompense, and when left idle it is not altogether adequate for meadows or for grazing land. Therefore this type, whether in tillage or fallow, is a source of grief to the husbandman and should be shunned as if it were plague-ridden ground; for the one type brings death, and this brings starvation, that most frightful attendant of death, if we may trust the Grecian Muses, who cry:

To die of hunger is the bitterest of fates.[a]

But now we shall turn our attention rather to the 8
more fertile soil, and our treatment of this is to be set forth under two heads—land in tillage, and woodland. We shall first speak of reducing a wooded area to an arable state, for the reason that the preparation of a field comes before its cultivation. As to an untilled piece of ground, then, let us consider whether it is dry or damp, shaded with trees or rough and stony; whether it is covered with rushes and grass or encumbered with fern-brakes or other bushy
growth. If it is damp, the superfluous moisture must 9
first be drained off with ditches. Of these we are familiar with two kinds—blind and open. In tracts of hard-packed and chalky soil they are left open; but where the ground is of looser texture some are made open and some of them, too, are covered over, though in such a way as to connect with the

[a] Homer, *Od.* XII. 342.

---

[5] in ora *Sobel*: in eas ora *R*, *vett. edd.*, *Lundström*: in ea hora (h *expunct.*) *S*: in ea ora *A*. in patentes ora hiantia caecarum competant *habent Ald.*, *Gesn.*, *Schn.*

fossarum competant. Sed[1] latius apertas summa parte declivesque et ad solum coartatas imbricibus supinis similes facere conveniet; nam quarum recta sunt latera, celeriter aquis vitiantur et superioris
10 soli lapsibus replentur. Opertae rursus occaecari debebunt sulcis in altitudinem tripedaneam depressis; qui cum parte dimidia lapides minutos vel nudam glaream receperint, aequentur superiecta terra, quae fuerat effossa. Vel si nec lapis erit nec glarea, sarmentis connexus velut funis informabitur in eam crassitudinem, quam solum fossae possit angustae
11 quasi accommodatam coartatamque capere. Tum per imum[2] contendetur, ut super calcatis cupressinis vel pineis aut, si eae non erunt, aliis frondibus terra contegatur, in principio atque exitu fossae more ponticulorum binis saxis tantummodo pilarum vice constitutis et singulis superpositis, ut eius modi constructio ripam sustineat, ne praecludatur umoris inlapsus atque exitus.

Nemorosi frutectosique tractus duplex cura est vel exstirpandis radicitus arboribus et removendis vel, si rarae sunt, tantum succidendis incendendisque
12 et inarandis. Ac saxosum facile est expedire lectione

[1] sed patentes latius *Schn.*: sed et petentes latius *Ald.*, *Gesn.*
[2] humum *M.*

---

[a] The text here translated accepts the emendation of Ragnar Sobel ("En Columellakonjektur," *Apophoreta Gotoburgensia Vilelmo Lundström Oblata* [Gothenburg, 1936], pp. 169–170), reversing the illogical position of covered and open ditches as found in most of the manuscripts and in

mouths of the open ditches.[a] But it will be best
to make open drains wider at the top, and sloping
and narrowing together at the bottom, like inverted
roof-tiles; for those whose sides are perpendicular
are quickly eroded by water and are filled in by the
slipping of the earth above. The covered ones, on 10
the other hand, are to be blinded by sinking trenches
to a depth of three feet, and then, after they have
received a filling half way up of small stones or clean
gravel, levelling them off by throwing over them the
dirt that was dug out. Or, if stones and gravel are not
available, a sort of cable of entwined brushwood will be
fashioned of such a thickness as the bottom of the
narrow trench may receive when it is fitted, so to speak,
and pressed down close. This will then be stretched 11
along the bottom, to be covered over with earth after
cypress or pine foliage—or, failing this, other
boughs—has been trampled down over it; there
being, both at the beginning and at the outlet of the
ditch, two stones set up, merely by way of supports,
with one stone laid on top of them in the fashion of
little bridges, that this sort of structure may hold
the banks in place and prevent the stoppage of water
at inlet and outlet.

There are two methods of handling a wooded and
bushy stretch of land: either by tearing out the trees
by the roots and removing them or, if they are few,
by simply cutting them down, burning them, and
ploughing them under. It is easy to clear stony 12

Lundstrom's text. Earlier editors read *ut in patentes ora hiantia caecarum competant*, "that the gaping mouths of the blind ditches may connect with those that are open." On the subject of ditching, *cf.* Cato, 43. 1, 155; and especially Pliny, *N.H.* XVIII. 47, and Palladius, VI. 3.

lapidum, quorum si magna est abundantia, velut quibusdam substructionibus partes agri sunt occupandae, ut reliquae emundentur, vel in altitudinem sulco depresso lapides obruendi; quod tamen ita
13 faciendum erit, si suadebit operarum vilitas.[1] Iunci et graminis pernicies[2] repastinatio est, filicis[3] frequens exstirpatio, quae vel aratro fieri potest; quoniam intra biennium saepius convulsa emoritur,[4] celerius etiam, si eodem tempore stercores et lupino vel faba conseras, ut cum aliquo reditu medearis agri vitio. Namque constat filicem sationibus et stercoratione facilius interimi.[5] Verum et si subinde nascentem falce decidas, quod vel puerile opus est, intra praedictum tempus vivacitas eius absumitur.
14 Sed iam expediendi rudis agri rationem[6] sequitur cultorum novalium cura, de qua mox quid censeam profitebor, si quae ante discenda sunt, arvorum studiosis praecepero.

Plurimos antiquorum, qui de rusticis rebus scripserunt, memoria repeto quasi confessa nec dubia signa pinguis ac frumentorum fertilis agri prodidisse dulcedinem soli propriam, herbarum et arborum
15 proventum, colorem[7] nigrum vel cinereum. Nihil de ceteris ambigo, de colore satis admirari non possum cum alios tum etiam[8] Cornelium Celsum, non solum agricolationis sed universae naturae

[1] utilitas *R aliquot.* [2] pernities *S, Lundström.*
[3] felicis *SA, Lundström.*
[4] *sic Lundström, praeeunte Madvig.*: convulsae moritur *vel* moriuntur *codd. et edd. vulgo, sed* convulsa *Schneider, Corrigenda.*
[5] interemi *S*[1]*A, Lundström.*
[6] ruris agricolationem *R plerique, vett. edd.*
[7] colorem *om. AR, vett. edd.*
[8] etiam *om. R, edd. ante Schn.*

ground by gathering up the stones; and if there is a great quantity of them, parts of the field must be used for building them into piles of some sort, so that the other parts may be cleared off, or the stones will have to be buried in a deep-dug trench. This should be done, however, only if the cheapness of labour makes it advisable. The bane of rushes and grass 13
is repeated grubbing, of the fern it is constant uprooting, which may be done also with the plough; for it dies out within two years' time if torn up repeatedly, and even sooner if at the same time you apply manure and sow with lupines or beans so as to have some return while remedying the defects of the field. For it is agreed that the fern is more easily destroyed by sowing and manuring; but even if you cut it down with the sickle (which is work even a child could do) as it sprouts out from time to time, within the aforesaid period its vigour is spent. But now, 14
after a consideration of the clearing of unbroken ground, comes the management of land newly brought under cultivation; and I shall set forth presently my own views on this, after I have given to those who are concerned with land in tillage some precepts on matters which must be learned first.

I recall that very many of the ancients who have written on agricultural topics have laid down as acknowledged and unquestioned evidence of fat and fertile grain-land the natural sweetness of the soil, its growth of herbage and trees, and its black or ashy colour. As to the other points I have no doubt; 15
but in the matter of colour I cannot marvel enough, not only that other writers but especially that Cornelius Celsus, a man of discernment not merely in

prudentem virum, sic et sententia et visu deerrasse, ut oculis eius tot paludes, tot etiam campi salinarum non occurrerent, quibus fere contribuuntur praedicti
16 colores. Nullum enim temere videmus locum, qui modo pigrum contineat umorem, non eundem vel nigri vel cinerei coloris, nisi forte in eo fallor ipse, quod non putem aut in solo limosae paludis et uliginis amarae aut in maritimis areis salinarum gigni posse laeta frumenta. Sed est manifestior hic antiquorum error, quam ut pluribus argumentis convincendus sit. Non ergo color tamquam certus auctor testis est
17 bonitatis arvorum; et ideo frumentarius ager, id est pinguis, magis aliis qualitatibus aestimandus est. Nam ut fortissimae pecudes diversos et paene innumerabiles, sic etiam robustissimae terrae plurimos et varios colores sortitae sunt. Itaque considerandum erit, ut solum quod excolere destinamus,
18 pingue sit. Per se tamen id parum est, si dulcedine caret; quod utrumque satis expedita nobis ratione contingit discere. Nam perexigua conspargitur[1] aqua glaeba manuque subigitur, ac si glutinosa est, quamvis levissimo tactu pressa inhaerescit et

picis in morem ad digitos lentescit habendo,

ut ait Vergilius, eademque inlisa humo non dissipatur, quae res nos admonet inesse tali materiae naturalem
19 sucum et pinguitudinem. Sed si velis scrobibus

[1] conspergitur *S*[2] *et R aliquot, edd. ante Lundström.*

---

[a] *Georg.* II. 250. Palladius (I. 5. 3) also considers this a test of fat soil; but Pliny (XVII. 27) remarks that stickiness is not a true test of fat soil, for potter's clay has the same quality.

husbandry but also in nature as a whole, went so far astray, both in his thinking and in his observation, that the many marshes and the many stretches of salt meadows, in which the above-mentioned colours are usually present, did not attract his notice. For our casual observations reveal no 16
place, provided it contains stagnant water, which is not of a black or ashy colour; unless perhaps I am myself mistaken in thinking that luxuriant grain crops cannot be produced in the soil of slimy swamp and brackish marshland or in a region of salt deposits along the seacoast. But this mistake of the ancients is too apparent to require refutation by further argument. It is not the colour, then, that is, so to speak, the infallible voucher and witness of goodness of ploughland; and for that reason grain- 17
land, that is rich land, is to be judged rather by other qualities. For, as the sturdiest of farm animals have been allotted different and almost countless colours, just so the strongest soils have them in very great number and variety. Accordingly, we must take care that the soil which we intend to cultivate is rich. Still this of itself is not sufficient if it lacks 18
sweetness; and we may come to know both qualities by a very easy method. For a clod is sprinkled with a little water and kneaded in the hand, and if it is viscous and cohesive when firmed with the slightest touch and,

> in the manner of pitch is shaped to the fingers in handling,

as Vergil says,[a] and does not crumble when dashed to the ground, this test informs us that there is in such earth a natural moistness and fatness. But when 19

egestam humum recondere et recalcare, cum aliquo
quasi fermento abundaverit, certum erit esse eam
pinguem; cum defuerit, exilem; cum aequaverit,
mediocrem. Quamquam ista, quae nunc rettuli,
non tam vera possint [1] videri, si sit pulla terra, quae
20 melius proventu frugum approbatur. Saporem [2]
quoque sic [3] dinoscemus: [4] ex ea parte agri, quae
maxime displicebit, effossae glaebae et in fictili vaso
madefactae dulci aqua permisceantur ac more
faeculenti vini diligenter colatae gustu explorentur;
nam qualem traditum ab eis rettulerit umor saporem,
talem esse dicemus eius soli.[5] Sed et citra hoc
experimentum multa sunt, quae et dulcem terram
et frumentis habilem significent, ut iuncus, ut
calamus, ut gramen, ut trifolium, ebulum, rubi, pruni
silvestres et alia complura, quae etiam indagatoribus
aquarum nota non nisi [6] dulcibus terrae venis edu-
21 cantur. Nec contentos esse nos oportet prima specie
summi soli, sed diligenter exploranda est inferioris
materiae qualitas, terrena necne sit. Frumentis
autem sat erit, si aeque bona suberit bipedanea
humus; arboribus altitudo quattuor pedum abunde
est. Haec cum ita exploraverimus, agrum sationibus

[1] possunt *M*, *Ald.*, *Gesn.*, *Schn.*
[2] Sapore *Ald.*, *Gesn.*, *Schn*
[3] sic *om. Gesn.*, *Schn.*
[4] dignoscemus, si ex *Ald.*, *Gesn.*, *Schn.*
[5] humi *M*.
[6] non tamen nisi *AR*, *vett. edd.*

---

[a] Such a soil test is mentioned also by Vergil (*Georg.* II. 226–237) and Palladius (*loc. cit.*). Pliny (*loc. cit.*) rejects the test as inconclusive.

[b] *Cf.* I. *Praef.* 24.

[c] On testing by tasting *cf. De Arb.* 3. 6; Vergil, *Georg.* II. 238–247; Palladius, *loc. cit.*

you try to put back and tread down in trenches the earth that has been removed, if there is an excess as by some sort of leavening, it will be a sure sign that the soil is fat; if it is insufficient, that it is poor; if it makes an even fill, that it is ordinary.[a] And yet the statements which I have just now made may seem not so trustworthy in the case of blackish earth (*pulla*),[b] which is better tested by its yield of crops. We shall also make distinctions of taste as follows: 20
from that part of the field which displeases us most, clods should be dug and soaked in an earthen vessel, then thoroughly mixed with fresh water and, after careful straining in the manner of dreggy wine, examined by tasting;[c] for, whatever is the taste transmitted from the clods to the water, such we shall take to be the taste of that soil. But, apart from this experiment, there are many signs which show that ground is sweet and suitable for grain—for example, the rush, the reed, grass, trefoil, the dwarf-elder, bramble bushes, wild plums, and many other things which are well known also to searchers for springs,[d] and which are not nourished except by veins of sweet water in the ground. And we should not be content 21
with the first appearance of surface soil, but should take pains to investigate the character of what lies beneath—whether it is earthy or not. It will be satisfactory for grain, however, if the soil below is equally good to a depth of two feet; for trees, a depth of four feet is sufficient.[e] When we have investigated these points as stated, we shall put our

[d] For directions as to the ancient methods of locating water, digging wells, and piping, see Vitruvius, *De Arch.* VIII, Chaps. 1 and 5–6, and Palladius, IX. 8–12.
[e] *Cf.* Palladius, I. 6. 11.

faciundis expediemus. Is autem non minimum exuberat, si curiose et scite subigitur. Quare antiquissimum est formam huius operis conscribere,[1] quam velut sectam legemque in proscindendis agris sequantur agricolae.

22 Igitur in opere boves arte iunctos habere convenit, quo speciosius ingrediantur sublimes et elatis capitibus ac minus colla eorum labefactentur iugumque melius aptum cervicibus insidat. Hoc enim genus iuncturae maxime probatum est. Nam illud, quod in quibusdam provinciis usurpatur, ut cornibus inligetur iugum, fere repudiatum est ab omnibus qui praecepta rusticis conscripserunt, neque immerito.
23 Plus enim queunt pecudes collo et pectore conari quam cornibus, atque hoc modo tota mole corporis totoque pondere nituntur; at illo retractis et resupinis capitibus excruciantur aegreque terrae summam partem levi admodum vomere sauciant. Et ideo minoribus aratris moliuntur, quia[2] non valent alte perfossa novalium terga[3] rescindere; quod cum fit, omnibus virentibus plurimum confertur,[4] nam penitus arvis sulcatis maiore incremento segetum arborumque
24 fetus grandescunt. Et in hoc igitur a Celso dissentio, qui reformidans impensam, quae scilicet largior est in amplioribus armentis,[5] censet et exiguis vomeribus et dentalibus terram subigere, quo minoris formae bubus id administrari possit; ignorans plus esse

[1] conscripsere *A et R plerique.*
[2] quia *S, Lundström*: qui *AR, et vulgo.*
[3] terra *AR.* [4] confert *Ald., Gesn., Schn.*
[5] armentis *edd.*: argumentis *SAR*: iugamentis *M.*

[a] *Cf.* Palladius, II. 3. 1. Pliny, though apparently in agreement with Columella (*N.H.* XVIII. 177), speaks of yoking by the head as customary in the Alps (*N.H.* VIII. 179).

field in readiness for planting; and it yields no trifling increase if it is worked with care and understanding. For this reason it is a matter of first importance to put a plan of this kind of work in writing, that husbandmen may adhere to it as a pattern and a law in the breaking up of their fields.

To proceed then, it is proper to have oxen closely 22
yoked while at work, so that they will move with a more stately gait, with lofty bearing and heads held high; also that their necks may be galled less, and that the yoke may sit more closely on their shoulders. This method of yoking is most approved; for the method in use in some provinces—fastening the yoke to the horns—has been condemned by almost all who have written precepts for husbandmen, and not without reason. For cattle can put forth more effort 23
with neck and shoulders than with the horns,[a] and in this way they exert themselves with the entire bulk of the body and its whole weight; but in the other way, with their heads pulled back and faces turned upward, they are tortured, and barely scratch the surface of the ground with a very light ploughshare. And it is for this reason that they work with smaller ploughs, because they are unable to tear up the surface of new ground and dig it deep; but when this is done, all growing things are greatly benefited, for when ploughlands are deeply furrowed the fruits of crops and trees swell with greater increase. On 24
this point, therefore, I disagree with Celsus, who, shrinking from the expense which is undoubtedly greater in the case of larger cattle, advises the breaking up of land with small shares and share-beams, so that it may be accomplished with oxen of smaller size; disregarding the fact that the revenue in fruit-

reditus in ubertate frugum quam impendii, si maiora mercemur armenta, praesertim in Italia, ubi arbustis atque oleis consitus ager altius resolvi ac subigi desiderat, ut et summae radices vitium olearumque vomeribus rescindantur, quae si maneant, frugibus obsint, et inferiores penitus subacto solo facilius
25 capiant umoris alimentum. Potest tamen illa Celsi ratio Numidiae et Aegypto convenire, ubi plerumque arboribus viduum solum frumentis seminatur; atque eius modi terram pinguibus harenis putrem velut cinerem solutam quamvis levissimo dente moveri satis est. Bubulcum autem per proscissum ingredi oportet alternisque versibus obliquum tenere aratrum et alternis recto plenoque sulcare, sed ita necubi crudum solum et immotum relinquat, quod agricolae
26 scamnum vocant; boves, cum ad arborem venerint, fortiter retinere ac retardare, ne in radicem maiore nisu vomis impactus colla commoveat, neve aut cornu bos ad stipitem vehementius offendat aut extremo iugo truncum delibet ramumque deplantet. Voce potius quam verberibus terreat, ultimaque sint opus recusantibus remedia plagae. Numquam stimulo lacessat iuvencum, quae res taetricum [1] calcitrosumque eum reddit, non numquam tamen admoneat

[1] quae res taetricum *scripsi, praeeunte ex parte Lundström* (q. r. taetratum): quae rescae tratum *SA*: q; reste (*vel* recte) tractum *R*: iuvencumque reste (*vel* recte) tractum *vett. edd.*: quod retrectantem *Gesn., Schn., praeeunte Ursino* (q. retractantem).

---

[a] The *arbustum* was a plantation of trees to which vines were trained.

[b] *Cf.* Varro, *L.L.* V. 135, *dens, quod eo mordetur terra.*

[c] *I.e.* a "skip" or "balk." On the matter of ploughs

fulness of crops outweighs the expense of buying
heavier draught animals, and especially in Italy,
where the land, being planted with vineyards [a] and
olives, wants to be broken and worked rather deep,
so that the uppermost roots of vines and olives, which
are detrimental to the yield if they are left, may be
cut off by the ploughshares, and that the deeper roots
may receive the nourishment of moisture more
readily when the ground is deeply worked. Still 25
Celsus' method may be suited to Numidia and
Egypt, where, as a rule, the land is destitute of trees
and is sown with grain; and soil of that sort, crumbling
with fat sands, and like loose ashes, is stirred sufficiently
with the lightest plough-point (*dens*).[b] The ploughman, moreover, must walk upon the broken ground
and in every other furrow must hold his plough slantwise, running alternate furrows with the plough upright and at its full depth, but in such a way as not
to leave anywhere any solid and unbroken ground,
which farmers call *scamnum*.[c] When the oxen come 26
to a tree, he must keep them firmly in hand and check
their pace, for fear that the driving of the ploughshare
with too great force against a root may jolt their
necks, and so that an ox may not strike a horn
violently against the bole of the tree, or graze the
trunk or break off a branch with the end of the yoke.
He should keep them in dread of his voice rather than
of his lash, blows being his last resort when they
balk at a task. He should never urge a bullock with
a goad, for this makes him irritable and inclined
to kick; yet he may urge him on now and then with a

and ploughing, particularly with reference to this chapter and the three following, see Fairfax Harrison, "The Crooked Plow," *Classical Journal* XI. 323–332.

27 flagello. Sed nec in media parte versurae consistat detque requiem in summa, ut spe cessandi totum spatium bos agilius enitatur. Sulcum autem ducere longiorem quam pedum centum viginti contrarium pecori est, quoniam plus aequo fatigatur ubi hunc
28 modum excessit. Cum ventum erit ad versuram, in priorem partem iugum propellat et boves inhibeat, ut colla eorum refrigescant, quae celeriter conflagrant, si adsidue stringuntur,[1] et ex eo tumor ac deinde ulcera invadunt. Nec minus dolabra quam vomere bubulcus utatur et praefractas stirpes summasque radices, quibus ager arbusto consitus implicatur, omnes refodiat ac persequatur.

III. Boves cum ab opere disiunxerit, substrictos confricet, manibusque comprimat dorsum et pellem revellat nec patiatur corpori adhaerere, quia et[2]
2 genus morbi maxime est armentis noxium. Colla subigat merumque faucibus, si aestuaverint, infundat; satis autem est singulis vini[3] sextarios praebere. Sed ante ad praesaepia boves religari non expedit, quam sudare atque anhelare desierint. Cum deinde tempestive potuerint vesci, non multum nec universum cibum, sed partibus et paulatim praebere convenit. Quem cum absumpserint, ad aquam duci

[1] si . . . stringuntur *scripsi*: nisi (*ex* -nt si?) . . . stringantur (astringantur *M*) *codd.*, *vett. edd.*, *Lundström*: refrigerentur *Ald.*, *Gesn.*, *Schn.*
[2] et *SAR*: id *edd. ante Schn.* [3] binos *Ald.*, *Gesn.*, *Schn.*

---

[a] *I.e.* the part of the neck embraced by the bow of the yoke.

whip. He should not stop in the middle of the 27 furrow, but should allow a rest at the end of it, so that the ox will exert himself more energetically the whole way in the hope of stopping. But to run a furrow more than one hundred and twenty feet in length is injurious to a beast, for he is wearied more than is right when he goes beyond this limit. When 28 the turning-point is reached, the ploughman should push the yoke forward and hold the oxen back, to allow their necks to cool off; for these quickly become inflamed if they are constantly bound, and as a result there arises a swelling and then running sores. And the ploughman should use the mattock no less than the ploughshare, and should dig up and hunt out all the broken stumps and surface roots with which a field is infested when it is planted with trees for supporting vines.

III. When the ploughman has unyoked his oxen after work, he should rub the lower parts that were bound,[a] knead the upper part[b] with his hands, and pull up the skin and not allow it to cling to the body; for this, too, is a kind of ailment very injurious to cattle.[c] He should rub down their necks 2 and pour unmixed wine down their throats if they are heated; and it is enough to give a pint of wine to each. But it is not proper for oxen to be tied to their cribs before they have stopped sweating and panting. Then, when they are in proper condition for feeding, it is best not to give them much feed, and not the whole amount at once, but to portion it out, a little at a time. When they have consumed this, they

[b] Lit., the back (of the neck), pressed by the bar of the yoke.

[c] An affliction called *coriago*, "hidebound." *Cf.* VI. 13. 2–3, and Vegetius, *Vet.* IV. 12. 1, for causes and treatment.

oportet sibiloque adlectari, quo libentius bibant, tum demum reductos largiore pabulo satiari.

Hactenus de officio bubulci dixisse abunde est. Sequitur ut tempora quoque subigendi arvi praecipiamus.

IV. Pingues campi, qui diutius continent aquam, proscindendi sunt anni tempore iam incalescente, cum omnis herbas ediderint neque adhuc earum semina maturuerint; sed tam frequentibus densisque sulcis arandi sunt, ut vix dinoscatur, in utram partem vomer actus sit, quoniam sic omnes radices herbarum
2 perruptae necantur. Sed et compluribus iterationibus sic resolvatur vervactum in pulverem, ut vel nullam vel exiguam desideret occationem,[1] cum seminavimus.[2] Nam veteres Romani dixerunt male subactum agrum, qui satis frugibus occandus sit.
3 Eum porro an recte aretur frequenter explorare debet agricola, nec tantum visu, qui fallitur non numquam superfusa terra latentibus scamnis, verum etiam tactu, qui minus decipitur cum solidi rigoris admota pertica transversis sulcis inseritur. Ea si aequaliter ac sine offensatione[3] penetravit, manifestum est totum solum deinceps esse motum; sin autem subeunti durior aliqua pars obstitit, crudum vervactum esse demonstrat. Hoc cum saepius bubulci fieri vident, non committunt scamna facere.

[1] occasionem *SA*, *et R plerique*.

[2] seminabimus *S*, *vett. edd.*: seminaverimus *vulgo ante Lundström*.

[3] offensione *Ald.*, *Gesn.*, *Schn.*

---

[a] *Vervactum* is defined by Varro (*R.R.* I. 44. 2) as land that sometimes rests between crops, while land that is worked every year is called *restibilis*. Pliny, *N.H.* XVIII. 76, *quod vere semel aratum est, a temporis argumento vervactum vocatur.*

[b] *Cf.* Palladius, II. 3. 2.

should be led to water and enticed by whistling to drink more freely, and then at length taken back to eat their fill of a more generous allowance of fodder.

It is enough to have discussed the duties of the ploughman up to this point. Our next step is to give directions also as to the seasons for breaking up ploughland.

IV. Rich plains which hold water for a considerable length of time are to be broken at a time of year when it is growing warm, after they have put forth all their vegetation and while the seeds of this vegetation have not yet ripened; but they should be ploughed with furrows so numerous and close together that it can hardly be told in what direction the ploughshare has been driven, for in this way all the roots of the growth are broken off and killed. But fallow 2
land [a] should be so pulverized by much re-ploughing that it will require no harrowing, or very little, after we have put in the seed. For the ancient Romans said that a field was poorly prepared when it had to be harrowed after the crop was in the ground. Furthermore, a farmer should examine it 3
frequently to see whether it is properly ploughed—and not merely by sight, which is sometimes mistaken when earth is scattered over unploughed skips that lie hidden, but also by touch, which is deceived the less when a strong and stiff pole is put to use and pushed into the furrows crosswise. If it goes in to a uniform depth and without striking anything, it is clear that all the ground has been stirred in turn; but if some harder spot obstructs its entrance, it shows that there is unbroken fallow. When ploughmen observe that this is done rather frequently, they are not guilty of leaving skips.[b] Wet

Igitur uliginosi campi proscindi debent post Idus
4 mensis Aprilis. Quo tempore cum arati fuerint,
viginti [1] diebus interpositis circa solstitium, quod
est nonum vel octavum Kalendas Iulias, iteratos esse
oportebit ac deinde circa Septembris Kalendas
tertiatos; quoniam in id tempus ab aestivo solstitio
convenit inter peritos rei rusticae non esse arandum,
nisi si magnis, ut fit non numquam, subitaneis
imbribus quasi hibernis pluviis terra permaduerit.
5 Quod cum accidit, nihil prohibet quo minus mense
Iulio vervacta subigantur. Sed quandoque [2] arabi-
tur, observabimus ne lutosus ager tractetur neve
exiguis nimbis semimadidus, quam terram rustici
variam cariosamque appellant; ea est cum post
longas siccitates levis pluvia superiorem partem
glaebarum madefecit, inferiorem non attigit. Nam
quae limosa versantur arva, toto anno desinunt posse
tractari nec sunt habilia sementi aut occationi aut
sationi; [3] at rursus, quae varia subacta sunt, continuo
6 triennio sterilitate adficiuntur. Medium igitur
temperamentum maxime sequamur in arandis agris,
ut neque suco careant nec abundent uligine; quippe
nimius umor, ut dixi, limosos lutososque reddit, at
qui siccitatibus aruerunt, expediri probe non possunt.

[1] viginti *om. AR, edd. ante Schn.*
[2] quandocumque *M, edd. ante Gesn.*
[3] sarritioni *Schn., praeeuntibus Ursino et Pontedera.*

[a] *I.e.* after April 13th. *Cf.* Palladius, V (*April*). 2. 4.
[b] June 23rd or 24th.
[c] September 1st.

champaign lands, then, should be broken after the Ides of April.[a] When they are ploughed at this 4
time, they should be gone over a second time after the passing of the twenty days around the solstice—which falls on the ninth or eighth day before the Calends of July[b]—and then a third time in the neighbourhood of the Calends of September;[c] for it is agreed among experts in husbandry that no ploughing should be done from the summer solstice up to this time. unless, as sometimes happens, the earth is soaked with heavy and sudden showers as if by winter rains. In this case there is no objection 5
to breaking fallow land in the month of July. But whenever the ploughing is done, we must be careful not to let a field be worked when it is muddy or half soaked from light rains—a condition of soil which farmers call *varia* and *cariosa*;[d] that is, when, after a long drought, a light rain wets the upper surface of the clods but does not reach the lower part. For ploughlands which are turned over when they are muddy cannot be worked for a whole year, and they are not fit for sowing or harrowing or planting; but, on the other hand, those which are ploughed when they are *varia* are visited with barrenness for three successive years.[e] Let us, then, above all, follow a 6
middle course in ploughing our lands, that they may neither be entirely wanting in dampness nor immoderately wet; for too much moisture, as I have said, makes them sticky and muddy, while those that are parched with drought cannot be properly loosened.

[d] *Cf.* Cato, 5. 6. Pliny (*N.H.* XVII. 34–35), commenting on Cato's precept, compares carious ground with the rottenness of wood, as being dry, spongy, full of holes, weak, unfruitful, and not fit for anything.

[e] *Cf.* Palladius, II. 3. 2–3.

Nam vel respuitur duritia soli[1] dens aratri, vel si qua parte penetravit, non minute diffundit humum, sed vastos caespites convellit; quibus obiacentibus impeditum arvum minus recte potest iterari, quia ponderibus glaebarum, sicut aliquis[2] obstantibus fundamentis vomis a sulco repellitur, quo evenit ut in iteratione quoque scamna fiant et boves iniquitate
7 operis maxime mulcentur. Accedit huc, quod omnis humus quamvis laetissima tamen inferiorem partem ieiuniorem habet, eamque attrahunt excitatae maiores glaebae; quo evenit ut infecundior materia mixta pinguiori segetem minus uberem reddat, tum etiam ratio rustici adgravatur exiguo profectu operis.
8 Iusta enim fieri nequeunt, cum induruit ager. Itaque siccitatibus censeo quod iam proscissum est iterare pluviamque opperiri, quae madefacta terra facilem nobis culturam praebeat. Sed iugerum talis agri quattuor operis expeditur; nam commode proscinditur duabus, una iteratur, tertiatur dodrante, in liram satum[3] redigitur quadrante operae. Liras autem rustici vocant easdem porcas, cum sic aratum est ut inter duos latius distantes sulcos medius
9 cumulus siccam sedem frumentis praebeat. Colles pinguis soli peracta satione trimestrium[4] mense Martio, si vero tepor caeli siccitasque regionis suade-

[1] solis *codd.*
[2] aliquibus *R pauci, edd. ante Lundström.*
[3] statim R *pauci, edd. ante Gesn.*
[4] trimestri *Ald., Gesn., Schn.*

---

[a] About three-fifths of an acre.
[b] Varro says (*R.R.* I. 29. 3) that the ridges between the furrows are called *porcae* because that soil produces (*porricit*) the grain.

For either the point of the plough is rejected by the hardness of the ground or, if it does enter at some spot, it does not break the soil into fine particles, but tears up huge clods; and when these lie in the way, the plough-land is under a handicap and cannot be properly worked at the second ploughing, because the ploughshare is thrown out of the furrow by the weight of the clods as though by some deep-seated obstructions, with the result that hard skips are left even in the re-ploughing and that the oxen are severely injured by the unevenness of the strain. Added to this is that all ground, though it be never 7
so rich, still has poorer soil underneath, and when the larger clods are turned up they bring this with them; the result being that the less productive soil, mixed with the richer, grows a less bountiful crop, and in addition the accounting of the farmer is made more difficult by the poor progress of his work; for the proper tasks cannot be completed when the ground is hard. For this reason my advice is, in dry 8
weather, to replough ground already broken, and to wait for rain which, by its soaking of the earth, makes cultivation easy for us. But a *iugerum* [a] of such land is prepared with four days' labour; for it is broken easily in two days, gone over a second time in one, a third time in three-fourths of a day, and is formed into ridges and sown in one-fourth of a day. These ridges, moreover, country folk call *porcae* [b] when the ground is ploughed in such a way that the earth heaped up between two widely separated furrows affords a dry bed for the grain. Hillsides where 9
the soil is rich should be broken after the sowing of the three-months crops is completed, in the month of March; or, if the warmth of the climate and the

bit, Februario statim proscindendi sunt. Deinde
ab Aprile medio usque in solstitium iterandi, terti-
andique Septembri circa aequinoctium; ac totidem
operis, quot uliginosi campi, excolitur iugerum talis
agri.

10 Sed[1] in arando maxime est observandum, semper
ut transversus mons sulcetur. Nam hac ratione
difficultas acclivitatis infringitur, laborque pecudum
et hominum commodissime sic minuitur. Paulum
tamen, quotiensque[2] iterabitur, modo in elatiora,
modo in depressiora clivi obliquum agi sulcum
oportebit, ut in utramque partem rescindamus
11 nec eodem vestigio terram moliamur. Exilis ager
planus, qui aquis abundat, primum aretur ultima
parte mensis Augusti, subinde Septembri sit iteratus
paratusque ad sementim[3] circa aequinoctium.
Expeditior autem labor eius modi solo est, eoque[4]
pauciores impenduntur operae; nam tres uni iugero
sufficiunt. Item graciles clivi non sunt aestate
arandi, sed circa Septembres Kalendas, quoniam si
ante hoc tempus proscinditur, effeta et sine suco
humus aestivo sole peruritur nullasque virium re-
liquias habet. Itaque optime inter Kalendas et
Idus Septembris aratur ac subinde iteratur, ut
primis pluviis aequinoctialibus conseri possit; neque
in lira, sed sub sulco talis ager seminandus est.

V. Prius tamen quam exilem terram iteremus,

[1] iugerum. Sed tali agro *Schn.*
[2] quotienscumque *edd. ante Lundström.*
[3] ad sementim *Lundström*: ac sementi *SA et R plerique*: sementi *vulgo.*
[4] *sic Lundström cum codd., ut videtur*: eo quod *M, et vulgo.*

---

[a] Sept. 1st. [b] Sept. 13th.

dryness of the region make it advisable, even in February. Then between the middle of April and the solstice they should be gone over a second time, and a third time in September around the equinox; and a *iugerum* of such ground is prepared with the same number of days labour as wet champaign land.

But especial care must be taken in the ploughing 10
always to run the furrow crosswise to the slope; for by this method the difficulty of the ascent is mitigated, and the toil of man and beast is thereby lessened most handily. Still, whenever it is reworked, the furrows should be run somewhat obliquely, now uphill, now downhill, so that we may tear up the ground in both directions and not work it in the same track.
Lean land which lies level and is well watered 11
should be ploughed for the first time during the latter part of the month of August, then gone over again a second time in September, and put in readiness for sowing about the time of the equinox. In ground of this sort, moreover, the work is easier, and for this reason fewer days of labour are expended; for three days are sufficient for one *iugerum*. Lean and sloping ground, likewise, is not to be ploughed in summer, but around the Calends of September;[a] for if it is broken before this time, the earth, being exhausted and destitute of moisture, is burned by the summer sun and has no reserves of strength. Therefore it is best to plough it between the Calends and the Ides of September,[b] and then to work it again immediately, so that it may be sown during the first rains of the equinox; and such land is to be sown, not in the ridges, but in the furrows.

V. Still, before we give lean land its second

stercorare conveniet; nam eo quasi pabulo gliscit. In campo rarius, in colle spissius, acervi stercoris instår quinque modiorum disponentur; atque in plano pedes intervalli quoquoversus octo, in clivo duobus minus relinqui sat erit. Sed id nobis decrescente luna fieri placet, nam ea res herbis liberat segetes. Iugerum autem desiderat, quod spissius stercoratur, vehes quattuor et viginti; quod rarius,
2 duodeviginti. Disiectum deinde protinus fimum inarari et obrui [1] convenit, ne solis halitu vires amittat et ut permixta humus praedicto alimento pinguescat. Itaque, cum in agro disponentur acervi stercoris, non debet maior modus eorum dissipari,[2] quam quem bubulci eodem die possint obruere.

VI. Quoniam sementi terram docuimus praeparare, nunc seminum genera persequamur.[3] Prima et utilissima sunt hominibus frumenta triticum et semen adoreum. Tritici genera complura cognovimus, verum ex iis maxime serendum est, quod robus dicitur, quoniam et pondere et nitore praestat.
2 Secunda conditio est habenda siliginis, cuius species in pane praecipua pondere deficitur. Tertium erit trimestre,[4] cuius usus agricolis gratissimus; nam ubi propter aquas aliamve causam matura satio est omissa, praesidium ab hoc petitur. Id porro[5] genus

[1] obrui *R pauci, et vulgo*: adrui *codd. plerique, Lundström.*
[2] dissupari *SA, Lundström.*
[3] persequemur *edd. ante Lundström.*
[4] trimenstre *S, Lundström.*
[5] porro *om. AR, edd. ante Lundström.*

---

[a] 1 *modius* = about 1 peck.
[b] One cart-load contained eighty *modii*; *cf.* XI. 2. 86 and Palladius, X. 1. 2.
[c] For the wheats, see Note on page 461.

ploughing, it will be best to manure it; for on such food, so to speak, it grows fat. On level ground piles of manure, about five *modii* [a] to the pile, should be placed farther apart, and on hilly land closer together: on the level it will suffice to leave an interval of eight feet each way, on a slope two feet less. My own preference is that this be done when the moon is waning, for this frees the crops from weeds. Furthermore, one *iugerum*, if manured heavily, requires twenty-four loads; [b] if lightly, eighteen. Then the manure, once it is spread, should be 2
ploughed in immediately and covered over, that it may not lose its strength from the heat of the sun and that the soil, being mixed with it, may grow fat on the aforesaid nourishment. And so, when piles of manure are distributed in a field, the number of those so scattered should not exceed what the ploughmen can dig in on the same day.

VI. Inasmuch as we have given directions for the preparation of the ground for sowing, let us now treat of the kinds of seed. The seeds of first importance and most useful to mankind are grains of wheat and emmer.[c] We know of several varieties of wheat; but of this number that called *robus* or "ruddy" is most suitable for sowing, because it is superior in both weight and brightness. Second 2
place must be given to *siligo* or winter wheat, which is of excellent appearance in bread [d] but lacking in weight. The third shall be the three-months wheat, the use of which is most gratifying to farmers; for when, because of rains or some other reason, an early sowing has not been made, recourse is had to

[d] Because of its whiteness; *cf.* II. 9. 13, and Pliny, *N.H.* *XVIII.* 86.

est siliginis. Reliquae tritici species, nisi si quos multiplex varietas frugum et inanis delectat gloria,
3 supervacuae sunt. Adorei autem plerumque videmus in usu genera quattuor: far, quod appellatur Clusinum, candidi oris[1] et nitidi; far, quod vocatur vennuculum rutilum atque alterum candidum, sed utrumque maioris ponderis quam Clusinum; semen trimestre, quod dicitur halicastrum, idque pondere
4 et bonitate est praecipuum. Sed haec genera tritici et adorei propterea custodienda sunt agricolis, quoniam raro quisquam ager ita situs est, ut uno semine contenti esse possimus, interveniente parte aliqua vel uliginosa vel arida. Triticum autem sicco loco melius coalescit, adoreum minus infestatur umore.

VII. Leguminum genera cum sint complura, maxime grata et in usu hominum videntur faba, lenticula, pisum, phaselus, cicer, cannabis, milium, panicum,[2] sesama, lupinum, linum etiam et hordeum, quia ex eo tisana[3] est. Item pabulorum optima sunt
2 Medica et faenum Graecum nec minus vicia; proxima deinde cicera et ervum et farrago, quae est ex hordeo. Sed de his prius disseremus quae nostra causa seminantur, memores antiquissimi praecepti quo monemur

[1] *sic distinxit Lundström*: candidioris *SR* (*ex* candidoris *corr. A*), *vett. edd.*: candoris *Ald.*, *Gesn.*, *Schn.*: candidioris grani et nitidi *Pontedera.*

[2] panicium *SA et R pauci.*

[3] tisana *SR plerique, Lundström*: tisanana *A*: ptisana *R pauci, Ald.*, *Gesn.*, *Schn.*: ptissana *vett. edd.*

this. This, again, is a variety of *siligo*. The other kinds of wheat, except for those who find pleasure in a great variety of crops and in idle vainglory, are superfluous. Of emmer, however, we commonly see 3
four varieties in use: the *far* which is called Clusian,[a] of a white and shiny appearance; that called *vennuculum*,[b] one kind reddish and the other white, but both of greater weight than the Clusian; the three-months *far*, called, *halicastrum*,[c] which is excellent both in weight and in goodness. But these kinds of 4
wheat and emmer should be kept by farmers for this reason, that seldom is any land so situated that we can content ourselves with one kind of seed, as some strip which is either swampy or dry cuts through it. Further, wheat grows better in a dry spot, while emmer is less harmed by moisture.

VII. Though there are very many kinds of pulse or legumes, those observed to be most pleasing and useful to man are the bean, the lentil, the pea, the cow-pea, the chick-pea, hemp, millet, panic grass, sesame, lupine, also flax and barley, because from the last named is made *tisana* [d] or barley-grits. Likewise of the fodder crops the best are Medic clover and fenugreek, and vetch no less so; and next in 2
order are chickling-vetch, bitter vetch, and mixed fodder made from barley. But of this number we shall first discuss those which are sown for our own sake,[e] keeping in mind that very ancient rule in which

[a] So called from Clusium, a town of Etruria, now Chiusi.

[b] The derivation of the word is not known.

[c] Or *alicastrum*, defined by Isidore (*Orig.* XVII. 3. 9) as similar to the Greek *alica*.

[d] Greek πτισάνη, hulled and crushed barley.

[e] As against fodder plants for animals; *cf.* II. 10. 24.

ut locis frigidis novissime, tepidis celerius. calidis ocissime [1] metamus.[2] Nunc autem proinde ac si temperatae regioni praecepta dabimus.

VIII. Placet nostro poetae adoreum atque etiam triticum non ante seminare quam occiderint Vergiliae. Quod ipsum numeris sic edisserit:

At si triticeam in messem robustaque farra
Exercebis humum solisque instabis aristis,
Ante tibi Eoae Atlantides abscondantur.

2 Absconduntur autem altero et tricesimo die post autumnale aequinoctium, quod fere conficitur VIIII Kal. Octobris; propter quod intellegi debet tritici satio dierum sex et quadraginta ab occasu Vergiliarum, qui fit ante diem nonum Kalendas Novembris ad brumae tempora. Sic enim servant prudentes agricolae, ut quindecim diebus prius quam conficiatur bruma, totidemque post eam confectam neque arent neque vitem aut arborem putent. Nos quoque

[1] frigidis ocissime t. c. calidis novissime *Schneider ex Catone* 34, *praeeunte Pontedera.*

[2] metamus *SA et R pauci, vett. edd.*: metamur *R nonnulli*: metemur *vel* metantur *vel* metam *alii*: sereremus (*alt.* re *expunct. M*) *M et Cod. Bononiensis* 2523: seramus *Ald., Gesn., Schn.*: iaciamus *Lundström.*

---

[a] The translation follows the MSS. and earliest editions, against *seramus* "sow" and *iaciamus* "cast" of more recent editors. Columella appears to be speaking of the harvest from the autumn sowing (*cf.* 9. 6, below; and Palladius, I. 34. 6), in which sowing the order would be reversed.

[b] *I.e.* the Pleiades, seven daughters of Atlas, in the constellation Taurus.

[c] Vergil, *Georg.* I. 219–221.

[d] Sept. 23rd under the Julian Reform of 46 B.C.; but *cf. circa VIII Kal. Oct.* (= Sept. 24) in IX. 14. 11.

we are warned to reap[a] in cold places last, in warm places sooner, and in hot places earliest of all. For the present, however, we shall give rules applicable to a temperate region.

VIII. Our poet holds that emmer and even wheat should not be sown before the setting of the Vergiliae,[b] a rule which he puts in verse as follows:

> But if for wheat or emmer you plough, intent on grain alone,
> Let Atlas' daughters at dawn be hid before the planting's done.[c]

Now they are "hidden" on the thirty-second day 2
after the autumnal equinox, which usually falls on the ninth day before the Calends of October;[d] by which it should be understood that the seed-time of wheat lasts for forty-six days—from the setting of the Vergiliae, which occurs on the ninth day before the November Calends,[e] up to the time of the winter solstice.[f] For wise husbandmen observe this rule to such an extent that, for fifteen days before the occurrence of the solstice and a like number afterwards, they do no ploughing and no pruning of vine or tree. We, too, do not deny that

[e] Oct. 24th; but Nov. 11th according to Pliny, *N.H.* XVIII. 225. Varro (*R.R.* I. 28. 2) reckons fifty-seven days between the setting of the Pleiades and the winter solstice.

[f] Columella puts the shortest day (*bruma*) of the year *circa VIII Kal. Ian.* (= Dec. 25; *cf.* IX. 14. 12), and, citing Hipparchus, *XVI Kal. Ian.* (= Dec. 17; *cf.* XI. 2. 94). But Columella's calendar is often confused. Some explanation may be found in his statement in IX. 14. 12, when treating of bees, that he follows the calendars of Eudoxus and Meton and the ancient astronomers as adapted to the public sacrifices and better known to husbandmen than the more exact reckonings of Hipparchus.

non abnuimus in agro temperato et minime umido
3 sementem sic fieri debere; ceterum locis uliginosis atque exilibus aut frigidis aut etiam opacis plerumque citra [1] Kalendas Octobris seminare convenire,

dum sicca tellure licet, dum nubila pendent,

ut prius convalescant radices frumentorum quam hibernis imbribus aut gelicidiis [2] pruinisve infestentur. Sed quamvis tempestive sementis confecta erit, cavebitur tamen ut patentes liras crebrosque sulcos aquarios, quos non nulli elices vocant, faciamus et omnem umorem in colliquias [3] atque inde extra
4 segetes derivemus.[4] Nec ignoro quosdam veteres auctores praecepisse ne seminarentur agri, nisi cum terra pluviis permaduisset; quod ego, si tempestive competat, magis conducere agricolae non dubito. Sed si, quod evenit non numquam, seri sunt imbres, quamvis sitienti solo recte semen committitur; idque etiam in quibusdam provinciis, ubi status talis caeli est, usurpatur. Nam quod sicco solo ingestum et inoccatum est, proinde [5] ac si repositum in horreo non corrumpitur; atque ubi venit imber, multorum dierum sementis uno die
5 surgit. Tremelius quidem adseverat, prius quam impluverit, ab avibus aut formicis sata non infestari, dum aestivis serenitatibus ager aret; idque etiam saepius nos experti verum adhuc esse [6] comperimus. Magis apte [7] tamen in eius modi agris adoreum

[1] circa *R aliquot.* [2] gelidis *SA et R aliquot, Lundström.*
[3] colloquias *R*: cloacas *M.*
[4] dirivemus *R aliquot, Lundström*: diruemus *SA.*
[5] perinde *M, et vulgo ante Lundström.*
[6] non *post* esse *add. Schn.*
[7] apte *omnes post ed. Reg.* 1496: alte *vel* alter *vel* alitur *codd.*

the sowing should be governed by this rule in land that is temperate and not at all moist; but in sections 3 that are wet and lean, or cold, or even shaded, it is usually proper to sow before the Calends of October,

> while the dry earth permits, while clouds are in suspense,[a]

so that the roots of the grain may gain strength before they are attacked by winter rains or cold or frost. But even though the sowing be finished in good season, still we must be careful to make wide ridges and frequent water-furrows, which some call *elices*, and to turn off all water into drains [b] and hence outside the grain-fields. And I am not unaware that some 4 ancient authorities have left directions that fields should not be sown except after the ground is well soaked with rain; and that this is to the greater advantage of the farmer, if it comes in due season, I have no doubt. But if the rains are late, as sometimes happens, the seed is safely intrusted to ground however thirsty; and that is actually the practice in certain provinces where such weather conditions exist. For seed that is put into dry ground and harrowed in, is no more injured than if it were stored away in a granary; and when the rain does come, the sowing of many days' standing sprouts up in one.[c] Tremelius, in fact, makes the statement 5 that seed sown before the rains begin is not injured by birds or ants when the soil is parched during the fair weather of summer, and I have even tried it rather frequently and have thus far found it to be true. However, in land of this sort it is more suitable to sow

[a] Vergil, *Georg.* I. 214. [b] *Cf.* Pliny, *N.H.* XVIII. 179.
[c] *Cf.* Pliny, *N.H.* XVIII. 203.

quam triticum scritur, quoniam folliculum, quo continetur, firmum et durabilem adversus longioris temporis umorem habet.

IX. Iugerum agri pinguis plerumque modios tritici quattuor, mediocris quinque postulat; adorei modios novem, si est laetum solum, si mediocre, decem desiderat. Nam quamvis de mensura minus auctoribus convenit, hanc tamen videri commodissimam docuit noster usus; quem si quis sequi recusat, utatur praeceptis eorum, qui uberem campum in singula iugera tritici, quibus [1] et adorei, octo modiis obserere praecipiunt atque hac portione mediocribus agris
2 semina praebenda censent. Nobis ne istam quidem, quam praediximus, mensuram semper placet servari, quod eam variat aut loci aut temporis aut caeli conditio; loci, cum vel in campis vel collibus frumentum seritur atque his vel pinguibus vel mediocribus vel macris; temporis, cum autumno aut etiam ingruente hieme frumenta iacimus, nam prima sementis rarius serere permittit, novissima spissius postulat; caeli, cum aut pluvium aut siccum est, nam illud idem quod prima sementis, hoc quod ultima
3 desiderat. Omne autem frumentum maxime campo patente et ad solem prono apricoque et soluto laetatur; collis enim quamvis granum robustius aliquanto, minus tamen tritici reddit. Densa cretosaque et uliginosa humus siliginem et far adoreum non incommode alit. Hordeum nisi solutum et siccum
4 locum non patitur. Atque illa vicibus annorum requietum agitatumque alternis et quam laetissimum

[1] tritici quinque, et *Ald.*, *Gesn.*, *Schn.*

[a] *I.e.* at the rate of about one and two-thirds bushels an acre.

emmer than wheat, as it has a husk enclosing it which is tough and resistant to moisture for a longer period.

IX. A *iugerum* of rich land usually requires four *modii* of wheat; [a] land of medium quality, five; it calls for nine *modii* of emmer if the soil is fertile, and ten if it is ordinary. For although there is little agreement among authorities as to the quantity, yet my own experience has shown that this amount seems best suited; and anyone who does not care to comply with this may follow the directions of those who instruct us to sow a rich field with eight *modii* of wheat a *iugerum*, and the same for emmer, and who hold that seed should be supplied to medium land in this proportion. My opinion is that not even the amount 2
which I have mentioned above is always to be held to, for the reason that conditions of place or season or weather cause it to vary: of place, according as the grain is sown on level ground or hillsides, and these, too, either fat or medium or lean; of season, according as we cast the seed in autumn or even at the onset of winter, for the earlier sowing allows a lighter seeding while the later requires it to be heavier; of weather, according as it is rainy or dry, for the former requires the same as the early sowing, and the latter the same as the late. Further, every sort of grain especially 3
delights in ground that is open and sloping toward the sun, warm and loose; for though hilly ground produces a somewhat stronger grain, it yields a smaller crop of wheat. Soil that is heavy, chalky, and wet is not unsuited to the growing of winter wheat and emmer. Barley tolerates no place except one that is loose and dry. And the first mentioned 4
grains require ground that lies fallow and is worked by turns in alternate years and that is as rich as

volunt arvum; hoc nullam mediocritatem postulat, nam vel pinguissima vel macerrima humo iacitur. Illa post continuos imbris, si necessitas exigat, quamvis adhuc limoso et madente solo sparseris, iniuriam sustinent; hoc si lutoso commiseris, emori-
5 tur. Siliginis autem vel tritici, si mediocriter cretosus uliginosusve ager est, etiam paulo plus quam, ut prius iam dixi, quinque modiis ad sationem opus est. At si siccus et resolutus locus idemque vel pinguis vel exilis est, quattuor; quoniam et e contrario macer tantundem seminis poscit, nam nisi rare
6 conseritur, vanam et minutam spicam facit. At ubi ex uno semine pluribus culmis fructificavit,[1] etiam ex rara segete densam facit. Inter cetera quoque non ignorare debemus quinta parte seminis amplius occupari[2] agrum consitum arbusto quam vacuum et apertum.

Atque adhuc de satione autumnali loquimur; hanc
7 enim potissimam ducimus. Sed est altera, cum cogit necessitas: semestrem[3] vocant agricolae. Ea locis praegelidis ac nivosis, ubi aestas est umida et sine vaporibus, recte committitur, ceteris admodum raro respondet. Quam tamen ipsam celeriter et utique ante aequinoctium vernum conveniet peragere; si vero locorum et caeli conditio patietur, quanto
8 maturius severimus, commodius[4] proveniet. Neque enim est ullum, sicut multi crediderunt, natura

[1] fruticavit *R aliquot, Ald., Gesn., Schn.*

[2] quintam partem (*AR*) . . . occupare (*R pauci*) *edd. ante Schn.*

[3] semestrem *S* et *R aliquot, vett. edd.*: semenstrem *A* et *R aliquot, Lundström*: triticum semestrem (semenstrem) *vel.* t. semestre (semenstre) *R cett.*: trimestrem *Ald., Gesn., Schn.*

[4] tanto commodius *Ald., Gesn.*; tanto *inclusit Schn.*

possible; while the last named wants no middling
ground, being sown either in very rich or very poor
soil. Even though you sow the first mentioned in
ground that is still muddy and wet after continuous
rains, if necessity so demands, it withstands the
injury; if you commit the last named to miry ground,
it dies. However, if the field is moderately chalky or 5
marshy, you need for a sowing of the white winter
wheat or common wheat somewhat more than the
five *modii* that I mentioned above. But if the
ground is dry and loose, no matter whether it be rich
or poor, only four; for, conversely, lean land requires
the same amount of seed, because if it is not sown
thinly it produces a small and empty head. But when 6
it forms a stool of several stalks from one seed it makes
a heavy stand even from a light sowing. Among
other things, too, we should not overlook the fact that
a field planted with trees for supporting vines requires
one fifth more seed than a treeless and open field.

We have been speaking thus far of the autumn
sowing, for this we regard as the most important.
There is another sowing, however, when necessity 7
requires it—what farmers call the "half-month
sowing."[a] This is practised to advantage in very cold
and snowy regions where the summer is damp and
free from intense heat, but in other places it very
seldom yields a return. And even in this sowing it
will be better to finish it quickly, and certainly before
the spring equinox; in fact, if conditions of ground
and of weather allow it, the sooner we sow the better
the result will be. For there is no seed that naturally 8
requires three months, as many have believed, and

[a] Or, perhaps better, *trimestrem* (" three-months sowing ").
Cf. Palladius, I. 6. 16; Pliny, *N.H.* XVIII. 69.

trimestre semen, quippe idem iactum autumno melius respondet. Sed[1] sunt nihilo minus quaedam aliis potiora, quae sustinent veris tepores, ut siligo et hordeum Galaticum et halicastrum granumque fabae Marsicae. Nam cetera robusta frumenta semper ante hiemem seri debent in regionibus temperatis.

Solet autem salsam non numquam et amaram uliginem vomere terra, quae quamvis matura iam sata manante noxio umore corrumpit et locis calenti-
9 bus[2] sine ulla stirpe seminum areas reddit. Ea glabreta[3] signis adhibitis notari convenit, ut suo tempore vitiis eius modi medeamur; nam ubi vel uligo vel alia quae[4] pestis segetem enecat,[5] ibi columbinum stercus vel, si id non est, folia cupressi convenit spargi et inarari. Sed antiquissimum est omnem inde umorem facto sulco deducere; aliter vana erunt praedicta remedia. Nonnulli pelle hyaenae satoriam trimodiam vestiunt atque ita ex ea, cum paulum immorata sunt semina, iaciunt non
10 dubitantes proventura, quae sic sata sint. Quaedam etiam subterraneae pestes adultas segetes radicibus subsectis enecant. Id ne fiat, remedio est aquae mixtus sucus herbae, quam rustici sedum appellant, nam hoc medicamine una nocte semina macerata iaciuntur. Quidam cucumeris anguinei umorem ex-

[1] Sed *om. SA, Schn.*

[2] glabrentibus *R pauci, et vulgo ante Schn.*

[3] ea (eam, ea in) glabreta *R plerique, et vulgo*: eam glaeba *SA*: eam (ea in *a*) gleba *ad*: eam glaebam *Lundström.*

[4] alia quae *S, Lundström*: aliquae *A*: aliqua *R, et vulgo.*

[5] negat *SA*.

[a] *Cf.* II. 6. 3.

in fact the same seed will do better when planted in the autumn. There are, nevertheless, certain seeds that do better than others in enduring the heat of spring, such as white wheat (*siligo*), Galatian barley, the three-months emmer,[a] and the grain of the Marsian bean; for the other hardy grains should always be sown before winter in temperate localities.

Further, the earth has a way, at times, of emitting a brackish and bitter ooze which blights even full-grown crops with its poisonous seepage and in warm localities leaves patches without even a single stalk from the seed. It is best that such bare spots be 9
indicated by the use of markers, so that we may take measures against faults of this kind in due season; for in a place where oozy ground or some other plague kills out the crop it is best that pigeon dung or, failing that, cypress foliage be scattered and ploughed in. But the very first thing to do is to draw off all free water by running a furrow; otherwise the aforesaid remedies will be useless. Some people wrap a three-*modius* sowing measure in the skin of a hyena and broadcast the seed from it after it has remained there a while, not doubting that seed sown in this way will do well.[b] Certain underground pests 10
also kill out mature crops by cutting off their roots. As a remedy against this they use the juice of a plant which country people call *sedum*,[c] mixed with water; for the seeds are sown after they have been soaked in this solution for one night. Some take the juice squeezed from the wild cucumber and the

[b] Compare with this paragraph Palladius, X. 3, and especially sec. 2, *Si modium, quo seretur, hyaenae pelle vestieris, et ibi aliquamdiu quod serendum est, esse patiaris, sata bene provenire feruntur.*

[c] The house-leek.

pressum et eiusdem tritam radicem diluunt aqua, similique ratione madefacta semina terrae mandant. Alii hac eadem aqua vel amurca insulsa, cum coepit infestari seges, perfundunt sulcos et ita noxia animalia summovent.

Illud deinceps praecipiendum habeo,[1] ut demessis segetibus iam in area futuro semini consulamus.
11 Nam quod ait Celsus, ubi mediocris est fructus, optimam quamque spicam legere oportet separatimque ex ea semen reponere; cum rursus amplior messis provenerit, quicquid exteretur, capisterio expurgandum erit, et semper, quod propter magnitudinem ac pondus in imo subsederit, ad semen reservandum. Nam id plurimum prodest, quia quamvis celerius locis umidis, tamen etiam siccis frumenta degenerant, nisi cura talis adhibetur.[2]
12 Neque enim dubium est ex robusto semine posse fieri non robustum; quod vero protinus ex levi[3] natum sit, numquam robur accipere manifestum est, ideoque Vergilius cum et alia tum et hoc de seminibus praeclare sic disseruit:

Vidi lecta diu et multo spectata labore
Degenerare tamen, ni vis humana quotannis
Maxima quaeque manu legeret; sic omnia fatis
In peius ruere ac retro sublapsa referri.

[1] habeto *R plerique.*
[2] *sic SA*[1], *Lundström*: adhibeatur *R, et vulgo.*
[3] exile *R, et vulgo ante Schn.*

[a] *Cf.* Varro, *R.R.* I. 2. 25. [b] *Georg.* I. 197–200.

crushed root of the same, dilute it with water, and after soaking the seeds in the same way they consign them to the earth.[a] Others sprinkle the furrows with this same liquid or with unsalted lees of oil, when the crop begins to be infested, and so drive off the destructive creatures.

The next direction that I have to offer is that when the crops have been harvested and are on the threshing-floor, we should consider the sowing that is to
follow. For, as Celsus remarks, when the harvest 11
is just ordinary we should select all the best heads and store the seed from them by itself; when, in turn, there is a more generous yield, everything that is threshed out should be cleaned with a sieve, and the grain that settles to the bottom because of its size and weight should always be kept for seed. This is a most beneficial measure because, while grain deteriorates more rapidly in damp places, it also does
so in dry places unless such pains are taken. For 12
there is no doubt that from strong seed there can be produced seed that has no strength; but it is obvious that what is produced continuously from weak seed can never acquire strength. For that reason Vergil, in treating of other matters, has also expressed himself very clearly on the subject of seeds, as follows;

Some I have seen deteriorate, though chosen with
great care
And long examination, if with toil of man
The largest were not hand-picked every year.
But so the will of Fate. All things are doomed
To hasten to the worse and, downward turned,
To take a backward course.[b]

13 Granum autem rutilum si, cum est diffissum,[1] eundem colorem interiorem habet, integrum esse non dubitamus; quod extrinsecus albidum, intus etiam candidum conspicitur,[2] leve ac vanum intellegi debet. Nec nos tamquam optabilis agricolis fallat siligo, nam hoc tritici vitium est et, quamvis candore praestet, pondere tamen vincitur. Verum in umido statu caeli recte provenit et ideo locis manantibus magis apta est. Nec tamen ea[3] longe nobis aut magna difficultate requirenda est, nam omne triticum solo uliginoso post tertiam sationem convertitur in siliginem.

14 Proximus est his frumentis usus hordei, quod rustici hexastichum, quidam etiam cantherinum appellant, quoniam et omnia animalia, quae ruri sunt, melius quam triticum pascit et hominem salubrius quam malum triticum,[4] nec aliud in egenis rebus magis inopiam defendit. Seritur soluta siccaque terra et vel praevalida vel exili, quia constat arva segetibus eius macescere;[5] propter quod pinguissimo agro, cuius nimiis[6] viribus noceri non possit, aut macro, cui nihil aliud, committitur.
15 Altero sulco seminari debet post aequinoctium, media fere sementi, si laeto solo, si gracili, maturius. Iugerum quinque modios occupabit.[7] Idque ubi

[1] diffusum *AR.*
[2] *sic Lundström cum codd.*: conspicitur candidum *vulgo.*
[3] ea *om. SA.*
[4] *alt.* pascit (cibat *M*) *post* triticum *add. R.*
[5] marcescere *A*[2]*R pauci, Lundström*: manascere *A*[1]: manescere *S.*
[6] nimis *SAa, Schn., Lundström.*

Further, if a red grain, when cut in two, shows the same colour throughout, we have no doubt that it is sound; but one that is whitish outside and is also seen to be white inside, that should be set down as light and lacking in substance. And let us not be misled into thinking that *siligo* is desirable for farmers; for this is a degenerate kind of wheat, and though superior in whiteness, it is inferior in weight. It does well, however, in a humid climate, and for that reason is better suited to springy places. Still we need not go a great distance or to great pains to find it; for in wet ground every kind of wheat turns into *siligo* after the third sowing. 13

Next to these grains in utility is that variety of barley which country people call *hexastichum*;[a] some also call it *cantherinum*[b] because it is a better food than wheat for all animals that belong on a farm, and is more wholesome for humans than is bad wheat; and in times of scarcity there is nothing better in guarding against want. It is sown in loose, dry ground, either very rich or poor, because it is agreed that land is weakened by crops of it; for this reason it is committed to a very fertile field, whose excessive strength cannot be impaired, or to a lean one to which nothing else is entrusted. The seed should be cast at the 15
second ploughing, after the equinox, about the middle of seed-time if the soil is rich, and earlier if it is poor. One *iugerum* will take five *modii* of seed. And when 14

[a] *I.e.* "six-rowed" barley.

[b] "horse-barley," from *cantherius*, a gelding (Varro, *R.R.* II. 7. 15).

---

[7] modii occupabunt *Ald.*, *Gesn.*, *Schn*; *sed* modiis occupabit *maluit Schn. in not.*, *ex Pallad.*, *Sept.* 4.

paulum maturuerit, festinantius quam ullum aliud frumentum demetendum erit; nam et fragili culmo et nulla vestitum palea granum eius celeriter decidit, isdemque [1] de [2] causis facilius teritur quam cetera. Sed cum eius messem sustuleris, optimum est novalia pati anno cessare; si minus, stercore saturare et omne virus, quod adhuc inest terrae, propulsare.

16 Alterum quoque genus hordei est, quod alii distichum, Galaticum nonnulli vocant, ponderis et candoris eximii, adeo ut tritico mixtum egregia cibaria familiae praebeat. Seritur quam pinguissimis, sed frigidis locis circa Martium mensem; melius tamen respondet si clementia hiemis permittit, cum seminatur circa Idus Ianuarias. Iugerum sex modios postulat.

17 Inter frumenta etiam panicum ac milium ponenda sunt, quamvis iam leguminibus ea contribuerim, nam multis regionibus cibariis eorum coloni sustinentur.[3] Levem solutamque humum desiderant, nec in sabuloso solo, sed in harena quoque proveniunt, modo umido caelo vel riguo solo; nam siccum

18 cretosumque reformidant. Ante ver seri [4] non possunt, quoniam teporibus maxime laetantur; ultima tamen parte Martii mensis commodissime terrae committuntur. Nec impensa gravi rationem [5] cultoris onerant, quippe sextariis fere quattuor iugerum implent; frequentem tamen exigunt sar-

[1] hisdemque *vel* his denique *R plerique.*
[2] de *om. Sa.*
[3] sustinerentur *A.*
[4] versari A^2R, *vett. edd.*
[5] sationem *vel* sartionem *R.*

[a] "two-rowed."

[b] The Sarmatians, says Pliny (*N.H.* XVIII. 100), lived chiefly on millet porridge, made with mare's milk or with blood drawn from the thigh of a horse; while the Ethiopians knew of no other grains than millet and barley. Panic was used by

this has ripened somewhat it should be harvested with more haste than any other grains, for, having brittle straw and grain that has no covering of chaff, it shatters quickly; and for the same reason it is more easily threshed than other grains. But when you have taken off a crop of it, it is best to let the ground lie fallow for a year; or if not, to saturate it with manure and drive out all the poison that still remains in the land. There is also a second variety of barley 16
which some call *distichum* [a] and others Galatian, of extraordinary weight and whiteness, so much so that when mixed with wheat it makes excellent food for the household. It is sown about the month of March in ground that is very rich but cold; it does better, however, if a mild winter allows it, when sown around the middle of January. One *iugerum* calls for six *modii.*

Panic and millet also should be counted among 17
grain crops, even though I have already listed them among the legumes, for in many countries the peasants subsist on food made from them.[b] They require a light, loose soil, and thrive not only in gravelly ground but also in sand, if only the climate is moist or the ground well watered; for they have a great dread of dry and chalky ground. They cannot 18
be sown before spring, for they are fond of warm weather above all; but they are intrusted to the earth to best advantage in the latter part of March. They do not burden the farmer's budget with a heavy expense, as about four *sextarii* are enough for a *iugerum*; and yet they demand repeated hoeing and

the people of Gaul and Aquitania, by the people of Italy beyond the Po, and was held in highest esteem by the nations of Pontus (*ibid.* 101).

tionem [1] et runcationem, ut herbis liberentur. Ea cum spicas ediderunt, prius quam semina hient aestibus,[2] manu carpuntur, et suspensa in sole cum adsiccuerunt,[3] reconduntur atque ita reposita peren-
19 nant diutius quam cetera. Panis ex milio conficitur, qui antequam refrigescat, sine fastidio potest absumi. Panicum pinsitum [4] et evolutum furfure, sed milium [5] quoque pultem quamvis in copia [6] maxime cum lacte [7] non fastidiendam praebet.

X. Quoniam de frumentis abunde praecepimus, de leguminibus deinceps disseremus.[8] Lupini prima ratio est, quod et minimum operarum absumit et vilissime emitur et maxime ex iis, quae seruntur, iuvat agrum. Nam vineis iam [9] emaciatis et arvis optimum stercus praebet ac vel effeto solo provenit vel repositum in granario patitur aevum. Boves per hiemem coctum maceratumque probe alit; famem quoque, si sterilitas annorum incessit, hominibus
2 commode propulsat. Spargitur statim ex area, atque id solum omnium leguminum non desiderat requiem in horreo,[10] sive Septembri mense ante aequinoctium seu protinus a Kalendis Octobribus crudis novalibus ingeras; et qualitercumque obruas, sustinet coloni neglegentiam. Teporem tamen autumni desiderat, ut celeriter confirmetur, nam si

[1] sarritionem *plerique edd. ante Lundström.*

[2] aestibus *om. SA.*

[3] *sic SAM, Lundström*: ad(as)siccaverunt vel ad(as)siccaverint *R plerique*: assiccaverint *vett. edd.*: assiccata fuerint *Ald., Gesn., Schn.*

[4] pinsatum *R plerique.*

[5] sed et milium *Ald., Gesn., Schn.*

[6] quavis in copia *Schn., praeeunte Pontedera*: quavis inopia *Ald., Gesn.*

[7] maxime cum lacte *om. S (in marg. man. alt.) A.*

weeding to make them free of weeds. When they have formed their heads, before the seeds crack open with the heat, they are gathered by hand, hung in the sun, and stored away after they have dried; and when stored in this fashion they keep longer than other grains. Bread is made of millet, and it may 19
be eaten without distaste before it cools. Panic, when ground and freed from bran, and millet as well, makes a porridge which, especially with milk, is not to be despised even in time of plenty.

X. Inasmuch as we have given sufficient instructions about grains, we shall next discuss the legumes. First consideration belongs to the lupine, as it requires the least labour, costs least, and of all crops that are sown is most beneficial to the land. For it affords an excellent fertilizer for worn-out vineyards and ploughlands; it flourishes even in exhausted soil; and it endures age when laid away in the granary. When softened by boiling it is good fodder for cattle during the winter; in the case of humans, too, it serves to ward off famine if years of crop failures come upon them. It is broadcast direct from the 2
threshing-floor, and it is the only one of all the legumes which does not require a rest in the bin, whether you sow it in unbroken fallow in the month of September before the equinox or immediately after the Calends of October; and whatever way you cover it, it withstands the carelessness of the farmer. Still it needs the mild temperature of autumn to become quickly established, for if it has not taken

---

[8] *sic S, Lundström* : disseramus *AR, et vulgo.*
[9] iam *om. SA.* [10] in horreo *om. SA.*

non ante hiemem convaluit,[1] frigoribus adfligitur.
3 Reliquum quod semini superest, in tabulatum, quo fumus pervenit, optime reponas,[2] quoniam si umor invasit, vermes gignit; qui simul atque oscilla lupinorum adederunt,[3] reliqua pars enasci non potest. Id, ut dixi, exilem amat terram et rubricam
4 praecipue, nam cretam reformidat limosoque non exit agro. Iugerum decem modios [4] occupat. Ab hoc recte phaselus terrae mandabitur vel in vetereto [5] vel melius pingui et restibili agro, nec amplius quattuor modiis iugerum obseretur.[6] Similis quoque ratio est pisi, quod tamen facilem et solutam terram desiderat tepidumque locum et caelum frequentis umoris. Eadem mensura iugerum vel modio minus quam phaselum licet obserere primo tempore sementis ab aequinoctio autumnali.[7]

5 Fabae pinguissimus locus vel stercoratus destinetur [8] et si veteretum erit in valle situm, quod a superiore parte sucum accipit. Prius autem iaciemus [9] semina, deinde proscindemus terram proscissamque in liram revocabimus occabimusque, quo altius largiore humo contegatur; nam id plurimum refert, ut radices enatorum seminum penitus de-
6 mersae sint. Sin autem proximae messis occupandum erit restibile, desectis stramentis quattuor

[1] convaluerit *R plerique, edd. ante Lundström*; *sed* convaluit *maluit Schn.*

[2] reponis *Ald., Gesn., Schn.*

[3] aediderunt *A*: edederunt *vel* ediderunt (*vett. edd.*) *R plerique*: ederunt *R pauci, Ald., Gesn.*

[4] modios (modios X *M*) *R pauci, vett. edd.*: modis S^1A: modiis *R plerique, Lundström*: modii occupant *Ald., Gesn., Schn.*

[5] veterio *SAM*: vervacto *Ald., Gesn.*

[6] observetur *A*: obseritur *R, edd. ante Schn.*

[7] autumni SA^1.

a strong hold before winter it is greatly injured by
the cold. It will be best to put away your left-over 3
seed in a loft where smoke can reach it, for if
dampness gets into it, it breeds worms; and when
they have once eaten away the embryo of the lupine
seed, the other part cannot germinate. The lupine
likes lean ground, as I have said, and especially
reddish soil; it has an intense dislike of chalky 4
ground and does not come up at all in a miry field.
One *iugerum* takes ten *modii*. Next after this it will
be proper to commit to the earth the kidney bean,
either in old fallow ground, or better in rich ground
that is tilled every year; the sowing of one *iugerum*
will require not more than four *modii*. The same may
be said of the pea, which desires, however, an easy
and loose soil, a warm situation, and a climate
where it often rains. The same quantity may be
sown to the *iugerum* as in the case of the kidney
bean, or one *modius* less, at the beginning of seed-time after the autumnal equinox.

A spot that is naturally very fertile or well manured 5
should be set aside for the common bean, and old
fallow lying in a valley and receiving moisture from
the higher ground. First, however, we shall cast the
seed, then furrow the ground, and after furrowing
reduce it to ridges and harrow it, to provide a deeper
and more abundant covering of loose earth; for it is
of the greatest importance that the roots of the
sprouting seed be sunk deep. But if we must use 6
restored land that has just borne a crop, after cutting
the straw we shall distribute twenty-four loads of

---

[8] destinatur *AR, edd. ante Lundström.*
[9] iactemus *R plerique*: alemus *SA.*

et viginti vehes stercoris in iugerum disponemus dissipabimusque [1] et similiter, cum semen crudo solo ingesserimus, inarabimus imporcitumque [2] occabimus; [3] quamvis sint, qui negent locis frigidis oportere occari fabam, quia exstantes glaebae a gelicidiis adhuc eam teneram vindicent et aliquem
7 teporem frigore laboranti praebeant. Sunt etiam qui putent in arvis hanc eandem vice stercoris fungi; quod sic ego interpretor, ut existimem non sationibus eius pinguescere humum, sed minus hanc quam cetera semina vim terrae consumere. Nam certum habeo frumentis utiliorem agrum esse, qui nihil quam
8 qui istam spicam [4] proximo anno tulerit. Iugerum agri, ut Tremelio quattuor, ut nobis videtur, fabae sex occupant modii,[5] si solum pingue sit, si mediocre, paulo amplius; eaque nec macrum nec nebulosum locum patitur, densa tamen humo saepe commode respondet. Media sementi pars seri et pars ultima debet, quae septimontialis satio dicitur; tempestiva frequentius, non numquam tamen sera melior est.
9 Post brumam parum recte seritur, pessime vere; quamvis sit etiam trimestris faba, quae mense Februario seratur, quinta parte amplius quam matura, sed

[1] dissipavimusque *SAa*.
[2] inporcitumque *A*[1], *Lundström*: im(in)porcatumq; *vel* importatunq; *R*: imporcatumque *edd. vulgo*.
[3] occupabimus *A*.
[4] siliquam *Ald.*, *Gesn.*, *Schn.*
[5] modiis *SA*: modiis *vel* modii si *R pauci*: modios *vel* modios si *R plerique*.

---

[a] Varro (*R.R.* I. 23. 3), for example, speaks of the use of the field bean for green manuring before the pods have formed.

[b] A sowing made at about the time of the festival of the Seven Hills (*Septimontium*), celebrated in December before the

manure to the *iugerum* and spread it; and just as before, when we have scattered the seed on the unbroken ground, we shall plough it in, form ridges, and harrow, though there are some who say that beans should not be harrowed in cold regions because the projecting clods shelter them from the frosts while they are still young and provide some warmth when they are suffering from the cold. There are 7
people, too, who think that in cultivated land this same plant takes the place of manure[a]—a belief which I take as meaning, not that the ground is enriched by the sowing of it, but that it uses up the strength of the soil less than other crops. For I am convinced that land which has borne no crop is better suited for grain than one which bore a crop of this legume the preceding year. A *iugerum* of land 8
requires four *modii* of beans, as Tremelius thinks, but six, in my opinion, if the ground is rich, and somewhat more if it is just ordinary; and it does not tolerate lean ground or a foggy situation, though it often does well on heavy soil. It should be sown, part at the middle of seed-time, and part at the end —the sowing called "septimontial."[b] The early sowing is more common, though the late one is sometimes better. There is little use in sowing it after the 9
winter solstice, and the very worst time is spring; although there is also a three-months bean which may be sown in February, using one-fifth more than for the early variety, but which yields scanty straw

solstice; *cf.* Varro, *L.L.* VI. 34, and Palladius, XIII (*Dec.* 1). The festival celebrated, not the union of the Seven Hills of complete Rome, but a much earlier union of the three spurs of the Palatine, the three spurs of the Esquiline, and the lower ground of the Subura.

exiguas paleas nec multam siliquam facit. Veteres itaque rusticos plerumque dicentes audio malle se
10 maturae[1] fabalia quam fructum trimestris. Sed quocumque tempore anni seretur, opera danda erit, ut quantum destinaverimus in sationem, tantum quinta decima luna, si tamen ea non transcurret eo die solis radios, quod Graeci ἀπόκρουσιν[2] vocant, si minus, quarta decima utique adhuc lunae crescente lumine spargatur, etiam si confestim totum semen operiri non poterit. Nihil enim nocebitur ei nocturnis roribus aliisve ex causis, dum a pecore et avibus
11 vindicetur. Priscis autem rusticis nec minus Vergilio prius amurca vel nitro macerari eam et ita seri placuit,

> laetior[3] ut fetus siliquis fallacibus esset
> et quamvis igni exiguo properata maderent.[4]

Nos quoque sic medicatam comperimus, cum ad maturitatem perducta sit, minus a curculione infestari. Sed et illud, quod deinceps dicturi sumus,
12 experti praecipimus.[5] Silente luna fabam vellito ante lucem; deinde cum in area exaruerit, confestim, prius quam luna incrementum capiat, excussam refrigeratamque in granarium conferto. Sic condita a curculionibus erit innoxia, maximeque ex leguminibus ea sine iumentis teri, sine vento purgari expedi-

[1] matura *R*, *edd. ante Schn.*
[2] *Graec. om., spat. relict., R plerique.*
[3] laetior *SAR*: grandior *M*, *codd. Verg.*
[4] maderet *S*, *Schn.*
[5] praecepimus *vel* praecipiemus *R plerique.*

---

[a] Vergil, *Georg.* I. 195–196.
[b] Palladius (VII. 3. 2) gives similar directions for the pulling of beans *luna minuente*, when the moon is waning. In connec-

and not many pods. And so I hear the old-time farmers commonly remark that they would rather have the bean straw of the early sowing than the beans of the three-months variety. But, whatever 10
the season of sowing, we must take care that the quantity allotted for seed be broadcast on the fifteenth day of the moon, provided only she does not on that day traverse the rays of the sun—what the Greeks call ἀπόκρουσις or "waning"; otherwise that it be sown in any case on the fourteenth day, while the light of the moon is still waxing, even though the whole amount of seed cannot be covered immediately. For no harm will come to it from nightly dews or other causes, if only it be protected from cattle and birds. The ancient husbandmen, 11
moreover, and Vergil too, held that it should first be soaked in oil lees or in nitre, and then sown,

> That the deceptive pods might have a larger fruit,
> Their seeds soon softened by even a little heat.[a]

We, too, have learned that seed so treated is less infested by weevils after it has reached maturity. And what we are about to say next, we offer as a precept from own experience: Gather beans 12
in the dark of the moon,[b] before dawn; and when they have dried on the threshing-floor, immediately, before the moon begins its waxing, beat them out, cool them, and carry them into the granary. When stored in this way they will not be harmed by weevils. And this one, especially, of the legumes, can be very easily threshed without the use of cattle, and cleaned

tion with this and much of the moon lore that follows, see Eugene Tavenner, "The Roman Farmer and the Moon," *Trans. Am. Phil. Assn.* XLIX. 67–82.

13 tissime sic poterit. Modicus [1] fasciculorum numerus resolutus in extrema parte areae colligetur,[2] quem per longissimum eius mediumque spatium tres vel quattuor homines promoveant pedibus et baculis furcisve [3] contundant; [4] deinde cum ad alteram partem areae pervenerint, in acervum culmos
14 regerant. Nam semina excussa in area iacebunt,[5] superque ea paulatim eodem modo reliqui fasciculi excutientur, ac durissimae quidem acus reiectae separataeque erunt a cudentibus, minutae vero, quae de siliquis cum faba resederint,[6] aliter secernentur. Nam cum acervus paleis granisque mixtus in unum fuerit congestus, paulatim ex eo ventilabris per longius spatium iactetur, quo pacto [7] palea, quae levior est, citra decidet, faba, quae longius emittitur, pura eo perveniet, quo ventilator eam iaculabitur.

15 Lentim modo semediata [8] luna usque in duodecimam solo tenui et resoluto vel pingui, sed [9] sicco maxime loco seri convenit; nam in flore facile luxuria et umore corrumpitur. Quae ut celeriter prodeat et ingrandescat, ante quam seritur,[10] fimo arido permisceri debet, et cum ita quatriduo [11] aut quinque diebus requieverit, spargi. Sationes eius duas servamus, alteram maturam per mediam sementim,
16 seriorem alteram mense Februario. Iugerum agri

[1] modius *SA*.
[2] collocetur *R aliquot, edd. ante Lundström.*
[3] furcillisve *R aliquot, Ald., Gesn., Schn.*
[4] contundat *SA*. [5] iacebant *SA*.
[6] resederunt *R, edd. ante Schn.*
[7] facto *Gesn., Schn., praeeunte Ursino.*
[8] *sic Lundström*: lenti modo semediata *SA*: Lentem semente (Lentis sementem *M*) media crescente *R, et vulgo*: Lentim modo a dimidiata *Schn.*
[9] *sic Lundström*: pingius et *SA*: pinguis sed *a*: pingui et *R, et vulgo.* [10] seratur *Ald., Gesn., Schn.*

without the aid of wind, as follows: Have a moderate 13
number of loose sheaves brought together at one end
of the threshing-floor, and let three or four men push
them along with their feet through the middle of the
floor the longest way, and beat them with sticks or
forks; then, when they reach the other end of the
floor, let them throw the stalks again into a pile.
For the seeds that have been beaten out will lie on 14
the floor, and the other bundles will be threshed out
on top of them, little by little, in the same manner.
For the hardest chaff will be knocked off and
separated by the beaters, but the fine chaff which
has fallen from the pods along with the beans will
be separated in another way: that is, when the mixture of chaff and seeds has been heaped together in
one pile, let it be tossed some distance away, a little
at a time, by winnowing-fans; and by this means the
chaff, being lighter, will fall short, and the beans,
which are thrown farther, will come clean to the spot
where the winnower throws them.

The lentil is properly sown only from the time of 15
the half-moon up to her twelfth day, in ground that
is lean and loose, or fat, but above all in a place that
is dry; for when in flower it is easily damaged
by rankness and moisture. To make it come out
quickly and make a good growth, it should be mixed
with dried manure before sowing, and then broadcast
after it has remained thus for four or five days. Our
practice is to make two sowings, the early one in the
middle of seedtime, and the later in the month of
February. A little more than one *modius* covers a 16

---

[11] quattuor *vel* quatuor *vel* IIII *R plerique*: quatuor *Ald.*, *Gesn.*

paulo plus quam modius occupat. Ea ne curculionibus absumatur—nam etiam dum est in siliqua exestur—curandum [1] erit, ut cum extrita sit, in aquam demittatur et ab inani, quae protinus innatat, separetur solida; tum in sole siccetur et radice silphi trita cum aceto adspargatur defriceturque [2] atque ita rursus in sole siccata et mox refrigerata recondatur, si maior est modus, in horreo, si minor, in vasis oleariis salsamentariisque; quae repleta cum confestim gypsata sunt, quandoque in usus prompserimus, integram lentim [3] reperiemus. Potest tamen etiam citra istam medicationem cineri mixta commode servari.

17 Lini semen, nisi si [4] magnus est eius in ea regione, quam colis, proventus et pretium proritat, serendum non est; agris enim praecipue noxium est. Itaque pinguissimum locum et modice umidum poscit. Seritur a Kalendis Octobribus in ortum Aquilae, qui est VII Idus Decembris. Iugerum agri octo modiis obseritur. Non nullis placet macro solo et quam spississimum semen eius committi, quo tenuius [5] linum proveniat. Idem etiam, si laeto solo seratur mense Februario, decem modios in iugerum iaci oportere dicunt.

18 Sesama, quae rigantur, maturius, quae carent umore, ab aequinoctio autumnali serenda sunt in

[1] extercorandum *R*: editur curandum *M*.
[2] oleo *post* defricetur *add. Schn. ex Catone* 116.
[3] lentem *R aliquot, edd. ante Lundström.*
[4] si *om. R, edd. ante Schn.*
[5] tenuius *Schn., Lundström*: tenui ut *SA*[1]: tenue *A*[2]*R, et vulgo.*

[a] Identified by Columella (VI. 17. 7; *cf.* XII. 7. 4, 59. 4) with *laserpitium*, laserwort. Pliny (*N.H.* XIX. 38–46) gives a long account of the history and uses of the plant.

iugerum of ground. To keep it from being destroyed by weevils—for they eat it even when it is in the pod—care must be taken that, as soon as it is threshed out, it be sunk in water, and that the sound grains be separated from the empty, which come at once to the surface; then that it be dried in the sun, sprinkled and rubbed with the bruised root of silphium[a] mixed with vinegar, and again dried in the sun; and presently, after cooling, that it be stored away—in the bin if the amount is rather large, or in olive jars and salt-fish jars if there is not much of it. If these are sealed with gypsum immediately upon being filled, we shall find the lentil sound whenever we take it out for use. Still, it can be kept satisfactorily without such treatment if mixed with ashes.

Flax-seed should not be sown unless it yields a heavy 17
crop and brings a good price in the region where you farm; for it is particularly hurtful to land. For this reason it requires a soil which is very rich and moderately moist. It is sown from the first of October to the rising of Aquila, which falls on the seventh day before the Ides of December.[b] A *iugerum* of land is sown with eight *modii* of it. Some hold that it should be sown in poor land, and very thickly, so that the flax may grow with a more slender stem. The same people also say that if it is sown in rich ground in February, ten *modii* should be broadcast to the *iugerum*.

Sesame[c] is to be sown earlier on well-watered 18
ground, and from the autumnal equinox to the Ides

[b] Dec. 7th.

[c] Perhaps to be identified with the gingili- or gingelly-plant.

Idus Octobres. Putre solum, quod Campani pullum vocant, plerumque desiderant; non deterius tamen etiam pinguibus harenis vel congesticia humo proveniunt, tantumque seminis quantum milium panicumque, interdum etiam duobus sextariis amplius in iugerum spargitur. Sed hoc idem semen Ciliciae Syriaeque regionibus ipse vidi mense Iunio Iulioque conseri et per autumnum, cum permaturuit, tolli.[1]

19 Cicer aut[2] cicercula, quae piso est similis, mense Ianuario aut Februario seri debet laeto loco caelo umido; quibusdam tamen[3] Italiae locis ante Kalendas Novembris seritur. Tres modii iugerum implent. Nec ullum legumen minus agro nocet, sed raro respondet, quoniam nec siccitates nec austros in flore sustinet; quae utraque incommoda fere eo
20 tempore anni sunt, quo deflorescit. Cicer, quod arietillum[4] vocatur, itemque alterius generis, quod Punicum, seri mense Martio toto potest caelo umido, loco quam laetissimo; nam etiam id terram laedit atque ideo improbatur a callidioribus agricolis. Quod tamen si seri debeat, pridie macerandum erit, ut celerius enascatur. Iugero modii tres abunde sunt.

21 Cannabis solum pingue stercoratumque et riguum vel planum atque umidum et alte subactum deposcit. In quadratum pedem seruntur grana sex eius

[1] colligi *M* : et per . . . tolli *om. SA.*
[2] Cicer aut *om. R plerique, Ald., Gesn., Schn.*
[3] tamen *om. SA.*
[4] arietillum *Lundström cum codd.* : arietinum *vulgo.*

[a] Oct. 15th.
[b] *Congesticia,* earth brought together from different places; *cf.* II. 15. 4–5; Palladius X. 7; Theophrastus, *De Caus. Plant.* III. 25.

of October[a] on ground that lacks moisture. It usually requires a loamy soil, such as the Campanians call *pullum*; still it thrives no less well even in rich sand or in mixed ground.[b] The same quantity of seed is sown to the *iugerum* as of millet and panic, sometimes even two *sextarii*[c] more. But I have seen this same seed sown in the months of June and July in districts of Cilicia and Syria, and harvested during the autumn, when it was fully ripe.

The chick-pea or the chickling-vetch, which has a resemblance to the pea, should be sown in January or February in rich soil if the weather is moist; though in some sections of Italy the sowing is made before the first of November. Three *modii* are sufficient for one *iugerum*. No legume is less hurtful to land; but it seldom does well, because, when in bloom, it cannot endure dry weather or south winds; and both these drawbacks usually attend the season when it drops its blossoms.[d] The chick-pea which is called *arietillum*,[e] and also one of another variety, called *Punicum*, may be sown during the whole month of March, if the weather is moist, in the most fertile soil; indeed, this kind is harmful to land and for that reason is not approved by the more expert farmers. If it must be sown, however, it should be soaked a day ahead to hasten its germination. Three *modii* are enough for one *iugerum*.

Hemp demands a rich, manured, well-watered soil, or one that is level, moist, and deeply worked. Six grains of this seed to the square foot are planted at

[c] 1 sextarius = about 1 pint.
[d] *Cf.* Palladius II (*Jan.*), 5.
[e] Pliny says (*N.H.* XVIII. 124) that it is so called because of its resemblance to the head of a ram (*aries*).

seminis Arcturo exoriente, quod est ultimo mense Februario, circa sextum aut quintum Kalendas Martias; nec tamen usque in aequinoctium vernum, si sit pluvius caeli status, improbe seretur.

22 Ab his leguminibus ratio est habenda napi[1] raporumque,[2] nam utraque rusticos implent. Magis tamen utilia rapa sunt, quia et maiore incremento proveniunt et non hominem solum, verum etiam boves pascunt, praecipue in Gallia, ubi hiberna cibaria praedictis pecudibus id holus praebet. Solum putre et solutum res utraque desiderat nec densa
23 nascitur humo. Sed rapa campis et locis umidis laetantur, napus devexam amat et siccam tenuique propiorem terram; itaque glareosis sabulosisque arvis melior exit,[3] locique proprietas utriusque semen commutat; namque in alio solo rapa biennio sata convertuntur in napum, in alio napus raporum accipit speciem. Riguis locis utrumque recte ab solstitio seritur, siccis ultima parte mensis Augusti vel prima Septembris. Subactum solum pluribus iterationibus aratri vel rastri largoque stercore satiatum postulant;
24 nam id plurimum refert, non solum quod melius ea proveniunt, sed quod etiam post fructum eorum sic tractatum etiam[4] solum segetes opimas facit. Iu-

[1] naporum *R, edd. ante Schn., qui* naporum *legit,* napi *defendit in not.*
[2] raparumque *Lundström, cum SA et R aliquot ut videtur.*
[3] meliorescit *M.*
[4] etiam *om. edd. ante Lundström.*

[a] *I.e.* Feb. 24th or 25th.
[b] *Cf.* Palladius, VIII. 2. 2. Pliny remarks that the Greeks (*N.H.* XVIII. 129) and medical men (*N.H.* XIX. 75) distinguished between "male" (round) and "female" (elongated) turnips or navews, the original sex and change of nature being determinable by thickness of sowing and quality of soil.

the rising of Arcturus, which means toward the end of February, about the sixth or fifth day before the Calends of March;[a] and yet no harm will be done in planting it up to the spring equinox if the weather is rainy.

After these legumes consideration must be given 22 to the navew and the turnip, as both of them are filling food for country people. The turnips, however, are more profitable, because they yield a greater increase and serve as food, not only for mankind, but also for cattle, especially in Gaul, where this vegetable provides winter fodder for the aforesaid animals. Both require a loamy, loose soil, and do not grow in heavy ground. Turnips, however, like level and 23 moist places, while the navew prefers ground that is sloping and dry with more of a tendency to leanness; and so it grows better in gravelly and sandy lands. The nature of the situation changes the seed of both: thus, turnips sown in one soil are changed into navews in two years' time, while in the other the navew likewise takes on the appearance of the turnip.[b] In well-watered situations both are properly sown after the summer solstice, in dry places at the end of August or the early part of September.[c] They demand a soil that is well prepared by repeated working with the plough or mattock and generously manured; for this is of the greatest importance, not 24 only because they themselves make a better showing but also because, after they are harvested, soil so treated produces luxuriant crops of grain. One

[c] Columella speaks also (XI. 3. 16 and 59) of a spring sowing, in February, for a summer crop, though the sowing in August was to be preferred.

gerum agri non amplius quattuor sextariis raporum seminis obserendum est; quarta parte amplius napi[1] spargendum, quia[2] non in ventrem latescit, sed tenuem radicem deorsum agit.

Atque haec hominum causa serenda censemus, illa deinde pecudum pabulorum genera complura, sicut Medicam, viciam, farraginem quoque hordeaceam et avenam, faenum Graecum nec minus ervum et ciceram; nam cetera neque enumerare et minus serere dignamur, excepta tamen cytiso, de qua dicemus[3] in iis libris, quos de generibus surculorum
25 conscripsimus. Sed ex iis, quae placent, eximia est herba Medica, quod semel seritur, decem annis omnibus deinde recte quater,[4] interdum etiam sexiens demetitur, quod agrum stercorat, quod omne emaciatum armentum ex ea pinguescit, quod aegrotanti pecori remedium est, quod iugerum eius toto anno
26 tribus equis abunde sufficit. Seritur ut deinceps praecipiemus. Locum, in quo Medicam proximo vere saturus es, proscindito circa Kalendas Octobris et eum tota hieme putrescere sinito; deinde Kalendis Februariis diligenter iterato et lapides omnes eligito[5] glaebasque offringito; postea circa Martium mensem tertiato et occato. Cum sic terram subegeris, in morem horti areas latas pedum denum, longas

[1] napis *AR, omnes ante Gesn.*
[2] qui *AR, vett. edd.*
[3] diximus *M.*
[4] Medica. quod cum semel seritur, decem annis durat; quod per annum deinde recte quater *Ald., Gesn., Schn.*
[5] eligito *SAR, vett. edd., Schn.* : elegito *Lundström* : egerito *Ald., Gesn.*

[a] Medic clover or lucern (alfalfa) is said to have come to Italy from Greece, where it was introduced from Media at the

iugerum of ground should be sown with not more than four *sextarii* of turnip seed; of the navew, one-fourth more is to be scattered, because it does not widen out into a globular shape but pushes its slender root straight down.

The above plantings are to be made, in our opinion, for the sake of man, and then come several kinds of cattle fodder, such as Medic clover,[a] vetch, mixed fodder of barley and oats, fenugreek, and also bitter vetch and chick-pea; for we do not think it worth while to enumerate the rest, and still less to sow them, excepting only the cytisus [shrub-clover] of which we shall speak in those books[b] which we have in writing on the various kinds of young shoots. But 25 of those which find favour the Medic plant is outstanding for several reasons: one seeding affords, for all of ten years thereafter, four harvestings regularly and sometimes six; it improves the soil; lean cattle of every kind grow fat on it; it has medicinal value for an ailing beast; and one *iugerum* of it provides abundant fodder for three horses for an entire year. It is sown as we shall next direct. In the place where 26 you are to sow Medic the following spring, break the ground about the first of October and allow it to mellow during the entire winter; then, at the beginning of February, work it again carefully, remove all stones, and break up the clods; after that, sometime in the month of March, plough it a third time and harrow it. When you have prepared the ground in this fashion, make divisions as you would in a

time of the Persian Wars with King Darius (Pliny, *N.H.* XVIII. 144).

[b] The cultivation of *cytisus* is discussed in V. 12 and *De Arb.* 28; it is tree-medick.

pedum quinquagenum facito, ut per semitas aqua ministrari possit aditusque utraque parte runcantibus
27 pateat. Deinde vetus stercus inicito, atque ita mense ultimo Aprili serito tantum, quantum ut singuli cyathi seminis locum occupent decem pedum longum et quinque latum. Quod ubi feceris, ligneis rastris—id enim multum confert—statim iacta semina obruantur; nam celerrime sole aduruntur. Post sationem ferro tangi locus non debet; atque, ut dixi, ligneis rastris sariendus et identidem runcandus est, ne alterius generis herba invalidam Medicam
28 perimat.[1] Tardius messim[2] primam eius facere oportebit, cum iam seminum aliquam partem eiecerit. Postea quam voles teneram, cum prosiluerit, deseces licet et iumentis praebeas, sed inter initia parcius, dum consuescant, ne novitas pabuli noceat; inflat enim et multum creat sanguinem. Cum secueris autem, saepius eam rigato; paucos deinde post dies, ubi coeperit fruticare,[3] omnis alterius generis herbas eruncato. Sic culta sexiens anno[4] demeti poterit et permanebit annis decem.

29 Viciae autem duae sationes sunt: prima, qua[5] pabuli causa circa aequinoctium autumnale serimus septem modios eius in unum iugerum; secunda, qua sex modios mense Ianuario vel etiam serius iacimus semini progenerando. Utraque satio potest cruda terra fieri, sed melius proscissa; idque genus prae-

[1] peremat *S¹A, Lundström*: perveniat *M.*
[2] messem *R aliquot, edd. ante Lundström.*
[3] fructificare *AR.*
[4] sexies in anno *R aliquot, edd. ante Lundström.*
[5] qua *omnes post Ursinum*: quam *codd.*

[a] 1 *cyathus* = about one-twelfth of a pint.

garden, ten feet wide and fifty feet long, to allow water to be supplied by way of the foot-paths and to provide a means of access on both sides for the weeders. Then spread old manure over it, and 27 at the end of April sow at the rate of one *cyathus* [a] of seed to a space ten feet long and five wide. When you have done so, the seed should be covered at once with wooden rakes—a matter of great importance—for the seed is very soon burned by the sun. After the seed is sown, the place should not be touched with iron; and so, as I have said, it must be hoed with wooden implements and repeatedly freed of weeds, so that no other kind of growth may kill out the weak Medic. It will be best to make the first cutting 28 rather late, after it has dropped some of its seed. Thereafter, when it has started up, you may cut it as tender as you please and feed it to stock, but somewhat sparingly at first, until they become accustomed to it, so that the novelty of the fodder may not harm them; for it causes bloating and greatly increases the blood supply. After cutting, water it rather frequently; then, a few days later, when it begins to send out new shoots, weed out all other kinds of growth. If cared for in this way, it can be cut six times a year and will last for ten years.[b]

Of vetch, however, there are two sowings: the first 29 about the time of the autumnal equinox, for the purpose of forage, in which we sow seven *modii* to the *iugerum*; the second in the month of January or even later, when we scatter six *modii* for the production of seed. Both sowings may be made on untilled land, but with better results on broken ground; and this

[b] Pliny (*loc. cit.*) gives it more than thirty years of life.

30 cipue non amat rores, cum seritur. Itaque post secundam diei horam vel tertiam spargendum est, cum iam omnis umor sole ventove detersus est, neque amplius proici debet, quam quod eodem die possit operiri; nam si nox incessit, quantulocumque umore, prius quam obruatur, corrumpitur. Observandum erit ne ante quintam et vicesimam lunam terrae mandetur; aliter satae fere limacem nocere comperimus.

31 Farraginem in restibili stercoratissimo loco et altero sulco serere convenit. Ea fit optima, cum cantherini hordei decem modiis iugerum obseritur circa aequinoctium autumnale, sed impendentibus pluviis, ut consita rigataque imbribus celeriter prodeat et confirmetur ante hiemis violentiam. Nam frigoribus cum alia pabula defecerunt, ea bubus ceterisque pecudibus optime desecta praebetur, et si depascere saepius voles, usque in mensem Maium sufficit.

32 Quod si etiam semen voles ex ea percipere, a Kalendis Martiis pecora depellenda et ab omni noxa defendenda est, ut sit idonea frugibus. Similis ratio[1] avenae est, quae autumno sata partim[2] caeditur in faenum vel pabulum dum adhuc viret, partim semini custoditur.[3]

33 Faenum Graecum, quod siliquam vocant rustici, duo tempora sationum habet, quorum alterum est Septembris mensis, cum pabuli causa seritur, isdem

[1] satio *R, edd. ante Schn.*

[2] quae autumno sata partim (*sed* qua autumno sata partim *in marg. A man. alt.*) *om. et post* viret *inserunt SA.*

[3] partim semini custoditur *om. SA.*

[c] *Farrago* is defined by Varro (*R.R.* I. 31. 5) as a mixture of barley, vetch, and legumes for green feed; *cf.* Pliny, *N.H.* XVIII 142.

species especially does not like dew at the time of sowing. For this reason it must be broadcast after 30 the second or third hour of the day, when all moisture has been dried up by sun or wind, and no more should be scattered than can be covered in the same day; for, if night comes on before it is covered, the least moisture spoils it. Care must be taken not to put it in the ground before the twenty-fifth day of the moon; otherwise we usually find that the slug damages the crop.

Mixed forage[a] should be sown in land that is 31 worked every year, very heavily manured, and twice ploughed. It turns out best when sown with ten *modii* of horse-barley to the *iugerum* about the autumnal equinox; but when rains are threatening, so that, being watered by showers after sowing, it may come up quickly and gather strength before the severe weather of winter. For in cold weather, when other forage has failed, this provides excellent cut fodder for oxen and other animals; and if you care to graze it frequently, it holds out even up to the month of May. If, however, you wish also to take 32 seed from it, cattle must be kept off after the first of March, and it must be protected from every kind of harm so as to be capable of bearing seed. The same method is applied to oats: they are sown in the autumn; some are cut for hay or for fodder while still green; and some are set apart for seed.

Fenugreek, which country people call *siliqua*,[b] has 33 two seasons for sowing: one of them in the month of September, when it is sown for fodder, on the same

[b] The texts of Pliny (*N.H.* XVIII. 140) read *silicia*, with variants *silica* and *sicilia*. Pliny's *siliqua* is carob.

diebus, quibus vicia circa aequinoctium, alterum autem mensis Ianuarii ultimi vel primi Februarii, cum in semen[1] seminatur; sed hac satione iugerum sex modiis, illa septem occupamus. Utraque cruda terra non incommode fit, daturque opera ut spisse aretur, nec tamen alte, nam si plus quattuor digitis adobrutum est semen eius, non facile prodit; propter quod non nulli prius quam serant, minimis aratris proscindunt atque ita iaciunt semina et sarculis adobruunt.[2]

34 Ervum autem laetatur loco macro nec umido, quia luxuria plerumque corrumpitur. Potest autumno seri nec minus post brumam Ianuarii parte novissima vel toto Februario, dum ante Kalendas Martias, quem mensem universum negant agricolae huic legumini convenire, quod eo tempore satum pecori sit noxium et praecipue bubus, quos pabulo suo cerebrosos reddat. Quinque modiis iugerum obseritur.

35 Cicera bubus ervi loco fresa datur in Hispania Baetica; quae cum suspensa mola divisa est, paulum aqua maceratur, dum lentescat,[3] atque ita mixta paleis succretis[4] pecori praebetur. Sed ervi duodecim librae satisfaciunt uni iugo, cicerae sedecim. Eadem hominibus non inutilis neque iniucunda est; sapori certe nihilo differt a cicercula, colore tantum discernitur, nam est obsoletior et nigro propior.

[1] semen *SAR, Lundström* : messem *R duo dett., et vulgo.*
[2] adruunt *S, Lundström* : adfruunt *A.*
[3] inlentescat *Ald., Lundström, cum codd. ut videtur.*
[4] *sic Lundström, cum codd. ut videtur* : subtritis *vulgo.*

[a] *Cf.* Pliny, *N.H.* XVIII. 139. [b] Andalusia.

days as vetch, near the time of the equinox; the other, however, at the end of January or early in February, when it is sown for seed; though we use six *modii* to the *iugerum* for the latter sowing, and seven for the former. Both sowings are made not without advantage before the ground is prepared, and care is taken that it be ploughed closely but not deeply, for if the seed is covered more than four fingers deep it does not easily come up; and for this reason some people break the ground with the smallest ploughs before sowing, and then scatter the seed and cover it with light hoes.

Bitter vetch, on the other hand, thrives on soil that 34
is lean but not moist, because it is usually spoiled by rankness. It may be sown in autumn and equally well after the winter solstice, in the latter part of January or all of February, if only before the first day of March. This whole month, farmers say, is not suited to this legume, because when sown at this time it is harmful to cattle, and especially to oxen, in which it causes brain-madness when they eat it.[a] It is sown five *modii* to the *iugerum*.

Crushed chickling-vetch instead of bitter vetch is 35
given to oxen in Hispania Baetica[b]: after being broken by a suspended[c] millstone it is soaked for a time in water, until it becomes soft, and in this condition, mixed with sifted chaff, it is fed to cattle. But twelve pounds of bitter vetch are sufficient for one yoke, and sixteen of chick-pea. This same chick-pea is not unsuited to human use, and is not unpleasant; in taste, at least, it differs not at all from the chickling-vetch, being distinguished merely by its colour, for it is more dirty-looking

[c] *I.e.* set for coarse grinding.

Seritur primo vel altero sulco mense Martio, ita ut postulat soli laetitia, quod eadem quattuor modiis, non numquam et tribus, interdum etiam duobus ac semodio iugerum occupat.

XI. Quoniam quando quidque serendum sit persecuti sumus, nunc quem ad modum quotque operis singula eorum, quae rettulimus, colenda sint demonstrabimus. Peracta sementi sequens cura est sartionis; de qua non convenit inter auctores. Quidam negant eam [1] quicquam proficere, quod frumenti radices sarculo detegantur, aliquae etiam succidantur ac, si frigora incesserint post sartionem, gelu frumenta enecentur; satius autem esse ea
2 tempestive runcari et purgari. Pluribus tamen sariri placet, sed neque eodem modo neque isdem temporibus usque quaque fieri; nam in agris siccis et apricis, simul ac primum sartionem pati queant segetes, debere eas permota terra adobrui, ut fruticare [2] possint. Quod ipsum ante hiemem fieri oportere, deinde post hiemem iterari; in locis autem frigidis et palustribus plerumque transacta hieme sariri nec adobrui, sed plana sartione terram permo-
3 veri. Multis tamen nos regionibus aptam esse hiemalem sartionem comperimus dumtaxat ubi et siccitas caeli et tepores permittunt, sed nec istud ubique fieri censemus, verum incolarum consuetudine uti. Sunt enim regionum propria munera, sicut Aegypti et Africae, quibus agricola [3] post sementim

[1] eam *om. SA.* [2] fructificare *AR.*
[3] agricolatio *R.*

and nearer black. It is sown at the first or second ploughing in the month of March, according as the richness of the soil requires, and the same consideration determines the amount—four *modii*, sometimes three, sometimes even two and a half to the *iugerum*.

XI. Since we have treated of the time at which each sowing should be made, we shall now show what method of cultivation is to be employed, and the number of days' labour required for each of the crops mentioned. After the sowing is finished, the next matter is that of hoeing, a point on which authorities are not agreed. Some say that this is of no advantage, because the roots of the grain are uncovered by the hoe and some of them are even cut off, and, if the weather is cold after the hoeing, the grain is killed by frost; but that it is better that weeding and cleaning be done at the proper season. Still there 2
are many who believe in hoeing, but that it should not be done everywhere in the same way and at the same time; thus, in dry and sunny fields, as soon as the crops can stand hoeing, they should be covered with well-stirred soil to enable them to bush out; and this should be done before winter, and then repeated after winter is past; while in cold and swampy places, usually after winter is over, they should be hoed without being covered over but having the earth thoroughly stirred by level hoeing. Nevertheless we find that winter hoeing is suited to 3
many regions, but only where dryness and warmth of climate permit, though we think it best not to practice even this everywhere but to conform to the ways of those who live in the neighbourhood. For countries have their own peculiar advantages, such as those of Egypt and Africa, where the farmer does

ante messem segetem non attingit, quoniam caeli conditio et terrae bonitas ea est ut vix ulla herba exeat nisi ex semine iacto, sive quia rari sunt imbres seu quia qualitas humi sic se cultoribus praebet.
4 In iis autem locis, ubi desideratur sartio, non ante sunt attingendae segetes, etiam si caeli status permittat,[1] quam cum sata sulcos contexerint. Triticumque et adoreum, cum quattuor fibras habere coeperint, hordeum, cum quinque, faba et cetera legumina, cum quattuor digitis a terra exstiterint, recte sarientur, excepto tamen lupino, cuius semini contraria est sartio, quoniam unam radicem habet, quae sive ferro succisa est seu vulnerata, totus
5 frutex emoritur. Quod etiam si non fieret, supervacuus tamen esset [2] cultus, cum sola haec res adeo non infestetur herbis, ut ipsa herbas perimat. At quae [3] aliae segetes vel umidae moveri possunt, melius tamen siccae sariuntur, quia sic tractatae non infestantur rubigine; hordeum vero nisi siccissi-
6 mum tangi non debet. Fabam multi ne sariendam quidem putant, quod et manibus, cum maturuerit, ducta secernatur a cetera runcatione [4] et internatae herbae faeno reserventur. Cuius opinionis etiam Cornelius Celsus est, qui inter ceteras dotes eius [5] leguminis hanc quoque enumerat, quod sublata faba faenum ex eodem loco secari posse dicat. Sed mihi videtur pessimi agricolae committere ut satis

[1] permittat *S, Lundström*: permittit *AR, et vulgo.*

[2] esset *ac, Ursinus, Gesn., Schn.*: erat *SA, Lundström*: erit *R, vett. edd.*

[3] At quae *Lundström*: atque *codd., Schn.*: at aliae segetes, quae *vulgo.*

[4] runca *SA*[1], *Lundström.*

[5] eius *om. R, edd. ante Schn.*

not touch his crop from the sowing until the reaping, for climatic conditions and the quality of the soil are such that scarcely any plant comes up except from seed that is sown; either because of the scarcity of rain or because the character of the soil so lends itself to those who cultivate it.[a] Moreover, in those 4
regions where hoeing is desirable, the crops are not to be touched before the growth has covered the furrows, even if the condition of the weather should allow it. It will be proper to hoe wheat and emmer as soon as they have put forth four blades, barley when it has five, and beans and other legumes when they stand four fingers above ground—with the exception, however, of the lupine, as hoeing is hurtful to its seedlings; for it has a single root, and if this is cut or injured by an iron tool, the whole plant dies. And even if this were not the case, cultivation would 5
still be unnecessary, for this one plant is so far from being troubled by weeds as actually to destroy them on its own account. Now other crops which may be worked when wet, are nevertheless hoed with better results when dry, because, when handled in this way, they are not attacked by rust; but barley must not be touched except when perfectly dry. Many people 6
think that beans should not be hoed at all, because, being pulled by hand when ripe, they may be separated from the other growth, and the grass that grows among them may be saved for hay. This is also the opinion of Cornelius Celsus, who counts this too among the other virtues of this legume when he says that after the beans are removed a cutting of hay may be taken from the same spot. But to me it seems the mark of a very poor farmer to allow grass

[a] *Cf.* Pliny, *N.H.* XVIII. 186.

herba proveniat; frugibus enim plurimum detra-
7 hitur, si relinquitur runcatio.[1] Neque[2] est rustici
prudentis magis pabulis studere pecudum quam
cibis hominum, cum praesertim liceat illa quoque
cultu pratorum consequi; adeoque fabam sariendam
censeo, ut existimem debere etiam ter sariri. Nam
sic cultam comperimus non solum multiplicare
fructum, sed et[3] exiguam portionem in valvulis
habere fresaeque eius et expurgatae modium paene
tam plenum esse quam integrae, quoniam vix minua-
8 tur mensura detractis putaminibus. Atque in totum,
sicut ante iam diximus, hiberna sartio plurimum
iuvat diebus serenis ac siccis post brumam confectam
mense Ianuario, si gelicidia non sint. Ea porro sic
debet fieri, ne radices satorum laedantur et ut potius
adobruantur cumulisque exaggerentur,[4] ut latius se
frutex culmi[5] diffundat. Id prima sartione fecisse
proderit, secunda oberit, quia cum pullulare[6] desiit[7]
9 frumentum, putrescit si adobrutum[8] est. Nihil
itaque amplius in iteratione quam remolliri[9] terra
debet aequaliter; eamque transacto aequinoctio
verno statim peragi oportet intra dies viginti, ante
quam seges in articulum eat, quoniam serius sarta
corrumpitur insequentibus aestivis siccitatibus et
caloribus. Subiungenda deinde est sartioni runcatio
curandumque ne florentem segetem tangamus, sed
10 aut ante[10] aut mox cum defloruerit. Omne autem

[1] runca *SA*, *Lundström*.
[2] neque enim *R*, *edd. ante Lundström*.
[3] et *om. AR*, *edd. ante Schn.* [4] exaggerantur *codd.*
[5] humi *R*, *edd. ante Lundström*.
[6] paululum *SA* : paulum *a*.
[7] desit *SA*, *Lundström*.
[8] adrutum *SA*, *Lundström*.
[9] *sic Schn.* : remoliri *Lundström*, *et vulgo*.

to grow among his crops, for it detracts greatly from the yield if weeding is neglected. And it is no mark 7
of a wise husbandman to be more concerned with fodder for cattle than with food for man, especially when he may obtain the former as well by cultivation of his meadows. I am so strongly in favour of hoeing beans as to think that they should actually be hoed three times. For we find that when cultivated in this way they not only multiply their yield but also have but little pod in proportion, and that a measure of them when shelled and cleaned is almost as full as before they were shelled, as the amount is scarcely diminished by the removal of the outer coverings.
And in general, as we have said before, winter hoeing 8
is of very great benefit on clear and dry days after the solstice is past, in the month of January, if there are no frosts. It should be done, besides, in such a way that the roots of the plants will not be damaged, but rather covered over and hilled up, so that the offshoots of the main stem may spread out farther. It will be beneficial to do this at the first hoeing, but harmful at the second, because grain rots if it is covered after
it has ceased to send out shoots. Therefore nothing 9
more should be done at the second hoeing than to loosen the ground evenly; and this should be done immediately after the vernal equinox is past, within twenty days, before the plant forms a joint, for when it is hoed later it is destroyed by the dry weather and heat of the ensuing summer. To the hoeing must be added the weeding, and we must take care not to touch a grain-field when it is in bloom, but either beforehand or soon after the blossoms have fallen.

---

[10] antea *R plerique, edd. ante Lundström.*

frumentum et hordeum, quicquid denique non duplici semine est, spicam a tertio ad quartum nodum emittit et, cum totam edidit, octo diebus deflorescit ac deinde grandescit diebus quadraginta, quibus post florem ad maturitatem venit. Rursus quae duplici semine sunt, ut faba, pisum, lenticula, diebus quadraginta florent simulque grandescunt.

XII. Et ut iam percenseamus, quot operis in aream perducantur ea, quae terrae credidimus, tritici modii quattuor vel quinque bubulcorum operas occupant quattuor, occatoris unam, sartoris duas primum et unam cum iterum sariuntur, runcatoris unam, messoris unam et dimidiam; in totum summam operarum decem et dimidiam. Siliginis modii quinque totidem operas desiderant. Seminis [1] modii novem vel decem totidem operas quot tritici modii quinque
2 postulant. Hordei modii quinque bubulci operas tres exigunt, occatoriam unam, sartoriam unam et dimidiam, messoriam unam: summam operarum sex et dimidiam. Fabae modii quattuor vel sex in vetereto duas operas bubulcorum detinent, at in restibili unam; occantur sesquiopera, sariuntur sesquiopera et una opera [2] iterum, tertium [3] sariuntur una opera, metuntur una: summa fit operarum octo
3 vel septem. Viciae modii sex vel septem in vetereto bubulcorum duas operas volunt, in restibili unam,

[1] Seminis *S*: si seminis *AR*: Sesamii *vel* Sesami *vulgo ante Schn.*; *sed Pontedera* adorei *proposuit*.

[2] sariuntur s. e. u. opera *Lundström*: sariuntur sex una opera *R plerique*; *om. SA*: sarriuntur sesquiopera, iterum sarriuntur una opera, et tertio una *vulgo*.

[3] tertium *add. Lundström*.

[a] *I.e.*, in modern botanical usage, dicotyledonous.

[b] The amount of seed required for sowing one *iugerum*; *cf.* II. 9. 1.

Now all grain and barley, in short everything that 10
is not of double seed,[a] sends out an ear from the third to the fourth joint; and when it has pushed out the entire spike it casts its bloom within eight days, and then continues to grow until it reaches maturity forty days after its flowering. On the other hand, those that are of double seed, such as beans, peas, and lentils, bloom in forty days and increase in growth for the same length of time.

XII. And now to reckon up the number of days' labour required to bring to the threshing-floor what we have committed to the earth, four or five *modii* of common wheat[b] take up four days' work of the ploughmen, one of the harrower, two of the hoer for the first hoeing and one for the second, one of the weeder, and one and a half of the reaper—a total of ten and one-half days of labour. Five *modii* of winter wheat require the same number of days. Nine or ten *modii* of emmer[c] call for as many days' work as five *modii* of common wheat. Five *modii* of barley require 2
three days' labour of the ploughman, one day of harrowing, one and a half of hoeing, and one of reaping—six and a half days in all. Four or six *modii* of beans use up two days' work of the ploughmen in old fallow ground, but one in land under cultivation; they are harrowed in a day and a half, hoed in a day and a half, hoed a second time in one day and a third time in one day, and harvested in one day—the total amounting to seven or eight days. Six or seven *modii* 3
of vetch want two days' labour of the ploughmen in old fallow, and one in ground that is kept under

[c] *Semen adoreum*, in combination or singly; *cf.* II. 6. 1, II. 9. 1.

item occantur una opera, metuntur una: summa fit operarum quattuor.[1] Ervi modii quinque totidem operis conseruntur, occantur una, item singulis sariuntur, runcantur, metuntur; quae cuncta sex operas occupant. Siliquae modii sex vel septem totidem operis obruuntur, metuntur una. Phaseoli modii quattuor obruuntur totidem operis, occantur
4 una, metuntur una. Cicerae vel cicerculae modii quattuor operas bubulcorum tres postulant, occantur una opera, runcantur una, velluntur una: summa fit sex operarum. Lentis sesquimodius totidem operis[2] obruitur,[3] occatur una, saritur duabus, runcatur una, vellitur una: summa fit operarum octo. Lupini modii decem obruuntur una, occantur una, metuntur una. Milii sextarii quattuor totidemque panici bubulcorum operas occupant quattuor, occantur operis tribus, sariuntur tribus; quot operis
5 carpantur, incertum est. Ciceris modii tres operis totidem seminantur, occantur duabus, sariuntur una, runcantur una, velluntur tribus: summa fit undecim operarum. Lini decem modii vel octo quattuor iugis conseruntur, occantur tribus,[4] runcantur una, velluntur tribus: summa fit undecim operarum. Sesami sextarii sex tribus iugis a proscissione coluntur,[5] occantur[6] operis quattuor, sariuntur quattuor

[1] *sic codd., Lundström:* vel trium *add. Ald., Gesn., Schn.*

[2] operas *R, edd. ante Lundström.*

[3] obruitur *add. Madvig, Lundström*; *om. SA, vett. edd.*: desiderat *R, Ald., Gesn., Schn.*

[4] operis tribus *Ald., Gesn. Schn.*

[5] coluntur *R, edd.*: tolluntur *SA, Lundström.*

[6] *post* occantur *verba* tribus runcantur una velluntur tribus summa fit *e sententia antecedente repetunt SA, teste Lundström:* occantur operis tribus, s. q., e. s. i. d., runcantur una, velluntur duabus. Summa fit *Schn. praeeunte Pontedera.*

cultivation; this likewise is harrowed in one day, and harvested in one day—the total amounting to [three or] four days' work. Five *modii* of bitter vetch are sown in the same number of days, harrowed in one day, and also hoed, weeded, and harvested in one day each—the total making up six days. Six or seven *modii* of fenugreek [a] are put in the ground with the same number of days' labour, and are harvested in one day. Four *modii* of cow-peas are put under ground in the same number of days, are harrowed in one day, and harvested in one. Four *modii* of 4
chickling-vetch or of the small chick-pea require three days' work of the ploughmen; they are harrowed in one day, weeded in one, and pulled in one—the total amounting to six days of work. A *modius* and a half of lentil is covered in the same number of days, harrowed in one, hoed in two, weeded in one, and pulled in one—the total coming to eight days' work. Ten *modii* of lupine are covered in one day, harrowed in one, and harvested in one. Four *sextarii* of millet and the same amount of panic take up four days' labour of the ploughmen, are harrowed in three days, and hoed in three; the number of days for gathering is not fixed.
Three *modii* of the chick-pea are sown in the same 5
number of days, harrowed in two days, hoed in one, weeded in one, and pulled in three—a total of eleven days' work. Eight or ten *modii* of flaxseed are sown with four days' ploughing, harrowed with three days' work, weeded with one, and pulled with three—the total amounting to eleven days' work. Six *sextarii* of sesame are cared for with three days' ploughing after the first breaking of the ground, four days of

[a] *Siliqua*, *cf.* II. 10. 33.

et sariuntur iterum duabus, metuntur duabus:
6 summa fit operarum quindecim. Cannabis seritur, ut supra docuimus, sed incertum est quantam impensam curamque desideret. At Medica obruitur non aratro, sed, ut dixi, ligneis rastellis. Iugerum agri eius occant duo,[1] sarit unus, metit unus.[2]

7 Hac consummatione operarum colligitur posse agrum ducentorum iugerum subigi duobus iugis bovum[3] totidemque bubulcis et sex mediastinis, si tamen vacet arboribus. At ubi[4] sit arbustum, tamen[5] eundem modum Saserna tribus hominibus adiectis adseverat probe satis excoli. Quae nos ratio docet sufficere posse iugum bovum tritici centum viginti quinque modiis totidemque leguminum, ut sit in assem[6] autumnalis satio modiorum ducentorum quinquaginta, et posthac nihilo minus conserantur[7] trimestrium modii[8] quinque et septua-
8 ginta. Hoc deinde sic probatur. Semina, quae quarto sulco seruntur in iugeribus viginti quinque, desiderant bubulcorum operas centum decem et quinque; nam proscinditur is agri modus, quamvis durissimi, quinquaginta operis, iteratur quinque et
9 viginti, tertiatur et conseritur quadraginta. Cetera[9] legumina occupant operas sexaginta, id est menses duos. Pluviales quoque et feriarum computantur, quibus non aratur, dies quinque et quadraginta; item peracta sementi, quibus requiescunt, dies

[1] occantur duabus *R*: occatur duabus *M, Ald., Gesn.*
[2] sarit una metit una *R*: sarritur una, metitur una *M, Ald., Gesn.*
[3] *sic SA, Lundström*: boum *R, et vulgo.*
[4] si *Ald., Gesn., Schn.*
[5] tamen *om. SA, edd. ante Lundström.*
[6] asse *Ursinus, Schn.*

harrowing, four of hoeing and two at the second hoeing, and two days of harvesting—a total of fifteen days. Hemp is sown as we have directed above, but 6
the amount of expense and attention required is not fixed. Medic, however, is put in the ground, not with the plough, but, as I have said, with small wooden rakes. One *iugerum* of this is harrowed by two men, hoed by one, and harvested by one.

From this summing up of the days of labour required 7
it is concluded that two hundred *iugera* of land can be worked with two yoke of oxen, the same number of ploughmen, and six common labourers, provided it be free of trees; but the same amount, when it is planted with trees, Saserna says can be satisfactorily cultivated with three additional men. This calculation shows us that one yoke of oxen can meet the requirements of one hundred and twenty-five *modii* of wheat and the same of legumes, so that the autumn sowing may total two hundred and fifty *modii*, and even after that seventy-five *modii* of three-months crops may still be sown. The proof of this is as 8
follows: Seeds that are sown at the fourth ploughing require, for twenty-five *iugera*, one hundred and fifteen days' labour of the ploughmen; for such a plot of ground, however hard, is broken in fifty days, re-ploughed in twenty-five, ploughed a third time and then sown in forty days. Other legumes 9
require sixty days, that is, two months. Forty-five days also are allowed for rainy weather and holidays, on which no ploughing is done; likewise thirty days after the sowing is finished, in which there is a period

---

[7] conseram *S*: conserant *A et R plerique*: conserat *Ald.*, *Gesn.*, *Schn.*

[8] modios *Ald.*, *Gesn.*, *Schn.*

[9] Cetera *om. Schn.*

triginta. Sic in asse fiunt octo menses et dies decem. Supersunt tamen de anno tres reliqui menses et dies quinque et viginti, quos absumamus [1] aut in satione trimestrium aut in vecturis faeni et pabulorum et stercoris aliorumque utensilium.

XIII. Sed ex iis, quae rettuli, seminibus idem Saserna putat aliis stercorari et iuvari agros, aliis rursus peruri et emaciari; stercorari lupino, faba, vicia, ervilia, lenti, cicercula, piso. De lupino nihil dubito atque etiam de pabulari vicia, si tamen eam viridem desectam confestim aratrum subsequatur et, quod falx reliquerit, prius quam inarescat,[2] vomis rescin-
2 dat atque obruat; id enim cedit pro stercore. Nam si radices eius desecto pabulo relictae inaruerunt,[3] sucum omnem solo auferent vimque terrae absument; quod etiam in faba ceterisque leguminibus, quibus terra gliscere videtur, verisimile est accidere, ut nisi protinus sublata messe [4] eorum proscinditur,[5] nihil iis segetibus, quae deinceps in eo loco seminari
3 debent, profuturum sit. Ac de iis quoque leguminibus, quae velluntur, Tremelius obesse ait maxime [6] solo virus [7] ciceris et lini, alterum quia sit salsae,[8] alterum quia sit [9] fervidae naturae, quod etiam Vergilius significat dicendo:

> Urit enim lini campum seges, urit avenae,
> Urunt Lethaeo perfusa papavera somno.

[1] absumimus *R plerique*.
[2] macrescat *vel* marcescat *R plerique*.
[3] inaruerunt *SA*, *Lundström*: inaruerint *R*, *et vulgo*.
[4] messes *SA*.
[5] proscinditur *codd.*, *Lundström*: proscindatur *vulgo*.
[6] maxime ait *R*. [7] virtus *A*.
[8] densae *S* dens (e *suprascr. man rec.*) *A*. [9] sit *om. S*.

[a] *Georg.* I. 77–78.

of rest. Thus the total amounts to eight months and ten days. Still there are left of the year three months and twenty-five days, which we may spend either in sowing three-months crops or in the hauling of hay, forage, manure, and of other useful things.

XIII. But of the crops that I have mentioned, the same Saserna thinks that land is fertilized and improved by some, and, on the other hand, that it is burned out and wasted by others; that it is fertilized by lupine, beans, vetch, bitter vetch, lentils, the small chickpea, and peas. As to the lupine I have no doubt, nor yet as to vetch when it is sown for fodder, provided, however, that after being cut green it be followed up immediately by the plough, and that the ploughshare cut up and bury, before it dries out, what is left by the sickle; for this takes the place
of manure. For if the roots are left to dry out after 2
the fodder is cut, they will draw all the moisture out of the soil and use up the strength of the land; and it is probable that this happens also in the case of beans and other legumes by which the ground appears to be enriched; so that, unless the ground is broken up at once after a crop of them has been taken off, it will be of no benefit to the crops which are to be planted
in that spot thereafter. Of those legumes, too, which 3
are harvested by pulling, Tremelius says that the poisons of the chickpea and of flax are most harmful to the soil, the one because it is of a salty nature, the other because of its burning qualities; and Vergil, too, points this out when he says:

> A field is burned by crops of flax, is burned by crops of oats,
> Is burned by crops of poppies with Lethaean slumber steeped.[a]

Neque enim dubium, quin et his seminibus infestetur ager sicut et[1] milio et panico. Sed omni solo, quod praedictorum leguminum segetibus fatiscit, una praesens medicina est, ut stercore adiuves et absump-
4 tas vires hoc velut pabulo refoveas, nec tantum propter semina, quae sulcis aratri committuntur, verum etiam propter arbores ac virgulta, quae maiorem in modum laetantur eius modi alimento. Quare si est, ut videtur, agricolis utilissimum, diligentius de eo dicendum existimo, cum priscis auctoribus, quamvis non omissa res,[2] levi tamen admodum cura sit prodita.

XIV. Tria igitur genera stercoris[3] sunt praecipue,[4] quod ex avibus, quod ex hominibus, quod ex pecudibus confit. Avium primum habetur quod ex columbariis egeritur, deinde quod gallinae ceteraeque volucres edunt, exceptis tamen palustribus aut nantibus, ut anatis[5] et anseris; nam id noxium quoque est. Maxime tamen[6] columbinum probamus, quod modice sparsum terram fermentare comperi-
2 mus; secundum deinde, quod homines faciunt, si et aliis villae purgamentis immisceatur, quoniam per se[7] naturae est ferventioris et idcirco terram perurit. Aptior est tamen surculis hominis urina, quam sex mensibus passus veterascere[8] si vitibus aut pomorum arboribus adhibeas, nullo alio magis fructus exuberat: nec solum ea res maiorem faciet[9] proventum,

[1] etiam *Ald., Gesn., Schn.*

[2] non omnes sares *SA.*

[3] stercoris genera *R.*

[4] praecipua *R pauci, et vulgo ante Schn.*

[5] anetis *SA, Lundström.* [6] autem *S.*

[7] per se *vulgo additur*; *om. codd. et Schn.*

[8] veterescere *Lundström cum codd. ut videtur.*

[9] facit *R aliquot, Ald., Gesn., Schn.*

For there is no doubt that a field is impaired by seeding it with these, just as it is by millet and panic. But for all ground that is exhausted by cropping the aforesaid legumes there is one remedy at hand, namely, to come to its aid with manure, and with this sustenance, so to speak, to restore the strength that has been taken from it; and this not only for the 4
sake of seed which is committed to the ploughed furrow, but also for trees and bushes, which thrive in greater measure on this kind of nourishment. Wherefore, if manuring is of the greatest advantage to the farmer, as it appears to be, I believe that it should be discussed with unusual care, inasmuch as this subject, though not overlooked by the ancient authorities,[a] has nevertheless been given very slight attention.

XIV. There are, then, mainly, three kinds of manure: that produced by birds, by humankind, and by cattle. Of bird dung that is considered first which is gathered from dove-cotes, and next is that which comes from hens and other fowl, excepting nevertheless marsh birds or swimming fowl, such as ducks and geese; for that is actually harmful. Still we especially commend pigeon dung, because we find that a moderate spreading of it causes the earth to ferment; and second to this is human excrement, if it is mixed 2
with other refuse of the farmstead, for by itself it is naturally rather hot and for that reason it burns the ground. Better suited to young shoots, however, is human urine; and if you let it age for six months and then apply it to vines or fruit trees, there is nothing that makes them bear more abundantly; and not only will this treatment produce a larger crop but also

[a] *Cf.* Cato, 36; Varro, *R.R.* I. 38. Of later authorities *cf.* Pliny, *N.H.* XVII. 50–57, and Palladius, I. 33.

sed etiam saporem et odorem vini[1] pomorumque
3 reddit meliorem. Potest et vetus amurca, quae salem non habet, permixta huic commode frugiferas arbores et praecipue oleas rigare, nam per se quoque adhibita multum iuvat. Sed usus utriusque maxime per hiemem est et adhuc vere ante aestivos vapores,[2]
4 dum etiam vites et arbores ablaqueatae sunt. Tertium locum obtinet pecudum stercus atque in eo quoque discrimen est; nam optimum existimatur, quod asinus facit, quia id animal lentissime mandit[3] ideoque facilius concoquit et bene confectum atque idoneum protinus arvo fimum reddit. Post haec, quae diximus, ovillum et ab hoc caprinum[4] est, mox ceterorum iumentorum[5] armentorumque. Deter-
5 rimum ex omnibus suillum habetur. Quin etiam satis proficit[6] cineris et favillae,[7] frutex vero lupini succisus optimi stercoris vim praebet. Nec ignoro quoddam esse ruris genus, in quo neque pecora neque aves haberi possint; at tamen inertis est
6 rustici eo quoque loco defici stercore. Licet enim quamlibet frondem, licet e vepribus et e viis[8] compitisque[9] congesta colligere, licet filicem[10] sine iniuria vicini, etiam cum officio decidere et permiscere

[1] vitis *SA*. [2] aestiuus tempores *A*.
[3] mandat *A*.
[4] quae diximus . . . caprinum *om. SA*.
[5] ceterum dum in iumentorum *SA*.
[6] proficit *Lundström*: profuit *R, cdd plerique*: prodicitur *S*: prodicit *A*.
[7] cineris usus et favillae *Ursinus, Gesn., Schn.*
[8] et e viis *om. R*.
[9] compitisque *Ald.*: conpitique *S*[1]*A*: compitibusque *R*.
[10] felicem *S*[1]*Aa, Lundström*.

it improves the flavour and the bouquet of the wine and the fruit. Also old oil lees, unsalted and mixed 3
with this, can be used to advantage in watering fruit-bearing trees, and especially olives; for even when applied alone the lees are very beneficial. But both of them are used chiefly during the winter and even in spring, before the heat of summer, while the ground is kept open around the vines and the trees.[a]
The dung of cattle holds third place, and in this too 4
there is a difference; for what the ass produces is considered best, because that animal chews very slowly and for that reason digests his food more easily, and he gives in return a manure that is well prepared and ready for the field immediately. After those that we have mentioned comes sheep dung, next is goat dung, and then that of other cattle and draught-animals. The dung of swine is considered the poorest of all. Moreover, the use of ashes and cinders is 5
reasonably beneficial, while cut lupine plants provide the strength of the best manure. And I am not unaware that there is a certain kind of countryside in which neither cattle nor fowl can be kept; but even in such a place it is the mark of a slothful husbandman to be destitute of fertilizer. For he may store up any 6
sort of leaves; he may gather any accumulated matter from bramble patches and from highways and byways; he may cut down his neighbour's fernbrakes without doing him harm, or even as a favour, and mix

[a] An operation formerly described by the convenient word "ablaqueation." *Cf.* Palladius, II. 1, *Ianuario mense locis temperatis ablaqueandae sunt vites, quod Itali excodicare apellant, id est circa vitis codicem dolabra terram diligenter aperire, et purgatis omnibus velut lacus efficere, ut solis teporibus et imbribus provocentur*; Isidore, *Orig.* XVII. 5. 31.

cum purgamentis cohortis, licet depressa fossa, qualem stercori reponendo primo volumine[a] fieri praecepimus, cinerem caenumque cloacarum et culmos ceteraque, quae everruntur, in unum congerere. Sed eodem medio loco robustam materiem defigere convenit, namque ea res serpentem noxiam[1]
7 latere in stercore prohibet. Haec ubi viduus pecudibus ager. Nam ubi greges quadrupedum versantur, quaedam cotidie, ut culina et caprile, quaedam pluviis diebus, ut bubilia et ovilia, debent emundari. Ac si tantum frumentarius ager est, nihil refert genera stercoris separare;[2] sin autem surculo et segetibus atque etiam pratis fundus est dispositus, generatim quoque[3] reponendum est, sicut caprarum et avium. Reliqua deinde in praedictum locum concavum egerenda[4] et adsiduo humore[5] satianda sunt, ut herbarum semina culmis ceterisque rebus
8 immixta putrescant. Aestivis deinde mensibus non aliter ac si repastines, totum stercilinum rastris permisceri oportet, quo facilius putrescat et sit arvis idoneum. Parum autem diligentis existimo esse agricolas, apud quos minores singulae pecudes tricenis diebus minus quam singulas itemque maiores denas vehes stercoris efficiunt[b] totidemque singuli homines, qui non solum ea purgamenta, quae ipsi corporibus edunt, sed et quae colluvies cohortis et

[1] serpentum noxam *Ald., Gesn.*
[2] separari *R, Ald , Gesn., Schn.*
[3] quodque *Ursinus, Schn.*
[4] egerenda *R, Lundström*: erigenda SA, *vett. edd.*: congerenda *vulgo.*
[5] adsiboum mores (more *A*) *SA*[1].

---

[a] I. 6. 21–22.
[b] So Varro, *R.R.* I. 38. 3; Pliny, *N.H.* XVII. 57.

them with the cleanings from his inclosure; he may sink a trench such as, in my first book,[a] I directed to be made for the storage of manure, and may heap together in one pile his ashes, sewer filth, straw, and other dirt that is swept out. But it is well to fasten a piece of oak wood in the middle of that same place, for this keeps the harmful serpent from hiding in the manure.[b] All this of land which is bereft of cattle; 7
for where herds of four-footed animals are kept, there are some places, such as the kitchen and the goat-sheds, which should be cleaned every day, and others, like the ox-stalls and sheepfolds, which are to be cleaned on rainy days. And if the ground is used merely for grain, it is of no importance to keep the different kinds of manure apart; but if the farm is laid out for a nursery, for grainfields, and also for meadows, the manure too must be stored separately, as that of goats and of birds. Then the rest of the refuse should be gathered into the hollowed-out place before mentioned, and it should be constantly saturated with moisture, so that the weed seeds mixed with the chaff and other matter may rot. Then 8
during the summer months the whole dunghill should be thoroughly stirred with rakes, just as if you were loosening the ground, so that it may decay more readily and be fit for the land. Moreover, I consider those farmers lacking in industry who have from each of the smaller animals less than one load [c] of manure in thirty days, and likewise ten loads from each of the larger ones; and the same amount from each person, for they can gather and heap together not only the waste matter from their own bodies, but also the dirt

[c] Columella, XI. 2. 86, speaks of one load (*vehis*) of manure as containing 80 *modii* (=about 20 bushels).

aedificii cotidie gignit, contrahere et congerere
9 possunt. Illud quoque praecipiendum habeo, stercus omne, quod tempestive repositum anno requieverit, segetibus esse [1] maxime utile, nam et vires adhuc solidas habet et herbas non creat; quanto autem vetustius sit, minus prodesse, quoniam minus valeat. Itaque pratis quam recentissimum debere inici, quod plus herbarum progeneret; idque mense Februario luna crescente fieri oportere, nam ea quoque res [2] aliquantum faeni fructum adiuvat. De cetero usu stercoris, qualis in quaque re debeat esse, tum dicemus, cum singula persequemur.

XV. Interim qui frumentis arva praeparare volet, si autumno sementem facturus est, mense Septembri, si vere, qualibet hiemis parte modicos acervos luna decrescente disponat,[3] ita ut plani loci iugerum duodeviginti,[4] clivosi quattuor et viginti vehes stercoris teneant; et ut paulo prius dixi, non antea dissipet
2 cumulos, quam erit saturus.[5] Si tamen aliqua causa eum [6] tempestivam stercorationem facere prohibuerit, secunda ratio est, ante quam sariat,[7] more seminantis ex aviariis pulverem stercoris per segetem spargere; si et is non erit, caprinum manu iacere atque ita terram sarculis permiscere. Ea res laetas segetes reddit. Nec ignorare colonos oportere reor,[8] sicuti refrigescere agrum, qui non stercoretur, ita peruri, si nimium stercoretur, magisque conducere

[1] repositum . . . esse *om. SA.* [2] res *om. SA.*
[3] disputat *SA.*
[4] duo et viginti *R* : duodecim *Gesn.*
[5] arturus *SA* : araturus *Schn., praeeunte Pontedera.*
[6] eum *om. R, edd. plerique.*
[7] sarias *R* : seras *Schn.*
[8] oportere (reor *s.* re *scr. man. alt. S*) *SAR* : oportet *edd. ante Lundström.*

which the yard and the buildings produce every day. I have also this further direction to give, that all 9
manure is most beneficial to crops when it has been stored in proper season and has rested for a year, for it still has its strength unimpaired and does not produce weeds; moreover, that the older it is, the less beneficial, because it has less strength. For this reason it should be spread on meadows while as fresh as possible, beeause it produces more grass; and this should be done in the month of February, while the moon is waxing, as this also contributes somewhat to the hay crop. As to the other use of manure, what sort is suitable for the several kinds of crops, we shall speak when we treat of them individually.

XV. Meanwhile, one who wishes to prepare his fields for grain should distribute manure in piles of moderate size while the moon is waning—in the month of September if he intends to sow in the autumn, at any time of winter if he is to sow in the spring—at the rate of eighteen loads to the *iugerum* on level ground and twenty-four on hilly land; and, as I said a little earlier,[a] he should not spread these heaps until he is ready to sow. Yet if anything 2
keeps him from applying manure at the proper time, a second method is, before hoeing, to scatter over the grainfield the pulverized droppings from the bird houses in the manner of one casting seed; and if there is none of this, to broadcast goat dung by hand and then stir the ground thoroughly with hoes. This produces luxuriant crops. And I think that husbandmen should not be unacquainted with the fact that as land grows cold when it is not manured, so it is burned if manured too heavily; and that it is of

[a] Chap. 5 of this book.

agricolae frequenter id potius quam immodice facere.
3 Nec dubium quin aquosus ager maiorem eius copiam, siccus minorem desideret, alter quod adsiduis umoribus rigens hoc adhibito regelatur, alter quod per se tepens siccitatibus hoc [1] adsumpto largioribus [2] torretur; [3] propter quod nec deesse ei talem mater-
4 iem nec superesse oportet. Si tamen nullum genus stercoris suppetet, multum proderit fecisse quod Marcum Columellam patruum meum, doctissimum et diligentissimum agricolam, saepe numero usurpasse memoria repeto, ut sabulosis [4] locis cretam ingereret, cretosis ac nimium densis sabulum, atque ita non solum segetes laetas excitaret verum etiam pul-
5 cherrimas vineas efficeret. Nam idem negabat stercus vitibus ingerendum, quod saporem vini corrumperet, melioremque censebat esse materiam vindemiis exuberandis congesticiam vel de vepribus vel denique aliam quamlibet arcessitam et advectam humum. Iam vero et ego reor, si deficiatur omnibus rebus agricola, lupini certe praesidium expeditissimum non deesse; quod cum exili loco [5] circa Idus Septembris sparserit et inaraverit idque tempestive vomere vel ligone succiderit, vim optimae stercora-
6 tionis exhibebit. Succidi autem lupinum sabulosis locis oportet, cum secundum florem, lubricosis,[6] cum tertium egerit. Illic, dum tenerum est, con-

[1] ad hoc *SA*.
[2] largiore *R, et vulgo ante Lundström.*
[3] tolleretur *SA*.
[4] pabulosis *SA*.
[5] sola *SA* : solo *Schn.*
[6] lubricosis *SA, Lundström* : rubricosis *R, et vulgo.*

greater advantage to the farmer to do this frequently rather than lavishly. And there is no doubt 3
that wet land requires a greater quantity of it, and dry land less—the one because, being chilled by constant moisture, it is warmed when manure is applied, and the other because, being naturally warm, it is parched by the increased aridity when this is added; for which reason such dressing should be neither deficient nor over-sufficient. If, however, no kind of 4
manure is available, it will be very helpful to follow the practice which I remember my uncle, Marcus Columella, a very learned and painstaking farmer, frequently employed: that is, to heap clay on gravelly ground, and gravel on ground that was clayey and too stiff, and in this way to grow not only luxuriant crops of grain but also very fine vineyards. For this same authority used to say that dung 5
should not be applied to vines, because it spoiled the flavour of the wine; and he thought that a better dressing for making a heavy vintage was humus, either that which accumulates around bramble-thickets, or in fact any earth obtained elsewhere and brought in. But my opinion nowadays is that if the farmer is destitute of everything, at any rate there is no lack of lupine, that very ready aid; and if he will scatter this on lean ground about the middle of September, plough it in, and at the proper time cut it up with the ploughshare or the mattock, it will have the effect of the best manure. The lupine should be 6
cut, moreover, in gravelly ground when it is in the second flower, and in sticky soils when it is in its third.[a] In the former case it is turned under while it is tender,

[a] Pliny, in describing the lupine, says (*N.H.* XVIII. 133) that it blooms three times.

vertitur, ut celeriter ipsum putrescat permisceaturque gracili solo; hic iam robustius, quod solidioris glaebas diutius sustineat et suspendat, ut eae solibus aestivis vaporatae resolvantur.

XVI. Atque haec arator exsequi poterit, si non solum quae rettuli genera pabulorum providerit, verum etiam copiam faeni, quo melius armenta tueatur, sine quibus terram commode moliri difficile est; et ideo necessarius ei cultus est etiam prati, cui veteres Romani primas in agricolatione tribuerunt.
2 Nomen quoque indiderunt ab eo, quod protinus esset paratum nec magnum laborem desideraret. Marcus quidem Porcius et illa commemoravit, quod nec tempestatibus adfligeretur ut aliae partes ruris minimeque[1] sumptus egens per omnis annos praeberet reditum neque eum simplicem, cum etiam in
3 pabulo non minus redderet quam in faeno. Eius igitur animadvertimus duo genera, quorum alterum est siccaneum, alterum riguum. Laeto pinguique campo non desideratur[2] influens rivus, meliusque habetur faenum, quod suapte natura sucoso gignitur solo, quam quod inrigatum aquis elicitur;[3] quae tamen sunt necessariae, si macies terrae postulat. Nam et in densa et resoluta humo, quamvis exili, pratum fieri potest, cum facultas inrigandi datur.
4 Ac nec campus concavae positionis esse neque collis praeruptae debet: ille ne collectam diutius contineat

[1] minimique *vulgo ante Lundström.*
[2] desideretur *SA.*
[3] suapte (suate *A*) natur aquis et eligitur (*cetera verba om.*) *SA.*

[a] So also Varro, *R.R.* I. 7. 10; Pliny, *N.H.* XVIII. 29; Isidore, *Orig.* XV. 3.
[b] Cato. But the passage is lost.

so that it may rot quickly and be mixed with the thin soil; in the latter case when it has grown stronger, so that it may hold up the more solid clods longer and keep them suspended, to be broken down when heated by the summer sun.

XVI. These things the ploughman will be able to accomplish if he makes provision not only for the varieties of forage crops which I have mentioned, but also for a supply of hay for the better maintenance of his cattle, without which it is difficult to work the land to advantage; and on that account the tending of a meadow is also required of him. To the meadow the ancient Romans assigned the leading rôle in
agriculture, and to it also they gave its name (*pratum*) 2
from the fact that it was immediately "ready" (*paratum*) [a] and did not require a great amount of toil. Marcus Porcius,[b] indeed, called to mind also the following considerations: that it is not damaged by storms like the other divisions of the farm, and that, though needing very little outlay, it yields a return year after year—and that not a single return, because
it pays no less in pasturage than in hay. We take 3
notice, then, of two kinds of meadows, the dry and the watered.[c] In level ground that is rich and fat there is no need of an inflowing stream, and hay which grows naturally on a moist soil is considered superior to that enticed by irrigation; though such watering is necessary if the leanness of the soil demands it. For a meadow can be laid down both in stiff and in loose soil, however poor, if the opportunity for irrigation
is offered. And it should not be a plain that slopes 4
inward, nor a hill with a steep pitch—the former that it may not hold too long the water which settles

[c] Cato, S. 1.

aquam, hic ne statim praecipitem fundat. Potest tamen mediocriter acclivis, si aut pinguis est aut
5 riguus ager, pratum fieri. At planities maxime talis probatur, quae exigue prona non patitur diutius imbres aut influentis rivos immorari, sed ut[1] quis eam supervenit umor, lente prorepit.[2] Itaque si palus in aliqua parte subsidens restagnat, sulcis derivanda est, quippe[3] aquarum abundantia atque penuria graminibus aeque est exitio.

XVII. Cultus autem pratorum magis curae quam laboris est. Primum ne stirpes aut spinas[4] validiorisve[5] incrementi herbas inesse patiamur, atque alias ante hiemem per autumnum exstirpemus, ut rubos, virgulta, iuncos, alias sic vellamus, ut[6] intuba ac solstitialis spinas; ac[7] neque suem velimus impasci, quoniam rostro suffodiat et cespites excitet, neque pecora maiora, nisi cum siccissimum solum est, quia udo demerguntur ungulae[8] et atterunt
2 scinduntque radices herbarum. Tum deinde asperiora[9] et pendula loca mense Februario luna crescente fimo iuvanda sunt, omnesque lapides et si qua obiacent falcibus obnoxia colligi debent ac longius exportari summittique pro natura locorum aut temperius aut serius. Sunt etiam quaedam prata situ vetustatis obducta, quibus mederi solent agri-

[1] sed ut] aut si *R*, *edd. ante Schn.*

[2] proripit *SR*, *Lundström.*

[3] qui et *SA*.

[4] cineras *SA*.

[5] validiorisque *R*, *edd. ante Lundström.*

[6] sic vellamus ut *Lundström*: sigilla /// mus u (t *suprascr. man. rec.*) *S*: sigillam usu *A*: si vellamus ut *R*: per ver evellamus *Ald.*, *Gesn.*, *Schn*

[7] intuba solstitialis ac (*cett. verba om.*) *SA*.

[8] demergunt ungulas *R*, *et vulgo ante Lundström.*

there, the latter that it may not immediately pour it
off in a torrent. However, if the ground has a gentle
slope and is either rich or moist, a meadow may be
laid down. But the place most approved is an even 5
surface which, having a slight slope, does not allow
rain or inflowing rivulets to stand too long; but when
any moisture reaches it, it gradually drains off. And
so if there is in any part of it a low and boggy place
where water stands, it must be drained with ditches;
for an oversupply and an undersupply of water are
equally destructive to grass.

XVII. The keeping up of meadows is, moreover,
a matter of care rather than of labour. In the first
place, we must not allow shrubs or thorn bushes or
weeds of rather vigorous growth to remain in them,
but before winter and throughout autumn we must
root out some of them, such as bramble-bushes,
thickets, and rushes, and pull up others like endive
and midsummer thorns; and we should not permit
swine to feed on them, as they root them up with their
snouts and tear up the sod, nor larger animals except
when the ground is very dry, because their hoofs,
sinking into the wet ground, bruise and cut the grass
roots. Then also the more rugged and elevated 2
sections should be enriched with manure in the month
of February, while the moon is waxing; and all stones
and any harmful objects that may lie in the way of the
sickle should be gathered up and carried some
distance away, and then, sooner or later, according
to the nature of the place, the meadows should be let
alone to grow to hay. There are also some meadows
covered with the mould of long neglect, and the old-

[a] asperiora *R pauci*: aspriora *SA, Lundström*: macriora *R aliquot, et vulgo.*

colae veteres[1] vel eraso musco seminibusque de tabulato superiectis vel ingesto stercore; quorum neutrum tantum prodest quantum si cinerem saepius
3 ingeras. Ea res muscum enecat. At tamen pigriora sunt ista remedia, cum sit efficacissimum de integro locum exarare. Sed haec, si prata accessimus,[2] facere debemus; sin autem nova fuerint instituenda vel antiqua renovanda—nam multa sunt, ut dixi, quae neglegentia exolescant et fiant sterilia, eaque expedit interdum etiam frumenti causa exarare, quia talis ager post longam desidiam laetas segetes
4 adfert—igitur eum locum, quem prato destinaverimus, aestate proscissum subactumque protinus[3] per autumnum rapis vel napo vel etiam faba conseremus; insequente deinde anno, frumento. Tertio diligenter arabimus omnesque validiores herbas et rubos et arbores, quae interveniunt, radicitus[4] exstirpabimus, nisi si[5] fructus arbusti id facere nos prohibuerit. Deinde viciam permixtam seminibus faeni seremus, tum glaebas sarculis resolvemus et inducta crate coaequabimus grumosque, quos ad versuram plerumque tractae faciunt crates, disiciamus[6] ita, necubi ferramentum faenisecis possit
5 offendere. Sed eam viciam non convenit ante desecare, quam permaturuerit et aliqua semina subiacenti solo iecerit. Tum faenisecas eam oportet recidere ac deinde rigari,[7] si fuerit facultas aquae et

[1] veteres *Lundström*: veteri *codd., et vulgo.*

[2] adcessimus *SA, Lundström*: cepimus *R plerique*: accepimus *Gesn., Schn.*: coepimus *vel* cepimus *vett. edd.*

[3] protinus *SA, Lundström*: sepius *R*: saepius *cett. edd.*

[4] interveniunt radicibus *SA, Schn.*

[5] si *om. SA.*

[6] disiciamus *Lundström, praeeunte Pontedera*: assicamus *vel* adsiccamus *codd. plerique*: dispiciemus *R duo dett.*: despiciemus *vett. edd.*: dissipabimus *vulgo.*

time farmers have a way of restoring them by
scraping off the moss and broadcasting seed from the
hayloft, or by applying manure; neither of which is so
effective as the frequent application of ashes. This
last treatment kills the moss completely. Still 3
these remedies are rather slow, whereas the most
effective measure is to plough the spot all over again.
The above are measures that we should take if we
have taken over meadows ready-made; but if new
ones are to be established or old ones restored—for
there are many, as I have said, which run down and
become barren through neglect, and it is expedient to
plough them up now and then for a grain crop,
because such land after long idleness produces luxuriant crops—we shall break up in the summer such 4
land as we have set apart for a meadow, work it continuously throughout the autumn, and seed it with
turnips or navews or even beans; then the following
year, with grain. In the third year we shall plough
thoroughly and dig out by the roots all the stouter
growth, brambles and trees, that stand in the way,
unless the fruitfulness of the set trees keeps us from
so doing. Next we shall sow vetch mixed with hayseed, then break the clods with hoes and level the
surface by drawing a brushwood drag over it, and
scatter the heaps of earth which the drags usually
form at the turnings, so that the mower's scythe may
not strike against anything. But it is not advisable 5
to cut this vetch until it is entirely ripe and has shed
some seed on the ground beneath it. Then the
mowers should cut it down, and the ground should
next be irrigated if there is a supply of water, but

---

[7] faenisecas e. o. r. a. d. rigari *Lundström* *alii alia.*

si tamen terra densior est; nam in resoluta humo non expedit inducere maiorem vim rivorum, prius quam conspissatum fuerit [1] et herbis colligatum solum,[2] quoniam impetus aquarum proluit terram nudatisque
6 radicibus gramina non patitur coalescere. Propter quod ne pecora quidem oportet teneris adhuc et subsidentibus pratis immittere, sed quotiens herba prosiluerit, falcibus desecare; nam pecudes, ut ante iam dixi, molli solo infigunt ungulas atque interruptas non sinunt herbarum[3] radices serpere et condensari. Altero tamen anno minora pecora post faenisicia permittemus admitti, si modo siccitas et
7 conditio [4] loci patietur. Tertio deinde cum pratum solidius ac durius erit, poterit etiam maiores recipere pecudes. Sed in totum curandum est, ut secundum Favonii exortum mense Februario circa Idus immixtis seminibus faeni macriora loca et utique celsiora stercorentur Nam editior clivus praebet etiam subiectis alimentum, cum superveniens imber aut manu rivus [5] perductus sucum stercoris in inferiorem partem secum trahit. Atque ideo fere prudentes agricolae etiam in aratis collem magis quam vallem stercorant, quoniam, ut dixi, pluviae semper omnem pinguiorem materiam in ima deducunt.

XVIII. Faenum autem demetitur optime ante

[1] fuerit om. *SA, edd. ante Lundström.*

[2] *sic Lundström*: conspissatum et herbis colligatum sit solum *vulgo.*

[3] herbarum *om. SA.*

[4] conducio *S*: conductio *A.*

[5] rivos *SA et R plerique, Lundström.*

only in case the ground is rather heavy; for in loose soil it is not wise to let in too heavy a flow of water before the ground is packed and bound together by vegetation, because the force of the water washes away the soil and, by exposing the roots, does not allow the grass to gain a foothold. It is for this reason 6
that one should not even turn his herds into meadows that are still soft and settling, but should cut the grass with sickles whenever it shoots up; for, as I have said before, cattle plant their hoofs in the soft ground and, cutting off the grass roots, do not allow them to spread and form a dense growth. In the second year, however, we shall allow the smaller animals to be turned in after the haymaking, if only dry weather and the condition of the ground will permit it. Then 7
in the third year, when the meadow is quite solid and firm, it will be in condition to receive even the larger cattle. But, in general, care must be taken that after the rising of Favonius [a] in February, about the middle of the month, the poorer spots and especially the higher places be given a coating of manure in which hayseed is mixed; for the more elevated slope supplies nourishment to the land that lies below when a pouring rain or a hand-conducted rivulet carries the liquid manure along with its own waters to the part below. And it is for this reason that wise farmers, even in ploughed land, manure a hillside more heavily than a valley, because, as I have stated, the rains are forever carrying all the richer matter down to the lowland.

XVIII. It is best, moreover, that hay be cut before

[a] Favonius, also called Zephyrus, was the gentle west wind, a harbinger of spring. *Cf.* VIII. 11. 7, *cum Favonii spirare coeperunt, id est ab Idibus Februariis ante Martium mensem.*

quam inarescat;[1] nam et largius percipitur et iucundiorem cibum pecudibus praebet. Est autem modus in siccando, ut neque peraridum neque rursus viride colligatur, alterum quod omnem sucum si amisit, stramenti vicem obtinet, alterum si nimium retinuit, in tabulato putrescit ac saepe, cum concaluit,[2] ignem creat et incendium. Non numquam etiam, cum faenum cecidimus, imber oppressit; quod si permaduit, inutile est udum movere, melius-
2 que patiemur superiorem partem sole siccari. Tunc demum convertemus et utrimque[3] siccatum coartabimus in strigam atque ita manipulos vinciemus. Nec omnino cunctabimur, quo minus sub tectum congeratur, vel si non competet, ut aut[4] in villam faenum portetur aut in manipulum colligatur,[5] certe quicquid ad eum modum, quem[6] debet, siccatum erit, in metas exstrui conveniet easque ipsas in angustissimos
3 vertices exacui. Sic enim commodissime faenum defendetur[7] a pluviis, quae etiam si non sint, non alienum tamen est praedictas metas facere, ut si quis umor herbis inest, exsudet atque[8] excoquatur in acervis. Propter quod prudentes agricolae quamvis iam inlatum tecto non ante componunt, quam per paucos dies temere congestum in se concoqui et defervescere patiantur. Sed iam faenisicia insequitur cura messis, quam ut recte possimus percipere, prius instrumenta praeparanda sunt, quibus fruges coguntur.

[1] arescat *SA*. [2] caluit *SAc*.
[3] siccari . . utrimque *om. SA*: utrimque *Ursinus*: utrunque *R*.
[4] aut *om. Schn.*
[5] manipulos colligatum *Schn.*
[6] quo *Ald., Gesn., Schn.*
[7] defenditur *R, edd. ante Lundström.*

it begins to wither, as a greater quantity of it is harvested and it affords a more agreeable food for cattle. But a middle course should be followed in the curing, that it be gathered neither when very dry nor, on the other hand, while still green—in the one case because it is no better than straw if it has lost all its sap, and in the other because, if it has kept too much of it, it rots in the loft and often, when it becomes heated, it breeds fire and starts a blaze. Sometimes, too, when we have cut our hay a rain surprises us; and if the hay is soaked through it is useless to move it while wet, but better to let the upper side of it dry out in the sun. Only then shall we turn it, and, when it is dry on 2
both sides, we shall bring it together in windrows and then bind it up in bundles. And above all we shall lose no time in putting it under cover; or, if it is not convenient for the hay to be carried to the farmstead or tied into bundles, it will be well at any rate that all of it that had been dried out to the proper extent be built up into cocks and that these be topped off with very sharp peaks. For by this method hay 3
is very conveniently protected from rains; and even if there is no rain, it is still not amiss to build the aforesaid cocks, so that any moisture remaining in the hay may sweat and dry out in the piles. For this reason wise husbandmen, even in the case of hay brought under cover, do not store it away until they have allowed it to heat and cool for a few days in a loose pile. But now after the haymaking comes attention to the grain harvest; and that we may properly gather it, we must first put in readiness the implements with which the crops are harvested.

---

[8] exsudet atque *om. SA.*

XIX. Area quoque si terrena erit, ut sit ad trituram satis habilis, primum radatur, deinde confodiatur,[1] permixtis paleis cum amurca, quae salem non accepit, et rigetur;[2] nam ea res a populatione murum formicarumque frumenta defendit. Tum aequata paviculis vel molari lapide condensetur et rursus superiectis paleis inculcetur atque ita solibus siccanda relin-
2 quatur. Sunt tamen, qui prati subiacentem Favonio[3] partem triturae destinant areamque demessa faba et iniecta[4] expoliunt; nam dum a pecudibus legumina proculcantur, etiam herbae ungulis atteruntur, atque ita glabrescit et fit idonea frumentis[5] area.

XX. Sed cum matura fuerit seges, ante quam torreatur vaporibus aestivi sideris, qui sunt vastissimi per exortum[6] Caniculae, celeriter demetatur;[7] nam dispendiosa est cunctatio, primum quod avibus praedam ceterisque animalibus praebet, deinde quod grana et ipsae spicae culmis arentibus et aristis
2 celeriter decidunt. Si vero procellae ventorum aut turbines incesserunt,[8] maior pars ad terram defluit; propter[9] quae recrastinari non debet, sed aequaliter flaventibus iam satis, ante quam ex toto grana indurescant, cum rubicundum colorem traxerunt,

[1] conficiatur *SA*.

[2] et rigetur *SA et R aliquot*: extricetur *Lundström*: extringetur *R plerique, vett. edd.*: aspergatur *Ursinus*: irrigetur *Schoettgen, et maluit Gesn.*: extergatur *vulgo*.

[3] prati subiacentem Favonio *Lundström, praeeunte Schn. in not.*: pratis obiacentem fabonio (b *in* v *mut. S*) *SA*: pratis obiacente favonio *R*: potius adiacentium fabalium *vulgo*.

[4] lecta *R, et vulgo ante Schn.*

[5] trituris *Ald., Gesn., Schn.*

[6] ortum *R, et vulgo ante Lundström.*

[7] demetur *SA*.

[8] incesserint *R, edd. ante Lundström.*

[9] propter *om. SA*.

XIX. The threshing-floor, too, if it is of earth, to be satisfactorily prepared for threshing should first be scraped, then dug thoroughly, with an admixture of chaff and oil lees which have not been salted, and moistened; for such treatment protects the grain from the ravages of mice and ants. Then, after being smoothed down, it should be packed hard with rammers or with a millstone, and, again strewn with chaff, it should be tramped down and left in this condition to be dried by the sun. There are people, however, who set aside for the threshing a piece of meadow land which is exposed to the west wind, and smooth off a threshing-place by cutting beans and throwing them on it; for while the legumes are being trampled out by the cattle the vegetation also is worn away by their hoofs, and in this way the place becomes bare and makes a suitable threshing-floor for grain.

XX. But when the grain is ripe it should be quickly harvested before it can be parched by the heat of the summer sun, which is most severe at the rising of the Dog-star;[a] for delay is costly—in the first place because it affords plunder for birds and other creatures, and, secondly, because the kernels and even the heads themselves quickly fall as the stalks and beards wither. And if wind-storms or cyclones strike it, 2
the greater part of it is lost on the ground; for which reason there should be no delay, but when the crop is even golden yellow, before the grains have entirely hardened and after they have taken on a reddish colour, the harvest should be gathered, so

[a] XI. 2. 53, *Septimo Kal. Augustas* (= July 26) *Canicula apparet.*

messis facienda est, ut potius in area et in acervo quam in agro grandescant frumenta. Constat enim, si tempestive decisa sint, postea capere incrementum.
3 Sunt autem metendi genera complura. Multi falcibus veruculatis atque iis vel rostratis [1] vel denticulatis medium culmum secant, multi mergis, alii pectinibus spicam ipsam legunt, idque in rara segete facillimum, in densa difficillimum est.

Quod si falcibus seges cum parte culmi demessa sit, protinus in acervum vel in nubilar [2] congeritur et subinde opportunius solibus [3] torrefacta proteritur.
4 Sin autem spicae tantummodo recisae sunt, possunt in horreum conferri et deinde per hiemem vel baculis excuti vel exteri pecudibus. At si competit ut in area teratur frumentum, nihil dubium est quin equis melius quam bubus ea res conficiatur et, si pauca iuga sunt, adicere tribulam et traheam [4] possis, quae res utraque culmos facillime comminuit. Ipsae autem spicae melius fustibus cuduntur [5]
5 vannisque expurgantur. At ubi paleis immixta sunt frumenta, vento separantur. Ad eam rem Favonius habetur eximius, qui levis aequalisque aestivis mensibus perflat; quem tamen opperiri lenti est agricolae,

[1] rostratis *ac* : nostratibus *SAR*, *vett edd.*
[2] nubilarium *Ald.*, *Gesn*, *Schn.* [3] solidibus *SA*.
[4] traheam *Lundström* . trahere *SAR* : traham *vulgo.*
[5] cuduntur *SA*, *Schn.* : tunduntur *R*, *Lundström, et vulgo.*

---

[a] *Cf.* Columella on olives (XII. 52. 18): *Plerique agricolae crediderunt, si sub tecto baca deponatur, oleum in tabulato grandescere; quod tam falsum est quam in area frumenta crescere.*

[b] Commentators are uncertain as to the nature and use of these implements. Festus (111 L) defines *mergae* as forks for lifting grain; so called because in the hands of the reaper they plunge into the grain just as diving birds (*mergi*) dive

that the grain may grow larger on the floor [a] and in the stack rather than in the field. For it is an established fact that, if cut at the proper time, it makes some growth afterwards. There are, furthermore, 3 several methods of reaping: many cut the straw in the middle with cradle-scythes, and these either bill-shaped or toothed; many gather the heads only with forks, and others with combs [b]—an operation which is very easy in a thin crop, but very difficult in a thick one.

But if the grain, with a part of the straw, is cut with sickles, it is at once gathered into a pile or carried into the shed,[c] and then after repeated drying in the sun, as opportunity offers, it is threshed. If, 4 however, the heads only are cut off they may be carried into the granary and then, during the winter, be beaten out with flails or trodden out by cattle. But if it is convenient to have the grain threshed on the floor, there is no doubt that this work is better done with horses than with oxen; and if you have few teams you may hitch to them a threshing-sledge and a drag, either of which very easily breaks up the straw. It is better, however, that the heads themselves be beaten with flails and winnowed with fans. But when the grain is mixed with the chaff it is cleaned 5 by the wind. The west wind is considered excellent for this purpose, as it blows gently and evenly in the summer months; but to wait for it is the mark of a

(*mergunt*) in pursuit of food. Others conjecture a sharp V-shaped contrivance which the user pushed before him in such a way as to catch and tear off the heads of the grain. The "comb" (*pecten*) is regarded by some as a rake; by others as an iron implement with comb-like teeth, used to clip off the heads of the standing grain. *Cf.* Varro, *R.R.* I. 50; Pliny, *N H.* XVIII. 296–297.

[c] *Cf.* I. 6. 24, with note.

quia saepe,[1] dum expectatur, saeva nos hiems deprendit. Itaque in area detrita frumenta sic sunt aggeranda ut omni flatu possint excerni. At si compluribus diebus undique silebit aura, vannis[2] expurgentur, ne post nimiam ventorum segnitiem vasta tempestas inritum faciat totius anni laborem.
6 Pura deinde frumenta, si in annos reconduntur, reteri[3] debent, nam quanto sunt expolitiora, minus a curculionibus exeduntur; sin protinus usui destinantur, nihil attinet repoliri, satisque est in umbra refrigerari et ita granario inferri. Leguminum quoque non alia cura est quam reliquorum frumentorum, nam ea quoque vel[4] statim absumuntur vel conduntur. Atque hoc supremum est aratoris emolumentum percipiendorum seminum quae terrae crediderit.[5]

XXI. Sed cum tam otii quam negotii rationem reddere maiores nostri censuerunt, nos quoque monendos esse agricolas existimamus, quae feriis facere quaeque non facere debeant. Sunt enim, ut ait poeta, quae

festis exercere diebus[6]
Fas et iura sinunt: rivos deducere nulla
Religio vetuit, segeti praetendere saepem,
Insidias avibus moliri, incendere vepres
Balantumque gregem fluvio mersare salubri.

[1] saepe *om. R et edd. ante Schn.* [2] manibus *SA.*

[3] reteri *R, Lundström*: reperiri *S*: repperiri *A*: repurgari *Ald., Gesn., Schn.*: repoliri *Pontedera.*

[4] *Post* vel *verba manifeste exciderunt SAR*: absumuntur statim vel *inserit Bononiensis* 2523: statim absumuntur vel *Ald., et deinceps omnes praeter Lundström, qui lacunam indicat.*

[5] crediderit *Lundström*: ceciderit *SA*: crediderat *R, cett. edd.*

[6] exercere festis diebus *SA.*

dilatory farmer, for often, while we are waiting, a raging storm surprises us. Therefore the threshed grain should be heaped on the threshing-floor in such a way that it can be winnowed with any gentle wind. But if the air is quiet in every quarter for many days, the grain should be cleaned with winnowing-fans, for fear that after excessive stillness of the winds a mighty storm may bring to naught the toil of an entire year.
Then the pure grain, if it is being laid away for a 6
term of years, should be threshed again, for the better it is scoured the less it is preyed upon by weevils; but if it is intended for immediate use, there is no need of a second cleaning and it is sufficient that it be cooled in the shade and so carried to the granary. The handling of legumes, too, differs not at all from that of other grains, for they also are either consumed at once or stored away. And this is the crowning reward of the husbandman—reaping the harvest of the seed that he has entrusted to the earth.

XXI. But inasmuch as our ancestors saw fit to render an account of their leisure hours as well as of their times of non-leisure,[a] I also believe that farmers should be advised of what they should do on holidays and what they should leave undone. For here are things which, as the poet says,

> Divine and human laws let be performed on festive
> days:
> No sacred law forbids to fetch the irrigating rills,
> A hedge along the field to stretch, for birds a
> snare to lay,
> And briars to burn, and bleating flocks to dip in
> wholesome stream.[b]

[a] Cicero remarks (*Pro Plancio*, 27) that this was a dictum of Cato in his *Origines*. [b] Vergil, *Georg.* I. 268–272

2 Quamquam pontifices negant segetem feriis saepiri debere; vetant quoque lanarum causa lavari[1] oves nisi si[2] propter medicinam. Vergilius quod[3] liceat feriis flumine abluere gregem praecipit et idcirco adicit "fluvio mersare salubri," id est salutari;[4] sunt enim vitia, quorum causa pecus utile
3 sit lavare. Feriis autem ritus maiorum etiam illa permittit: far pinsere,[5] faces incidere, candelas sebare, vineam conductam colere, piscinas, lacus, fossas veteres tergere et purgare, prata sicilire, stercora aequare, faenum in tabulata componere, fructus oliveti conductos cogere, mala, pira, ficos pandere, caseum facere, arbores serendi causa collo vel mulo clitellario adferre; sed iuncto advehere non permittitur nec adportatas[6] serere neque terram aperire
4 neque arborem conlucare, sed ne sementem quidem administrare, nisi prius catulo feceris, nec faenum secare aut vincire aut vehere; ac ne vindemiam quidem cogi per religiones pontificum feriis licet nec ovis tondere, nisi si catulo feceris. Defrutum quoque facere et vinum defrutare licet. Uvas itemque olivas conditu[7] legere licet. Pellibus oves vestiri

[1] lavare *SA*. [2] si *om. R, edd. ante Lundström.*

[3] qui *Gesn., Schn.*

[4] id est salutari *om. R aliquot, Ald., Gesn., Schn.*

[5] faro (farao *A*) instare *SA*.

[6] adportatas *Warmington*: adportata *vel* apportata *R, edd.*: adportare *SA*.

[7] condituí *R plerique, Ald., Gesn., Schn.*

---

[a] The ancient authorities frequently speak, for example, of dipping sheep as a preventive of scab.

[b] *Cf.* Cato, 2. 4.

[c] *Sicilire* is defined by Varro (*R.R.* I. 49. 2) as cutting with a sickle the tufts of grass which the mowers have passed over.

[d] Not the regular pruning (*putatio*), but the removal of superfluous foliage to admit the light (*conlucare, sublucare*).

And yet the pontiffs assert that a grain-field should 2
not be fenced on holidays; they also forbid the washing of sheep for the good of the fleece, except as a curative measure. Vergil is instructing us as to the lawfulness of washing the flock in a river on holidays, and for that reason he adds "to dip in wholesome stream"—that is, in a healing stream; for there are ailments because of which it is expedient to bathe the cattle.[a] Furthermore, the religious observances 3
of our forefathers permit these tasks also on holidays:[b] the braying of spelt; the cutting of torches; the dipping of candles; the tilling of a leased vineyard; the clearing out and cleaning of fish-ponds, cisterns, and old ditches; the sickling[c] of meadows; the spreading of manure; the storing of hay in the loft; the gathering of the fruits of a leased olive-grove; the spreading of apples, pears, and figs to dry; the making of cheese; the carrying of trees for planting, either on our own shoulders or with a pack mule. But it is not permitted to haul them with a yoked animal, nor to plant them after they are transported, nor to open the ground, nor to thin a tree;[d] and not to assist 4
in the sowing either unless you have first sacrificed a puppy, nor to cut hay or bind it or haul it; and it is not permissible either by the ordinances of the priests for the vintage to be gathered on feast days, nor to shear sheep, unless you have sacrificed a puppy. It is also lawful to make boiled must and to boil wine. To gather grapes and olives for preserving is likewise lawful. It is not lawful to clothe sheep with skins.[e]

[e] Certain breeds of fine-wooled sheep were jacketed with skins to keep their fleeces free from dirt, etc.; Varro, *R.R.* II. 2. 18; Pliny, *N.H.* VIII. 47. Columella devotes a chapter (VII. 4) to the care of these delicate animals.

non licet. In horto quicquid holerum causa facias, omne licet. Feriis publicis hominem mortuum
5 sepeliri [1] non licet. M. Porcius Cato mulis, equis, asinis nullas esse ferias ait, idemque boves permittit coniungere lignorum et frumentorum advehendorum causa. Nos apud pontifices legimus feriis tantum denicalibus [2] mulos iungere non licere, ceteris licere.

Hoc loco certum habeo quosdam, cum solemnia festorum percensuerim,[3] desideraturos lustrationum ceterorumque sacrificiorum, quae pro frugibus fiunt,
6 morem priscis usurpatum. Nec ego abnuo docendi curam, sed differo in eum librum, quem componere in animo est, cum agricolationis totam disciplinam praescripsero. Finem interim praesentis disputationis faciam dicturus exordio sequente, quae de vineis arbustisque prodidere veteres auctores quaeque ipse mox comperi.

[1] sepelire *vel* sepellire *R plerique.*
[2] denicalibus *R pauci dett.*: dentalibus *M*: devivalibus *S*: denibalibus *A*: dominicalibus *R plerique.*
[3] percensuerint *SA*.

---

[a] But Columella omits Cato's exception, "unless they fall on family festivals"; *cf.* Cato, 138, *Mulis, equis, asinis feriae nullae, nisi si in familia sunt.*

[b] Holidays celebrated by the family in honour of its deceased members; *cf.* Paul. Fest. 61 L, *Denicales feriae colebantur, cum hominis mortui causa familia purgabatur. Graeci enim νέκυν mortuum dicunt*; and Fest. 282 L,

Anything that you may do in your garden for the good of your vegetables is lawful. It is not lawful to bury a dead person on public feast days. Marcus Porcius 5
Cato says that there are no holidays for mules, horses, and asses;[a] the same authority permits the yoking of oxen for the purpose of hauling wood and grain. We ourselves have read in the books of the pontiffs that only on the holidays called *Denicales*[b] is it unlawful to have mules in harness, but on other holidays it is lawful.

I am well aware that at this point, after my survey of the observances of feast days, some people will miss the customs observed by the ancients in the matter of purificatory ceremonies and other offerings which are made for the good of the crops.[c] And I 6
am not declining the task of offering this instruction, but am postponing it for that book[d] which I intend to put together after I have written precepts on the whole science of agriculture. Meanwhile I shall bring the present discussion to an end, having in mind to tell in the next book what ancient authorities have handed down on the subject of vineyards and of tree-plantations, and what I myself have since discovered.

Privatae feriae vocantur sacrorum propriorum, velut dies natales, operationis, denecales. See also Cicero, *De Leg.* 2. 55, and Cincius *ap.* Gellius XVI. 4. 4.

[c] *Cf.* Cato 141; Vergil, *Georg.* I. 338 f.

[d] This proposed volume, if ever written, has been lost.

BOOK III

LIBER III

I "Hactenus arvorum cultus," ut ait praestantissimus poeta. Nihil enim prohibet nos, Publi Silvine, de iisdem[1] rebus dicturos celeberrimi carminis auspicari[2] principio.[3] Sequitur arborum cura, quae pars rei rusticae vel maxima est. Earum species diversae et multiformes sunt: quippe varii generis, sicut auctor idem refert,

> nullis hominum cogentibus ipsae
> Sponte sua veniunt;

2 multae[4] etiam nostra manu satae procedunt. Sed quae non ope humana gignuntur, silvestres ac ferae, sui cuiusque[5] ingenii poma vel semina gerunt; at quibus labor adhibetur, magis aptae sunt frugibus.

De eo igitur prius genere dicendum[6] est quod nobis alimenta praebet. Idque tripertito[7] dividitur. Nam ex surculo vel arbor procedit, ut olea; vel frutex, ut palma campestris; vel tertium[8] quiddam[9] quod nec arborem nec fruticem proprie dixerimus,

[1] isdem *SA* : hisdem *c.*
[2] aut spicari *A.*
[3] principio *Ursinus, Schn.* : principia *SAacM, Ald., Gesn.*
[4] multa *Ac* : *et deinde* sata *vett. edd.*
[5] cuique *SAac.*
[6] discendum *SA.*
[7] tripertito *SAa* : tripartito *cM, et vulgo.*
[8] tertius *SAac* : tercius *M.* [9] quidam *aM.*

BOOK III

I. "Thus far of the tillage of the land," as says that most excellent poet.[a] For, Publius Silvinus, as we are about to speak on the same topics, there is nothing to keep us from beginning under good omens with the opening words of that most renowned poem. There follows the management of trees, which is a most important part of rural husbandry. They are diverse in kind, and of many shapes; for trees of various sorts, as the same author relates,

of their own will come forth,
By mortals not constrained;[b]

and many, too, grow from seed planted by our own hand.[c] But those that are propagated without 2
human aid, the wild and untamed, bear fruits or seeds according to their several natures; while those on which labour is spent are fitted for a greater yield.

I must speak first, then, of that kind which supplies us with food. And of this there is a threefold division: for from a small shoot there comes forth either a tree, as the olive; or a shrub, as the palm of the plains; or a third something which we can properly call neither tree nor shrub, as is the vine.

[a] Vergil, *Georg.* II. 1. [b] *Georg.* II. 10–11.
[c] *Cf. Georg.* II. 14, *Pars autem posito surgunt de semine.*

3 ut est vitis. Hanc nos ceteris stirpibus iure prae-
ponimus, non tantum fructus dulcedine, sed etiam
facilitate per quam omni paene regione et omni
declinatione mundi, nisi tamen glaciali vel prae-
fervida, curae mortalium respondet, tamque felix
campis quam collibus provenit, et in densa non minus
quam in resoluta, saepe etiam gracili; atque pingui
4 et macra,[1] siccaque et uliginosa. Tum sola maxime
utramque [2] patitur intemperiem caeli vel sub axe
frigido, vel aestuoso procellosoque. Refert tamen
cuius generis aut quo habitu vitem pro regionis
statu colere censeas. Neque enim omni caelo solove
cultus idem, neque est unum stirpis eius genus:
quodque praecipuum est ex omnibus non facile
dictu [3] est, cum suum cuique regioni magis aut minus
5 aptum esse [4] doceat usus. Exploratum tamen
habebit prudens agricola genus vitis habile campo,
quod nebulas pruinamque sine noxa perfert; colli,
quod siccitatem ventosque patitur. Pingui et uberi
dabit agro gracilem vitem, nec natura nimis fecundam; macro feracem; terrae densae vehementem,
multaque materia frondentem; resoluto et laeto
solo, rari sarmenti. Humido loco sciet non recte
mandari fructus [5] teneri et amplioris acini,[6] sed
callosi [7] et angusti frequentisque vinacei; [8] sicco
recte contribui diversae quoque [9] naturae semina.
6 Sed et post haec non ignorabit dominus loci, plus

[1] et macra *Schn.* : macria (et *om.*) *S* : matria (et *om.*) *A* : materia *ac* (et *om.*) *M* : terra (et *om.*) *vulgo.*

[2] utramque *edd. ante Schn.*: utrumque *a*: utrunque *M*: utcumque *SAc, Schn.*

[3] dictum *ScM, vett. edd.*

[4] aptum esse *edd.*: apud se *SAacM.*

[5] fructum *SAac, vett. edd.*

[6] acinis *SA.*

[7] calli *S*: galli *AacM.*

[8] vinaceis *ac.*

[9] quoque *om. SAac.*

This last we rightly set above all other woody-plants, 3
not only for the sweetness of its fruits, but also because of the readiness with which in nearly every country and every climate, except, however, the icy cold or burning hot, it responds to human care; it thrives on plain as well as hillside, in compact soil no less than in loose, often also in thin land, in fat ground and lean, in dry ground and wet; and it 4
alone has the greatest endurance of both sorts of intemperate weather—either under a cold sky or one that is hot and stormy. Nevertheless an important consideration is the variety and the habit of the vine which you propose to cultivate, in relation to the conditions of the region. For its cultivation is not the same in every climate and in every soil, nor is there only one variety of that plant; and which kind is best of all is not easy to say, since experience teaches that to every region its own variety is more or less suited. Still the wise 5
farmer will have discovered by test that the kind of vine proper for level country is one which endures mists and frosts without injury; for a hillside, one which withstands drought and wind. He will assign to fat and fertile land a vine that is slender and not too productive by nature; to lean land, a prolific vine; to heavy soil, a vigorous vine that puts forth much wood and foliage; to loose and rich soil, one that has few canes. He will know that it is not proper to commit to a moist place a vine with thin-skinned fruit and unusually large grapes, but one whose fruit is tough-skinned, small, and full of seeds; and that plants of a different nature are properly entrusted to a dry site. But in addition 6
to this the proprietor of the place will not be un-

posse qualitatem caeli frigidam vel calidam, siccam vel roscidam, grandinosam ventosamque vel placi-
7 dam, serenam vel nebulosam:[1] frigidaeque aut nebulosae duorum generum vites aptabit, seu praecoques, quarum maturitas frugum praecurrit hiemem; seu firmi durique acini, quarum inter caligines uvae deflorescunt, et mox gelicidiis ac pruinis, ut aliarum[2] caloribus, mitescunt. Ventoso quoque et tumultuoso statu caeli fidenter easdem tenaces ac duri acini committet. Rursus calido teneriores uberioresque concredet. Sicco destinabit eas quae pluviis aut continuis roribus putrescunt; roscido, quae siccitatibus laborant; grandinoso quae foliis duris latisque sunt, quo melius protegant fructum. Nam placida et serena regio nullam non recipit; commodissime tamen eam, cuius vel uvae vel acini celeriter decidunt.

8 At[3] si voto est eligendus vineis locus et status caeli, sicut censet verissime Celsus, optimum est solum nec densum nimis nec resolutum, soluto tamen propius; nec exile nec laetissimum, proximum tamen uberi; nec campestre nec praeceps, simile tamen edito campo; nec siccum nec uliginosum, modice tamen roscidum; quod fontibus non in summo non in profundo terrae scaturiat, sed ut vicinum radicibus
9 umorem sumministret—eumque nec amarum nec salsum, ne saporem vini corrumpat, et incrementa

[1] nubilosam *M.* [2] alie *M*: aliae *Ald.*, *Gesn.* [3] ac *SAaM.*

aware that the nature of the climate—cold or warm, dry or moist, subject to hail and wind or calm, clear or foggy—is a more potent influence. To cold or 7
foggy conditions he will adapt two varieties of vine, either the early ripe, whose fruits mature before cold weather, or those with firm and hard berries, whose clusters drop their blossoms during the foggy season and are presently ripened by freezing weather and frosts, as those of other grapes are ripened by warmth. To a windy and unsettled climate also he will boldly commit the same hardy vines and those of the hard-berried variety. On the other hand, he will entrust to a warm climate the more delicate and heavier-bearing sorts. For a dry climate he will select such as are rotted by rains or continual dews; for a dewy one, those that suffer in dry weather; for one subject to hailstorms, those that have tough and broad leaves for the better protection of the fruit. A calm and clear-skied region does not refuse to admit any kind of vine, though most suitably one whose clusters or berries fall quickly.

But if your own wishes are to be considered in 8
the selection of site and climate for your vineyards, the best soil, as Celsus very rightly believes, is neither too compact nor loose, but closer to the loose type; neither poor nor excessively rich, but nearest to the fertile kind; neither flat nor steep, but like plain-land with a rise; neither dry nor wet, but moderately moist; one which does not abound in springs, either on the surface or in the depths of the earth, but which supplies the roots with moisture close at hand—and that neither bitter 9
nor brackish, lest it spoil the flavour of the wine

virentium veluti quadam scabra rubigine [1] coerceat, si modo credimus Vergilio dicenti,

> Salsa autem tellus, et quae perhibetur [2] amara,
> Frugibus infelix; ea nec mansuescit arando,
> Nec Baccho genus aut pomis sua nomina servat.

10 Caelum porro neque nivale [3] vinea, sicut praedixi, nec rursus aestuosum [4] desiderat, calido tamen potius quam frigido laetatur; imbribus magis quam serenitatibus offenditur; et solo sicco quam nimis pluvioso [5] est amicior; perflatu modico lenique [6] gaudet, procellis obnoxia est. Atque haec maxime probabilis est caeli et soli qualitas.

II. Vitis autem vel ad escam vel ad defusionem [7] deponitur. Ad escam non expedit instituere vineta, nisi cum tam suburbanus est ager, ut ratio postulet inconditum fructum mercantibus velut pomum vendere. Quae cum talis est conditio, maxime praecoques et duracinae, tum denique Purpureae et Bumasti, Dactylique et Rhodiae, Libycae quoque et Cerauniae;

[1] tubicine *a*.
[2] prohibetur *aM*.
[3] nivale *Sa, vett. edd.*: in valle *c*: nequẽ vale *A*: hyemale *M*: glaciale *vulgo*.
[4] aestivosum *A*, *vett. edd.*: estivosum *ac*.
[5] pluvioso *SA*, *vett. edd.*: pluvio *acM*, *Ald.*, *Gesn.*, *Schn.*
[6] per flatum odii colonique *A*.
[7] *sic SA*, *Schn.*: ad effusionem *acM*, *et vulgo*.

---

[a] *Georg.* II. 238–240.
[b] *Duracinae*: Pliny suggests (*N.H.* XIV. 14) that the name was derived from the toughness of the skin.
[c] So called from the round and swelling appearance of their clusters (*cf.* μαστός, breast, and βου- indicating largeness). Varro, *R.R.* II. 5. 4, refers to this grape as *bumamma* (cow's udder); *cf.* Pliny, *N.H.* XIV. 15, *tument vero mammarum*

and check the growth of the vines' greenery with a kind of scaly rust, if only we believe Vergil when he says,

> Unkind to crops is salty ground, and what is bitter called;
> It is not tamed by ploughman's toil, nor does it keep unstained
> The good repute of Bacchus' child and other fruits' fair name.[a]

Furthermore, as I have said before, a vineyard does 10
not want an icy climate nor, on the other hand, one that is burning hot, though it thrives better in warm weather than in cold. It is harmed more by rain than by clear weather, and is more kindly disposed to a dry soil than to one that is subject to too much rain. It delights in moderate and gentle breezes, but is liable to injury from squalls. And this is the character of climate and soil that is most commendable.

II. Further, the grape is planted either for eating or for the pouring forth of its juice. It is not profitable to establish vineyards for food unless the plot is so close to a city that conditions warrant the selling of the raw grapes to marketers, as we do other fruit. When this is the case, the early ripe and hard-berried[b] varieties are especially to be planted, and then the Purple and the Bumast (full-breasted),[c] the Dactyl (date-shaped)[d] and the Rhodian, and the Libyan and the Cerau-

modo Bumasti; and *ibid.* 40, *Purpureae, cognomine Bumammiae.*

[d] *Cf.* Pliny, *N.H.* XIV. 15, *praelongis Dactyli porriguntur acinis.*

2 nec solum quae iucunditate saporis, verum etiam quae
specie commendari possint,[1] conseri debent, ut Ste-
phanitae, ut Tripedaneae, ut Unciariae, ut Cydonitae;
item quarum uvae temporibus hiemis durabiles vasis
conduntur, ut Venuculae, ut nuper in hos usus
3 exploratae Numisianae. At ubi vino consulimus,
vitis eligitur, quae et in fructu valet et in materia,
quod alterum ad reditus coloni, alterum ad diuturni-
4 tatem stirpis plurimum confert. Sed ea tum praecipua est, si nec nimis [2] celeriter frondet, et primo
quoque tempore deflorescit, nec nimis [3] tarde
mitescit; quin etiam pruinas et caliginem et carbunculum facile propulsat, eademque nec imbribus
5 putrescit,[4] nec siccitatibus abolescit. Talis nobis
eligatur vel mediocriter fecunda, si modo is locus
habetur, in quo gustus nobilis pretiosusque fluit;
nam si sordidus aut vilis est, feracissimam quamque
serere conducit, ut multiplicatione frugum reditus
6 augeatur. Fere autem omni statu locorum cam-
pestria largius vinum sed iucundius adferunt collina;
quae tamen ipsa modico statu caeli magis exuberant
Aquiloni prona, sed [5] sunt generosiora sub Austro.

[1] possunt *S*. [2] minus *SAc*, *vett. edd.* [3] minus c.
[4] harescit *SA*. [5] pronas et *SAa*.

---

[a] Isidore (*Orig.* XVII. 5. 17) says that they were so named because of their fiery red colour (*cf.* κεραυνός, lightning).

[b] From στέφανος, crown. So called, says Pliny (*N.H.* XIV. 42), because the leaves run between the berries, to resemble a coronet.

[c] The name is derived from the size of the vine; Pliny, *N.H.* XIV. 41.

[d] Called *Unciales* by Pliny (*loc. cit.*), from the weight of their grapes.

[e] From their quince-like flavour; or from Cydonia in Crete.

nian;[a] and not only those that can be recommended 2 for agreeableness of flavour, but also those whose appearance can commend them, such as the Stephanitan (coronary),[b] the Tripedanean (three-foot kind),[c] the Unciarian (ounce-weight),[d] and the Cydonitan (quince-grape);[e] likewise those vines whose grapes keep well in winter and are stored in jars, as the Venuculan,[f] and the Numisian, which has recently been proved for this purpose. But when our interest is in the wine, a vine is 3 selected which is both heavy in yield and strong in wood, because the one contributes greatly to the income of the husbandman, and the other to the durability of the stock. But such a vine is 4 especially good if it does not put forth leaves too quickly, if also it casts its flowers very early in the season and does not ripen too slowly; moreover, if it easily withstands frosts and fog and blight, does not rot in rainy weather, and does not shrivel up in times of drought. A vine of this sort, though only 5 moderately fruitful, should be our choice, if only we have a piece of ground where the flavour of the wine is distinguished and costly; for if it is of poor quality or low in price, it is best to plant the most prolific vines, so that our revenues may be increased by the greater quantity of the yield. Moreover, in nearly 6 every type of place champaign slopes produce the larger quantity of wine, but hill lands the better flavoured; and in a temperate climate hills that slope to the north are more productive, while those with a southern exposure yield a superior quality.

[f] Also called Sirculan; sec. 27, below, and Pliny, *N.H.* XIV. 34. On their preserving qualities see XII. 45. 1; Pliny, *loc. cit.*; Horace, *Serm.* II. 4. 71.

7 Nec dubium, quin sit ea nonnullarum vitium natura, ut pro locorum situ bonitate vini modo vincant modo superentur.[1] Solae traduntur Amineae excepto caeli statu nimis frigido ubicumque sint, etiam si degenerent, sibi comparatae, magis aut minus probi gustus vina praebere, et ceteras omnis sapore
8 praecedere. Eae [2] cum sint unius nominis, non unam speciem gerunt. Duas germanas cognovimus, quarum minor ocius et melius deflorescit, habilis arbori nec non iugo: illic pinguem terram, hic mediocrem desiderat, longeque praecedit maiorem,
9 quia et imbres et ventos fortius patitur. Nam maior celeriter in flore corrumpitur, et magis in iugis quam in arboribus. Ideoque non est [3] vineis apta, vix etiam arbusto, nisi praepingui et vivida [4] terra; nam nec mediocri valet, multoque minus in exili. Prolixarum frequentia materiarum foliorumque et uvarum et acinorum [5] magnitudine dignoscitur, internodiis quoque rarior. Largis fructibus a minore superatur, gustu non vincitur. Et hae quidem utrae-

[1] *sic vett. edd., Schn.*: vincat (vincant *a*) modo superetur *SAacM, Ald., Gesn.*
[2] Ea *SAacM.*
[3] est in *Aac, vett. edd.*
[4] vivida *SAacM, Schn. in not., Sobel*: uivida *vel* humida *plerique.*
[5] et acinorum *om. SA.*

[a] Highly praised by all authorities; but see especially Chap. 9, below, and Pliny, *N.H.* XIV. 21–22. Isidore (*Orig.* XVII. 5. 18) says that it is called Aminean *quasi sine mineo, id est sine rubore,* producing a white wine.

And there is no doubt that the nature of some 7
vines is such that in the quality of their wine they sometimes excel, sometimes are excelled, according to their situation. The Aminean varieties [a] alone, except where the climate is exceedingly cold, and even if they decline in quality in comparison with their best, are said to provide wines of more or less true taste and to surpass all other varieties in flavour.
Though they bear one name, they are not of the same 8
appearance. We know of two "sister" vines, of which the smaller is earlier and better in casting its blossoms and may be trained to tree and trellis [b] alike. On the tree it requires rich ground; on the trellis, ordinary soil. And it far surpasses the larger variety by reason of its sturdier endurance of rain
and wind. For the larger sort is quickly spoiled in 9
the blossom, and more so on trellises than on trees; and on this account it is not suitable for vineyards, and hardly fit for an arbustum [c] except in ground that is very rich and vigorous; for it does not thrive in ordinary ground, and much less so in lean ground. It is distinguished by its great amount of rank woody growth and the large size of its leaves, clusters, and berries; it is also longer from joint to joint. In quantity of fruit it is surpassed by the smaller variety; it is not outdone in flavour. And both

[b] Lit. "yoke" (*iugum*), defined by Varro (*R.R.* I. 8. 1) as the support fastened cross-wise to the upright props (*pedamenta*), thus forming a frame or trellis.

[c] *Vinea* denotes the vineyard proper, in which the vines were either allowed to trail along the ground or were supported by frames or trained to stand upright beside props; *De Arb.* 4. 1. The *arbustum* was a plantation of lopped-off trees (preferably poplar, elm, and ash), upon which the vines were trained and festooned from tree to tree, see V. 6, *De Arb.* 16.

10 que Amineae. Verum et aliae duae geminae ab eo quod duplices uvas exigunt, cognomen trahunt[1] austerioris[2] vini, sed aeque perennis. Duarum[3] minor vulgo notissima, quippe Campaniae celeberrimos Vesuvii colles Surrentinosque vestit. Hilaris inter aestivos Favonii flatus Austris adfligitur.
11 Ceteris itaque partibus Italiae non tam vineis quam arbusto est idonea, cum praedictis regionibus commodissime iugum sustineat. Materiam fructumque, nisi quod duplicem, non absimilem minori germanae gerit, sicut maior gemina maiori[4] germanae; quae tamen minor hoc melior est, quod fecundior etiam mediocri solo, nam illam nisi praepingui non respon-
12 dere iam dictum est. Lanatam quoque Amineam quidam maxime probant, quae hoc vocabulum non ideo usurpat, quod sola ex omnibus Amineis, verum quod praecipue canescit lanugine. Sane boni vini, sed lenioris[5] quam superiores, crebram quoque materiam fundit; atque ideo propter pampini densitatem saepe parum[6] recte deflorescit, eadem-
13 que maturo fructu celeriter putrescit. Super hunc numerum, quem rettulimus, singularis habetur Aminea maiori geminae[7] non dissimilis, prima specie

[1] cognomen trahunt *SA* : gemelle vocantur *aM* : exigunt gemelle vocantur cognomen trahunt *c* : geminae, quae a. e. q. d. u. exigunt, gemellae vocantur, austerioris etc. *Ald.*, *Gesn.*

[2] austeris *SA*, *Sobel.*

[3] duarum *SAacM* : earum *edd.* : quarum *Sobel.*

[4] maiori *defenderunt Gesn. et Schn.*: minori *SAacM*, *cett. edd.*

[5] levioris *Ald.*, *Gesn.*

[6] parum saepe *SAacM*.

[7] gemine *M*, *edd.*: germane *Sc*: germanae *a*: germinae *A*.

[a] Modern Sorrento.

[b] *I.e.* is trained to the trellis (*iugum*).

of these, to be sure, are Aminean vines. But there 10
are two other vines, called "twins," which derive
their name from their producing of double clusters;
they yield a harsher wine, but keep equally well.
The smaller of the two is everywhere very well
known, because it covers those most famous slopes
of Vesuvius and of Surrentum [a] in Campania. It
is sprightly amid the western breezes of summer,
but downcast in southern winds; and so in other 11
sections of Italy it is suitable, not so much for vineyards, as for the arbustum, although in the regions
above mentioned it bears the yoke [b] very well. It
produces wood and fruit—except for its double
clusters—not unlike the smaller "sister" vine,
just as the larger "twin" is like the larger "sister";
but the smaller vine is the better in that it is more
fruitful even in ordinary soil, for I have already
said that the other does not yield except in very
rich ground. Some also approve very highly the 12
"woolly" Aminean, which acquires this epithet
not from the fact that it alone, of all the Aminean
varieties, is hoary with down, but because it is
especially so. A producer of exceedingly good wine,
though mellower than those above mentioned, it
also makes a rank growth; and for this reason,
because of the compactness of its foliage, it often does
not cast its blossoms perfectly, and it also rots quickly
after the fruit has matured. In addition to the 13
number that we have mentioned, there is included
a "single" [c] Aminean not unlike the larger "twin"—

[c] Seemingly a vine with single clusters, in contrast to the double-clustered "twin" (sec. 10, above). But *singularis habetur* may mean "there is held to be of outstanding merit."

pampini et trunci, sed vini sapore aliquanto inferior, quamvis generosissimis sit proxima,[1] praeferenda etiam propriis virtutibus. Nam et feracior[2] et flore melius exuitur, spissasque et albidas uvas ac tumidioris acini gerit, gracili arvo non desciscit, atque
14 ideo inter uberrimas vites numeratur. Nomentanae vini nobilitate subsequuntur Amineas, fecunditate vero etiam praeveniunt; quippe cum se frequenter impleant et id, quod ediderunt, optime tueantur.[3] Sed earum quoque feracior est minor, cuius et folium parcius scinditur, et materia non ita rubet ut maioris, a quo colore rubellanae[4] nuncupantur. Eaedemque faeciniae, quod plus quam ceterae faecis adferunt.
15 Id tamen incommodum repensant uvarum multitudine, quas et in iugo sed et in arbore melius exhibent. Ventos et imbres valenter sufferunt, celeriter deflorescunt, et ideo citius[5] mitescunt, omnis incommodi patientes praeter caloris. Nam quia minuti acini et durae cutis uvas habent, aestibus contrahuntur. Pinguique[6] arvo maxime gaudent, quod ubertatem aliquam natura gracilibus[7] et exilibus uvis praebere
16 valet. Frigidum ac roscidum solum et caelum[8] commodissime sustinent Eugeniae, dum sunt in Albano colle, nam mutato loco vix nomini suo

[1] proximo *SA* : proxime *Ald* : proximae *Gesn.*
[2] feracior est *edd.* : est *om. codd.*
[3] tueantur *M* : tuentur *SAac.*
[4] rubellanae *SAa* : rubellane *c* : rubellianae *M*, *et vulgo.*
[5] cito *SAa.*
[6] Pinguique *SAacM* : Pingui *edd.*
[7] gracilibus *om. S* : gracili et *A.*
[8] et caelum *om. SAa.*

a vine of first rank in the appearance of leafy shoots and stock, but somewhat inferior in the flavour of its wine; though even so it ranks next to the most outstanding varieties and is even to be preferred for qualities of its own. For it is more fruitful, it is better in casting its flowers, it bears compact light-coloured clusters of plumper grapes, it does not degenerate in poor land, and consequently it is counted among the most profitable vines. The 14
Nomentan vines [a] follow close after the Amineans in excellence of wine, but in productivity they even take the lead; and naturally so, since they are often loaded full and keep exceedingly well what they have produced. But of these, too, the smaller is the more prolific; its leaf is not so deeply cleft, and its wood is not so red as that of the larger variety—from which colour the vines are called *rubellanae*. These vines are also called *faeciniae* from the fact that they make more dregs (*faeces*)
than other varieties. Still they make up for this 15
disadvantage in the greater number of their clusters, which they produce even on a trellis but better on a tree. They endure winds and rains valiantly, drop their flowers early, and therefore ripen sooner. They bear up under every adversity except that of heat; for, having small-berried and tough-skinned clusters, they shrivel in high temperatures. They delight most of all in rich land, which can add some fullness to clusters that are naturally scanty and
small. The Eugenians endure a cold, dewy ground 16
and climate very well as long as they remain on the Alban hills; for in a changed situation they hardly

[a] From Nomentum, an ancient Sabine town, now Mentana; *cf.* Pliny, *N.H.* XIV. 23.

respondent; nec minus Allobrogicae, quarum vini
17 iucunditas cum regione mutatur. Magis etiam
dotibus tres Apianae [1] commendantur, omnes feraces
iugoque et arboribus satis idoneae, generosior tamen
una, quae nudis foliis est. Nam duae lanatae quamvis frondibus et palmitum pari facie fluxurae qualitate
sunt dispariles, cum tardius altera recipiat [2] cariem
18 vetustatis. Pingui solo feracissimae, mediocri quoque fecundae; praecoquis fructus, ideoque frigidis
locis aptissimae; vini dulcis, sed capiti nervisque,
venisque [3] non aptae.[4] Nisi mature lectae pluviis
ventisque et apibus adferunt praedam, quarum
vocabulo propter hanc populationem cognominantur.
Atque hae pretiosi gustus celeberrimae.

19 Possunt tamen etiam secundae notae vites proventu et ubertate commendari, qualis est Biturica,
qualis basilica,[5] quarum minorem coccolobin [6] vocant
Hispani, longe omnium primis utraeque proximae.
Nam et vetustatem vinum earum patitur, et ad
20 bonitatem aliquam per annos venit. Iam vero ipsae
fecunditate praestant omnibus, quas ante rettuli,
tum etiam patientia; quippe turbines imbresque
fortissime sustinent, et commode fluunt, nec deficiunt
macro solo. Frigora melius quam umores sustinent,
umores commodius quam siccitates, nec caloribus

[1] appianae *SA* : appiane *acM*.
[2] recipiat *M* : recipiet *SA* : recipit *ac*.
[3] venisque *om. SA*.
[4] apti *Ursinus*.
[5] balisca *S* : basilisca *Aa*.
[6] coccolobin *Sobel* : coccolovin *S* : coccoloum *Aa* : cocco-
lubem *c* : coccolleum *M* · cocolubem *edd*.

---

[a] εὐγενής, "well-born"; *cf.* Pliny, *N.H.* XIV. 25.
[b] *Ibid.* 26.

answer to their own name.[a] The same is true of the Allobrogian [b] vines: the agreeableness of their wines is affected by a change of region. The three 17
Apian [c] also are recommended for their great qualities; all of them fruitful and quite suitable for the trellis and for trees, though the one with bare leaves is superior. For the two lanate varieties, though of like appearance as to leaves and branches, differ in the quality of their juice, as one of them is slower in acquiring flatness of taste from long keeping. They are very prolific in rich ground, 18
and fruitful also in average soil; their fruit ripens early, and for that reason they are very well suited for cold localities; they yield a sweet wine, but are not good for the head, sinews, and veins. If they are not gathered at the proper time they become the prey of rains, winds, and bees; and it is because of this plundering that they are surnamed from the word meaning "bees" (*apes*). And these are the vines most renowned for their precious flavours.

There are, nevertheless, vines of second quality 19
which can be commended for their growth and fruitfulness, such as the Bituric [d] and the Basilic, the smaller of which the Spaniards call *coccolobis*,[e] —both of them by far the closest to the very best; for their wine stands long keeping and attains some degree of excellence with age. And in fact they 20
surpass in productiveness all that I have mentioned above, and also in hardiness; for they withstand storms and rain with the greatest fortitude, they have a good amount of juice, and do not fail in lean ground. They endure cold better than wetness, and wetness better than dryness, and yet they are

[c] *Ibid.* 24. [d] *Ibid.* 27. [e] *Ibid.* 30.

21 tamen contristantur. Visula[1] deinde ab his et minor Argitis terrae mediocritate laetantur; nam in pingui nimiis viribus luxuriant; in macra tenues et vacuae fructu veniunt; amiciores iugo quam arboribus, sed Argitis etiam in sublimibus fertilis
22 vastis materiis et uvis exuberat. Humillimis tabulatis aptior Visula brevem materiam, durum folium et latum exigit, cuius amplitudine[2] fructus suos optime adversus grandinem tuetur; qui tamen nisi primo quoque tempore maturi legantur, ad terram decidunt; humoribus etiam priusquam defluant,
23 putrescunt. Sunt et Helvolae, quas non nulli varias appellant, neque purpureae neque nigrae, ab helvo,[3] nisi fallor, colore vocitatae. Melior est nigrior abundantia vini, sed haec sapore pretiosior. Color acinorum in neutra conspicitur aequalis. Utraque[4] candidi musti alterna vice annorum plus aut minus adferunt.[5] Melius arborem, sed et iugum commode vestiunt. Mediocri quoque solo fecundae, sicut Pretiae minor et maior. Sed eae[6] generositate vini magis commendantur, et frequentibus materiis
24 frondent et cito maturescunt. Albuelis[7] utilior, ut ait Celsus, in colle quam in campo; in arbore quam in iugo; in summa arbore quam in ima;[8]

[1] vis ulla *ac*: visullae *SA*: Vissule *M*: Visulae *edd. ante Gesn.*

[2] altitudinem *Aac*: altıtudine *M*.

[3] ab helvo *om. a*: ab herbo *c*: ab albo *AM*.

[4] aequalis atque utraque *AacM*.

[5] auferunt *SA*.

[6] eae *edd.*: haec, *et deinde* commendatur *SA*: sed et *ac*: sed et haec *M*.

[7] aldi uelis *SA*: alius uel his (bis *a*) *ac*: alia est his *M*.

[8] in minima *ac*: in anima *A*.

[a] Pliny, *N.H.* XIV. 28.

not bothered by heat. Next after these are the Visula [a] and the smaller Argitis,[b] which thrive in ground of middling quality; for they make a rank growth in rich ground because of their excessive vigour, while in lean ground they grow spindling and are devoid of fruit. They have a greater fondness for the trellis than for trees, though the Argitis is productive even on high supports and makes a luxuriant growth of wood and grape clusters. The 22
Visula, better suited to very low frames, makes little wood but tough and broad leaves, whose size affords the fruit very good protection against hail; but if this is not gathered as soon as it is ripe, it falls to the ground; and in wet weather it rots even before it falls off. There are also the Helvolans,[c] which 23
some call *variae* (variegated); they are neither purple nor black, and get their name, if I mistake not, from their dun (*helvus*) shade. The one which is more nearly black is the better as to quantity of wine, while the other is more highly prized in the matter of flavour. In neither of them does the colour of the berries appear to be uniform. Both yield white must in greater or smaller quantity every year. They make a better covering on a tree, though doing well on a trellis. They are productive also in mediocre soil, as are the smaller and larger Pretians.[c] But the latter are commended more highly for the quality of their wine, and they put forth much wood and foliage and ripen quickly. The Albuelis,[d] as 24
Celsus says, is more profitable on a hill than on a plain; on a tree than on a trellis; and at the top

[b] Vergil, *Georg.* II. 99–100. *Argitisque minor, cui non certaverit ulla | Aut tantum fluere aut totidem durare per annos.*

[c] Pliny, *N.H.* XIV. 29. [d] *Ibid.* 31.

ferax et materiae frequentis et uvae. Nam quae Graeculae vites sunt, ut Mareoticae, Thasiae, Psithiae, Sophortiae, sicut habent probabilem gustum, ita nostris regionibus et raritate uvarum et acinorum exiguitate minus fluunt. Inerticula tamen nigra, quam quidam Graeci amethyston [1] appellant, potest in secunda quasi tribu esse, quod et boni vini est et innoxia,[2] unde etiam nomen traxit, quod iners habetur in tentandis nervis, quamvis gustu non sit hebes.[3]

25 Tertium gradum facit earum Celsus, quae fecunditate sola commendantur: ut tres Helvenacae,[4] quarum duae maiores nequaquam minori bonitate et abundantia musti pares habentur. Earum altera, quam Galliarum incolae marcum [5] vocant, mediocris vini; et altera quam longam appellant, eandemque canam,[6] sordidi vini nec tam largi quam ex numero
26 uvarum prima specie promittit. Minima et optima e tribus facillime folio dinoscitur, nam rotundissimum omnium id gerit; atque est laudabilis, quod siccitates maxime perfert; quod frigora sustinet, dum tamen

[1] amethyston *omnes post Beroaldum*: amarcion *SA*: amaricion *c*: amarition *M*, *vett. edd.*: amarciem *a*.

[2] quod et . . . innoxia *om. SA*.

[3] habilis *SAaM*.

[4] helvenace *M*: hennacae (-e *a*)*SAa*: henirace *c*: Helvenaciae *vulgo*.

[5] marcum *SAacM*, *Schn. in not.*, *Sobel*: emarcum *cett.* *Deinde* mediocris vineis (*SAa*) *defendit Sobel*.

[6] canam *Sobel*: cauam *SAac*: canaram *M*: avaram *edd.*

---

[a] ἀμέθυστος, "not drunken." *Cf.* the amethyst as a supposed remedy against drunkenness. On the name and quality of the vine, *cf.* Pliny, *N.H.* XIV. 31. and Isidore, *Orig.* XVII. 5. 24.

of the tree than at the lower part. It produces much wood and many clusters. For those Greekling vines—such as the Mareotic, the Thasian, the Psithian, and the Sophortian—though they have an agreeable taste, still in our localities they yield little juice because of the looseness of the bunches and the small size of the berries. Nevertheless the black Inerticulan, which certain Greeks call *amethystos*,[a] may be placed in the second tribe, so to speak, because it makes good wine and is harmless; from this fact, too, it takes its name, because it is considered inactive (*iners*) in its effect on the sinews, although not dull in taste.

25 Celsus makes a third class of those vines which are commended for fruitfulness alone, such as the three Helvenacans,[b] of which the two larger are considered by no means equal to the smaller in the quality and quantity of their must. One of them, which people who live in Gaul call *marcus*,[c] produces ordinary wine; and the other, which they designate as the "long vine" and also the "white vine," yields a wine of low grade and of no such quantity as the number of its clusters promises at first glance. The 26
smallest and best of the three is very readily recognized by its leaf, for it bears the roundest leaf of all of them; and it is praiseworthy because it endures drought best of all, because it bears cold

[b] *Cf.* Pliny, *N.H.* XIV. 32–33.

[c] Sobel (*Stud. Colum.*, 47–48) points out the long standing error of editors and lexicographers in reading *emarcum*, without MS. authority, as a "Gallic" word. Rejecting also Schneider's interpretation of the word as Fr. *marc*, Sobel, comparing modern "Alexander" apples, "Victoria" plums, "Williams" pears, etc., proposes the familiar Roman praenomen to produce "Marcus" grapes.

sine imbribus sit; quod non nullis locis etiam vinum eius in vetustatem diffunditur; quod praecipue sola macerrimum quoque solum fertilitate sua com-
27 mendat. Ut Spionia[1] dapsilis musto sed[2] amplitudine magis uvarum quam numero fertilis, ut Horconia,[3] ut Murgentina eademque Pompeiana, ut Numisiana, ut Venucula eademque Scirpula[4] atque Sticula,[5] ut nigra Fregellana, ut Merica,[6] ut Rhaetica, ut omnium quas cognovimus copiosissima Arcelaca
28 maior, a multis Argitis[7] falso existimata. Nam has nuper mihi cognitas, Pergulanam[8] dico et Irtiolam Fereolamque, non facile adseverem quo gradu habendae sint; quod etsi satis fecundas scio, nondum tamen de bonitate vini, quod adferunt, iudicare potui. Unam etiam praecoquem vitem nobis ante hoc tempus incognitam Graeca consuetudine Dracontion vocitari comperimus, quae fecunditate iucunditateve Arcelacae Basilicaeque et Bituricae comparari possit,
29 generositate vini Amineae. Multa praeterea genera sunt vitium, quarum nec numerum nec appellationes

[1] scipionia *SM* : scipioni ad apsilis *A* : scipioni adapsilis *a*: spioni allapsilis *c* : At spionia *plerique edd. ante Schn.*

[2] musto sed *c, vett. edd.* : mustos sed *SAa* : musto et *M, et vulgo.*

[3] horconia *Sobel* : holconia *S* : holcani aut *A* : holcoma *a* : holcama *cM* : holgonia aut *vett. edd.* : olcaginia *vulgo.*

[4] scuritula *a* . sartula *c* : fertula *M* : scircitula *Pontedera* : Pompeiana . . . scirpula *om SA.*

[5] rabucula *SAa* : rubicula *cM.*

[6] mettica *SAaM* : atthica c.

if only it is free from rain, because in some regions its wine is racked off for long keeping, and especially because it alone gives a good name to even the poorest of soil by reason of its own fertility. [Celsus 27
includes also] such as the Spionian, rich in must but fruitful in the size rather than the number of its clusters; such as the Horconian,[a] the Murgentine,[a] which is the same as the Pompeian, the Numisian, the Venuculan, also called Scirpulan and Sticulan;[b] such as the black Fragellan, the Merican, the Rhaetian, and that most prolific of all vines within our acquaintance, the greater Arcelacan,[c] wrongly considered by many to be the Argitis. For as to 28
those that have recently come to my knowledge—I mean the Pergulan, the Irtiolan, and the Fereolan—I could not easily declare with certainty in what class they are to be considered; for, though I know that they are passably fruitful, I have not been able as yet to pass judgment on the quality of the wine that they produce. We have discovered also that there is an early-ripe vine, hitherto unknown to us and called *Dracontion* after the Greek fashion, which may be compared in fruitfulness and agreeableness to the Arcelacan, the Basilic, and the Bituric vines, and in its high quality to the Aminean. There are, 29
besides, many sorts of vines of which we can relate

[a] *Cf.* Pliny, *N.H.* XIV. 35.
[b] Pliny, *N.H.* XIV. 34.
[c] Not mentioned as such by other writers.

---

[7] argillis *SA*.
[8] nuper gulanam (mihi cognitas per- *om.*) *SA*.

cum certa fide referre possumus. Neque enim,[1] ut ait poeta,

numero comprendere[2] refert;
Quem qui scire velit, Libyci velit aequoris idem
Discere[3] quam multae Zephyro turbentur[4] harenae:

30 quippe universae regiones regionumque paene singulae partes habent propria vitium genera, quae consuetudine sua denominant;[5] quaedam etiam stirpes cum locis vocabula mutaverunt; quaedam propter mutationem locorum, sicut supra diximus, etiam qualitate sua decesserunt, ita ut dinosci non possint. Ideoque in hac ipsa Italia, ne dicam in tam diffuso terrarum orbe, vicinae[6] nationes nominibus earum
31 discrepant, variantque vocabula. Quare prudentis magistri est eius modi nomenclationis aucupio, quo potiri nequeat,[7] studiosos non demorari; sed illud in totum praecipere, quod et Celsus ait et ante eum Marcus Cato, nullum genus vitium conserendum esse nisi fama, nullum diutius conservandum nisi experimento,[8] probatum. Atque ubi multa invitabunt regionis commoda, ut nobilem vitem conseramus, generosam requiremus, inquit Iulius Graecinus; ubi nihil erit aut non multum quod[9] proritet, feracitatem potius sequemur, quae non eadem portione

[1] enim *om. SA, Sobel.*

[2] numero comprendere *M, Verg. edd.*: numero comprehendere *a, edd.*: numerum comprehendere (comprehende refert *S*, comprehendere fert *A*) *SAc, Sobel.*

[3] dicere *SAacM.*

[4] turbentur *Sobel, Verg. edd.*: turbent' *S*: turbem *A*: versentur *acM, edd.*

[5] denominant *SAacM*: nominant *edd*

[6] etiam *post* vicinae *add. vulgo*: *om. SAacM, vett. edd.*

[7] nequeat *SAacM, vett. edd.*: nequeant *vulgo.*

[8] experimendo *SA.*

[9] quo *SA.*

neither the number nor the names with assurance. And, indeed, as the poet says,[a]

> to know their number is of no concern.
> One who would know of this might also wish to learn
> How many grains of Libyan sand by western breeze are stirred.

For all countries and almost all separate districts 30 of those countries have their peculiar types of vines, which they designate according to their own fashion; some vine-stocks also have changed their names along with the places where they are grown; and some, as I said above, have so far departed from their peculiar character, through a change of place, as to be unrecognizable. And so in our own Italy, not to speak of the whole far-flung world, neighbouring peoples disagree in the names of vines, and their designations vary. Therefore it is a mark of the wise 31 teacher not to retard his students with quibbling over a list of names of a sort which it is impossible to master, but in general to lay down as a precept what Celsus says, and Marcus Cato before him—that no kind of vine should be planted except that approved by common report, and that none should be kept for any length of time unless proved by test. And where the many advantages of a particular region invite us to plant a superior vine, we shall search out one of good origin, says Julius Graecinus; where there is nothing at all or not much to encourage us, we shall look rather for fruitfulness, which is not excelled in worth to the same degree that it excels

[a] Vergil, *Georg.* II. 104–106.

32 vincitur pretio quam vincit abundantia. Sed de hac sententia, quamquam et ipse paulo ante idem censuerim, quid tamen arcanius iudicem, suo loco mox dicam. Propositum est enim docere qua ratione vineae pariter feraces et pretiosae fluxurae possint constitui.

III. Nunc prius quam de satione vitium disseram, non alienum puto velut quoddam fundamentum iacere disputationi futurae, ut ante perpensum et exploratum habeamus an locupletet patrem familiae vinearum cultus. Est enim paene adhuc supervacuum de his conserendis praecipere, dum quod prius est, nondum concedatur an omnino sint habendae. Idque adeo plurimi dubitent, ut multi refugiant et reformident talem positionem ruris, atque optabiliorem pratorum possessionem pascu-
2 orumque vel silvae caeduae iudicent; nam de arbusto etiam inter auctores non exigua pugna fuit, abnuente Saserna genus id ruris, Tremelio maxime probante. Sed et hanc sententiam suo loco aestimabimus.[1] Interim studiosi agricolationis hoc primum docendi sunt, uberrimum esse reditum vinearum. Atque ut omittam veterem illam felicitatem arvorum,[2] quibus et ante iam Cato Marcus, et mox Varro Terentius, prodidit singula iugera vinearum sescenas urnas vini praebuisse—id enim maxime adseverat in primo libro rerum rusticarum Varro—nec una regione

[1] estimavimus *S* : extimabimus *ac* : existimabimus *M*.
[2] arborum *SA*[1].

[a] *I.e.* the lower quality of the prolific vine is more than offset by the quantity of its yield. [b] *I.e.* the *arbustum*.

[c] Varro, *R.R.* I. 2. 7, quoting Cato, *Origines*.

[d] 1 *urna* = ½ *amphora* = about 3.42 U.S. (2.85 Brit.) gallons.

in abundance of yield.[a] But as for this opinion, though I myself was of the same mind not long ago, I shall soon tell in the proper place what my more private judgment is. For it is my purpose to teach the method by which vineyards may be managed so as to be at the same time fruitful and productive of a wine that will bring a good price. 32

III. Now, before discoursing on the planting of vines, I think it not out of place to lay down, as a sort of foundation for the coming discussion, the principle that we would have carefully weighed and investigated in advance whether viticulture will enrich the proprietor; for it is well-nigh purposeless as yet to give directions for planting vines, as long as the prior question is not yet affirmatively answered—whether vines should be kept at all. And most people would be doubtful on this point, to such an extent that many would avoid and dread such an ordering of their land, and would consider it preferable to own meadows and pastures, or woodland for cutting; for in the matter of ground planted 2
with trees for the support of vines [b] there has been no little dispute even among authorities, Saserna being unfavourable to this kind of land, and Tremelius approving it most highly. But we shall make an appraisal of this opinion in its proper place. Meanwhile those devoted to the study of agriculture must be informed of one thing first of all—that the return from vineyards is a very rich one. And to pass over the old-time fertility of the land, of which Marcus Cato long ago, and Terentius Varro [c] more recently, recorded that each *iugerum* of vineyard yielded six hundred *urnae* [d] of wine—for Varro so declares most emphatically in the first book of his *Res Rusticae*—

provenire solitum, verum et in Faventino [1] agro
3 et in Gallico, qui nunc Piceno contribuitur; his certe
temporibus Nomentana regio celeberrima fama est
inlustris, et praecipue quam possidet Seneca, vir
excellentis ingenii atque doctrinae, cuius in praediis
vinearum iugera singula culleos octonos reddidisse
plerumque, compertum est. Nam illa videntur
prodigialiter in nostris Ceretanis accidisse, ut aliqua
vitis apud te excederet uvarum numerum duorum
milium et apud me octingenae [2] stirpes insitae intra
biennium septenos culleos peraequarent; ut primae
vineae centenas amphoras iugeratim praeberent, cum
prata et pascua et silvae, si centenos sestertios in
singula iugera efficiant, optime domino consulere
4 videantur. Nam frumenta maiore [3] quidem parte [4]
Italiae quando cum quarto responderint, vix meminisse possumus.[5] Cur ergo res infamis est? Non
quidem suo sed hominum inquit vitio Graecinus:
primum, quod in explorandis seminibus nemo adhibet
diligentiam, et ideo pessimi generis plerique vineta
conserunt; deinde sata non ita nutriunt, ut ante

[1] florentino *Sa*: flor. *expunct. et* faventino *in marg. A.*
[2] octingenae *SAcM*: ottingene *a*: octogenae *vulgo.*
[3] maiorem *SAa, Sobel.*
[4] partem *SA, Sobel.*
[5] possimus *S* (*in* possumus *corr.*) *A, Sobel.*

---

[a] Mod. Faenza.
[b] A strip of land running along the Adriatic coast of Italy.
[c] Lucius Annaeus Seneca, the philosopher.
[d] 1 *culleus* = 20 *amphorae* = about 137 U.S. (114 Brit.) gallons.
[e] See Introd., p. xi.
[f] Perhaps the two *iugera* of grafted vines mentioned in III. 9. 6. For the varying number of vines planted to the *iugerum*, see V. 3.

and that this was the customary yield not in one district alone but also in the country around Faventia[a] and in the Ager Gallicus,[b] which is now annexed to Picenum; in our own times, at any rate, the 3 neighbourhood of Nomentum is illumined by a most distinguished reputation; and especially that part owned by Seneca,[c] a man of outstanding genius and erudition, on whose estates it is learned that every *iugerum* of vineyard has yielded commonly eight *cullei*.[d] For the things that happened in our Ceretanum[e] seem to have been in the nature of a prodigy, in that a certain vine on your place exceeded the number of two thousand clusters, and with me, that eight hundred grafted stocks of less than two years[f] yielded seven *cullei*, or that first-class vineyards produced a hundred amphorae[g] to the *iugerum*, when meadows, pastures, and woodland seem to do very well by the owner if they bring in a hundred *sesterces*[h] for every *iugerum*. For we 4 can hardly recall a time when grain crops, throughout at least the greater part of Italy, returned a yield of four for one.[i] Why, then, is viticulture in disrepute? Not, indeed, through its own fault, but because of human failings, says Graecinus; in the first place because no one takes pains in searching after cuttings, and for that reason most people plant vineyards of the worst sort; and then they do not nourish their vines, once planted, in such a way as

[g] 1 *amphora* = about 6·84 U.S (5·70 Brit.) gallons.

[h] 1 *sestertius* = about 4 cents.

[i] Varro, in the preceding century, speaks (*R.R.* I. 44. 1–2) of grain yields of 10 for 1 (*cum decimo*) in some parts of Italy, of 15 for 1 (*cum quinto decimo*) at some places in Etruria, and of reported yields of a hundredfold (*cum centesimo*) around Sybaris in Italy and at certain places in Syria and Africa

convalescant ac prosiliant, quam retorrescant; sed
5 et si forte adoleverint, neglegenter colunt. Iam illud a principio nihil referre censent, quem locum conserant; immo etiam seligunt [1] deterrimam partem agrorum, tamquam sola sit huic stirpi maxime terra idonea, quae nihil aliud ferre possit. Sed ne ponendi quidem rationem aut perspiciunt, aut perspectam exsequuntur. Tum etiam dotem, id est instrumentum, raro vineis praeparant; cum ea res, si omissa sit, plurimas operas nec minus arcam patris
6 familiae semper exhauriat. Fructum vero plerique quam uberrimum praesentem consectantur, nec provident futuro tempori, sed quasi plane in diem vivant, sic imperant vitibus, et eas ita multis palmitibus onerant, ut posteritati non consulant. Haec omnia vel certe plurima ex his cum commiserunt, quidvis malunt quam suam culpam confiteri; queruntur que non respondere sibi vineta, quae vel per avaritiam vel inscientiam [2] vel per neglegentiam
7 perdiderunt. At si qui [3] cum scientia sociaverint [4] diligentiam, non, ut ego existimo, quadragenas vel certe tricenas,[5] sed ut Graecinus, minimum computans licet, inquit, amphoras vicenas percipient [6]

[1] sedeligunt *S, Sobel.*
[2] inscientiam *cM, vett. edd.*: inscientia *a*: inscientia quae perdiderunt *SA*[1]: inscitia *vulgo*
[3] quis *SAac*: *om. M.*
[4] sociaverit *SAcM, vett. edd.*
[5] *sic Gesn., Schn.*: tricenas vel quadragenas certe *ante Gesn.*: tricenas v. c. ducenas *SA*: tricenas vel ducenas (decenas *cM*) certe *acM.*
[6] percipiant *SA*[1]: percipiunt *a*: percipiet *M.*

to let them gain strength and shoot out before they
wither; and if they do happen to grow, they are careless in the matter of cultivation. Even at the very 5
start they think that it makes no difference what
kind of ground they plant; or rather they pick out
the very worst section of their lands, as though
such ground alone were particularly fit for this
plant because incapable of producing anything else.
Either they do not understand even the method of
setting them or else they fail to put it into practice when they do understand it. Then too, they
seldom have the dowry [a]—that is, the equipment—
in readiness for their vineyards; though this, if neglected, uses up many days of toil and puts a constant
drain on the coffers of the proprietor. Most people, 6
in fact, strive for the richest possible yield at the
earliest moment; they make no provision for the time
to come, but, as if living merely from day to day,
they put such demands upon their vines and load
them so heavily with young shoots as to show no
regard for succeeding generations. After commit-
ting all these acts, or at any rate most of them,
they would rather do anything at all than admit
their own guilt; and they complain that their vineyards do not yield them a return—vineyards which
they themselves have ruined through greed, or
ignorance, or neglect. But any who combine 7
painstaking care with scientific knowledge receive,
not forty, or at least thirty according to my reckoning, but, as Graecinus says, though setting the
lowest estimate, twenty *amphorae* from every *iugerum*,

[a] An expression borrowed from the marriage custom of providing a portion for the bride, for the vine was proverbially "wedded" to its supporting tree.

ex singulis iugeribus, omnis istos, qui faenum suum et holera amplexantur, incremento patrimonii facile superabunt. Nec in hoc errat; quippe ut diligens ratiocinator[1] calculo posito videt id[2] genus agrico-
8 lationis maxime rei familiari conducere. Nam ut amplissimas impensas vineae poscant, non tamen excedunt septem iugera unius operam vinitoris, quem vulgus quidem parvi aeris, vel de lapide noxium posse comparari putat; sed ego plurimorum opinioni dissentiens pretiosum vinitorem in primis esse censeo. Isque licet sit[3] emptus sex, vel potius sestertiis octo milibus, cum ipsum solum septem[4] iugerum totidem milibus nummorum partum, vineasque cum sua dote, id est cum pedamentis et viminibus, binis milibus in singula iugera positas duco, fit tamen[5] in assem consummatum pretium sestertiorum viginti
9 novem milium. Huc accedunt semisses usurarum sestertia tria milia et quadringenti octoginta nummi biennii temporis, quo velut infantia vinearum cessat a fructu. Fit in assem summa sortis et usurarum triginta duorum milium quadringentorum octoginta nummorum. Quod quasi nomen si ut faenerator cum debitore ita rusticus cum vineis suis fecerit, eius summae ut in perpetuum praedictam usuram semissium dominus constituat, percipere[6] debet in annos singulos mille nongentos[7] quinquaginta sestertios nummos; qua computatione vincit tamen reditus septem iugerum, secundum opinionem Graecini, usuram triginta duorum milium quadringentorum

[1] diligenter ratiocinator *SA*[1]: diligenter ratiocinatio *Sobel.*
[2] videre et id *SA*[1]: videt et id *c.*
[3] sit licet *SAa.*
[4] septem *edd.* · octo *SAacM, vett. edd.*
[5] tamen *SAacM, vett. edd.*: tum *vulgo.*
[6] praecipere *c.* [7] noningentos *ac.*

they will easily outdo in the increase of their ancestral estates all those who hold fast to their hay and pot-herbs. And he is not mistaken in this; for, like a careful accountant, he sees, when his calculations are made, that this kind of husbandry is of the greatest advantage to his estate. For, admitting 8
that vineyards demand a very generous outlay, still seven *iugera* require the labour of not more than one vinedresser, upon whom people in general set a low value, thinking that even some malefactor may be acquired from the auction-block;[a] but I, disagreeing with the opinion of the majority, consider a high-priced vinedresser of first importance. And supposing his purchase price to be 6000 or, better, 8000 *sesterces*, when I estimate the seven *iugera* of ground as acquired for just as many thousands of *sesterces*,[b] and that the vineyards with their dowry—that is, with stakes and withes—are set out for 2000 *sesterces* per *iugerum*, still the total cost, reckoned to the last farthing, amounts to 29,000 *sesterces*.
Added to this is interest at six per cent. per annum, 9
amounting to 3480 *sesterces* for the two-year period when the vineyards, in their infancy as it were, are delayed in bearing. The sum total of principal and interest comes to 32,480 *sesterces*. And if the husbandman would enter this amount as a debt against his vineyards just as a moneylender does with a debtor, so that the owner may realize the aforementioned six per cent. interest on that total as a perpetual annuity, he should take in 1950 *sesterces* every year. By this reckoning the return from seven *iugera*, even according to the estimate of Graecinus, exceeds the

[a] Lit the stone, or stone platform, at which slave auctions were held. [b] *I.e.* 7000.

10 octoginta nummorum. Quippe ut deterrimi generis
sint vineae, tamen si cultae, singulos utique culleos
vini singula earum iugera peraequabunt; utque
trecentis nummis quadragenae urnae veneant,[1] quod
minimum pretium est annonae, consummant tamen
septem cullei sestertia duo milia et centum nummos:
11 ea porro summa excedit usuram semissium. Atque
hic calculus quem posuimus, Graecini rationem
continet. Sed nos exstirpanda vineta censemus,
quorum singula iugera minus quam ternos culleos
praebent. Et adhuc tamen sic computavimus, quasi
nullae sint viviradices, quae de pastinato eximantur;
cum sola ea res omnem impensam terreni pretio
suo liberet, si modo non provincialis sed Italicus ager
12 est. Neque id cuiquam[2] dubium esse debet, cum
et nostram et Iulii Attici rationem dispexerit.[3] Nos
iam[4] enim vicena milia malleorum per vineae iugerum
inter ordines pangimus. Ille minus quattuor milibus
deponit: cuius ut vincat ratio, nullus tamen vel
iniquissimus locus non maiorem quaestum reddet
13 quam acceperit impensam; siquidem, ut cultoris
neglegentia sex milia seminum intereant,[5] reliqua tamen decem milia tribus milibus nummorum libenter
et cum lucro redemptorum erunt.[6] Quae summa
tertia parte superat duo milia sestertiorum, quanti
constare iugerum vinearum praediximus; quamquam
nostra cura in tantum iam processit, ut non inviti

[1] teneant *c*.
[2] cuiquam *om. SA, sed add. in marg. A.*
[3] dispexerit *SAacM, et plerique*: dispunxerit *Schn.*
[4] iam *om.* SA^1. [5] ingerunt *acM, et in marg. A.*
[6] redemptorum erunt SA^1, *Schn.*: redemptor emerit A^2*acM, et plerique.*

[a] Rooted cuttings. [b] See Chap. 6, sec. 3, below.

interest on 32,480 *sesterces.* For, assuming that the 10
vineyards are of the very worst sort, still, if taken
care of, they will yield certainly one *culleus* of wine
to the *iugerum*; and even though every forty urns
are sold for 300 *sesterces*, which is the lowest market
price, nevertheless seven *cullei* make a total of 2100
sesterces—a sum far in excess of the interest at six
per cent. And these figures, as we have given 11
them, take account of the calculations of Graecinus.
But our own opinion is that vineyards which yield
less than three *cullei* to the *iugerum* should be rooted
out. And, even so, we have made our calculations
up to this point as if there were no quicksets[a] to be
taken from the trenched ground; though this item
alone, at a favourable price, would clear the entire
cost of the land, if only the land belongs, not to the
provinces, but to Italy. And no one should be 12
skeptical of this statement when he distinguishes
between my method and that of Julius Atticus;
for I am now planting between the rows 20,000
mallet-shoots[b] to every *iugerum* of vineyard, while
he sets out four thousand fewer.[c] Assuming that
his way is the better one, still no ground, even
the most unfavourable, will fail to yield a return
exceeding the expense incurred; since, even though 13
6000 of the plants die through the carelessness of
the vinedresser, still the remaining 10,000 will be
purchased by contract-vineyardists, cheerfully and
at a profit, for 3000 *sesterces.* This sum exceeds
by one third the 2000 *sesterces* which we have
named above as the cost of planting one *iugerum*
of vines, and yet our own management has now
progressed to the point where husbandmen are not

[a] *Cf.* Chap. 16, sec. 3, below.

sestertiis sescenis[1] nummis singula[2] milia vivira-
14 dicis a me rustici mercentur. Sed vix istud alius
praestiterit. Nam nec quisquam nobis facile crediderit tantam in agellis esse nostris abundantiam
vini quantam tu, Silvine, novisti. Mediocre itaque
vulgatumque pretium viviradicis posui, quo celerius
nullo dissentiente perduci possent in nostram sententiam, qui propter ignorantiam genus hoc agricola-
15 tionis reformidant. Sive ergo pastinationis reditus
seu futurarum spes vindemiarum cohortari nos debet
ad positionem vinearum. Quas quoniam docuimus
rationis esse conserere, nunc institutionis earum
praecepta dabimus.

IV. Cui vineta facere cordi est, praecipue caveat
ne alienae potius curae quam suae credere velit,
neve mercetur viviradicem. Sed genus surculi[3]
probatissimum domi conserat, faciatque vitiarium
ex quo possit agrum vineis vestire. Nam quae
peregrina[4] ex diversa regione semina transferuntur,
minus sunt familiaria nostro solo quam vernacula;
eoque velut alienigena reformidant mutatam caeli
2. locique positionem. Sed nec certam generositatis
fidem pollicentur, cum sit incertum, an is, qui con-
seruerit ea, diligenter exploratum probatumque
genus surculi deposuerit. Quamobrem biennii spatium longum esse minime existimandum est, intra

[1] sescenis *S*: sexcenis *Aac*: sexenis *M*: sexcentis *vulgo*.
[2] singulis *SAa*, *vett. edd.*: singuli *c*.
[3] surculis *S* (*alt.* s *expunct.*) *A*.

averse to purchasing quicksets from me at a price
of six hundred *sesterces* a thousand. But anyone 14
else will hardly go beyond the above-named figure;
for no one will readily take our word for it that there
is such a quantity of wine upon our small pieces of
ground as you, Silvinus, know to be the case. For
that reason I have quoted the average and customary
price of quicksets, so that those who, through want
of knowledge, avoid this branch of husbandry, may
be brought over more quickly to my opinion with
no dissenting vote. Therefore either the revenue 15
from ground prepared for planting or the hope of
vintages to come should encourage us in the planting of vines. And now that we have shown that it
is consistent with good business to plant them, we
shall offer directions for putting them in order.

IV. One who has it at heart to make plantations of vines should guard especially against the willingness to entrust them to another's care in preference to his own; and he should not buy quicksets. But he should plant at home shoots of the sort most approved, and should make a nursery of vines from which he may clothe his land with vineyards. For foreign cuttings, transplanted from a different locality, are less at home in our soil than are the native varieties, and for that reason, being strangers, so to speak, they dread a change of climate and
situation; and also they offer no definite assurance 2
of quality, seeing that it is uncertain whether the one who has planted them has set out shoots of a carefully tested and approved variety. Therefore a period of two years must be considered the mini-

[4] perenna (peregryna *in marg. A*) *SA*.

quod utique tempestivitas seminum respondet; cum semper, ut dixi, plurimum rettulerit exquisiti
3 generis stirpem deposuisse. Post haec deinde meminerit accurate locum vineis eligere; de quo cum iudicaverit, maximam diligentiam sciat adhibendam pastinationi. Quam cum peregerit, non minore cura vitem conserat, et cum posuerit[1] summa sedulitate culturae serviat; id enim quasi caput et columen est impensarum, quoniam in eo consistit, melius an sequius terrae mandaverit paterfamilias pecuniam quam[2] in otio tractare. Igitur unum quodque eorum quae[3] proposui, suo iam persequar ordine.

V. Vitiarium neque ieiuna terra neque uliginosa faciendum est, sucosa tamen ac mediocri potius quam pingui; tametsi fere omnes auctores huic rei laetissimum locum destinaverunt. Quod ego minime reor esse pro agricola; nam depositae stirpes[4] valido solo, quamvis celeriter comprehendant atque prosiliant, tamen cum sunt viviradices factae, si in peius[5] transferantur, retorrescunt nec adolescere
2 queunt. Prudentis autem coloni est ex deteriori terra potius in meliorem, quam ex meliore in deteriorem transferre. Propter quod mediocritas in electione loci maxime probatur, quoniam in confinio boni malique posita est. Sive enim postmodum necessitas postulaverit[6] tempestiva semina ieiuno

[1] seruerit *acM*, *et in marg A*.
[2] quam *om. SAacM*, *vett. edd.*
[3] quod *S*.
[4] spinae SA^1.
[5] si in peius] si impetus *SA* : sint priusquam *c*, *edd. ante Gesn.* : et fractae sunt priusquam *in marg. A* : et fractae priusquam *M*.
[6] postulat SA^1 : postularit A^2a.

mum time within which the quality of the cuttings can certainly show itself; though, as I have said, it has always been of the greatest importance to set out stock of carefully selected origin. Next after this 3
he should remember to make a careful choice of a site for his vineyards; and when he has come to a decision on this point he should know that the greatest pains must be employed in trenching the ground. After he has finished the trenching he should use no less care in the planting of the vine, and after the planting he should attend with greatest diligence to the matter of cultivation; for this is, so to speak, the chief and crowning point of the investment, since on it rests the decision as to whether it has been better or worse for the proprietor to commit his money to the soil rather than to employ it in idleness. Therefore I shall discuss in their proper order each of those matters which I have proposed.

V. A vine-nursery should be established in ground that is neither hungry nor wet, but moist and of medium quality rather than fat; though nearly all authorities have designated a very fertile soil for this purpose. This I consider as not at all to the advantage of the husbandman; for even though the cuttings quickly take root and shoot up when planted in strong soil, yet if transferred to poorer soil when they become quicksets, they wither and cannot grow to maturity. Moreover, it is the mark 2
of a wise husbandman to transplant from poorer ground to better rather than from better to poorer. For this reason an intermediate quality is most approved in the choice of a site, because it stands on the border line between good and bad. For if necessity afterwards demands the setting of the

solo committere, non magnam sentient[1] differentiam, cum ex mediocri materia[2] in exilem translata sunt; sive laetior ager conserendus est, longe celerius in
3 ubertate coalescunt. Rursus tenuissimo solo vitiarium facere minime rationis est, quoniam malleolorum pars maior deperit, et quae superest, tarde fit idonea translationi. Ergo mediocris et modice siccus ager vitiario[3] est aptissimus; isque bipalio prius subigi debet, quae est altitudo pastinationis,[4] cum in duos pedes et semissem convertitur humus; ac deinde tripedaneis relictis spatiis, per quae semina excolantur, in singulis ordinibus, qui ducenos quadragenos pedes obtinent,[5] sesceni[6] malleoli pangendi
4 sunt. Is numerus consummat per totum iugerum seminum milia quattuor et viginti.[7] Verum hanc curam praevenit inquisitio et electio malleolorum. Nam ut saepe iam rettuli, quasi fundamentum est praedictae rei, probatissimum genus stirpis deponere.

VI. Sed electio dupliciter facienda est; non enim solum fecundam esse matrem satis est, ex qua semina petuntur, sed adhibenda ratio est subtilior, ut ex his partibus trunci sumantur, quae et genitales sunt et
2 maxime fertiles. Vitis autem fecunda, cuius pro-

[1] sentiunt *SAac, vett. edd*
[2] materia *SAacM*, *vett. edd.*: terra *vulgo.*
[3] seminari *SA*, *sed* vitiario *in marg. A.*
[4] pastionis *S.*
[5] optime (optinent *in marg. A*) *SAa.*
[6] sexceni *ac, et in marg. A*: sexeni *M*: septeni *SA*: sexcenteni *plerique edd.*: octogeni *Schn.*
[7] milia quattuor (quatuor *ac*) et viginti *SAacM, plerique edd.*: millia tria et ducenta *Schn*

---

[a] The *bipalium* had a cross-bar fitted to the handle at some distance above the blade, which allowed the spade to be pushed

young plants at the proper time in lean ground, they will be conscious of no great change when transferred from mediocre to poor soil; or if a more fertile field is to be planted, they gain strength far more quickly in the rich ground. On the other hand, 3
it is not at all consistent with reason to make a nursery of vines in the very poorest ground, since the majority of the slips die, and such as do survive are slow in becoming fit for transplanting. A piece of average and moderately dry ground, then, is best suited for the nursery; and it should first be worked with the trenching-spade,[a] which equals the depth of the trenching when the ground is turned up to two and one-half feet. Then, leaving three-foot spaces for the cultivation of the plants, 600 cuttings are to be set in each of the rows which measure 240 feet. This number makes a total of 24,000 plants to the 4
iugerum.[b] But the examination and choice of shoots takes precedence of this care. For, as I have often said before, the planting of the most approved kind of stock is the foundation, so to speak, of the aforesaid matter.

VI. But the choice must be made with two considerations in mind; for it is not enough merely that the mother vine from which the cuttings are sought should be prolific, but a more discriminating method must be employed, that they may be taken from those parts of her body which are both generative and especially fruitful. Moreover, the prolific vine 2

by the foot two spits deep—twice the depth of the ordinary spade (*pala*).

[b] The *iugerum* would thus measure 240 × 120 feet (V. 2. 3), and the cuttings would be set about five inches apart in the row.

geniem studemus summittere, non tantum debet eo aestimari, quod uvas compluris exigit, potest enim trunci vastitate id accidere et frequentia [1] palmitum; nec tamen eam feracem dixerim, cuius singulae uvae [2] in singulis sarmentis conspiciuntur. Sed si per unumquemque pampinum maior numerus uvarum dependet; si ex singulis gemmis compluribus materiis cum fructu germinat; si denique etiam e duro virgam [3] aliquibus [4] racemis citat; si etiam nepotum fructu [5] gravida est; ea sine dubitatione ferax
3 destinari debet legendo malleolo. Malleolus autem novellus est palmes innatus prioris anni flagello, cognominatusque ad similitudinem,[6] quod in ea parte, qua [7] deciditur ex vetere sarmento, prominens utrimque mallei speciem praebet. Hunc ex fecundissima stirpe [8] legendum censemus omni tempore quo vineae putantur, ac super terram gemmis tribus vel quattuor extantibus diligenter obruendum loco modice umido non uliginoso; dum tamen antiquissimum sit considerare ne vitis, ex qua is sumitur, ancipitem floris habeat eventum, ne difficulter acinus [9] ingrandescat, ne aut praecoquem [10] aut serae maturitatis fructum adferat. Nam illa volucribus,

[1] accidere frequentis *SA*[1]. [2] vite *c*.
[3] etiam me dura virgo *SA* : etiam in dura virga *a*.
[4] aliquis *SA*.
[5] nec totum fructum *SA*.
[6] a similitudine rei *acM*, *et vulgo ante Schn.*
[7] qua *S*, *Schn.* : quae *A*, *et vulgo* : que *acM*.
[8] statione *SA*. [9] acinis *SAc*.
[10] praecoquis *SAc* : percoquis *a*.

whose offspring we wish to rear should not be valued merely because it puts forth grape clusters in great quantity, for this may be due to the large size of the stock and the great number of fruiting canes;[a] though I should not call that a fruitful vine where only one cluster is seen to each cane. But if a larger number of clusters hang upon every young shoot; if from every eye on its many mature branches it sprouts out with fruit; if, finally, it also puts out from its firm wood a green shoot with some clusters; if, too, it is heavy with the fruit of its secondary shoots;[b] such a vine, fruitful beyond doubt, should be marked out for the gathering of mallet-shoots. The mallet-shoot, moreover, is a young shoot grow- 3
ing out of a cane of the year before; it is named according to its resemblance, because, projecting on both sides in that part where it is cut from the old branch, it has the appearance of a mallet. Our opinion is that this should be taken from the most prolific stock every time that the vines are pruned, and carefully planted, with three or four eyes showing above ground, in soil that is moderately moist but not wet; if only it be our first consideration that the vine from which the shoot is taken be not uncertain in its flowering, that its berries have no difficulty in growing big, and that it bear fruit which is neither early nor too late in ripening. For the former is damaged by birds, and the latter by

[a] *Cf.* V. 6. 29; Festus, 246 L, "*palmites*" *vitium sarmenta appellantur, quod in modum palmarum humanarum virgulas quasi digitos edunt*; Isidore, *Orig.* XVII. 5. 9.

[b] *Nepotes*, laterals or secondary shoots, lit. "grand-children" of the *flagellum* or cane in the order *flagellum-pampinus-nepos*, springing from the axil of the *pampinus* or leaf-stalk.

4 haec etiam tempestatibus hiemis infestatur. Tale porro genus non una [1] comprobatur vindemia; potest enim vel anni proventu vel aliis de causis etiam naturaliter infecunda vitis semel exuberare. Sed ubi plurium [2] velut emeritis annorum stipendiis fides surculo constitit, nihil dubitandum est de fecunditate. Nec tamen ultra quadriennium talis extenditur inquisitio; id enim tempus fere virentium generositatem declarat,[3] quo sol in eandem partem signiferi per eosdem [4] numeros redit, per quos cursus sui principium ceperat.[5] Quem circuitum meatus dierum integrorum mille quadringentorum sexaginta unius ἀποκατάστασιν [6] vocant studiosi rerum caelestium.

VII. Sed certum habeo, P. Silvine, iamdudum te tacitum requirere cuius generis sit ista fecunda vitis, quam nos tam accurate describimus, anne [7] de his aliqua significetur, quae vulgo nunc [8] habentur feracissimae. Plurimi namque Bituricam, multi Spioniam. quidam Basilicam, non nulli Arcelacam
2 laudibus efferunt. Nos quoque [9] haec genera testimonio nostro non fraudamus,[10] sunt enim largissimi vini; sed proposuimus docere vineas eius modi conserere, quae nec minus uberes fructus praedictis generibus adferant, et sint pretiosi saporis, velut

[1] non una] naturae *SA*.
[2] plurium *Ald.*, *Schn.*: plurimis *SAa*, *Gesn.*: pluribus *cM*.
[3] desiderat *a*.
[4] signiferi per eosdem] signifer eosdem *SA*: signi per eosdem *acM*.
[5] coeperat *A*, *et vulgo ante Schn.*
[6] *graec. om. spat. relict. acM*, *deinde* id est (*in abbr.*) reversionem vocant *a*.
[7] ac ne *A*, *Ald.*, *Gesn.*: ne *a*.
[8] non *cM*, *Ald.*, *Gesn.*
[9] efferunt. Nos quoque *om. SA*.

wintry storms as well. Moreover, such a kind of 4
vine is not proved by one vintage; for even a vine that is naturally unfruitful may produce an abundant yield a single time, either because of the bountifulness of the year or for other reasons. But when confidence in the slip has been established by the completion of several years of campaigning, as it were, there can be no doubt as to its fruitfulness. Yet such an examination is not carried beyond a period of four years; for the quality of plants usually becomes manifest in that period of time during which the sun returns to the same division of the zodiac through the same signs by which it began its circuit—a periodical course of fourteen hundred and sixty-one entire days, which students of celestial matters call ἀποκατάστασις.[a]

VII. But I am sure, Publius Silvinus, that you have long been inquiring in your own mind to what variety that fruitful vine belongs which we are at such pains to describe—whether one of those which are commonly regarded as most prolific nowadays is meant. For very many people are high in their praise of the Bituric, many of the Spionian, some of
the Basilic, and several of the Arcelacan. We, too, 2
do not deprive these varieties of our approbation, for they yield a very great quantity of wine; but we have resolved to teach the planting of vines of a sort that will produce fruit in no less abundance than the above-mentioned varieties, and that have

[a] *apocatastasis*, meaning the "restoration" of a previous condition.

---

[10] *sic acM*: non fraudamus *om. SA*: non fraudamus testimonio nostro *vulgo*.

Aminei, vel certe non procul ab eo gustu. Cui nostrae sententiae scio paene omnium agricolarum diversam esse opinionem, quae de Amineis inveterata longo iam tempore convaluit, tamquam
3 natali[1] et ingenita sterilitate laborantibus: quo magis nobis ex alto repetita compluribus exemplis firmanda ratio est, quae desidia nec minus imprudentia colonorum damnata, et velut ignorantiae tenebris occaecata luce veritatis caruit. Quare non intempestivum est nos ad ea praeverti, quae videntur hunc publicum errorem corrigere posse.[2]

VIII. Igitur si rerum naturam, Publi Silvine, velut acrioribus mentis oculis intueri velimus, reperiemus[3] parem legem fecunditatis eam[4] dixisse virentibus, atque hominibus ceterisque animalibus; nec sic aliis nationibus regionibusve proprias tribuisse dotes ut aliis in totum similia munera denegaret. Quibusdam gentibus numerosam progenerandi[5] sobolem dedit, ut Aegyptiis et Afris, quibus gemini partus familiares ac paene sollemnes sunt; sed et Italici generis esse voluit eximiae fecunditatis Albanas
2 Curiatiae[6] familiae trigeminorum matres. Ger-

[1] naturali *c.*

[2] quae spectandae sint qualitas in eo solo quod vineis destinaveris *post* posse *inserunt SAc, et in rubr. M.*

[3] reperiamus *S*: repperiamus *A.*

[4] eadem *A.*

[5] generandi *SA, vett. edd.*

[6] Curiatiae *edd.*: aequitiae *SA*: equitiae *acM.*

---

[a] Pliny (*N.H.* VII. 33) mentions several cases of multiple births, including the famous sets of triplets, the Roman Horatii and the Alban Curiatii (Livy, I. 24–26). A woman in the Peloponnesus, he says, four times gave birth to quintu-

a rich flavour like that of the Aminean, or at least not far from that taste. I am aware that the belief of nearly all agriculturists is at variance with my way of thinking; a belief which, as regards Aminean vines, has become deep-rooted and has gained strength through length of time, as though they suffered from a native and inborn unfruitfulness. For this reason there is greater necessity on our part 3 of fortifying with many examples a method recalled from times past—a method which, being condemned through the slothfulness as well as the indiscretion of husbandmen and obscured, as it were, by the darkness of ignorance, has been deprived of the light of truth. The time is not unsuitable, then, for us to turn our attention first to considerations which seem able to correct this general misunderstanding.

VIII. Therefore, Publius Silvinus, if we will look at nature through the keener eyes of the mind, so to speak, we shall find that she has established an equable law of fertility for all green things even as for human beings and other living creatures; and that she has not so bestowed special endowments upon some nations or regions as to deny like gifts altogether to others. To some peoples she has granted the gift of producing numerous progeny, as to the Egyptians and Africans, with whom the birth of twins is common and almost an annual occurrence; but of Italian stock, too, she has willed that there be women of extraordinary fertility—Alban women of the Curiatian family, mothers of three children at one birth.[a]

plets, while an Egyptian woman produced septuplets. The fertility of the Egyptians is attributed to their drinking of the waters of the *fetifer* (fertilizing) Nile.

maniam decoravit altissimorum hominum exercitibus; sed et alias gentes non in totum fraudavit praecipuae staturae viris. Nam et Cicero[1] testis est Romanum fuisse civem Naevium Pollionem pede[2] longiorem quam quemquam longissimum; et nuper ipsi videre potuimus in apparatu pompae Circensium ludorum Iudaeae gentis hominem proceriorem celsissimo
3 Germano. Transeo ad pecudes. Armentis sublimibus insignis Mevania est, Liguria parvis; sed et Mevaniae bos humilis et Liguriae non numquam taurus eminentis[3] staturae conspicitur. India perhibetur molibus ferarum mirabilis; pares tamen in hac terra vastitate beluas progenerari quis neget, cum intra moenia nostra natos animadvertamus
4 elephantos? Sed ad genera frugum redeo. Mysiam Libyamque largis aiunt abundare frumentis, nec tamen Apulos Campanosque agros opimis[4] defici segetibus; Tmolon et Corycon flore croceo,[5] Iudaeam et Arabiam pretiosis odoribus inlustrem haberi; sed nec nostram civitatem praedictis egere stirpibus, quippe compluribus locis urbis iam casiam frondentem conspicimus, iam tuream plantam, florentisque[6]
5 hortos myrrha et croco. His tamen exemplis nimi-

[1] M. Tullius Cicero *vulgo*: M. Tullius *deest codd., vett. edd.*
[2] pedem *SAcM.*
[3] eminenti *SA.*
[4] optimis *SA, vett. edd.*
[5] flore croceo *Aac, vett. edd., Gesn.*: flore roceo *S*: florere croco *Schn. et alii.*
[6] tam maturae (-e *a*) ampliatam frontisque (florentesque *a*) *SAa.*

She has adorned Germany with armies of exceedingly tall men; but she has not wholly deprived other nations of men of exceptional stature. For Cicero bears witness that there was once a Roman citizen, Naevius Pollio,[a] who was a foot taller than the tallest of other men; and recently we ourselves might have seen, among the exhibits of the procession at the games in the Circus, a man of the Jewish race who was of greater stature than the tallest German. I pass to cattle. Mevania[b] is famous for its herds of tall cattle, Liguria for small; but an ox of low stature is seen now and then in Mevania, and a bull of towering proportions in Liguria. India is said to excite astonishment for the hugeness of its wild animals; yet who will deny that beasts of equally vast size are bred in this land, when we consider that elephants are brought forth within our own walls? But I return to various kinds of crops. They say that Mysia and Libya produce enormous quantities of grain, but that the fields of Apulia and Campania are not wanting in rich crops; that Tmolus and Corycus[c] are considered famous for the saffron-flower, and Judea and Arabia for their precious scents; but that our own community is not destitute of the aforesaid plants, for in many sections of the city we see at one time cassia putting forth its leaves, again the frankincense plant, and gardens blooming with myrrh and saffron. Surely these examples

(margin: 2 beside line 1; 3 beside "of greater stature…"; 4 beside "But I return…"; 5 beside "with myrrh…")

[a] *Cf.* Pliny, *N.H.* VII. 74. It has been conjectured that the source of the story is a lost work of Cicero, *De Admirandis*, mentioned by Pliny, *N.H.* XXXI. 12.

[b] Modern Bevagna in Umbria, a region long famous for its huge white cattle.

[c] Tmolus, a mountain in Phrygia, *cf.* Vergil, *Georg.* I. 56. Corycus, a town and promontory in Cilicia.

ium admonemur, curae mortalium obsequentissimam esse Italiam, quae paene totius orbis fruges adhibito studio colonorum ferre didicerit; quo minus addubitemus[1] de eo fructu, qui velut[2] indigena pecularisque et vernaculus est huius soli. Neque[3] enim dubium est[4] Massici Surrentinique et Albani, atque Caecubi agri vites omnium, quas terra sustinet, nobilitate[5] vini principes esse.

IX. Fecunditas ab his forsitan desideretur; sed et haec adiuvari potest cultoris industria. Nam si, ut[6] paulo ante rettuli, benignissima rerum omnium parens natura quasque gentis atque terras ita muneribus propriis ditavit, ut tamen ceteras non in universum similibus dotibus fraudaret, cur eam dubitemus etiam in vitibus praedictam legem servasse? Ut quamvis earum genus aliquod praecipue fecundum esse voluerit, tamquam Bituricum aut Basilicum,[7] non tamen sic Amineum sterile reddiderit ut ex multis milibus eius ne paucissimae quidem vites fecundae, tamquam in Italicis hominibus Albanae
2 illae sorores, reperiri possint. Id[8] autem cum sit verisimile,[9] tum etiam verum esse nos docuit experimentum, cum et in Ardeatino agro, quem multis temporibus ipsi ante possedimus, et in Carseolano itemque in[10] Albano generis Aminei vites notatas[11]

[1] addubitemus *acM, Brusch., Sobel*: adubitemus *A* (a *in ras.*) *S*: dubitemus *Schn.*: addubitamus *Ald., Gesn.*

[2] velut *acM, edd.*: vel *SA, Sobel.*

[3] Neque *om. SAa.* [4] est *om. SAaM.*

[5] nobilitate *M*: quia (non c) nobilitate *ac*: non vilitate *S*: non utilitate *A*: in nobilitate *edd.*

[6] *sic vulgo*: nam sicut *acM*: nisi aut *SA.*

[7] valiscum *SAac.* [8] ita *SA.*

[9] sint avari simile *SA.*

[10] in *om. SA, Sobel.*

remind us that Italy is most responsive to care bestowed by mankind, in that she has learned to produce the fruits of almost the entire world when her husbandmen have applied themselves to the task. Therefore our doubts should be lessened as to that fruit which is a native, as it were, belonging to and born of our soil. For there is no doubt that, of all the vines that the earth sustains, those of the Massic, Surrentine, Alban, and Caecuban lands hold first place in the excellence of their wine.

IX. The fruitfulness of these vines may leave something to be desired, but even this may be aided by diligence on the part of the vine-dresser. For, as I said a little before, if nature, that most bounteous parent of all things, has endowed every people and land with their own peculiar gifts, though in such a way as not to deprive others entirely of like endowments, why should we doubt that she has observed the aforesaid rule also in the case of vines? So that, although she has willed that some varieties be especially prolific, such as the Bituric and Basilic, yet she has not made the Aminean variety so barren that, of many thousands of them, there may not be found at least a very few fruitful vines, just as those Alban sisters among the humankind of Italy. Not 2
only would this be highly probable, but what is more, experience has taught us the truthfulness of it; for on my place at Ardea, which I owned many years ago, and also on my estates at Carseoli and Alba,[a] I had marked vines of the Aminean variety,

[a] Ardea, Carseoli, and Alba were ancient towns of Latium.

---

[11] notatas *Sa, Sobel*; *quam lectionem probavit Schn.*: notatis *A*: notas *cM*: huiusmodi notae *vulgo*.

habuerimus, numero quidem perpaucas, verum ita fertiles ut in iugo singulae ternas urnas praeberent, in pergulis autem singulae denas amphoras perae-
3 quarent. Nec incredibilis debet in Amineis haec videri fecunditas.[1] Nam quemadmodum Terentius Varro, et ante eum Marcus Cato posset [2] adfirmare, sescenas [3] urnas priscis cultoribus singula vinearum iugera fudisse, si fecunditas Amineis defuisset, quas plerumque solas antiqui noverant? Nisi si putamus ea quae nuper ac modo plane [4] longinquis regionibus arcessita [5] notitiae nostrae sunt tradita, Biturici generis aut Basilici vineta eos coluisse, cum vetustissimas quasque vineas adhuc existimemus Amineas.
4 Si quis ergo tales, quales paulo ante possedisse me rettuli, Amineas pluribus vindemiis exploratas notet, ut ex his malleolos feracissimos eligat, possit is pariter generosas vineas et uberes efficere. Nihil enim dubium est quin ipsa natura subolem matri similem esse voluerit. Unde etiam pastor ille in Bucolicis ait,

> Sic canibus catulos similes, sic matribus haedos
> Noram.[6]

5 Unde sacrorum certaminum studiosi pernicissimarum quadrigarum [7] semina diligenti observatione custodiunt, et spem futurarum victoriarum concipiunt propagata subole generosi armenti. Nos quoque

[1] videri fecunditas *SAacM* : fecunditas videri *vulgo*.
[2] posset *SAac* : possent *vulgo*.
[3] sescenas *scripsi* (*cf.* III. 3. 2) : sexenas *M* : sexcentenas *a*, *edd.* : septenas *SAc*.
[4] plane *edd.* : palaeae *S* : paleae (-e *ac*) *AacM*.
[5] accersita *SAacM*
[6] Noram *om. SAac, vett. edd.*
[7] quadrigenarum *SA* : *om. c*.

very few in number, to be sure, but so fruitful that on a trellis each of them yielded three *urnae*, while on pergolas they produced ten *amphorae* to each vine. And this fruitfulness in Aminean vines 3 should not seem beyond belief. For how could Terentius Varro, and Marcus Cato before him, maintain that every *iugerum* of vineyard yielded the old-time husbandmen six hundred *urnae* of wine,[a] if fruitfulness was wanting in the Amineans—the only vines, for the most part, with which the ancients were acquainted? Unless, despite our belief up to this time that our most ancient vines are the Amineans, we are to suppose that they cultivated vineyards of the Bituric or Basilic varieties, vines which, being but recently indeed imported from far distant countries, have just come to our notice. Therefore if anyone would, for several vintages, 4 search out and mark such Aminean vines as I have said were in my possession not long ago, so as to take from them the most fertile cuttings, he could produce vineyards of equal excellence and productiveness. For there is no doubt that nature herself has decreed that the offspring shall resemble the mother. Hence it is, too, that the shepherd in the *Bucolics* says,

> So whelps like dogs; so kids, I knew,
> Were like unto their dams.[b]

And hence those who contend in the sacred games 5 protect with watchful care the progeny of their swiftest race-horses, and upon the multiplying of offspring of noble stock they base their hope of future victories. We too, for a reason like theirs

[a] *Cf.* Chap. 3, sec. 2, above. [b] Vergil, *Ecl.* I. 23.

pari ratione velut Olympionicarum equarum, ita feracissimarum Aminearum seminibus electis largae vindemiae spem capiamus. Neque est quod temporis tarditas quemquam [1] deterreat; nam quidquid
6 morae est, in exploratione surculi absumitur. Ceterum cum fecunditas vitis comprobata est, celerrime insitionibus ad maximam numerum perducitur. Eius rei testimonium tu praecipue, Silvine,[2] perhibere nobis potes, cum pulchre memineris, a me duo iugera vinearum intra tempus biennii ex una praecoque vite, quam in Ceretano [3] tuo possides, insitione
7 facta consummata. Quemnam igitur existimas vitium numerum intra tantundem temporis interseri posse duorum iugerum malleolis, cum sint ipsa duo iugera unius vitis progenies? Quare si, ut dixi, laborem et curam velimus adhibere, facile praedicta ratione tam feraces Aminei generis vineas constituemus, quam Biturici aut Basilici: tantum rettulerit,[4] ut in transferendis seminibus similem statum caeli locique et ipsius vitis habitum observemus; quoniam [5] plerumque degenerat surculus, si aut situs agri aut aeris qualitas repugnat, aut etiam si ex arbore in
8 iugum defertur. Itaque de frigidis in frigida, de calidis in similia, de vineis [6] in vineas transferemus. Magis tamen ex frigido statu stirps [7] Aminea potest calidum sustinere, quam ex calido frigidum; quoniam cum omne vitis genus tum maxime praedictum

[1] tarditas quam quemquam *c*.
[2] Silvine *SAacM* : Publi Silvine *edd.*
[3] cereno (ta *suprascr. A*) *SA* : cerretano *ac*.
[4] rettulit *A*. [5] cum *acM*, *vett. edd.*
[6] vinetis *SAacM*. [7] stirpis *ac* : status stirpis *SA*.

[a] By grafting scions of the proved vine on a large number of unproved stocks.

in selecting the progeny of victorious Olympic mares, should base our hope of a bountiful vintage upon the selection of progeny of the most fruitful Amineans. And there is no reason why the tediousness of the time required should discourage anyone; for any delay that occurs is taken up in the testing of the shoot. But when the fruitfulness of the 6
vine has been proved, it is very quickly raised to a very large number by ingrafting.[a] You especially, Silvinus, can bear me out in this, since you will readily recall that I completed the planting of two *iugera* of vineyard within two years time by making grafts from one early-ripe vine belonging to you on your place at Caere.[b] What number 7
of vines, then, do you think could be grafted within the same length of time with shoots taken from two *iugera*, when these two *iugera* are themselves the offspring of one vine? Therefore, as I have said, if we will exercise industry and care we shall easily, by the aforesaid method, establish vineyards of Aminean vines as fruitful as those of the Bituric or Basilic varieties: only it will be of importance, in transplanting the sets, to give heed to like conditions of climate and situation and to the habit of the vine itself; since a cutting is usually impaired in quality if the situation of the ground or climatic conditions are distasteful to it, or even if it is transferred from tree to trellis. Accordingly, we shall 8
transplant from cold places to cold, from warm to the like, and from open vineyards to open vineyards. Yet Aminean stock can better endure the change from a cold to a warm situation than from a warm to a cold; because every kind of vine, and especially that

[b] See Chap. 3, sec. 3, above.

naturaliter laetatur tepore potius quam frigore.
9 Sed et qualitas soli plurimum iuvat, ut ex macro aut mediocri transducatur in melius. Nam quod adsuetum est pingui, nullo modo maciem terrae patitur, nisi saepius stercores. Atque haec de cura eligendi malleoli praecepimus; nunc illud proprie specialiter,[1] ut non solum fecundissima[2] vite, sed et vitis[3] parte feracissima semina eligantur.

X. Feracissima autem semina sunt, non ut veteres auctores crediderunt,[4] extrema pars eius,[5] quod caput vitis appellant, id est, ultimum et productissimum flagellum; nam in eo quoque falluntur agricolae. Sed erroris est causa prima species et numerus uvarum, qui plerumque conspicitur[6] in[7] productissimo sarmento. Quae res nos decipere non[8] debet; id enim accidit non palmitis ingenita fertilitate, sed loci opportunitate, quia reliquas trunci partes umor omnis et alimentum quod a solo ministratur, transcur-
2 rit, dum ad ultimum perveniat. Naturali enim spiritu omne alimentum virentis quasi quaedam anima per medullam trunci veluti siphonem,[9] quam diabeten vocant mechanici, trahitur in summum; quo cum pervenerit,[10] ibi consistit, atque consumitur. Unde etiam materiae vehementissimae reperiuntur aut

[1] specialiter *inclusit Gesn. veluti glossam*: spectabitur *Ursinus.*

[2] ex *ante* fecundissima *acM, et vulgo*; *om. SA, Sobel.*

[3] sed et vitis *SAac, vett. edd., Sobel*: sed e vitis *M*: sed etiam e vitis *vulgo.*

[4] crediderunt *SAac, Brusch.*: tradiderunt *M, plerique cett. edd.*

[5] est *SAa*: *om. cM.* [6] conficitur *S.*

[7] in *om. SA, deinde* prudentissimo *A.* [8] non *om. SAc.*

[9] per (*om. SAacM, vett. edd.*) siphonem *vulgo*: si fons *SA*, *ad* si fonnem *corr. A.*

[10] pervenit *SA*^{1}.

just mentioned, has a natural fondness for warmth rather than cold. But the quality of the soil, too, is 9
of very great assistance, so that the transfer should be made from lean or ordinary ground to a better sort; for a vine which has been accustomed to rich soil can in no way endure lean ground unless you manure it rather frequently. And these precepts we have given, in general, as to care in the choice of cuttings; next it is proper to advise in particular that slips be selected, not only from the most prolific vine, but also from the most fruitful part of that vine.

X. Now, the most fruitful cuttings are not, as ancient authorities supposed, the extreme part of the vine—what they call its head, that is, the outermost and most extended shoot; for in this also husbandmen are mistaken. But the reason for this misapprehension lies in the prime appearance of the shoot and in the number of clusters very often seen on the longest branch. But we should not be deceived in this matter; for it comes about, not through the natural fertility of that branch, but through favourableness of location; because all the moisture and nourishment that is supplied by the soil courses through the other portions of the stem until it arrives at the tip. For by natural respiration all 2
the nourishment of a green plant is drawn, as a sort of vital breath, into the highest point, passing through the pith of the stem as though through a siphon, which mechanics call *diabetes*;[a] and when it arrives at that point, it halts there and is consumed. Hence it is that the most vigorous growth is found either in

[a] So called, no doubt, because the liquid passes through (δια + βαίνω) the outstretched legs of the siphon.

3 in capite vitis aut in crure vicino radicibus. Sed et hae steriles,[1] quae e duro citantur,[2] ac duplici ex causa robustae[3] sunt, quod a fetu vacant, quodque ex proximo terrae integro atque inlibato suco aluntur; et illae fertiles ac firmae, quia e tenero prorepunt, et quidquid, ut supra dixi, ad eas alimenti pervenit, individuum est. Mediae sunt macerrimae, quia transcurrit hinc parte aliqua interceptus,
4 illinc ad[4] se tractus umor. Non debet igitur ultimum flagellum quasi fecundum observari, etiam si plurimum adferat, siquidem loci ubertate in fructum cogitur; sed id sarmentum quod media vite situm, nec importuna quidem parte deficit, ac numeroso fetu benignitatem suam ostendit. Hic surculus translatus rarius degenerat, quoniam ex deteriore statu meliorem sortitur; sive enim pastinato deponitur, sive trunco inseritur, largioribus satiatur[5]
5 alimentis quam prius, cum esset in egeno. Itaque custodiemus ut e[6] praedictis locis, quos umeros rustici vocant, semina legamus, ea tamen quae attulisse[7] fructum antea[8] animadverterimus.[9] Nam si fetu vacua sint, quamvis laudabilem partem vitis nihil censemus ad feracitatem conferre malleolo. Quare vitiosissima est eorum agricolarum opinio, qui

[1] stirpes *cM, edd. ante Schn.*
[2] duro utantur (e *om.*) *SA.*
[3] probate *acM* : probatae *edd. ante Schn.*
[4] a *c, edd. ante Schn.* : in lineas etractus *a.*
[5] largioribus satiatur *om. SA.*
[6] e *SA* : a *acM, All., Gesn.* : ex *Schn.*
[7] ea quae tamen tulisse (utilisse *A*) *SA* : ea *om. cM, edd. ante Schn.* : tamen *om. a.*
[8] antea *om. SAaM.*
[9] animadvertemus *SA.*

[a] Lit. "leg."

the head of the vine or in the main stem [a] close to the roots. More than that, the latter shoots, those that 3
spring from the hard wood, are sterile, and yet they have a two-fold reason for their vigour, in that they do not bear fruit, and because they derive their nourishment from the full and undiminished flow of sap next to the ground; and the former are fruitful and strong because they sprout from young wood, and because, as I stated above, any nourishment that comes to them is not shared with others. The intermediate shoots are the leanest because the sap hastens past them, being partially cut off below and drawn to itself above. Therefore the leading shoot 4
should not be regarded as fruitful even though it may bear much fruit, since it is forced into bearing by the fertility of its situation; but that branch should be considered fruitful which, situated in the middle of the vine, does not fail in even that unfavourable place but displays its bounteousness through numerous offspring. Such a shoot, when transplanted, seldom degenerates, since it passes from a worse to a better lot; for whether set out in trenched ground, or grafted on a stock, it is fed fat with nourishment in greater abundance than before, when it was on scant rations. Accordingly, we shall take pains 5
to select propagating shoots from the places just mentioned, which country people call *umeri*,[b] but such canes as we shall have previously observed to have borne fruit. For if they are destitute of fruit, our opinion is that this part of the vine, much as it is to be commended, contributes nothing to the fruitfulness of the cutting. It is, therefore, a very mistaken notion that is held by those farmers who believe that

[b] *I.e.* "shoulders." *Cf. De Arb.* 3. 1, 20. 1.

minimum referre credunt quot[1] uvas sarmentum habuerit, dum et[2] ex vite fertili legatur et non ex duro trunco enatum, quod pampinarium vocant.

6 Haec autem opinio, quae orta est ex inscientia[3] seminum eligendorum, primum parum fecundas vineas, deinde etiam nimis steriles reddit. Quis enim omnino iam per tam longam seriem annorum agricolae malleolum legenti[4] praecepit ea, quae paulo ante rettulimus? Immo quis non imprudentissimum quemque, et eum qui nihil aliud operis facere valeat, huic negotio delegat? Itaque ex hac consuetudine veniunt imprudentissimi ad rem maxime necessariam, deinde etiam infirmissimi; nam inutilissimus[5] quisque, ut dixi, qui nullum alium laborem
7 ferre queat, huic officio applicatur. Is porro etiam si quam scientiam eligendi malleoli habet, eam propter infirmitatem dissimulat, ac superponit; et ut numerum, quem vilicus imperavit, explere possit, nihil curiose nihil religiose administrat. Unumque est ei propositum, peragere laboris sui pensum; cum tamen, ut et sciat, et quod sciat[6] exsequatur, hoc solum praeceptum a magistris accipit,[7] ne pampi-

[1] quod *SAac.*

[2] et *SA, Sobel*; *om. acM, edd.*

[3] inscientia *SAcM, vett. edd.*: scientia *a*: inscitia *vulgo.*

[4] agricolae m. legenti *AcM, et vulgo*: agricola m. legentibus *Sa, Schn.*

[5] infirmissimi nam inutilissimus *ScM*: infirmissimam inultissimus *a*: ad rem . . . infirmissimi *om.*, *deinde* nam inutilissimus *A*. infirmissimi. Nam et inutilissimus *Ald., Gesn.*: in firmissimam inutilissimus *vett. edd.*: infirmissimus et inutilissimus *Schn.*

[6] sciat *SAacM*: scit *vulgo.*

[7] accipit *SAac, vett. edd.*: accepit *M, Ald., Gesn.*: acceperit *Ursinus, Schn.*

it makes very little difference how many clusters a branch may have borne, if only it is taken from a fruitful vine and is not one that sprouted from the hard wood of the stock,—what they call *pampinarium*.[a]

This notion, however, arising from ignorance in the 6
matter of selecting cuttings, causes vineyards to have, first, too little fruitfulness, and then too much barrenness. For who, indeed, over what is now a long span of years, has laid down for the farmer, as he was selecting his cuttings, these precepts which we have just now set forth? More than that, who does not assign to this occupation whoever is least intelligent, and one who is not strong enough to perform any other task? As a result of this practice the men who are most lacking in intelligence enter into an occupation that is especially indispensable, and also those most lacking in strength; for, as I have said, it is the least useful fellow, one who can do no other work, who is put to this task.[b]
Such a person, moreover, even if he has some know- 7
ledge of the selection of shoots, conceals that knowledge and lays it aside because of his lack of strength; and that he may have the full number which the overseer has ordered, he does nothing carefully, nothing conscientiously. The one thing that he keeps before him is to get done with the task that is set; when, even though he may both know and carry out what he knows, he receives from his masters one precept

[a] A leaf-branch, or stock-branch. *Cf.* V. 6. 29; and Pliny, *N.H.* XVII. 181, *Sic duo genera palmitum: quod e duro exit materiamque in proximum annum promittit, pampinarium vocatur aut, ubi supra cicatricem est, fructuarium; alterum ex anniculo palmite semper fructuarium.*

[b] *Cf.* I. *Praef.* 12; I. 9. 4–5.

nariam virgam deplantet, cetera omnia ut seminibus contribuat.

8 Nos autem primo [1] rationem secuti, nunc etiam longi temporis experimentum, non aliud semen eligimus, nec frugiferum esse ducimus nisi quod in parte genitali fructum attulerit. Nam illud quidem, quod loco sterili laetum robustumque sine fetu [2] processit, fallacem fecunditatis imaginem
9 praefert,[3] nec ullam generandi vim possidet. Id procul dubio verum esse ratio nos admonet, si modo, ut in corporibus nostris propria sunt officia cuiusque membri, sic et frugiferarum [4] stirpium partibus propria munia. Videmus hominibus inspiratam velut aurigam rectricemque membrorum animam, sensusque iniectos [5] ad ea discernanda, quae tactu, quaeque naribus auribusque et oculis indagantur; [6] pedes ad gressum compositos, bracchia ad complexum. Ac ne per omnes vices ministeriorum vagetur insolenter oratio, nihil aures agere valent quod est oculorum, nihil oculi quod [7] aurium; nec generandi
10 quidem data est facultas manibus aut plantis. Sed quod hominibus ignotum voluit esse genitor universi,[8] ventre protexit, ut divina praedita ratione rerum aeterna [9] opifex, quasi quibusdam secretis corporis in arcano atque operto sacra illa spiritus

[1] primo *SAacM* : primum *vulgo*.
[2] fructu *ac*.
[3] praebet *a*, *vett. edd.* : prebet *M*.
[4] membris propria sunt officia et frugiferarum *S* : officia. Et frugiferarum (cuiusq. membri sic propria sunt officia *suprascr.*) *A*.
[5] sensus in lectos *SAa*.
[6] indignantur *a*.
[7] oculorum, nihil oculi quod *om. SA*.
[8] universis *S*, *Sobel*.

alone—not to break off the stock-branch but to add everything else to the supply of cuttings.

But we, having at first taken reason as a guide, 8
and now a long period of experimentation as well, choose no shoot, and consider none to be fruitful, except one that has borne fruit in the generative part of the vine. For one that has come forth in a barren place, luxuriant and strong but destitute of offspring, offers a deceptive appearance of fruitfulness but possesses no generative power. Common 9
sense teaches us that this is undoubtedly true, if only, as in our own bodies every member has its peculiar functions, so too the parts of fruit-bearing stocks have their proper duties. We know that human beings have a soul breathed into them as a charioteer and guide of their members, and that senses were implanted in them for the perception of those impressions which are discovered by touch, by smell, by hearing, and by seeing; that feet were devised for walking and arms for embracing. And that my discourse may not wander without restraint over all the relations of sensory functions, the ears can effect nothing that belongs to the eyes, and the eyes nothing that belongs to the ears; nor, indeed, is the power of procreation bestowed upon the hands or the feet.
But the father of the universe concealed in the belly 10
that which he willed should be unknown to mankind, in order that the eternal creatress[a] of things, endowed with divine understanding, might mingle in certain hidden parts of the body, as it were, in mystery

[a] *I.e.* Nature; *cf.* I. *Praef.* 2; Pliny, *N H.* XXXI. 1.

---

[9] aeterna *SA*, *vett edd.*, *Sobel*: eterna *acM*: aeternus *vulgo*.

elementa cum terrenis primordiis[1] misceret, atque
hanc[2] animantis machinae[3] speciem effingeret.
11 Hac lege pecudes ac virgulta progenuit; hac vitium
genera figuravit, quibus eadem ipsa mater ac parens
primum radices velut quaedam fundamenta iecit, ut
iis quasi pedibus insisterent.[4] Truncum deinde
superposuit velut quandam staturam corporis et
habitus; mox ramis diffudit quasi brachiis; tum
caules et[5] pampinos elicuit velut palmas, eorumque
alios fructu donavit, alios fronde sola vestivit ad
protegendos tutandosque partus.

12 Ex his igitur, ut supra diximus, si non ipsa membra
genitalia conceptu atque fetu gravida sed tamquam
tegmina et umbracula eorum, quae fructibus vidua
sunt, legerimus, umbrae scilicet non vindemiae
13 laboraverimus.[6] Quid ergo est? Cur quamvis non
sit e duro pampinus sed e tenero natus, si tamen
orbus est, etiam in futurum quasi sterilis damnatur a
nobis? Modo enim disputatio nostra colligebat
unicuique corporis parti proprium esse attributum
officium, quod scilicet ei convenit; ut malleolo
quoque, qui opportuno loco natus est, fecunditatis
14 vis adsit, etiam si interim cesset a partu. Nec ego
abnuerim hoc me instituisse argumentari; sed et
illud maxime profiteor, palmitem quamvis frugifera
parte enatum, si fructum non attulerit, ne vim quidem

[1] primordii *S, Sobel.*
[2] hanc *edd.*: hoc *codd., Sobel.*
[3] macine *A*: imagine, *et deinde* specie *S*: imagine (specie) *Sobel.*
[4] insisteret *SAacM.*
[5] caules et *om. SAa*: et *om. cM.*
[6] laboravimus *Aa*

---

[a] *Cf.* Cicero, *Tusc. Disp.* I. 18. 42, I. 20. 47.

and concealment, those sacred elements of the soul with terrestrial principles,[a] and fashion this sort of living machine. By this law she produced cattle and 11
trees; by this she fashioned the various kinds of vines, for which this same mother and parent first laid, as it were, certain foundations of roots upon which they might stand, as upon feet. Then upon these she placed the trunk, corresponding in a way to the upright carriage and appearance of a body; in the next place she caused it to spread out with branches as if with arms; and then she drew forth stems and shoots corresponding to hands, of which she endowed some with fruit and clothed others with leaves alone for the protection and safe-keeping of their progeny.

If, then, from these vines, as I have said above, we 12
select, not those parts which are capable of conception and heavy with young, but their coverings and sunshades, so to speak, which are destitute of fruit, our toil will certainly have been spent for shade and not for a harvest of grapes. What, then, is my point? 13
Why, if a shoot is destitute of offspring, even though it be sprung, not from hard wood, but from young, do we condemn it as sure to be barren also in time to come? Just now, indeed, our reasoning inferred that every part of the body has assigned to it a peculiar function which is manifestly appropriate to that part; so that a vine shoot, too, if sprung from a favourable place, may have in it the power of fruitfulness even though it be remiss in bearing for a time. I would not deny that I have taken it 14
upon myself to prove this point; but I declare most emphatically that a rod, even though sprung from a fruit-bearing part of the vine, does not even possess

fecunditatis habere. Nec hoc illi sententiae repugnat.[1] Nam et homines quosdam non posse generare, quamvis omni[2] membrorum numero constante, manifestum est; ne sit incredibile, si genitali loco virga nata fructu careat, carituram quoque[3] fetu.

15 Itaque ut ad consuetudinem agricolarum revertar, eiusmodi surculos, qui nihil attulerint,[4] spadones appellant; quod non facerent, nisi suspicarentur inhabiles frugibus. Quae et ipsa appellatio rationem mihi subiecit non eligendi malleolos quamvis probabili parte vitis enatos, si fructum non tulissent, quamquam et hos ipsos[5] sciam non in totum sterilitate affectos. Nam confiteor pampinarios quoque, cum e duro processerint,[6] tempore anni sequentis adquirere fecunditatem, et ideo in resecem summitti,
16 ut progenerare possit. Verum eiusmodi partum comperimus non tam ipsius resecis quam materni esse muneris. Nam quia inhaeret stirpi suae, quae est natura ferax, mixtus adhuc parentis elementis,[7] et fecundis[8] partus[9] seminibus ac velut altricis uberibus eductus, paulatim fructum ferre condiscit. At quae citra naturae quandam pubertatem immatura

[1] repugnant *Aa* : repugnet *c*.
[2] omni *SAa* : omnium *cM*, *edd.*
[3] *sic codd., vett. edd.* : quoque esse fetu *vulgo*.
[4] tulerint *SA*.
[5] ipsos *om. AacM*.
[6] processerint *acM*, *vett. edd.* (*cf. IV.* 21. 3): e duroto cesserint (ceserint *S*) *SA* : prorepserint *vulgo*.
[7] elementis *SacM*, *vett. edd.*, *Sobel* : elimentis *A* : alimentis *vulgo*.
[8] fecundis (foecundis *vett. edd.*) *SAa*, *Sobel* : foecundi *cM*, *et vulgo*
[9] partus *SaM*, *et vulgo* : pastus *Ac*, *vett. edd.*, *Sobel*.

the power of productiveness if it has not itself borne fruit. And this statement is not at variance with the former opinion. For it is evident that some men are incapable of procreation even though they have the full number of members; so that it should not be beyond belief that a cane sprung from a generative place, if devoid of fruit at present, will be devoid of progeny in the future also.

And so, to return to the usage of the farmers, they 15
give the name *spadones* or eunuchs [a] to that sort of shoots which have produced nothing; which they would not do if they did not suppose them to be incapable of bearing. It is this very appellation that suggested to me a reason for not choosing mallet-shoots,[b] even though they were sprung from an approved part of the vine, if they had not borne fruit; although I understand that even these are not entirely affected with barrenness. For I admit that stock-shoots [c] too, though they have come out of the hard wood, acquire fruitfulness the following season; and for that reason they are reduced to a single spur,[d] so that it may have strength for bearing fruit. But we find that offspring of this sort owes 16
not so much to the spur itself as to the munificence of the mother vine. For because it clings to its own stock, which is naturally fruitful, still mingling with the elements of its parent,[e] born of prolific seed and reared, so to speak, at the breasts of a nurse, it learns little by little to produce fruit. But when a slip is torn from the stock prematurely and unseasonably,

[a] *Cf.* Isidore, *Orig.* XVII. 5. 6, *Spadones sunt surculi fruge carentes, ex ipsa appellatione, quod sint inhabiles fructu et sterilitate affecti*; Pliny, *N.H.* XIII. 38.

[b] See III. 6. 3.

[c] See III. 10. 5.

[d] *Cf.* IV. 21. 3.

[e] *Cf.* Chap. 10, sec. 10, above.

atque intempestiva planta direpta trunco vel terrae vel etiam stirpi recisae inseritur, quasi puerilis aetas ne ad coitum quidem nedum ad conceptum habilis, vim generandi vel in totum perdit, vel certe minuit.
17 Quare magnopere censeo in eligendis seminibus adhibere curam, ut e [1] fructuosa parte [2] vitis palmites legamus eos qui futuram fecunditatem iam dato [3] fructu promittunt; nec tamen contenti simus singulis uvis, maximeque probemus eos [4] qui numerosissimis fetibus conspiciuntur. An non [5] opilionem laudabimus ex ea matre subolem propagantem, quae geminos enixa sit; et caprarium summittentem fetus earum pecudum, quae trigemino partu commendantur? Videlicet quia sperat [6] parentum fecundi-
18 tati responsuram. Et nos sequemur in vitibus hanc ipsam rationem, tanto quidem magis quod compertum habemus naturali quadam malignitate desciscere interdum quamvis diligenter probata semina; idque nobis poeta velut surdis veritatis inculcet dicendo,[7]

> Vidi lecta diu, et [8] multo spectata labore
> Degenerare tamen, ni vis humana quotannis
> Maxima quaeque manu legeret. Sic omnia fatis
> In peius ruere, ac retro sublapsa referri.

[1] uti *acM, et vulgo ante Schn.* [2] curam . . . parte *om. S.*
[3] toto *cM, et vulgo ante Schn.* [4] eos *om. SAacM.*
[5] non *om. SAac, vett. edd.*
[6] *sic Pontedera, Schn.*: speret *SA*: speret et *a*: semper et *c*: semper *M*: quasi semper sit *cett. edd.*
[7] incolcet diligendo *SA*: indulget dicendo c.
[8] Vidi lecta diu, et] videlicet adiuvet *A*.

[a] Here a general term including any propagative portion of a plant, true seeds, cuttings, quicksets, layers, etc. (except buddings and grafts).

without regard to a certain maturity required by nature, and is either planted in the ground or even grafted on a shortened stock, just as the age of childhood is capable not even of coition and much less of conception, so it either suffers complete loss of its generative power or at any rate has less of it. Therefore I think that we should take especial care, 17 in the choice of cuttings, to select from a fruitful part of the vine those shoots which, by having already produced fruit, give promise of future productiveness; and yet we should not be satisfied with single clusters, but should especially approve those shoots which are conspicuous for the greatest number of offspring. Or shall we not commend the shepherd who multiplies the progeny of a dam that has borne twins, and the goatherd who breeds the young of those animals which are noted for bearing three at one birth? For he hopes, of course, that the offspring will match the productiveness of their parents. In the matter of 18 vines we also shall follow this very method, and the more so because we have found out that seeds,[a] even though carefully tested, sometimes degenerate through some natural malignity; and this the poet would impress upon us, as if we were deaf to the truth, in saying,

> Some seeds I've seen, though chosen with time and care,
> Degenerate still, unless with human hand
> The largest were selected every year.
> But so it is; it is the will of fate
> That all things backward turn, all things deteriorate.[b]

[b] Vergil, *Georg.* I. 197–200.

Quod non tantum de seminibus leguminum, sed in tota agricolationis ratione [1] dictum esse intellegendum
19 est. Si modo longi temporis observatione comperimus, quod certe comperimus, eum malleolum, qui quattuor uvas tulerit, deputatum et in terram depositum, a fecunditate materna sic degenerare ut interdum singulis, non numquam etiam binis uvis
20 minus adferat; in quantum autem censemus defecturos [2] eos, qui binos aut fere singulos fetus in matre tulerint, cum etiam feracissimi translationem saepe reformident? [3] Itaque huius rationis demonstratorem magis esse me quam inventorem, libenter profiteor, ne quis existimet fraudari maiores nostros laude merita. Nam id ipsum sensisse [4] eos non dubium est, quamvis nullo alio scripto proditum, exceptis quos rettulimus numeros [5] Vergili, et sic [6] tamen ut de seminibus leguminum praecipiatur.
21 Cur enim aut e duro natam virgam, aut etiam ex fecundo malleolo, quem ipsi probassent, decisam sagittam repudiabant, si nihil interesse ducebant ex quo loco semina legerentur? Num [7] quia vim fecunditatis certis quasi membris inesse non dubitabant, idcirco pampinarium et sagittam velut inutiles ad deponendum prudentissime damnaverunt? Quod si ita est, nihil dubium est multo

[1] agricolatione spatione *SA*: in totam agricolationis rationem *M*, *et vulgo ante Schn.*: in tota agricolationis satione *Sobel.*

[2] despecturos *SAc*, *vett. edd.*

[3] formident *SAa*, *vett. edd.*

[4] censuisse *M*, *Ald.*, *Gesn.*

[5] numeros *S*, *Schn*: numeris *A*: metris *acM*: quae r. metris *plerique edd.*

[6] hic *ac*, *edd. ante Schn.*

[7] Nunc *SAcM*, *Ald.*, *Gesn.*

It is to be understood that this was said, not merely of the seeds of legumes, but of the whole matter of agriculture. If only we have discovered by a long 19
period of observation, as we certainly have discovered, that a shoot which has borne four clusters, when it is cut off and put into the ground, degenerates so far from the fruitfulness of the parent stock as to produce sometimes one, occasionally even two clusters fewer than before, to what extent do we think that 20
they will fall short which have produced two clusters or usually one on the parent stock, when even the most fruitful shoots often dread transplanting? And so I gladly profess myself a demonstrator of this method, rather than its inventor, lest anyone should think that our ancestors are unjustly deprived of the praise that is their due. For there is no doubt that they knew of it, even though it has been handed down in no writing except those lines of Vergil which we have quoted, and yet in such a way as to give directions for the seed of legumes.[a] For why did they 21
reject the rod sprung from the hard wood, or even the "arrow"[b] cut from the fruitful mallet-shoot which they had approved, if they considered that it made no difference from what place the cuttings were gathered? Was it because they had no doubt that the power of fruitfulness was present in certain members, so to speak, that they very wisely condemned the stock shoot and the arrow as useless for planting? If this is the case, there is no doubt that

[a] Columella seems to refer to his previous quotation of Vergil (*Georg.* I. 197–200) in II. 9. 12.

[b] The arrow is defined in Chap. 17, sec. 2, of this book; *cf.* Isidore, *Orig.* XVII. 5. 7, *Sagittam rustici vocant novissimam partem surculi sive qui longius recessit a matre et quasi prosilivit, seu quia acuminis tenuitate teli speciem praefert.*

magis ab his improbatum esse etiam illum palmitem,
22 qui frugifero loco natus fructum non attulisset. Nam si sagittam, id est superiorem partem malleoli, vituperandam censebant, cum esset eadem pars surculi frugiferi, quanto magis vel ex optima [1] vitis parte natum flagellum, si est sterile, improbatum ab his ratio ipsa declarat? Nisi tamen, quod est absurdum, crediderunt eum [2] translatum et abscissum a sua stirpe, destitutumque materno alimento, frugiferum, qui in [3] ipsa matre nequam fuisset.[4] Atque haec et forsitan pluribus dicta sint [5] quam exigebat ratio veritatis; minus tamen multis quam postulabat prave detorta et inveterata opinio rusticorum.

XI. Nunc ad reliquum ordinem propositae disputationis redeo. Sequitur hanc eligendi malleoli curam pastinationis officium, si tamen ante de qualitate soli constiterit. Nam eam quoque plurimum et bonitati et largitati frugum conferre, nihil dubium est. Ac prius quam ipsum solum [6] perspiciamus, illud antiquissimum censemus, rudem potius eligendum agrum, si sit facultas, quam ubi fuerit seges aut
2 arbustum. Nam de vinetis quae longo situ exoleverunt, inter omnes auctores constitit pessima esse si

[1] opima *cM*.
[2] eum *aM, Sobel*: cum *c, vett. edd.*: eam *SA*: id *vulgo*.
[3] qui in *scripsi*: quia in *Sobel*: frugifero quin *SAac vett. edd.*: frugiferoq; in *M*: frugiferum, quod in *vulgo*.
[4] fuisse *SAacM, Sobel*.
[5] sint *SA*: sunt *acM, et vulgo*.
[6] solum *om. Aac, et omnes ante Schn.*

[a] This special preparation of the ground, called *pastinatio*, consisted of deep digging or trenching. Ground so prepared was called *pastinatum*, *pastinatio* or *pastinum*. Palladius (II. 10. 1), like Columella below (Chap. 13), speaks of three kinds of trenching: complete trenching of the ground,

they disapproved far more of that cane which, though sprung from a bearing part, had borne no fruit. For if they thought that the arrow—that is, the 22
uppermost part of a mallet-cutting—was deserving of censure even though it was a part of a bearing shoot, how much more does mere common sense show that they would have disapproved of a slip, if it is sterile, even though it be sprung from the best part of the vine? Unless—and this is absurd—they believed that one which had been worthless on the mother vine would be fruitful when transplanted and cut off from its stock and deprived of its maternal sustenance. It may be that this has been told at greater length than a statement of the truth required; but even so, in fewer words than were demanded by the badly distorted and deep-rooted notion of country people.

XI. I now return to what remains of the topics proposed for systematic discussion. The business of preparing the ground[a] comes next, after this attention to the choice of cuttings, provided, however, that agreement has been reached beforehand as to the quality of the soil. For there is no doubt that this, too, contributes in very great measure to the goodness and abundance of the fruit. And before considering the soil itself, we think it a matter of very first importance that land hitherto untilled, if we have such, should be chosen in preference to that upon which there has been a crop of grain or a plantation of trees and vines. As to vineyards 2
which have become worthless through long neglect, it is agreed by all authorities that they are worst of

trenching in long strips or furrows (*sulci*), and trenching in short strips or planting-holes (*scrobes*).

reserere velimus, quod et inferius solum plurimis[1] radicibus sit impeditum ac velut irretitum, et adhuc non amiserit virus et cariem illam vetustatis, quibus hebetata quasi aliquibus venenis humus torpeat.[2]
3 Quam ob causam silvestris ager praecipue est eligendus, qui etiam si frutectis aut arboribus obsessus est, facile extricatur, quod suapte natura quaecumque gignuntur, non penitus nec in profundum radices agunt, sed per summam[3] terrae dispergunt atque deducunt; quibus ferro recisis atque exstirpatis, parum[4] quod superest inferioris soli rastris licet effodere et in fermentum congerere atque componere. Si tamen rudis terra non sit, proximum[5] est vacuum arboribus arvum. Si nec hoc est, rarissimum arbustum vel olivetum, melius tamen vetus olivetum[6]
4 quod non fuerit maritum, vineis destinatur. Ultima est, ut dixi, conditio restibilis vineae. Nam si necessitas facere cogit, prius quidquid est residuae vitis exstirpari debet; deinde totum solum sicco[7] fimo, aut si id non sit, alterius generis quam recentissimo stercorari, atque ita converti, et diligentissime refossae[8] omnes radices in summum regeri atque comburi; tum[9] rursus vel stercore vetusto, quia non gignit herbas, vel de vepribus egesta humo pasti-
5 natum large contegi. At ubi pura novalia et ab

[1] plurimis *SAc*: pluribus *aM, edd.*
[2] torreat *SA*.
[3] summam *Aac, vett. edd.*: summa *SM*: summum *vulgo.*
[4] parum *M, edd. vulgo*: purum *SAac, Schn.*
[5] componere: si tamen rudis terra non sit. proximum *Schn.*
[6] melius . . . olivetum (*in marg. M*) *om. a, Ald., Gesn.*
[7] sicco *om. SAa.*
[8] refossae *Schn.*: refossas *SAacM, et vulgo.*
[9] tum *acM, vett. edd.*: tunc *vulgo*: comburitur (tum *om.*) *SA*.

all if we wish to replant them, because the lower soil is imprisoned in a tangle of many roots, as if caught in a net, and has not yet lost that infection and rottenness of old age by which the earth is deadened and numbed as if by some poison or other.[a] For this reason a piece of wild land is an 3
especially good choice, and even if occupied with bushes or trees it is easily cleared, because all things that spring up naturally do not push their roots far nor to a great depth, but spread and extend them through the surface soil; and when they are cut off with the axe and are rooted out, the little that remains in the lower soil may be dug up with mattocks and brought together and heaped up for fermentation. But if you should have no unbroken ground, the next choice is ploughed land that is free of trees. Failing this, there is allotted to vineyards a plantation of trees and vines standing very far apart, or an olive grove—but preferably old olive trees which have not been wedded to vines. Last of all, as I have said, is the renewing 4
of a worn-out vineyard. Now if circumstances make this necessary, all remaining parts of the vines should first be rooted out; then all the ground should be fertilized with dry dung or, if this is not available, with the freshest manure of another sort; and so it should be turned over, and all the unearthed roots must be very carefully brought to the surface and burned; and then again the dug ground should be covered generously either with old manure, because that does not produce weeds, or with earth brought from the bramble thickets. But where 5

[a] In *De Arb.* 3. 5, Columella advises against the replanting of old vineyard ground until after it has rested ten years.

arboribus sunt libera, considerandum est ante quam pastinemus, surcularis necne sit terra; idque facillime exploratur per stirpes, quae sua sponte proveniunt. Neque enim est ullum tam viduum solum virgultis ut non aliquos surculos progeneret, tamquam piros silvestres et prunos, vel rubos certe; nam haec quamvis genera spinarum sint, solent tamen fortia
6 et laeta et gravida fructu consurgere. Igitur si non retorrida nec scabra, sed levia et nitida, et prolixa fecundaque viderimus, eam intellegemus [1] esse terram surcularem.

Sed hoc in totum ad [2] illud, quod vineis praecipue est idoneum, proprie considerandum, ut prius rettuli, si facilis est humus et modice resoluta, quam diximus [3] pullam vocitari; nec quia sola ea, sed quia sit
7 habilis maxime vinetis. Quis enim vel mediocris agricola nesciat etiam durissimum tofum vel carbunculum, simulatque sit confractus [4] et in summo regestus,[5] tempestatibus et gelu nec minus aestivis putrescere caloribus ac resolvi; eumque [6] pulcherrime radices vitium per aestatem refrigerare, sucumque retinere; quae res alendo surculo sunt accommodatissimae? Simili quoque de causa probari solutam glaream calculosumque agrum et mobilem lapidem? si tamen haec pingui glebae permixta sunt, nam
8 eadem ieiuna maxime culpantur. Est autem, ut

[1] intelligemus *M, et vulgo*: intellegimus *SA*: intelligimus *ac*.

[2] totum ad illud *SAacM, et vulgo*: totum: at illud *Schn.*

[3] dicimus *SAac, vett. edd.*

[4] simulatque sit confractus *scripsi*: simulatque situm confractum SA: simul atque si sint confracti *ac, vett. edd.*: simulatque sunt confracti *M, Ald., Gesn., Schn.*

[5] summus regestus *SA*: summo regesti *acM, et vulgo.*

there is clean fallow, free from trees, we must consider before working it whether or not the land is suitable for young vine-shoots; and this is most easily discovered through the sprouts that come up of their own accord. For there is no soil so destitute of shrubs as not to produce some shoots, such as wild pears and plums or at least brambles; for even though these are varieties of thorns, still it is their common habit to grow up strong and thrifty and
heavy with fruit. Therefore, if we observe that they 6
are not shrivelled and scaly, but smooth and bright, tall and prolific, then we shall know that the ground is suitable for young shoots.

But in the matter of what is especially suited to vines, this point in general deserves special consideration, as I have stated before, if the soil is easily worked and moderately loose in texture—what we have said is called *pulla*; not because such soil alone is proper for vineyards, but because it is
especially so. For who, though he be but an 7
ordinary farmer, does not know that even the hardest tufa or toph-stone, once it is broken in pieces and thrown up on the surface, is softened and loosened by storms and cold no less than by summer's heat; and that during hot weather it is very effective in cooling the roots of the vines and in holding moisture—conditions most suitable for the nourishing of the young shoot? And that for a like reason free gravel, pebbly ground, and loose stones are approved? on condition, however, that they are mixed with fat soil, for they meet with the greatest disapproval in
lean ground. Moreover, the flint-stone also, in my 8

[6] eumque *SAacM*, *vett. edd.*: eosque *Ald.*, *Gesn.*, *Schn.*

mea quoque fert opinio, vineis amicus etiam silex, cui[1] superpositum est modicum terrenum, quia frigidus et tenax umoris per ortum caniculae non patitur[2] sitire radices. Hyginus quidem secutus Tremelium praecipue montium ima, quae a verticibus defluentem humum receperint,[3] vel etiam valles quae fluminum alluvie et inundationibus concreverint, aptas esse vineis adseverat, me non
9 dissentiente. Cretosa humus utilis habetur viti: nam per se ipsa creta, qua utuntur figuli, quamque nonnulli argillam vocant, inimicissima est; nec minus ieiunus sabulo, et quidquid, ut ait Iulius Atticus, retorridum surculum facit, id autem solum vel uliginosum est vel salsum, amarum[4] etiam, vel siticulosum et pararidum. Nigrum tamen et rutilum sabulonem, qui sit vividae[5] terrae permixtus, probaverunt antiqui; nam carbunculosum agrum, nisi stercore adiuves, macres vineas efficere dixerunt.
10 Gravis est rubrica, ut idem Atticus ait, et ad comprehendendum radicibus iniqua. Sed alit eadem vitem, cum tenuit, verum est in opere difficilior, quod neque umentem fodere possis, quod sit glutinosissima, nec nimium siccam, quia ultra modum praedura.

XII. Sed ne nunc per infinitas terreni species evagemur, non intempestive commemorabimus[6] Iuli Graecini conscriptam velut formulam, ad quam posita est aestimatio terrae[7] vinealis. Idem enim

[1] cum *SAacM*. [2] patiatur *SAa, vett. edd*

[3] recipeient *SAacM*.

[4] vel salsum vel amarum *acM, Gesn.* ; *deinde* etiam *om.* c.

[5] vividae *SA, Schn.* : humide *acM*, *et* humidae *vulgo*.

[6] commemoravimus *SAa* : connumeravimus *c*.

[7] aestimatio terrae *scripsi* : estimatio (*pr.* est *om.*) referre terrae *S* : imitatio referre (refferre *A*) terre *Aac* : mutatio fere terre *M* : limitatio terrae *Ald., Gesn., et Schn., qui* ad quam

opinion, is friendly to vineyards when it is moderately well covered with earth, because, being cold and retentive of moisture, it does not allow the roots to thirst during the rising of the Dog-star. Hyginus indeed, following Tremelius, asserts that the bases of mountains, which have received the soil that washes down from their summits, or even valley lands that have been formed by the soil deposits of rivers and floods, are especially suited for vineyards; and I do
not disagree. Clayey soil is considered serviceable 9
for the vine: but, by itself, the clay which potters use, and which some call *argilla*,[a] is most unfriendly; and no less so is hungry gravel and, as Julius Atticus says, everything that makes a shrivelled shoot—that being soil which is either wet or salty, or sour too, or thirsty and extremely dry. Still the ancients approved black and reddish sand when mixed with vigorous earth; for they said that ground containing red toph-stone, unless aided with manure, produced
puny vines. Ruddle, as the same Atticus says, is 10
heavy and does not offer roots an easy hold. But the same soil is nourishing to the vine when once it has obtained a hold, though it is more difficult to work, since you cannot dig it when wet because it is very sticky, nor when too dry because it is hard beyond measure.

XII. But that we may not now wander through the endless varieties of soil, it will be not out of place to call to mind a standard rule, as it were, of Julius Graecinus which has been laid down for the appraisal of land suitable for vineyards. For that same

[a] *Cf.* ἄργιλλος, from ἀργής, white.

aestimatio referetur terrae vinealis *in nota coniecit et in Corrigend. in Comment.* ad quam iusta aestimatio *scripsit.*

Graecinus sic ait: Esse aliquam terram calidam vel frigidam, umidam vel siccam, raram vel densam, levem aut gravem, pinguem aut macram; sed neque nimium calidum solum posse tolerare vitem, quia inurat, neque praegelidum, quoniam velut stupentes et congelatas radices nimio frigore moveri non sinat; quae tum demum se promunt, cum modico tepore[1]
2 evocantur: umorem terrae iusto maiorem putrefacere deposita semina; rursus nimiam siccitatem destituere plantas naturali alimento, aut in totum necare, aut scabras et retorridas facere: perdensam humum caelestis aquas non sorbere, nec facile perflari, facillime perrumpi, et praebere rimas, quibus sol ad radices stirpium penetret; eandemque[2] velut conclausa et coartata semina comprimere atque
3 strangulare: raram supra modum velut per infundibulum transmittere imbres, et sole ac vento penitus siccari atque exarescere:[3] gravem terram vix ulla cultura vinci, levem vix ulla sustineri: pinguissimam et laetissimam luxuria, macram ac tenuem ieiunio laborare. Opus est, inquit, inter has tam diversas inaequalitates magno temperamento, quod in corporibus quoque nostris desideratur, quorum bona valetudo calidi et frigidi, umidi et aridi, densi et rari certo et
4 quasi examinato[4] modo continetur.[5] Nec tamen hoc temperamentum in terra, quae vineis destinetur, pari momento libratum esse debere ait, sed in alteram

[1] tēpore *S*: tempore *Aac*.

[2] eandemque *M*, *Ursinus*, *Schn.*: eademque *SAac*, *et plerique*.

[3] exarescere *SAacM*: exolescere *vett. edd. et Schn., qui hanc lectionem defendit*.

[4] examinati *SA*: continuato *a*.

[5] contineatur *SAa*.

Graecinus speaks as follows: That some land is hot or cold, damp or dry, loose or compact, light or heavy, fat or lean; but that soil which is excessively hot cannot support the vine, because it burns it, nor can the very cold soil, because it allows no action of the roots when they are benumbed and chilled, as it were, by excessive cold,—for they extend themselves only when they are drawn out by moderate warmth: that soil of more than the proper moisture 2
causes rotting of the plants that are set, while, on the other hand, excessive dryness deprives the plants of their natural sustenance and either kills them entirely or makes them scaly and shrivelled: that very compact ground does not absorb the rains, does not readily allow the circulation of air, is very easily broken through, and affords cracks through which the sun penetrates to the roots of the plants; and the same binds and chokes the plants, which are, so to speak, imprisoned and confined: that soil 3
which is immoderately loose allows rains to pass through it as through a funnel, and is then completely dried out and parched by sun and wind: that heavy ground can hardly be subdued by any cultivation, while light ground can hardly be kept up by any: that the fattest and most fertile soil suffers from rankness of growth, the lean and poor soil from barrenness. There is need, he says, of much intermixture among these so different extremes, as is requisite also in our own bodies, whose well-being depends on a fixed and, so to speak, balanced proportion of the hot and the cold, the moist and the dry, the compact and the loose. And yet, in the case 4
of land which is designed for vineyards, he says that this proportion should not be placed in equipoise but

partem propensius; ut calidior terra sit quam frigidior, siccior quam umidior, rarior quam densior, et si qua sunt his similia, ad quae contemplationem
5 suam dirigat, qui vineas instituet. Quae cuncta, sicut ego reor, magis prosunt, cum suffragatur etiam status caeli: cuius quam regionem[1] spectare debeant vineae, vetus est dissensio, Saserna maxime probante solis ortum, mox deinde meridiem, tum occasum; Tremelio Scrofa praecipuam positionem meridianam censente; Vergilio de industria occasum sic repudiante,[2]

Neve tibi ad solem vergant vineta cadentem;

Democrito et Magone laudantibus caeli plagam septentrionalem, quia existiment ei subiectas feracissimas fieri vineas, quae tamen bonitate vini
6 superentur. Nobis in universum praecipere optimum visum est ut in locis frigidis meridiano vineta subiciantur, tepidis orienti advertantur; si tamen non infestabuntur Austris Eurisque,[3] velut orae maritimae in Baetica. Sin autem regiones praedictis ventis[4] fuerint obnoxiae, melius Aquiloni vel Favonio committentur; nam ferventibus provinciis, ut Aegypto et Numidia, uni septentrioni rectius opponentur. Quibus omnibus diligenter exploratis, tum demum pastinationem suscipiemus.

[1] regionem quam *SAacM*.
[2] repudiantem *SAac*.
[3] aeris quae (que *a*) *SAa*.
[4] praedicti sunt is (his *A*) *SA*.

[a] *Georg.* II. 298.

should incline more in one direction or the other, so that the land may be rather warm than cold, rather dry than wet, rather loose than compact, and so on in any like matters to which one who plants vineyards should direct a careful gaze. All of this, in my 5
opinion, is of greater advantage when climatic conditions also are favourable: and in this matter there is long-standing disagreement as to what quarter of the heavens the vineyards should face, Saserna favouring the east especially, and next to that the south, and then the west; Tremelius Scrofa thinking a southern exposure superior to all others, Vergil explicitly rejecting the west in the words,

> Nor slope your vineyards toward the setting sun;[a]

and Democritus and Mago commending the northern quarter of the heavens, because they think that vineyards exposed to it become the most productive, even though they may be surpassed in the quality of their wine. To us it has seemed best to direct in 6
general that vineyards have, in cold regions, a southern exposure, and that in warm ones they face the east; on condition, however, that they are not harassed by the south and south-east winds, as are the maritime coasts of Baetica. If, however, your tracts are subject to the aforementioned winds, it will be better to entrust them to the north or the west wind; but in hot provinces, such as Egypt and Numidia, they will be exposed more properly to the north alone. And now that all these matters have been carefully examined, we shall take up at last the trenching of the ground.[b]

[b] See III. 11. 1, note.

XIII. Eius autem ratio cum Italici generis futuris agricolis tum etiam provincialibus tradenda est; quoniam in longinquis et remotis fere regionibus istud genus vertendi et subigendi agri minime usurpatur, sed aut scrobibus aut sulcis plerumque
2 vineae conseruntur.[1] Quibus autem [2] mos est scrobibus deponere, fere per tres longitudinis, perque duos pedes in altitudinem cavato solo, quantum latitudo ferramenti patitur, malleolos utrimque iuxta latera fossarum consternunt, et adversis scrobium [3] frontibus curvatos erigunt; duabusque gemmis supra terram eminere passi [4] reposita humo cetera coaequant: quae faciunt in eadem linea intermissis totidem pedum scamnis, dum peragant ordinem.
3 Tum deinde relicto spatio, prout cuique mos est vineas colenti [5] vel aratro vel bidente, sequentem ordinem instituunt. Et si fossore tantum terra versetur, minimum est quinque pedum interordinium, septem maximum; sin bubus et aratro, minimum est septem pedum, satis amplum decem.
4 Nonnulli tamen omnem vitem per denos pedes in quincuncem disponunt, ut more novalium terra transversis adversisque sulcis proscindatur. Id genus vineti non conducit agricolae, nisi ubi laetissimo solo vitis amplo incremento consurgit. At qui pastinationis impensam reformidant, sed aliqua tamen

[1] *Post* conseruntur *omnes habent* Scrobibus vineta sic ponuntur, *quae ex lemmate orta Schneider inclusit.*

[2] autem (aūt *A*) *SAacM, vett. edd.*: vitem *Ald., Gesn., Schn.*

[3] scrobum *SAac.*

[4] passim *ac, vett. edd.*

[5] colenti *SAcM, et plerique*: colendi *a, Ursinus, Schn.*

XIII. Now the method of doing this must be handed down, not only to future husbandmen of the Italian race, but also to those from the provinces; for in countries that are far distant and quite remote this particular way of turning and subduing a field is very little practised, but the vines are set for the most part either in planting-holes or in furrows. Those, 2
moreover, whose habit it is to set the vine in planting-holes, after excavating the earth for about three feet in length and two in depth—to as great a width as that of the iron spade permits, lay the shoots on both sides along the walls of the ditches and bend them to stand erect at the opposite ends of the holes; and then, allowing two eyes to project above ground, they replace the earth about it and level off the rest. This they do in the same line, leaving undug skips of the same number of feet, until they come to the end of the row. Then leaving a space, according to each 3
man's habit of cultivating with either plough or two-pronged mattock, they set the next row. And if the earth is merely turned by a spade-man, the minimum distance between rows is five feet, and seven is the maximum; but if with oxen and plough, the minimum is seven feet, while ten is large enough. Yet 4
some set all their vines at ten-foot intervals, in the form of a quincunx,[a] so that the ground may be broken up by diagonal and cross ploughing in the manner of fallow land. This sort of vineyard is not to the advantage of the farmer except where, in very fertile soil, the vine is of large growth. But those who dread the expense of trenching the ground, and yet wish to

[a] An arrangement in blocks of five, like the cinque on a die. In this way any five in the same position form a square, with the fifth in the centre. See Chap. 15, secs. 1–2, below.

parte pastinationem imitari student, paribus alternis omissis spatiis[1] senum pedum latitudinis sulcos dirigunt,[2] fodiuntque et exaltant in tres pedes, ac per latera fossarum vitem vel malleolum disponunt.
5 Avarius quidam dupondio et dodrante altum sulcum, latum pedum quinque faciunt; deinde ter tanto amplius spatium crudum relinquunt, atque ita sequentem sulcum infindunt.[3] Quos cum per definitum vineis[4] locum fecerunt, in lateribus sulcorum viviradices vel decisos quam recentissimos palmites novellos erigunt, consitis compluribus inter ordinaria semina malleolis, quos postea quam convaluerint crudo solo quod omissum est transversis scrobibus propagent, atque ordinent vineam paribus intervallis. Sed eae, quas rettulimus, vinearum sationes, pro natura et benignitate cuiusque regionis aut usurpandae aut repudiandae sunt nobis.

6 Nunc pastinandi agri propositum est rationem tradere. Ac primum omnium ut[5] sive arbustum sive silvestrem locum vineis destinaverimus, omnis frutex atque arbor erui et summoveri debet, ne postea fossorem moretur, neve iam pastinatum solum iacentibus molibus imprimatur et exportantium
7 ramos atque truncos ingressu proculcetur. Neque enim parum refert suspensissimum esse pastinatum et, si fieri possit, vestigio quoque inviolatum; ut mota aequaliter humus novelli seminis radicibus,

[1] *sic SAacM, et plerique*: spatiis omissis *Schn.*

[2] derigunt *SAc*: derigant *a.*

[3] infindunt *SAaM, Sobel*: infundunt *c, vett. edd.*: infodiunt *Ald., Gesn. Schn.*

[4] vineis *SAacM*: vinetis *edd. omnes.*

[5] *sic Schn.*: omnẽ ut *S*: ut omnem *Aac, vett. edd.*: ut omne *M*: Ac primum ex omni sive arbustivo, sive silvestri loco, quem vineis *Ald., Gesn.*

imitate that trenching in some measure, run straight
furrows to a width of six feet, leaving alternate
strips of equal width; then they dig the furrows
and deepen them to three feet, and place the vines
or shoots along the sides of the hollows. Some, 5
with greater saving of expense, make a furrow two and
three-fourths feet deep and five feet wide; then,
leaving three times as much unbroken ground, they
cut the next furrow. When they have done this
throughout the whole plot set aside for vines, they set
upright in the sides of the furrows either quicksets
or young vine-branches as freshly cut as possible,
putting in among the plants set in the regular rows
a great number of cuttings which, after they have
gained strength, they may propagate in cross-trenches
in the ground which was left unbroken, and so arrange their vineyards in rows at equal distances.
But these methods of planting vineyards, as we have
given them, are ours to employ or reject according
to the nature and favourableness of each region.

It is now my intention to hand down the method 6
of trenching a piece of ground. And first of all,
when we have marked out a site for vineyards,
whether it be a plantation of trees or natural woodland, every bush and tree should be rooted out and
removed, so as not to be a hindrance to the digger
thereafter, and that the ground already trenched
may not be pressed down by heavy masses lying upon
it and trodden down by the coming and going of those
who carry off the branches and tree trunks. For it is of 7
no little importance that trenched ground be in a very
loose state and, if possible, not violated even by a foot-
print; so that the earth, being evenly stirred, may
give way gently to the roots of the young plant in

quamcumque in partem prorepserint, molliter cedat, nec incrementa duritia sua reverberet, sed tenero velut in nutritio sinu recipiat, et caelestes admittat imbres eosque alendis seminibus dispenset, ac suis omnibus partibus ad educandam prolem novam conspiret.

8 Campestris locus alte duos pedes et semissem infodiendus est, acclivis regio tres; praeruptior vero collis vel in quattuor pedes vertendus, quia cum a superiore parte in inferiorem detrahitur humus, vix iustum pastinationi praebet regestum, nisi multo editiorem ripam quam in plano feceris. Rursus depressis vallibus minus alte duobus pedibus deponi vineam non placet. Nam praestat non conserere quam in summa terra suspendere; nisi si tamen scaturigo [1] palustris obvia sit,[2] sicut in agro Ravennate, plus quam sesquipedem prohibeat infodere.

9 Primum autem praedicti operis exordium est, non ut huius temporis plerique faciunt agricolae, sulcum paulatim exaltare et ita secundo vel tertio gradu pervenire ad destinatam pastinationis altitudinem; sed protinus aequaliter linea posita rectis [3] lateribus perpetuam fossam educere et post tergum motam humum componere, atque in tantum deprimere,

10 donec altitudinis mensuram datam ceperit.[4] Tum per omne spatium gradus aequaliter movenda linea est; obtinendumque ut eadem latitudo in imo reddatur quae coepta est in summo. Opus est autem perito ac vigilante exactore, qui ripam erigi

[1] nisi si (*om. ac*) tamen scaturigo (scaturrigo *SA*) *SAac, vett. edd.*: nisi tamen si scaturigo *M, Ald., Gesn.*: nisi si statim uligo *Schn.*

[2] sit (fit *A*) *codd., vett. edd.*: *om. vulgo.*

[3] erectis *acM*.

[4] coeperit *SA*.

whatever direction they creep out, not repelling their growth by its hardness, but taking them into its tender nourishing bosom, as it were, admitting the rains of heaven and dispensing them for the sustenance of the plants, and acting with all its members in harmony for the rearing of its new offspring.

A level field should be dug two and one-half feet 8
deep, a sloping region three feet; but a steeper hill should be turned to a depth of four feet, because when earth is carried down from a higher to a lower place, the amount thrown back is barely sufficient for trenching unless you make the bank much higher than on level ground. On the other hand, in sunken valleys it is not proper to set the vine less than two feet deep. For it is better not to plant it at all than to leave it suspended on the surface of the earth; except, however, when marshy ground stands in the way, as in the district about Ravenna, and prevents digging deeper than a foot and a half. It 9
is, moreover, a first principle of the aforesaid operation not to deepen the furrow little by little, as is the practice of most farmers of our time, and so by a second or third gradation to arrive at the intended depth of trenching; but, running a line evenly forward, to extend a continuous trench with perpendicular sides and to pile the earth together behind you as it is removed, and to sink the trench down until it has reached the prescribed measure of depth. Then the line must be moved evenly over the 10
whole extent of the gradation; and you must see to it that the width is made the same at the bottom as it was started at the top. There is need, too, of an experienced and watchful overseer to give orders that the bank be made plumb and the furrow

iubeat, sulcumque vacuari, ac totum spatium crudi soli cum emota iam terra committi, sicut praecepi priore[1] libro, cum arandi rationem traderem, monendo[2] necubi scamna omittantur, et quod est durum
11 summis glaebis obtegatur. Sed huic operi exigendo quasi quandam machinam commenti maiores nostri regulam fabricaverunt, in cuius latere virgula prominens ad eam altitudinem, qua deprimi sulcum oportet, contingit summam ripae partem. Id genus mensurae ciconiam vocant rustici. Sed ea quoque fraudem recipit, quoniam plurimum interest utrum eam pronam an rectam ponas. Nos itaque huic machinae quasdam partes adiecimus, quae contendentium litem disputationemque dirimerent.
12 Nam duas regulas eius latitudinis, qua[3] pastinator sulcum facturus est, in speciem Graecae litterae X[4] decussavimus,[5] atque ita mediae parti, qua regulae committuntur, antiquam illam ciconiam infiximus, ut tamquam suppositae basi ad perpendiculum normata insisteret; deinde transversae, quae est in

[1] priore *codd.*, superiore *edd.*
[2] monendo *om. SA*, *vett. edd.*: movendo *ac.*
[3] qua *om. SAac.*
[4] grecae chi littere (X *in marg.*) *S*: X *om. AacM.*
[5] decusabimus *SAac*: densavimus *M.*

[a] II. 2. 25, 4. 3.
[b] "Middle" as the meaning here of *latus* (side) is defended by Gesner and accepted generally by other commentators.
[c] This measuring device is not mentioned by other writers, though Isidore (*Orig.* XX. 15. 3) says that the Spaniards gave the name *ciconia* to a well sweep (*tolleno*) because the motion of the sweep, in drawing water, resembled the actions of the stork. Palladius (II. 10. 4) speaks of the use of the *virga* alone as a measure of the depth of trenched ground. It appears that the ancient *ciconia* here mentioned was in the form of the letter T, standing, like a stork, on one leg; though

cleared, and that all the ground not yet thrown up be added to the earth already moved; just as I directed in the preceding book,[a] when I was handing down the methods of ploughing, in my warning that no ridges or skips should be left anywhere and that there should be no hard part covered over with surface clods. But our ancestors, devising a cer- 11
tain kind of instrument for the measuring of this work, have fashioned a straight bar and on the side [b] of it a small rod which, when reaching down to the depth to which the furrow should be sunk, touches the uppermost part of the bank. This sort of measuring device farmers call *ciconia* or stork.[c] But this too is open to fraud, because it makes a very great difference whether you place it slantwise or in an upright position. For this reason we have added certain parts to this contrivance, to do away with quarrels and disputes of contending parties. For we have 12
fastened [d] two pieces crosswise in the form of the Greek letter X and of a spread equal to the width to which the trencher intends to make his ditch, and to the middle point, where the pieces are joined, we have fastened that old-fashioned *ciconia* in such a way as to stand at a right angle to it as upon a sub-base; then upon the transverse rod, which is on the side,

commentators disagree as to whether, in use, it was placed upright, inverted, or on its side. Columella's improvement, by the addition of X-shaped cross-pieces (his *stella*), has also puzzled the commentators: some attach these pieces, at the point of intersection, to the base of the T and on the same plane; others think of the X as being in a horizontal position, *i.e.* lying flat on the ditch-bottom, with the T standing at right angles to it. The latter explanation seems the more probable, if text and translation are correct.

[d] *decussare* = to make a *decussis*, Roman numeral ten.

latere, virgulae fabrilem libellam superposuimus.[1] Sic compositum organum cum in sulcum demissum est, litem domini et conductoris sine iniuria diducit.[2]
13 Nam stella, quam diximus Graecae litterae faciem obtinere, pariter imae fossae solum metitur atque perlibrat, quia sive pronum seu resupinum est, positione machinae deprehenditur; quippe praedictae virgulae superposita libella alterutrum ostendit nec patitur exactorem operis decipi. Sic permensum et perlibratum opus in similitudinem vervacti semper procedit; tantumque spatii linea promota occupatur quantum effosus [3] sulcus longitudinis ac latitudinis obtinet. Atque id genus praeparandi soli probatissimum est.

XIV. Sequitur opus vineae conserendae, quae vel vere vel autumno tempestive deponitur: vere melius, si aut pluvius aut frigidus status caeli est, aut ager pinguis, aut campestris et uliginosa planities; rursus autumno, si sicca, si calida est aeris qualitas, si exilis atque aridus campus, si macer praeruptusve collis. Vernaeque positionis dies fere quadraginta sunt ab Idibus Februariis usque in aequinoctium; rursus autumnalis ab Idibus Octob. in Kalendas Decembres.
2 Sationis autem duo genera, malleoli vel viviradicis, quod utrumque ab agricolis usurpatur; et in provinciis magis malleoli, neque enim seminariis student

[1] supposuimus *ac*
[2] deducit *S*[1]*AcM*, *et omnes ante Gesn.*
[3] et fusus *SAac*: effusus *M*.

[a] The line and plummet, sometimes suspended from the apex of a triangular frame, formed a simple level (*libella*).

[b] *I.e.*, the new land, when so trenched in successive strips of the same dimensions, comes gradually to resemble a field that is kept in cultivation, though temporarily out of production.

we have fastened a workman's plumb-line.[a] When the instrument so constructed is let down into the trench, it settles all dispute between master and contractor without injustice to either. For the star, 13
which we have said has the appearance of the Greek letter, measures the ground at the bottom of the trench and at the same time tests its exact level, because, if there is any slope downward or upward, it is detected by the position of the instrument; for the plumb-line that is placed on the aforementioned rod shows the one or the other and does not allow the overseer of the work to be deceived. The work so measured and levelled off progresses always towards a likeness to tilled fallow; and as the line is moved ahead, as much space is taken up as is occupied by the length and breadth of the trench that has been dug.[b] And this method of preparing ground is most approved.

XIV. There follows the task of planting the vine; it is properly set out either in spring or in autumn; preferably in the spring if the weather is rainy or cold, or if the land is either fat or flat and wet plain; in autumn, on the other hand, if the atmosphere is dry or warm, if it is a poor and dry plain or a lean and steep hill. There are about forty days of the spring planting, from the Ides of February[c] up to the equinox; and of the autumn planting, from the Ides of October to the Calends of December.[d] Moreover, 2
there are two kinds of planting, with cuttings or with quicksets, both of which are in use by farmers; and in the provinces more use is made of the cutting, for they do not concern themselves with nurseries

[c] Feb. 13. [d] Oct. 15–Dec. 1.

nec usum habent faciendae viviradicis. Hanc sationem cultores Italiae plerique iure improbaverunt,
3 quoniam plurimis dotibus praestat viviradix: nam minus interit, cum et calorem et frigus, ceterasque tempestates propter firmitatem facilius sustineat; deinde adolescit maturius. Ex quo[1] evenit ut celerius quoque sit tempestiva edendis fructibus; tum etiam nihil dubium est saepius[2] translatam.[3] Potest tamen malleolus protinus in vicem viviradicis conseri soluta et facili terra; ceterum densa et gravis utique vitem desiderat.

XV. Seritur ergo prius emundata inoccataque et aequata pastinatione, macro solo quinis pedibus inter ordines omissis, mediocri senis. In pingui vero septenum pedum spatia danda sunt, quo largiora vacent intervalla per quae frequentes prolixaeque materiae diffundantur. Haec in quincuncem vinearum metatio expeditissima ratione conficitur: quippe linea per totidem pedes, quot destinaveris interordiniorum spatiis, purpura vel quolibet alio conspicuo colore insuitur; eaque sic denotata per repastinatum[4] intenditur, et iuxta purpuram calamus defigitur.[5]
2 Atque ita paribus spatiis ordines diriguntur. Quod deinde cum est factum, fossor insequitur, scrobemque alternis omissis in ordinem spatiis a calamo ad proximum calamum non minus altum quam duo pedes et semissem planis locis refodit, acclivibus in

[1] ex quo *M, Ald., Gesn., Schn.*: quod *SAac, vett. edd.*
[2] saepius *om. a.*
[3] translatam *Ursinus*: translatum *codd., et vulgo.*
[4] repastinationem *c.* [5] deficitur *SA.*

[a] Because the quickset, having an established root system, is planted in a greater variety of soils than is the rootless cutting. [b] *Cf* Palladius, III. 9. 10.

and have no experience in the making of quicksets. This kind of planting has been disapproved with good reason by most vinedressers of Italy, because the quickset is superior in very many particulars:
for it is less likely to die, since, because of its strength, 3
it has a readier endurance of heat and cold and other kinds of weather; and, in the next place, it reaches maturity earlier. The result is that it also comes more quickly into condition to bear fruit; and besides, there is no doubt that it is more generally transplanted.[a] Still, a cutting may be set immediately in loose and light ground, in place of a quickset; but ground that is compact and heavy certainly requires a rooted vine.

XV. The planting, then, is made preferably in prepared ground that is well cleaned and harrowed and levelled off, leaving five feet between the rows in lean ground, and six feet in medium soil. But in fat soil intervals of seven feet must be allowed, so as to leave greater space of open ground over which the numerous and far-reaching branches of firm wood may spread themselves. This laying-out of vineyards in quincunx arrangement is accomplished by a very quick method: for a line is stitched with purple or some other striking colour at intervals of the same number of feet as you have determined upon for the distance between rows; and when so marked it is stretched along the dug ground, and a reed
is thrust in beside each bit of purple. In this way the 2
rows are equally spaced.[b] When this has been done, the digger follows and, leaving spaces by turns along the rows, he digs a trench from one reed to the next, not less than two and one-half feet deep on the level, two and three-fourths feet on sloping

dupondium[1] et dodrantem, praecipitibus etiam in tres
pedes. In hanc mensuram scrobibus depressis
viviradices ita deponuntur ut a media scrobe singulae
in diversum sternantur, et contrariis frontibus fos-
3 sarum ad calamos erigantur. Satoris autem officium
est, primum quam recentissimam, et si fieri possit,
eodem momento quo serere velit, de seminario
transferre plantam diligenter exemptam et integram;
deinde eam velut veteranam vitem totam exputare,
et ad unam materiam firmissimam redigere, nodosque
et cicatrices adlevare; si quae etiam radices, quod
maxime cavendum est ne fiat in eximendo, labora-
verint,[2] eas amputare; sic deinde curvatam deponere
ne duarum vitium radices implicentur. Id enim
vitare facile est per imum solum iuxta diversa latera
fossarum dispositis paucis lapidibus, qui singuli[3]
4 non excedant quinquelibrale pondus. Hi videntur,
ut Mago prodit, et aquas hiemis et vapores aestatis
propulsare radicibus: quem secutus Vergilius tutari
semina et muniri[4] sic praecipit:

Aut lapidem bibulum aut squalentes infode conchas.

et paulo post:

Iamque reperti
Qui saxo super atque ingentis[5] pondere testae
Urgerent:[6] hoc effusos munimen ad imbres,
Hoc ubi hiulca siti findit canis aestifer arva.

[1] dipondium *c*: dipundium *SA*: clipundium *a*.
[2] lavoverint *SA*: levaverint *c*, *vett. edd.*
[3] singulis *Aac*. [4] munire *SAaM*.
[5] ingenti *S*: repertis (reperti *a*) qui super atque incentis (vincentis *c*, in gentis *a*) *Aac*
[6] teste urgeret *M*: testa urgetur *S*: testa re urgetur *A*: testa reurgetur *ac*; *deinde* et fusos *SAac*.

---

[a] *Cf. De Arb.* 4. 4 and Palladius, III. 10. 2–3.
[b] *Georg.* II. 348. [c] *Ibid.* 350–353.

land, and even three feet in steep places. After the trenches are put down to this depth, the quicksets are set in such a way that they are laid flat, each by itself and in opposite directions from the middle of the trench, and raised upright alongside the reeds at opposite ends of the ditches. But the planter's 3
duty is, first, to transfer the plant from the nursery in as fresh condition as possible, and, if this can be done, at the very moment that he wishes to plant it—removing it carefully and without mutilation; then to prune it all over like an old vine, reducing it to one very strong cane of firm wood and smoothing off the knots and scars; also, if any roots have been injured—and especial care must be taken that this does not happen in removing the vine—to cut them off; and then to set out the plant, bending it in such a way that the roots of two vines may not be intertwined. For this is easy to avoid by placing along the bottom, close to the opposite sides of the trenches, a few stones whose weight should not exceed five pounds each.[a] These 4
seem, as Mago records, to ward off the winter's wetness and the summer's heat from the vine roots. Vergil, agreeing with Mago, teaches the safeguarding and strengthening of young plants in these words:

> With them you bury scaly shells or moisture-drinking stone.[b]

and, a little later,

> And some are found who cover them with rock or heavy tile,
> Thus offering shelter 'gainst the driving rains, and shelter, too,
> When sultry Dog-star splits the fields that lie agape with thirst.[c]

5 Idemque Poenus auctor probat vinacea permixta stercori depositis seminibus in scrobe admovere,[1] quod illa provocent et eliciant novas radiculas: hoc per hiemem frigentem et umidam [2] scrobibus inferre calorem tempestivum,[3] ac per aestatem virentibus alimentum et umorem praebere.[4] Si vero solum cui vitis [5] committitur, videtur exile, longius arcessitam pinguem humum scrobibus inferre censet: quod an expediat, regionis annona operarumque ratio nos docebit.

XVI. Exigue umidum pastinatum sationi convenit; melius tamen vel arido quam lutoso semen committitur. Idque cum supra summam scrobem compluribus internodiis productum est, quod de cacumine superest, duabus gemmis tantum supra terram relictis amputatur, et ingesta humo scrobis completur.[6] Coaequato deinceps [7] pastinato malleolus ordinariis vitibus interserendus; [8] cumque sat erit medio spatio, quod vacat inter vites, per unam lineam
2 depangere.[9] Sic enim melius et ipse convalescet,[10] et ordinariis seminibus modice vacuum solum ad culturam praebebitur. In eadem deinde linea, in qua viviradix obtinebit ordinem suum, praesidii

[1] *sic Schn.*: in scrobem admovere *M*: scrobe an movere *S*: scrobeam (strobeam *a*) movere *Aac*: scrobem vires movere *Ald*, *Gesn.*

[2] et humidam *M*: ut humidam *vulgo*: ut (et *ac*) humum *SAac, vett. edd.*

[3] tempestivum *M, et vulgo*: tempestate *SAac*: calorem: tempestate *ac, vett. edd.*

[4] praebeat (prebeat *Sa*) *SAac, vett. edd.*

[5] civitatis *SAac.*

[6] completur *Ald., Gesn.*: completus *codd., Schn.*

[7] *sic. codd., Ald., Gesn.*: coaequatur; deinceps *Schn.*: scrobibus completis coaequato. Deinceps *vett. edd.*

[8] est *add. vulgo*; *om. codd.*

The same Carthaginian author approves an application of grape-husks mixed with dung when the plants are set in the trench, on the ground that they encourage and draw out new rootlets; saying that this gives a suitable warmth to the trenches during the cold and wet weather of winter, and supplies the growing plants with nourishment and moisture in summer. But if the ground to which the vine is committed seems to be lean, his advice is that rich soil be brought from some distance and put into the trenches. Whether this is profitable the annual yield of the region and an estimate of the labour involved will teach us. 5

XVI. Trenched ground is suitable for planting when it is slightly moist; and yet it is better to commit the plant to it even when dry than when it is muddy. And when the plant extends several joints above the upper edge of the trench, that part of the top which projects above is cut off, leaving only two eyes above ground, and the trench is filled by throwing the earth into it. Then, after the trenched ground is levelled off, the mallet-cutting is to be planted between the rows of vines. It will be sufficient to set this in a single line in the centre of
the space that lies vacant between the vines; for in 2
this way the cutting itself will regain its strength the better, and the ground will be left moderately free for the cultivation of the plants in the rows. Then, in the same line in which the quickset is arrayed, five mallet-shoots are to be set for each

---

[9] depangere *M, et vulgo*: depingere *SAac, vett. edd.*
[10] convalescit *codd.*

causa, quorum ex numero propagari[1] possit in locum demortuae vitis, quinque malleoli pangendi sunt per spatium pedale; isque pes ita medio interordinio sumitur ut ab utraque vite[2] paribus intervallis
3 distet.[3] Tali consitioni Iulius Atticus abunde putat esse malleolorum sedecim milia. Nos tamen plus quattuor milibus conserimus, quia neglegentia cultorum magna pars deperit, et interitu seminum cetera, quae virent, rarescunt.

XVII. De positione surculi non minima disputatio fuit inter auctores. Quidam totum flagellum, sicut erat matri detractum, crediderunt sationi convenire;[4] idque per gemmas quinas vel etiam senas partiti, complures taleolas terrae mandaverunt. Quod ego minime probo; magisque assentior his auctoribus qui negaverunt esse idoneam frugibus superiorem partem materiae, solamque eam quae est iuncta cum vetere sarmento probaverunt. Ceterum omnem
2 sagittam repudiaverunt. Sagittam rustici vocant novissimam partem surculi, sive quia longius recessit a matre, et quasi emicuit atque prosiluit, seu[5] quia cacumine attenuata praedicti teli speciem gerit.
3 Hanc ergo prudentissimi agricolae negaverunt conseri debere, nec tamen sententiae suae rationem nobis prodiderunt; videlicet quia ipsis in re rustica multum callentibus prompta erat et ante oculos

[1] propagari *Gesn.*, *Schn.*: propagare *codd.*
[2] vite *S*, *Schn.*: parte *Ald.*, *Gesn.*: *om. AacM*, *vett. edd.*
[3] distet *SAacM*: distent *edd.*
[4] convenire *M*: convenirent *SAac.*
[5] seu *SAcM*: sive *a*, *et vulgo.*

[a] Isidore (*Orig.* XVII. 5. 7) defines *sagitta* in the same terms; but Pliny has a different explanation (*N.H.* XVII. 156), *tertium genus adiectum etiamnum expeditius sine calce, quod*

foot of space, as reserves from whose number it may be possible to set a slip in place of a vine that has died; and this foot is taken from the middle space between the rows in such a way as to be equally distant from the vines on either side. Julius Atticus 3
considers 16,000 cuttings enough for this kind of planting. But we plant 4000 more, because a large number of them are lost through the carelessness of the vinedressers, while the rest, that do thrive, are thinned out by the deaths of the young plants.

XVII. On the matter of setting the shoot there has been no little dispute among authorities. Some have held that the whole rod, just as it was pulled from the parent vine, is proper for planting; and dividing this into sections with five or even six eyes each, they committed the several slips to the earth. This I by no means approve, agreeing rather with those authorities who have said that the upper part of the branch is not suitable for bearing fruit, and who gave their approval rather to that part which is joined to the old branch. But they wholly rejected the "arrow." Farmers give the name "arrow" to 2
the extreme portion of a shoot, either because it has withdrawn farther from its mother and has, so to speak, shot out and darted away from her, or because, being drawn out into a point, it bears a resemblance to the aforesaid missile.[a] Our wisest 3
husbandmen have said, then, that the arrow should not be planted, and yet they have failed to give us the reason for their opinion; obviously because to those men of much experience in agricultural affairs that reason was obvious and almost laid bare before

sagittae vocantur, cum intorti panguntur, iidem cum recisi nec intorti, trigemmes.

paene exposita. Omnis enim fecundus pampinus intra quintam aut sextam gemmam fructu exuberat, reliqua parte quamvis longissima vel cessat vel perexiguos ostendit racemos. Quam ob causam sterilitas cacuminis iure ab antiquis incusata est. Malleolus autem sic ab iisdem pangebatur ut novello
4 sarmento pars aliqua veteris haereret. Sed hanc positionem damnavit[1] usus. Nam quicquid ex vetere materia relictum erat, depressum atque obrutum celeriter umore putrescebat, proximasque radices teneras et vixdum prorepentes[2] vitio suo enecabat;[3] quod cum acciderat, superior pars seminis retorrescebat. Mox Iulius Atticus et Cornelius Celsus, aetatis nostrae celeberrimi auctores, patrem atque filium Sasernam secuti, quicquid residui fuit ex vetere palma per ipsam commissuram, qua nascitur materia nova, raserunt,[4] atque ita cum suo capitulo sarmentum depresserunt.

XVIII. Sed Iulius Atticus praetorto capite et recurvato, ne pastinum[5] effugiat, praedictum semen demersit. Pastinum autem vocant agricolae ferramentum bifurcum, quo semina panguntur. Unde etiam repastinari dictae sunt vineae veteres quae refodiebantur, haec enim propria appellatio restibilis vineti erat; nunc antiquitatis imprudens consuetudo

[1] damnabit *Ac.*

[2] prorepentes *edd.*: propeientis *SA* : proparentis *acM.*

[3] enecabat *M* : enecarat *ac, et corr. ex* enegarat *S*: enacarat *A.*

[4] raserunt *SAac, vett. edd.* : resecuerunt *vulgo.*

[5] pastinum *Ald., Gesn., Schn.*: pastinatum *SAacM, vett. edd.*

---

[a] Here = the thick end or butt of the mallet-cutting, like the "head" of a mallet.

the eyes. For every fruiting cane bears in abundance within the limits of the fifth or sixth bud; while in the remaining portion, however great its length, it is either entirely lacking in fruit or displays very small clusters. For this reason the barrenness of the tip was justly censured by the ancients. Moreover, the mallet-shoot was so planted by these same ancients that some part of the old branch remained fixed to the new. But experience has condemned this kind 4
of planting. For all that was left of the old wood quickly rotted with the moisture after it was set and covered with earth, and by the damage to itself it killed the tender roots lying next to it and scarcely creeping out as yet; and when this happened, the upper part of the plant would wither. Afterwards Julius Atticus and Cornelius Celsus, the most distinguished authorities of our time, following the example of the Sasernas, father and son, smoothed off every remaining bit of the old branch at the very joint where the new wood begins, and so they set the slip, tip and all.

XVIII. But Julius Atticus pressed the aforesaid plant into the ground with its head[a] twisted and bent so that it might not slip away from the trench-fork. The name *pastinum* or trench-fork, by the way, is given by farmers to that two-pronged implement of iron with which the plants are set.[b] Hence even old vineyards which were turned by the spade for a second time were said to be "repastinated," this term belonging properly to a vineyard that was restored; but modern custom, ignorant of ancient usage, applies the term "repastinated" to

[b] Cf. Isidore, *Orig.* XX. 14. 8.

quicquid emoti soli vineis praeparatur, repastinatum vocat. Sed redeamus [1] ad propositum.

2 Vitiosa est, ut mea fert opinio, Iulii Attici satio, quae contortis capitibus malleolum recipit; eiusque rei vitandae non una ratio [2] est. Primum quod nulla stirps ante quam deponatur vexata et infracta melius provenit quam quae integra et inviolata sine iniuria deposita est; deinde quicquid recurvum et sursum versus spectans [3] demersum est, cum tempestivum eximitur, in modum hami repugnat obluctanti fossori, et velut uncus infixus solo, ante quam extrahatur, praerumpitur. Nam fragilis est ea parte materia, qua torta et recurvata, cum deponeretur, ceperat vitium; propter quod praefractam maiorem partem
3 radicum amittit. Sed ut incommoda ista praeteream, certe illud, quod est inimicissimum, dissimulare nequeo; nam paulo ante, cum de summa parte sarmenti disputarem, quam sagittam dixeram vocitari, colligebam fere intra quintam vel sextam gemmam, quae sint proximae veteri sarmento,
4 fructum edi.[4] Hanc ergo fecundam partem consumit, qui contorquet malleolum; quoniam et ea pars, quae duplicatur, tres gemmas vel quattuor obtinet, et reliqui duo vel tres fruccuarii oculi penitus in terram deprimuntur,[5] mersique non materias sed radices creant. Ita evenit ut [6] quod in sagitta non

[1] redeamus *M, edd.*: *om. SAac, et inclusit Schn.*
[2] ut narratio *Aac.*
[3] spectans *M, et vulgo*: spectant *SA*: spectat *ac, vett. edd.*

any ground that is stirred and prepared for vineyards. But let us return to the subject before us.

Quite wrong, in my opinion, is the method of planting employed by Julius Atticus, which allows mallet-cuttings with bent and twisted heads; and there is more than one reason for avoiding this practice: in the first place, because no stem which is damaged and broken before it is put into the ground thrives better than one that is planted whole without suffering any injury; and in the second place, anything that is curved back and tending upward at the time of planting resists the efforts of the digger, in the manner of a hook, when the time comes for taking it up, and like a barb fixed in the ground it is broken off before it can be pulled out. For the wood is brittle in that section where it received injury when twisted and bent at the time of planting, and for this reason it loses the majority of its roots, which are broken off. But, even though I pass over these disadvantages, surely I cannot conceal a point that is most hurtful; for a short time ago, while speaking of the uppermost part of the shoot, which I said was called the arrow, I observed that fruit is generally put forth within the limits of the fifth or sixth eye nearest to the old branch. Therefore one who bends the shoot destroys this productive part; because that part which is doubled over contains three or four eyes, and the remaining two or three fruit-bearing eyes are pressed deep into the earth, and when so buried they produce, not wood, but roots. Thus it comes about that, what we

2 (margin, beside "Quite wrong")

[4] fructum edi *Schn. ex coniect. Gesn.*: fructu medii *SAac*: fructus medii *M, edd. ante Schn.*

[5] deprimantur *SAacM*. [6] ut *edd.*: sed *SAacM*.

serenda[1] vitaverimus id sequamur in eiusmodi malleolo, quem necesse est longiorem facere[2] si volumus detortum depangere. Nec dubium quin gemmae cacumini proximae, quae sunt infecundae, in eo relinquantur, ex quibus pampini pullulant[3] vel steriles[4] vel certe minus feraces, quos rustici vocant
5 racemarios. Quid quod plurimum interest ut malleolus, qui deponitur, ea parte qua est a matre decisus, coalescat, et celeriter cicatricem ducat? Nam si id factum non est, velut per fistulam ita per apertam vitis medullam nimius umor trahitur, idemque truncum cavat; unde formicis aliisque animalibus, quae putrefaciunt crura vitium, latebrae praebentur. Hoc autem evenit retortis seminibus; cum enim per exemptionem imae partes eorum praefractae sunt, apertae medullae deponuntur; atque inrepentibus aquis praedictisque animalibus celeriter senescunt. Quare pangendi optima est ratio recti malleoli, cuius imum caput, cum consertum est bifurco pastini, angustis faucibus ferramenti facile continetur ac deprimitur; idque sarmentum sic demersum[5] citius coalescit. Nam et radices e capite, qua recisum est, emittit, eaeque cum accreverunt cicatricem obducunt, et alioquin plaga ipsa deorsum spectans non tantum recipit umorem quantum illa quae reflexa et resupina more infundibuli per medullam transmittit quicquid aquarum caelestium superfluxit.[6]

[1] *sic Schn. cum Pontedera*: in salictam conseranda (-o *A*) *SA*: in salictam (-a) conserando *ac*: in salicto conserendo *M*, *et vulgo ante Schn.*

[2] *sic codd*: facere longiorem *edd.*

[3] pampinus (panpinus *SA*) pullat (expullat *c*, expullulat *M*) *codd.*

[4] sterilis *et deinde* feracis (ferax *M*) *SAacM*.

[5] demersum *SAacM*: depressum *edd. vulgo.*

have avoided in not planting the arrow, we comply
with in the case of a mallet-cutting of this sort, which
we must make longer if we wish to plant it twisted.
Nor is there any doubt that the buds next to the tip,
which are unfruitful, are left on it; from which sprout
young shoots, either barren or at least less fruitful,
which farmers call *racemarii*. And furthermore, it 5
is of the greatest importance that a cutting which is
set in the ground should heal over and quickly form
a callus at the point where it is cut from the mother
vine. For, if this does not happen, excessive
moisture is drawn up through the open pith of the
vine, as though through a tube, and makes the stock
hollow; and the result is that hiding-places are
provided for ants and other creatures that cause
the lower part of the vine-stalk to rot. And this
also happens when plants are bent back; for when
their lower sections are broken in taking them up,
they are planted with the pith exposed; and when
water and the aforementioned animals creep into
them, they soon waste away. Therefore the best 6
method is to plant a straight cutting, whose butt
end, when caught in the two prongs of the trench-
ing-fork, is easily held in the narrow jaws of the
implement and so thrust into the ground; and a
cutting that is set in this way heals over sooner.
For it puts out roots from the butt, where it was
cut off, and these cover the callus as they grow;
and, besides, the wound itself, looking downwards,
does not admit as much moisture as the one which,
being bent back and facing upwards, conveys through
its pith, as though through a funnel, all the rains that
fall upon it.

[6] superfluit *cM, et vulgo ante Schn.*

XIX. Longitudo, quae debeat esse malleoli, parum certa est, quoniam sive crebras gemmas habet, brevior faciendus est; seu raras, longior. Ac tamen[1] nec maior pede nec dodrante minor esse debet: hic ne per summam[2] terrae sitiat aestatibus; ille ne depressus altius cum adoleverit, exemptionem difficilem praebeat. Sed haec in plano. Nam in clivosis, ubi terra decurrit, potest palmipedalis
2 deponi. Vallis et uliginosi campi situs patitur[3] etiam trigemmem, qui est paulo minor dodrante, longior utique semipede. Isque non ab eo trigemmis dictus est quod omnino trium oculorum est, cum fere circa plagam, qua matri abscisus est, plenus sit germinum;[4] sed quod his exceptis quibus est frequens in ipso capite tres deinceps articulos totidemque gemmas habet. Super cetera illud quoque sive malleolum sive viviradicem serentem praemoneo, ne semina exarescant, immodicum ventum solemque vitare, qui uterque non incommode arcetur obiectu
3 vestis aut cuiuslibet densi teguminis.[5] Verumtamen praestat eligere sationi silentis vel certe placidi spiritus diem. Nam sol umbraculis facile depellitur.

Sed illud etiam, quod nondum tradidimus, ante quam disputationi clausulam imponamus, dicendum est: uniusne[6] an plurium generum vites habendae sint, eaeque[7] separatae ac distinctae specialiter, an

[1] Ac tamen *SAac*: Attamen *M*, *edd.*

[2] summam *SAacM*, *vett. edd.*: summa *Ald.*, *Gesn.*, *Schn.*

[3] situ sentitur *Aac*: situs seritur *M*: situ serimus *vulgo ante Schn.*

[4] germinum *SAacM*: gemmarum *edd.*

[5] teguminis *SAaM*. tegminis *c*, *et vulgo.*

[6] uniusne *S*, *Schn.*: ne *Aa*: ut *c*: utrum *M*: *om. vett. edd.*

[7] eaeque *M*, *et vulgo*: aeque *SA*, *vett. edd.*: que *a*: ut quare *c*.

XIX. The length that a cutting should have is not absolutely fixed, since it should be made shorter if its eyes are close together, or longer if they are far apart. Still, it should be not more than a foot nor less than nine inches in length: lest in the latter case, being at the surface of the earth, it dry out in hot weather; while in the former case, if set too deep, it may make removal difficult after it has made some growth. But the above applies to planting in level ground. For on hillsides, where the land falls off rapidly, it may be set to a depth of a foot and a palm. A 2
situation in a valley or a wet plain allows even a cutting of three buds, which is a little less than nine inches but in any case more than half a foot in length. And this cutting is called "three-budded," not from the fact that it consists of three eyes in all—since it is usually full of sprouts about the wound where it was cut from its mother—but because, apart from those buds with which it is crowded at the butt, it has three joints in succession and the same number of buds. In addition, I offer this advice also to one who is planting either the cutting or the rooted vine—to avoid excessive wind and sun, lest the plants dry out; and both of these are warded off without inconvenience by throwing a garment or any sort of thick covering around the plants. However, it is better to 3
choose for the planting a day when the air is still or at least stirring but lightly. For the sun is easily kept off by canopies.

But, before putting an end to this discussion, we must speak of a matter which we have not yet touched upon—whether vines of one or several kinds are to be kept, and whether these are to be separated and kept apart, sort by sort, or jumbled

confusae et mixtae catervatim. Prius disseremus de eo quod primum proposuimus.

XX. Prudentis igitur agricolae est vitem, quam praecipue probaverit, nulla interveniente alterius notae[1] stirpe conserere, numerumque quam maximum eius semper augere. Sed et[2] providentis est diversa quoque genera deponere. Neque enim umquam sic mitis ac temperatus est annus, ut nullo incommodo vexet aliquod vitis genus: sive[3] siccus est, id quod umore proficit,[4] contristatur; seu pluvius, quod siccitatibus gaudet; seu frigidus et pruinosus, quod non est patiens uredinis; seu fer-
2 vens,[5] quod vaporem non sustinet. Ac ne nunc mille tempestatum iniurias persequar, semper est aliquid quod vineas offendat. Igitur si unum genus severimus, cum id acciderit quod ei noxium est, tota vindemia privabimur; neque enim ullum erit subsidium, cui diversarum notarum stirpes non fuerint.[6]
3 At[7] si varii generis vineta fecerimus, aliquid ex iis inviolatum erit quod fructum perferat. Nec tamen ea causa nos debet compellere ad multas vitium varietates: sed quod iudicaverimus eximium genus, id quantae possimus[8] multitudinis efficiamus; quod deinde proximum a primo; tum quod est tertiae notae vel quartae quoque. Eatenus velut athletarum[9] quodam contenti simus tetradio;[10] satis est

[1] nota *SAac.* [2] et *S, Schn.*: *om. reliqui.*

[3] enim *add. vulgo*: *deest codd.*

[4] quod (h)umore proficit *Ald., Gesn. Schn.*: *om. SAa, et* umore proficit *om. cM.*

[5] perurens *S.*

[6] diversarum . . . fuerint *om. SAac, vett. edd.*: cui . . . fuerint *om. M.*

[7] Ad *SA* : et *c* : Quod *Schn.*

[8] possimus *SAaM, Sobel*: possumus *vulgo.*

together and intermingled, one with another. We shall deal first with the question first proposed

XX. It is, then, the part of a wise farmer to plant that vine which he especially approves, with no shoot of any other sort standing between, and always to increase the number of that vine as far as possible. But it is also the part of a man of foresight to set out different kinds as well. For there is never a year so mild and temperate as not to inflict some injury upon some variety of the vine: if it is dry, that kind which thrives on moisture is damaged; if rainy, that which delights in dry weather; if cold and frosty, that which cannot endure blighting cold; or if hot, that which cannot bear heat. And, not to run 2
through, at this time, a thousand rigours of the weather, there is always something to work harm to vineyards. Therefore, if we plant but one kind, when that thing happens which is hurtful to that kind, we shall be deprived of the whole vintage; for he who is without plants of different sorts will have no reserve supply. But if we make plantings 3
of various kinds of vines, some of them will escape injury to produce a yield. And yet this reason should not force us to many varieties of vines· but what we have judged to be an extraordinary variety, that we should produce in as great numbers as possible; then that which is next to the first choice, and after that the kind which is of third or even fourth rank. So far let us be content with a sort of quartet, so to speak, of champion vines; for it is quite enough to

[9] athletarum *Schn.*: letarum *SacM*: laetarum *A*: lectarum *vulgo*.

[10] *sic Gesn.*, *Schn.*: tetradeo *vett. edd.*: tetartaeo *Ald.*: conten simus tetra deo *S*: contempsimus tetradeo *AacM*.

enim per quattuor vel summum quinque genera vindemiae fortunam opperiri.

4 De altero, quod mox proposueram, nihil dubito quin per species digerendae vites disponendaeque sint in proprios hortos, semitis ac decumanis distinguendae: non quod aut ipse potuerim[1] a meis familiaribus hoc obtinere, aut ante me quisquam eorum, qui[2] quam maxime id probaverit,[3] effecerit. Est enim omnium rusticorum operum difficillimum, quia et summam diligentiam legendis desiderat seminibus, et in his[4] discernendis maxima[5] plerumque felicitate et prudentia opus est; sed interdum, quod ait divinus auctor Plato, rei nos pulchritudo trahit vel ea consectandi, quae propter infirmitatem
5 commortalis[6] naturae consequi nequeamus. Istud tamen, si aetas suppetat et scientia facultasque cum voluntate congruant, non aegerrime perficiemus;[7] quamvis non minimo[8] aetatis spatio perseverandum sit, ut magnus numerus per aliquot annos discernatur. Neque enim omne tempus permittit eius rei iudicium; nam vites, quae propter similitudinem coloris aut trunci flagellorumve uvae[9] dinosci nequeunt, maturo fructu foliisque declarantur. Quam tamen diligentiam nisi per ipsum patrem familiae exhiberi
6 posse non adfirmaverim; nam credidisse vilico vel

[1] potueram *codd., et plerique ante Schn.*
[2] qui *om. codd.* [3] probabit *codd., vett. edd.*
[4] in his *Schn.*: nihis *S*: nihil *Aac*: non nihil *M, et vulgo.*
[5] in quo maxima *M, Ald., Gesn.*
[6] conmortales *SAa.* [7] perficiamus *SAac.*
[8] *sic SAac, Schn.*: non (ron *M*) omnino minimo *M, et vulgo.*
[9] flagellorum uvae *Sobel*: f. vaenue *SA*: f. venue *ac*: f. hieme *M*: flagellorumve *edd.*

[a] *Cf.* Palladius, III. 9. 11.

await the luck of the vintage with four varieties, or five at the most.[a]

As for the other point, which I had next proposed, 4 I have no doubt that vines should be separated according to their species and set in their proper plots, and marked off by foot-paths and boundary lines;[b] not that I myself have been able to obtain this of my household, or that any one of those before me accomplished it, however much he may have approved. For this is the most difficult of the farmer's tasks, because it requires the utmost care in the selection of plants, and in separating them there is need, for the most part, of the greatest good fortune combined with wisdom. But sometimes, as the divine author Plato says, the beauty of a thing attracts us to the pursuit even of those ends to which, because of the frailty of human nature, we cannot attain. And yet if our 5 years suffice, and if our knowledge and means are in accord with our desires, we shall accomplish the task without great difficulty; though we must persist for more than a brief portion of our lives, so that a large number may be classified over a period of several years. For not every period of time permits a decision in this matter, seeing that vines which cannot be distinguished because of their likeness in colour or stock or shoots or berry make themselves known by the ripening of their fruit and by their foliage. Nevertheless, I would not say that this care can be employed by anyone except the head of the family; for it is folly to intrust it to an overseer or vine- 6

[b] Palladius (*loc. cit.*) speaks to the same effect. Pliny (*N.H.* XVII. 169) gives directions as to the size of the various plots and the widths of intervening roads or paths. *Cf.* also Columella, IV. 18.

etiam vinitori,[1] socordia [2] est, cum, quod longe sit facilius, adhuc perpaucissimis agricolis contigerit ut nigri vini stirpe careant, quamvis color uvae possit vel ab imprudentissimo deprehendi.

XXI. Illa tamen una mihi ratio suppetit, celerrime quod proposuimus efficiendi, si sint veteranae vineae, ut separatim surculis [3] cuiusque generis singulos hortos inseramus: sic paucis annis multa nos milia malleolorum [4] ex insitis percepturos, atque ita discreta semina per regiones consituros nihil dubito.
2 Eius porro faciendae rei nos utilitas multis de causis compellere potest: et ut a levioribus incipiam, primum, quod ad omnem rationem [5] vitae non solum agricolationis sed cuiusque disciplinae prudentem delectant impensius ea, quae propriis generibus distinguuntur, quam quae passim velut abiecta et
3 quodam acervo confusa sunt: deinde quod vel alienissimus rusticae vitae, si in agrum tempestive [6] veniat, summa cum voluptate naturae benignitatem miretur, cum istinc Bituricae fructibus opimis, hinc paribus Helvolae respondeant; [7] illinc Arcelaca cursus,[8]

[1] vilici(villici *c*) vel etiam vinitoris *SAac, et* (*sc.* diligentiae) *Sobel.*

[2] socordia *a* : socordio *SA* : secordi *c* : secordis *M, Ald., Gesn.* : socordis *Schn.* : socordiae *Sobel.*

[3] separatim surculis *Ursinus, Schn.* : separarum (sepera-torum *a,* seperate *M,* seperare *c*) surculorum *SAacM* : separatorum surculorum *Ald., Gesn.* : separatos sulcorum *vett. edd.*

[4] malleolum *SA* : malleorum insitis *acM.*

[5] ad omnem (omne *A*) rationem (ratione *Ac*) *SAacM, et vulgo* : in omni ratione *Schn.*

dresser, since—what would be easier by far—it has been the lot of very few farmers as yet to be free from stock that produces black wine, though the colour of the grape may be detected even by the most inexperienced person.

XXI. Nevertheless, one method suggests itself to me of accomplishing very quickly what we have proposed: that, if we have old vineyards, we should ingraft individual plots with slips of every sort, each kind by itself. Thus I have no doubt that within a few years we shall obtain many thousands of cuttings from the grafted vines, and that we shall set in separate blocks the plants so distinguished from one
another. Moreover, the advantage of doing this 2
may urge us on for many reasons: in the first place, to begin with the less important, because in respect to every concern of life, not only in farming but in every branch of study, the wise man delights more in those things which are separated into their proper kinds than in those which are thrown helter-skelter, so to speak, and jumbled together into a common
heap: and in the second place, because even the 3
man who is quite unversed in country life, if he should enter a field at the proper time, would marvel most pleasurably at the benevolence of nature, when on the one side the Bituric vines with their rich fruits correspond to the Helvolans, with like fruit, on the other side; when the Arcelacans turn his course to

---

[6] tempestive *SAac, vett. edd.*: tempestive consitum *M, et vulgo.*

[7] opimis (opinis *SA*) hic paribus heluo respondent *SAacM*: opimae hinc pares iis helvolae respondeant *vulgo.*

[8] arcelaca cursus *Sobel*: arcela cursus *SAac*: arcelane cursus *M*: arcellae, rursus *Ald., Gesn.*: arcelacae, rursus *Schn.*

illinc Spioniae Basilicaeve convertant,[1] quibus alma tellus annua vice velut aeterno quodam puerperio laeta mortalibus[2] distenta musto demittit[3] ubera. Inter quae patre favente Libero fetis[4] palmitibus vel generis albi vel flaventis ac rutili vel purpureo nitore micantis, undique versicoloribus pomis gravidus
4 collucet Autumnus. Sed haec quamvis plurimum delectent,[5] utilitas tamen vincit voluptatem. Nam et pater familiae libentius ad spectaculum rei suae, quanto est ea luculentior, descendit; et, quod de sacro numine poeta dicit,

Et quocumque deus circum caput egit honestum,

verum quocumque domini praesentia et oculi[6] frequenter accessere, in ea parte maiorem in modum fructus exuberat. Sed omitto illud, quod indescriptis etiam vitibus contingere potest; illa quae sunt maxime spectanda, persequar.

5 Diversae notae stirpes nec pariter deflorescunt nec ad maturitatem simul perveniunt. Quam ob causam, qui separata generibus vineta non habet, patiatur alterum incommodum necesse est, ut aut serum[7] fructum cum praecoque elevet,[8] quae res mox acorem facit; aut si maturitatem serotini expectet,[9]

[1] convertant *SAacM*, *vett. edd.*, *Sobel*: conveniant *vulgo*.

[2] leta (laeta *edd.*) mortalibus *M*, *et vulgo*: laeta mortis *S*: laetam ortibus (h *supra* o *scr.*) *A*: letam ortibus (hortibus *a*) *ac*: laeta in hortis *Sobel*.

[3] demit *S*: distamusto demit *Aa*: dicta musto demit *c*.

[4] foetis *vulgo*: petis *SAacM*, *vett. edd.*

[5] delectant *Aac*.

[6] praesentia et oculi *Sobel*: presenti et oculi *SAac*: praesente et oculos *M*: praesentis oculi *edd.*

[7] serum *om. SAac*, *vett. edd.*

[8] preco quae lebat *SA*: percoque elebat *a*.

[9] expectes *SAac*.

the one side and the Spionians or Basilicans to the other side, whereby the fostering earth each year, as if delighting in never-ending parturition,[a] extends to mortals her breasts distended with new wine. Meanwhile, as father Bacchus is propitious to the pregnant vine-branches, either of the white or yellow variety, and of the ruddy kind or that which gleams with purple sheen, on every hand Autumnus glows, laden with his fruits of changing hue. But though 4
all these give the greatest delight, still profit prevails over pleasure. For the head of the household comes down the more willingly to feast his eyes upon his wealth in proportion to its splendour; and, as the poet says of the sacred deity,

Wheresoever the god has turned his goodly head,[b]

truly, wherever the person and eyes of the master are frequent visitors, there the fruit abounds in greater measure.[c] But, dismissing this statement, which is applicable also to vines not grouped according to their kinds, I shall proceed with those matters which are most deserving of notice.

Vine-plants of different kinds do not cast their 5
blossoms at the same time, nor do they reach the time of ripening together. For this reason, the man who does not have his vineyards divided according to their kinds must suffer one or the other of these disadvantages: either he must gather the late fruit along with the early ripe, which soon causes sourness; or, if he awaits the ripening of the late fruit, he may

[a] *Cf.* X. 145, 157.
[b] Vergil, *Georg.* II. 392. The god is Bacchus.
[c] *Cf.* IV. 18. 1; Palladius, I. 6. 1, *Praesentia domini provectus est agri.*

amittat vindemiam praecoquem, quae [1] plerumque populationibus volucrum pluviisque aut ventis laces-
6 sita dilabitur. Si vero interiectionibus capere cuiusque generis fructum aveat, primum necesse est ut neglegentiae vindemiatorum aleam [2] subeat; neque enim singulis totidem antistitores possit dare,[3] qui observent quique praecipiant ne acerbae uvae [4] demetantur.

Deinde etiam quarum vitium maturitas competit, cum diversae notae sint, melioris gustus ab deteriore corrumpitur confususque in unum multarum sapor vetustatis impatiens fit. Atque ideo necessitas cogit agricolam musti annonam experiri,[5] cum plurimum pretio accedat si venditio vel in annum vel in aestatem
7 certe differri possit. Iam illa generum separatio summam commoditatem habet, quod vinitor cuique facilius suam [6] putationem reddet, cum scit cuius notae sit hortus quem deputat: [7] idque in consemineis vineis observari difficile est, quia maior pars putationis per id tempus administratur quo vitis neque folium notabile gerit. Ac [8] multum interest pluresne an pauciores materias pro natura cuiusque stirpis vinitor summittat, prolixisne flagellis incitet an

[1] quae *om. SAacM.*

[2] interiectionibus . . . aleam] *sic vulgo, sed Ald. et Gesn.* interiectibus *habent et* neglegentiae *omittunt*: interiectionibus fructum capere (carpare *in* carpere *mut. S*) genus suerit (genusuerit *A*, gensuerit *in* censuerit *mut. S*, suerit *om. a*) primum neglegentiae (neglıgentıe *ac*) vindemiatoris (vindemmıatorıs *a*) alaeam (aliam *a*, alacam *c*) *SAac*: interiectıbus fructum capere genus vetuit primum neglıgentiam vindemıatoris alaeam *M*.

[3] antistitores possit dare *Sobel*: antistiores possit dare clare *a*) *SAacM*: antıstes dare potest *vulgo.*

[4] *post* uvae *vulgo add.* cum maturis, *in uncis Schn.*: *om. SAacM*, *Sobel.*

lose the early vintage, which, being assailed by the plunderings of birds and by rains or winds, usually comes to ruin. But if he should wish to gather the 6 fruit of each kind at intervals of time, he must first take the risk of carelessness on the part of the vintagers; for it would be impossible to assign the same number of overseers, one to each man, to watch over them and give orders that the sour grapes shall not be gathered.

Moreover, when vines of different kinds ripen at the same time, the taste of the better kind is spoiled by the worse, and the flavour of many, when blended into one, becomes intolerant of age. And so necessity forces the farmer to market his wine when it is new, though it would bring a better price if the selling could be put off for a year, or at least until summer. Now the separating of varieties, 7 mentioned above, has a very great advantage, in that the vinedresser can more readily give each its proper pruning when he knows the particular sort in that plot which he is pruning; and this is a difficult practice to observe in vineyards that are planted with many sorts of vines, because the greater part of the pruning is done during the time when the vine is not even bearing distinctive foliage. And it makes a great difference, according to the nature of each stock, whether the vinedresser allows the growth of more or fewer canes, whether he is encouraging the growth of the vine by leaving long shoots or re-

[5] expedire *Ald.*, *Gesn.*

[6] *sic SAac, vett. edd.*: suam cuique facilius *vulgo*.

[7] disputat *a*: deputet *Ald.*, *Gesn.*

[8] Ac *SAacM*: At *vulgo*.

8 angusta putatione vitem coerceat. Quin etiam quam caeli partem spectet genus quodque vineti plurimum refert. Neque enim omne [1] calido statu, nec rursus frigido laetatur; sed est proprietas in surculis, ut alii meridiano axe convalescant, quia sint calori aptiores;[2] alii septentrionem desiderent, quia contristentur [3] aestu; quidam temperamento laetentur
9 orientis vel occidentis. Has differentias servat pro situ et positione locorum, qui genera per hortos separat. Illam quoque non exiguam sequitur utilitatem, quod et laborem vindemiae minorem patitur et sumptum. Nam ut quaeque virescere [4] incipiunt, tempestive leguntur, et quae nondum maturitatem
10 ceperunt uvae, sine dispendio differuntur; nec pariter vetus [5] atque tempestivus fructus praecipitat vindemiam, cogitque pluris operas quantocumque pretio conducere. Iam et illud magnae dotis est, posse gustum cuiusque generis non mixtum sed vere merum condere, ac separatim reponere, sive est ille Bituricus seu Basilicus seu Spionicus.[6] Quae genera cum sic diffusa sunt, quia nihil intervenit diversae naturae quod repugnet perpetuitati,[7] nobilitantur, neque enim post annos quindecim vel paulo plures

[1] omni *SAac.*, *edd. ante Gesn.*

[2] sin⟨t⟩ calori ⟨apti⟩ores *coniecit L. A. Post*: sincaloriores *S*: in sicaloriores *A*: nisi calidiores *ac*: *om. M*: sunt calidiores *vett. edd.*: rigore vitiantur *Ald., Gesn., Schn.*: *num* sint caloris avidiores?

[3] contristentur *SAac, edd. ante Schn.*: contristantur *Schn.*: quia sint . . . contristentur *om. M.*

[4] *sic scripsi*: ut que quae virescere (*ex* viresgere *corr.*) *S*: ut quae quiescere *A*. ut que vinescere *a*: ut que quiescere *c*: ut quaeque restire *M*: ut quaeque maturescere *Schn.*: ut quae maturescere *Ald*, *Gesn.*

[5] vetus *SAacM*: vietus *Schn.*

[6] spiniosus *SA*: spinosus *acM.*

tarding it by close pruning. Moreover, it is of very 8
great importance what quarter of the heavens every kind of vineyard faces. For not every kind thrives in a hot situation nor, on the other hand, in a cold one; but it is a peculiarity inherent in young vines that some thrive exposed to the south because they are better adapted to warmth, while others want a northern exposure because they are damaged by heat; and certain kinds delight in the moderate temperature of an eastern or western exposure.
One who separates the various sorts by sections has 9
regard to these differences as to situation and setting. He also gains no small advantage in that he is put to less labour and expense for the vintage; for the grapes are gathered at the proper time, as each variety begins to grow ripe,[a] and those that have not yet reached maturity are left until a later time
without loss; nor does the simultaneous ageing and 10
ripening of fruit precipitate the vintage and force the hiring of more workmen, however great the cost. Now this also is a great advantage, to be able to preserve the flavour of every variety—not blended, but true and genuine—and to put it away by itself whether it be Biturican or Basilican or Spionian. These varieties, when racked off in this fashion, attain the rank of nobility, because nothing of a different sort enters in to counteract their keeping qualities; for even after fifteen years or a little

[a] For Columella's method of determining the ripeness of grapes, see XI. 2. 67–69.

[7] perpetuitati *Schn.*: per vetustatem *vel* perpetuitate *Ursinus*: perpetua tamen *SAa*: perpetuo tamen *c*: per potus tamen *vulgo*.

deprehendi potest[1] ignobilitas in gustu; quoniam fere omne vinum eam qualitatem sortitum est ut
11 vetustate acquirat bonitatem. Quare, ut dicere instituimus, utilissima est generum dispositio; quam si tamen obtinere non possis, secunda est ratio, ut diversae notae non alias conseras vites quam quae saporem consimilem fructumque maturitatis eiusdem praebeant. Potes[2] etiam, si te cura pomorum tangit, ultimis ordinibus in ea vineti fine qua subiacet septentrionibus, ne cum increverint obumbrent, cacumina ficorum pirorumve et malorum depangere, quae vel inseras interposito biennii spatio, vel si generosa sint, adulta transferas. Hactenus[3] de positione vinearum.

Superest pars antiquissima, ut praecipiamus etiam cultus earum, de quibus sequenti volumine pluribus disseremus.

[1] possit *SAac*.

[2] Potes etiam *M*, *et maluit Schn.*: Posset iam *SAac*: Potes iam *vulgo*.

[3] Hactenus *S*, *Schn.*: Haec *A*, *et vulgo*: hoc *a*: hec *c*: Nunc *M*.

longer no trace of inferiority can be detected in their flavour, because almost every wine has the property of acquiring excellence with age. There- 11
fore, as we proposed to show, the orderly distribution of varieties is of the greatest advantage; and yet, if you cannot effect such an arrangement, the next best method is to plant no vines of different sorts except those which have a similar flavour and produce fruit that reaches maturity at the same time. Furthermore, if you are interested in fruit trees, you may set the tops of fig or pear or apple trees at the very ends of the rows on that side of the vineyard which lies to the north, so that they may not shade it when they grow up; and after two years' time you may graft them or, if they are of superior quality, you may transplant them as mature trees. So much for the planting of vineyards.

There still remains that part of most importance—that we give directions also for their cultivation, and of this we shall treat at length in the book that follows.

BOOK IV

LIBER IV

I. Cum de vineis conserendis librum a me scriptum, Publi Silvine, compluribus agricolationis studiosis relegisses,[1] quosdam repertos esse ais,[2] qui cetera quidem nostra praecepta laudassent, unum tamen atque alterum reprehendissent: quippe seminibus vineaticis nimium me profundos censuisse fieri scrobes adiecto dodrante super altitudinem bipedaneam, quam Celsus et Atticus prodiderant; singulasque viviradices singulis adminiculis parum prudenter contribuisse, cum permiserint idem illi auctores minore sumptu geminis materiis unius seminis[3] diductis duo continua per ordinem vestire pedamenta.

Quae utraque reprehensio[4] ambiguam[5] magis
2 habet aestimationem quam veram. Etenim, ut
quod prius proposui prius refellam, si contenti
bipedanea scrobe futuri sumus, quid ita censemus
altius pastinare tam humili mensura vitem posituri?
Dicet aliquis, "ut sit inferior tenera subiacens terra,
quae non arceat, nec duritie sua repellat novas
3 irrepentes radiculas." Istud quidem contingere[6]

[1] relegisse *SAac*: relegissem *M*. [2] ais *om. SAacM*.

[3] m. u. s *om. AacM et omnes ante Schn.*: *deinde* deductis *AacM, vett. edd.*

[4] reprehensio *S, Schn.*: *om. AacM, plerique edd.*

[5] ambiguam *cM, edd. ante Schn.*· abiaram *SA*: abieram *a*: avaram *Schn.* *Post* ambiguam *inserunt cM* nisi antiquitus ita dici solitum erat.

BOOK IV

I. You say, Publius Silvinus, that when you had read over to several students of agriculture the book which I have written on the planting of vineyards, some persons were found who, indeed, had praise for the rest of our teachings, though they criticized one or two: in that I advised the making of excessively deep trenches for vine plants by adding three-fourths of a foot to the two-foot depth which Celsus and Atticus had recorded; and that I had shown little wisdom in assigning each quickset to its individual support when those same authors allowed them, at less expense, to clothe two successive props in the same row with the branches of one vine separated into two parts.

Both these objections are based upon false reasoning rather than true judgment. For, to refute first 2
what I first proposed, if we are to be content with a two-foot trench, why are we of such a mind as to work the ground deeper when we intend to set the vines at so shallow a depth? Some one will say, " So that there may be a lower layer of soft ground underneath which will not, by its hardness, check the young creeping rootlets or thrust them back." It is possible, indeed, to accomplish that end also if the 3

[6] continere *Aac.*

potest etiam, si ager bipalio moveatur et deprimatur
scrobis in regesto, quod est fermentatum plus
dupondio semisse; nam semper in plano effosa et
regesta[1] humus tumidior[2] est quam gradus soli
crudi. Nec[3] sane positio seminum praealtum sibi
4 cubile substerni desiderat; verum abunde est semipe-
daneam consitis resolutam vitibus terram subiacere,[4]
quae velut hospitali atque etiam materno sinu recipiat
incrementa virentium. Exemplum eius rei capiamus[5] in arbusto, ubi cum scrobes defodimus, admo-
5 dum exiguum[6] pulveris viviradici subicimus. Verior
igitur causa est depressius pastinandi, quoniam iugata
vineta melius consurgunt altioribus demersa[7] scrobibus. Nam bipedanei vix etiam provincialibus
agricolis approbari possint,[8] apud quos humili statu
vitis plerumque iuxta terram coercetur; cum quae
iugo destinetur,[9] altiore fundamento stabilienda sit,
quando si[10] modo scandit excelsius, plus alimenti
6 terraeque desiderat. Et ideo in maritandis arboribus
nemo minorem tripedanea scrobem vitibus comparat.
Ceterum illa parum prudens[11] agricolarum studio:
praecipua esse[12] commoda humilis positionis, quod et

[1] effosa et regesta *scripsi* (*cf.* XI. 3. 10), *praeeunte Schn., not.*: refusos sed egesta *SAa* : refusos sed et gesta *c* : infusius egesta *M* : refusius egesta *vulgo.*

[2] humus dior (clior *c*) *SAcM* : humidior *a.*

[3] quam *S.*

[4] subiacere *cM, vett. edd.*. subiaceret *SAa* : subiicere *vulgo.*

[5] capimus *S.*

[6] exigui *SAac, edd. ante Schn.*

[7] demersa *scripsi* : demessa *S* : dimissa *Aac* : demissa *M, edd.*

[8] possint *SAac* : possunt *M, edd.*

[9] destinetur *SAacM, vett. edd.* : destinatur *Ald., Gesn*, *Schn.*

[10] *sic scripsi cum Schn., not.*: si modo quando *SAa, vett. edd.* : et (*om. c*) si modo (quando *om.*) *c, et vulgo* : si quõ qñ *M.*

[11] prudens *SAacM, vett. edd., Sobel* : prosunt *Ald., Gesn., Schn.*

[12] esse *SAa, Sobel* : esset *c* : *om. M, Ald., Gesn., Schn.*

ground is stirred with the trenching-spade[a] and the trench sunk in the upturned earth, which is swollen to more than two feet and a half;[b] for always, in level ground, earth that is thrown out and then back again swells higher than the level of the unbroken ground. And surely the setting of plants does not require that a very deep bed be spread beneath them; but it is sufficient that half a foot of loose earth lie 4
beneath the planted vines, that it may, so to speak, receive the increase of the growing plants into its hospitable—I might say even maternal—bosom. Let us take an instance of this in the arbustum[c] where, after digging planting-holes, we throw a very small bit of dust under the quickset. There is, then, a 5
truer reason for trenching the ground deeper, in that "yoked"[d] vineyards grow up better when planted in deeper holes. For two-foot holes could hardly be approved even by farmers in the provinces, with whom a vine is usually of low stature and kept close to the ground; while one that is intended for the yoke (trellis) must be steadied by a deeper foundation, since if it merely climbs higher, it demands more nourishment and more earth. And on this 6
account, in wedding vines to trees, no one prepares a planting-hole less than three feet deep for the vines. But it is with little insight into the interests of husbandmen, that he remarks that there are peculiar advantages in shallow planting, in that

[a] *I e.*, to a depth of about two feet. *Cf.* III. 5. 3, note; XI. 3 11; *De Arb.* 1. 5.

[b] As prescribed for level ground. On the various depths of trenching and the proportionate swelling of the earth, see, e.g., III. 13. 8, XI. 3. 10.

[c] See III. 2. 9, note.

[d] *I.e.* vines trained to *iuga* (yokes). See III. 2. 8, note.

celeriter adolescant semina quae non fatigentur[1] multo soli pressa pondere, fiantque uberiora quae leviter suspensa sint. Nam utraque ista Iuli Attici ratio convincitur exemplo arbustivae positionis, quae scilicet multo validiorem fertilioremque stirpem reddit; quod non faceret,[2] si laborarent altius
7 demersa semina. Quid quod pastinati[3] humus, dum est recens soluta laxataque, velut fermento quodam intumescit? cum deinde non longissimam cepit vetustatem, condensata subsidit,[4] ac velut innatantes radices vitium summo solo destituit? Hoc autem minus accidit nostrae sationi, in qua maiore mensura vitis demittitur. Nam quod in profundo semina frigore laborare dicuntur, nos
8 quoque non diffitemur. Sed non[5] est dupondii et dodrantis altitudo, quae istud efficere possit; cum praesertim, quod paulo ante rettulimus, depressior arbustivae vitis satio tamen effugiat praedictum incommodum.

II. Alterum illud, quod minori impensa[6] duos palos unius seminis flagellis censent[7] maritari, falsissimum est.[8] Sive enim caput ipsum demortuum est, duo viduantur statumina, et mox viviradices totidem substituendae sunt, quae numero suo rationem cultoris onerant: sive tenuit,[9] et ut saepe evenit,

[1] fatigantur *AacM, et vulgo ante Schn.*

[2] faceret *SAaM, Sobel*: facerent *vulgo; deinde* si non laborarent *Aac, et vulgo ante Schn.*

[3] pastinati *SAacM, Sobel*: repastinata *vulgo.*

[4] subsidet *M*: subsidii *SAac, vett. edd.*

[5] non *om. SAa, vett. edd.*

[6] impensa *M*: pensa *SAac.*

[7] flagellis censet *M*: flagelliscent *SAac.*

[8] falsum est *M, edd. ante Schn.*: est *om. SAac.*

[9] tenuit *S, Sobel*. lenuit (*ut vid.*) *Aa*: leniit *c*: vivit *edd.*

plants grow up quickly when they are not wearied and pressed down by a great weight of soil, and that plants which are lightly supported become more productive. For both these arguments of Julius Atticus are overthrown by the case of planting beside trees, which obviously makes the vine much stronger and more fruitful; which would not be the case if the plants were suffering from being sunk too deep.
What answer is there to this—that the soil of a 7
trenched plot, while it is newly broken up and loosened, swells up as though by some process of leavening? and then, when it has taken on no great length of age, it is packed, and settles, and leaves the roots of the vines swimming,[a] so to speak, on the surface of the ground? But this does not happen to my way of planting, in which the vine is put down to a greater depth. Now, as to the argument that deep-set plants are said to suffer from cold, this too we do not
deny. But a depth of two and three-fourths feet is 8
not such that it can produce that effect; especially since, as we said a little before, the vine, though planted deeper beside a tree, still escapes the aforesaid discomfort.

II. The other point, their belief that two stakes are wedded with the shoots of one plant at less expense, is most falsely taken. For if the actual root dies, two props are bereft, and presently there must be a substitution of the same number of quicksets, which, by their number, burden the accounts of the vinedresser; or, if it takes hold and, as often happens, is of a black

[a] Cf. Quintilian, X. 7. 28, *innatans illa verborum facilitas in altum reducetur, sicut rustici proximas vitis radices amputant, quae illam in summum solum ducant, ut inferiores penitus descendendo firmentur.*

vel nigri est generis vel parum fertilis, non in uno sed in pluribus pedamentis fructus claudicat. Quamquam etiam generosae stirpis vitem sic in duos palos divisam rerum rusticarum prudentiores existimant
2 minus fertilem fore, quia cratem factura sit. Et idcirco veteres vineas mergis propagare potius quam totas sternere idem ipse Atticus praecipit; quoniam mergi mox facile radicentur,[1] ita ut quaeque vitis suis radicibus tamquam propriis fundamentis innitatur. Haec autem, quae toto est prostrata corpore cum inferius solum quasi cancellavit atque irretivit, cratem facit et pluribus radicibus inter se conexis angitur,[2] nec aliter quam si multis palmitibus gravata
3 deficit. Quare per omnia praetulerim duobus potius seminibus depositis, quam unico periclitari, nec id velut compendium consectari, quod in utramque partem longe maius adferre possit dispendium. Sed iam prioris libri disputatio repetit a nobis promissum sequentis exordium.

III. In omni genere impensarum, sicut ait Graecinus, plerique nova opera fortius auspicantur quam tuentur perfecta. Quidam, inquit, ab inchoato domos exstruunt, nec peraedificatis cultum adhibent. Nonnulli strenue fabricant navigia, nec consummata perinde instruunt armamentis ministrisque. Quosdam emacitas in armentis, quosdam exercet in
2 comparandis mancipiis: de tuendis[3] nulla cura

[1] radicentur *Sobel*: radicantur *vulgo*: redigentur *SAac*: redigantur *M*.

[2] angitur *S*: an igitur *AacM*.

[3] *sic Schn.*: mancipi isdem tuendis *S*: m. de emptuendis *A*: m. intuendis *a*: mancipiis: sed iisdem tuendis *cM*, *plerique edd.*

[a] *I.e.*, whether the plant dies, or lives as an inferior vine.

sort or not sufficiently productive, the fruit falls short, not on one prop alone, but on more than one. And men of more than ordinary insight into agricultural affairs think that even a vine of noble stock, when it is so divided upon two stakes, will be less fruitful because it is sure to form a mat of intertwined roots. For this reason the very same Atticus 2
directs us to propagate old vineyards by layers rather than by spreading the whole vines flat, because layers soon and easily strike root so that each vine rests upon its own roots as though upon proper foundations. But a vine that has its whole body laid flat, by making a sort of lattice-work and entanglement of roots in the soil beneath, forms a mat and is choked by the intertwining of over-many roots, and it fails just as if it were burdened with many branches. Therefore I should prefer, on every 3
account, to risk the setting of two plants rather than one, and not to pursue as gain a course which, considered from either side,[a] may bring far greater loss. But now the argument of the previous book demands of us the beginning of the next as promised.

III. In every sort of costly enterprise, just as Graecinus says, most men enter upon new works with more vigour than they maintain them when finished. Some, he remarks, erect houses from the very foundation, and then fail to bestow care upon the finished buildings. Some are active in the building of ships, but do not fit them out accordingly with gear and crews when they are completed. Some have a fondness for the buying of cattle, and some for acquiring slaves; but they are moved by no concern over the keeping of them. Many also, by their inconstancy, 2

tangit. Multi etiam beneficia quae in amicos contulerunt, levitate destruunt. Ac ne ista, Silvine, miremur, liberos suos nonnulli nuptiis votisque quaesitos avare nutriunt, nec disciplinis aut ceteris corporis excolunt instrumentis. Quid his colligitur? Scilicet plerumque simili genere peccari etiam ab agricolis, qui pulcherrime positas vineas, antequam
3 pubescant, variis ex causis destituunt: alii sumptum annuum refugientes, et hunc primum reditum certissimum existimantes, impendere nihil; quasi plane fuerit necesse vineas facere, quas mox avaritia desererent. Nonnulli magna potius quam culta vineta possidere pulchrum esse ducunt.[1] Cognovi iam plurimos, qui persuasum haberent agrum bonis ac malis rationibus
4 colendum. At ego, cum omne genus ruris, nisi diligenti[2] cura sciteque exerceatur, fructuosum[3] esse non posse iudicem, tum vel maxime vineas. Res enim est tenera, infirma, iniuriae maxime impatiens, quae plerumque nimia laboret[4] ubertate; consumitur enim, si modum non adhibeas,[5] fecunditate sua. Cum tamen aliquatenus se confirmavit et veluti iuvenile robur accepit, neglegentiam sustinet.
5 Novella vero, dum adolescit, nisi omnia iusta perceperit, ad ultimam redigitur[6] maciem, et sic intabescit ut nullis deinceps impensis recreari possit. Igitur

[1] dicunt *SAcM*.
[2] diligentis *SA*.
[3] fructui *SAa*, *vett. edd.*
[4] nimio (enimio *a*) labore et *acM*: nimio labore et ubertate consumitur peritque *vulgo ante Schn.*
[5] habeas *SAa*.
[6] reducitur *acM*.

undo the kindnesses that they have done to their friends. And that we may not wonder at these statements, Silvinus, some men are niggardly in the nurture of their children—objects of their marriage ties and solemn prayers—and do not look to their improvement through the training of the mind or through the general furnishings of the body. What is the inference from all this? Obviously that errors of like nature are commonly made by husbandmen also, who for various reasons abandon their most beautifully planted vineyards
before they reach the age of bearing, some shrinking 3
from the yearly expense and thinking it the first and surest income to have no outgo at all; as if they were under an absolute necessity of making vineyards, only to quit them presently because of their greed. Some consider it a fine thing to have extensive rather than well-tended vineyards. I have known a very great number also who were convinced that their land must be cultivated, whether by good methods or bad.
But my judgment would be, not only that every kind 4
of land cannot be profitable unless it is worked skilfully and with painstaking care, but that this is especially true of vineyards. For the vine is a tender thing, weak, and exceedingly intolerant of ill treatment, and it commonly suffers from over-productiveness; for, unless you place a limit upon it, it is exhausted by its own fertility. And yet when it has strengthened itself somewhat and has, as it were, taken on
the vigour of youth, it endures neglect. But a newly 5
planted vine, unless it receives every proper care while it is growing up, is reduced to extreme emaciation, and it pines away to such a degree that it can never be restored by any expenditure thereafter.

summa cura ponenda sunt quasi fundamenta, et ut membra infantium a primo statim die consitionis formanda; quod nisi fecerimus, omnis impensa in cassum recidat, nec praetermissa cuiusque rei tempestivitas revocari queat.

Experto mihi crede, Silvine, bene positam vineam bonique generis et bono cultore numquam non cum
6 magno faenore gratiam reddidisse. Idque non solum ratione sed etiam exemplo nobis idem Graecinus declarat eo libro, quem de vineis scripsit,[1] cum refert ex patre suo saepe se audire solitum, Paridium quendam Veterensem vicinum suum duas filias et vineis consitum habuisse fundum; cuius partem tertiam nubenti maiori filiae dedisse in dotem, ac nihilo minus aeque magnos fructus ex duabus partibus eiusdem fundi percipere solitum; minorem deinde filiam nuptum collocasse in dimidia parte reliqui agri, nec sic ex pristino reditu detraxisse. Quod quid convincit? Melius[2] scilicet postea cultam esse tertiam illam fundi partem quam antea universam.[3]

IV. Et nos igitur, Publi,[4] magno animo vineas ponamus, ac maiore studio colamus. Quarum consitionis sola illa commodissima ratio est, quam priore tradidimus exordio, ut facta in pastinato scrobe vitis a media fere parte sulci prosternatur, et ad

[1] eo libro . . . scripsit *om. SA.*
[2] convicit (convincit *c*) nisi melius *acM* : quo quid coniicit? nisi melius *vulgo ante Schn.*
[3] universa sunt *SA.*
[4] Silvine *add. Ald., Gesn., Schn.* : *om. SAacM.*

[a] III. 15. 2.

Therefore the foundations, so to speak, must be laid with the greatest care, and from the very first day of its planting it must be moulded into shape, just as the bodies of young children must be shaped; and if we have failed to do this, the whole outlay comes to naught, and once neglected the proper time for each operation cannot be recalled.

Believe it from my experience, Silvinus, that a vineyard well planted, of good kind, and under the care of a good vine-dresser, has never failed to make recompense with big interest. And the same Grae- 6
cinus makes this clear to us, not only by argument but also by example, in that book which he wrote on the subject of vineyards. He relates that he often used to hear his father say that a certain Paridius Veterensis, his neighbour, had two daughters, and also a farm planted with vineyards; that he presented one-third of this farm to the older daughter as a dower when she married, and that, none the less, he used to take equally large yields from the remaining two-thirds of the farm; that he next married off the younger daughter with a half portion of the land that was left, and, even so, took away nothing from its old-time revenue. What does this prove? Why, obviously, that that one third of the farm was better tended afterward than the whole farm had been before.

IV. And so, Publius, let us plant our vineyards with great resolve, and tend them with greater zeal. And the most convenient method of planting them is that one alone which we proposed in the preceding book:[a] that, after making a planting-hole in prepared ground, the vine be laid flat from about the middle point of the trench, and that its firm

frontem eius ab imo usque recta materies exigatur calamoque applicetur; id enim praecipue observandum est, ne similis sit alveo scrobis, sed ut expressis angulis velut ad perpendiculum frontes eius dirigantur.
2 Nam vitis supina et velut recumbens[1] in alveo deposita, postea quum[2] ablaqueatur, vulneribus obnoxia est. Nam dum exaltare fortius orbem ablaqueationis fossor studet, obliquam vitem plerumque sauciat et non numquam praecidit. Meminerimus ergo usque ab imo scrobis solo rectum adminiculo sarmentum applicare et ita in summum perducere. Tum cetera, ut priore libro praecepimus. Ac deinde[3] duabus gemmis super extantibus terram coaequare. Deinde malleolo inter ordines posito crebris fossionibus[4] pastinatum resolvere
3 atque in pulverem redigere. Sic enim optime et viviradices et reliqua semina, quae deposuerimus, convalescent, simul ac[5] tenera humus nullis herbis irrepentibus umorem stirpibus praebuerit, nec duritia soli novellas adhuc plantas velut arto[6] vinculo compresserit.

V. Numerus autem vertendi soli bidentibus, ut verum fatear, definiendus non est, cum quanto

[1] et velut recumbens *om. SA.*
[2] quum *Gesn., Schn.*: quam *SAacM.*
[3] Ac deinde] et *SA, vett. edd.*
[4] positionibus (fossionibus *suprascr. S*) *SA.*
[5] si mollis ac *acM, et vulgo ante Schn.*
[6] arcto *M, et vulgo*: alto *SA*: arto alto *a*: arecto c.

wood be raised straight up from the very bottom along the end of the trench and fastened to a reed. For especial care must be taken that the planting-hole be not trough-shaped, but that its ends be drawn up straight, as though to a plumb-line, with clear-cut angles. For a vine that lies slantwise and is set 2
in a trough in a leaning posture, so to speak, is subject to damage thereafter when the ground is loosened around it;[a] for the digger, in his eagerness to deepen the circle of loosened ground, usually wounds a vine that is aslant, and sometimes he cuts it off.[b] We shall remember, then, to fasten the sprig straight up to its prop from the very bottom of the hole, and so bring it to the surface. Then in other matters, to do as we directed in the preceding book; and next, leaving two eyes standing above ground, to level off the surface. Then, after planting the mallet-cutting between the rows, to loosen the trenched ground anew by frequent digging and reduce it to powder. For it is in this way that quick- 3
sets and other plants that we have set out will best gain strength, when once the softened earth supplies moisture to the roots without allowing weeds to creep in, and when the hardness of the soil does not choke the still tender plants as though with close-fitting bonds.

V. Moreover, to confess the truth, no limit should be set to the number of times that the ground is to be turned by the hoes, since it is agreed that the more

[a] The operation of loosening the soil about the roots of a plant, to admit air and moisture, is summed up in the convenient, though now obsolete, word "ablaqueation." *Cf.* II. 14. 3, note *a*.

[b] So Palladius, II. 10. 3.

crebrior sit, plus prodesse fossionem conveniat. Sed quoniam impensarum ratio modum postulat, satis plerisque[1] visum est, ex Calendis Martiis usque in Octobres tricesimo[2] quoque die novella vineta confodere, omnesque herbas et praecipue gramina exstirpare, quae nisi manu eliguntur et in summum reiciuntur, quantulacumque parte adobruta sunt, reviviscunt, et vitium semina ita perurunt, ut scabra atque retorrida efficiant.

VI. Ea porro, sive malleolos[3] seu viviradices deposuimus, optimum est ab initio sic formare, ut frequenti pampinatione supervacua detrahamus;[4] nec patiamur plus quam[5] in unam materiam vires et omne alimentum conferre. Primo tamen bini pampini summittuntur, ut sit alter subsidio si alter
2 forte deciderit. Cum deinde paulum induruere[6] virgae, tum singulae[7] detrahuntur. Ac ne quae relictae sunt procellis ventorum decutiantur, molli et laxo vinculo adsurgentes subsequi conveniet, dum claviculis suis quasi quibusdam manibus adminicula
3 comprehendant. Hoc si operarum penuria facere prohibebit[8] in malleolo, quem et ipsum pampinare

[1] plerique *SAc.*
[2] tricensimo *SA* : trigesimo *acM.*
[3] malleolo *SAac* : malleolo seu viviradice *vulgo ante Schn.*
[4] detrahamur *Sa* : detramur *A* : detrahantur *M, et vulgo ante Schn.*
[5] quam *om. Schn.*
[6] induere (*sed corr. A*) *SAc.*
[7] *sic SAacM, vett. edd.*: deteriores singulae *Ald., Gesn., Schn.*
[8] prohibebit *SAcM* : probibet *a, edd.*

[a] March 1st.

frequent it is, the more beneficial is the digging. But, since consideration for expenses demands some limit, it has seemed sufficient to most people to dig newly planted vineyards every thirtieth day from the Calends of March [a] up to October, and to root out all weeds and especially grasses; for these, unless pulled out by hand and thrown on the surface, return to life when any least part of them is covered with earth, and so scald the vine-plants as to make them scaly and shrivelled.

VI. Furthermore, whether we have planted cuttings or quicksets, it is best to train the vines from the beginning in such a way as to remove superfluous growth by frequent leaf-pruning, not allowing them to bestow their strength and all their nourishment upon more than one branch of firm wood.[b] Yet two shoots are allowed to grow at first, that one may be a reserve if the other should happen to die. Later, when the green branches have 2
hardened somewhat, one of each pair is removed. And that those which are left may not be beaten off by squalls of wind, it will be best to follow them up, as they grow, with a soft and loose band, until they catch hold of their props with their tendrils as though with hands.[c] If shortage of workmen prevents the 3
carrying out of this kind of labour in the case of the

[b] Palladius, VI. (May) 2, gives similar instructions for the trimming away of useless foliage (*pampinatio*), and adds, like Columella (IV. 7. 1), that the task should be performed at a time when the young twigs snap easily with pressure of the fingers. *Cf.* Varro, *R.R.* I. 31. 2; Col. IV. 27. 6, 28. 1, with note.

[c] *Cf.* Cicero, *De Sen.* 15. 52, *Vitis quidem, quae natura caduca est et, nisi fulta est, fertur ad terram, eadem, ut se erigat claviculis suis quasi manibus, quicquid est nacta, complectitur.*

censemus, at certe in ordinariis vitibus utique obtinendum est, ne pluribus flagellis emacientur, nisi si propaginibus futuris prospiciemus;[1] sed ut singulis materiis serviant, quarum incrementa elicere debebimus,[2] applicato longiore adminiculo, per quod proprepant in tantum ut sequentis anni iugum
4 exsuperent et in fructum curvari possint. Ad quam mensuram cum increverint, cacumina infringenda sunt, ut potius crassitudine convalescant quam supervacua longitudine attenuentur. Idem tamen sarmentum, quod in materiam summittimus, ab imo usque in tres pedes et semissem pampinabimus,[3] et omnes eius intra id spatium nepotes enatos saepius de-
5 cerpemus.[4] Quicquid deinde supra germinaverit, intactum relinqui oportebit.[5] Magis enim conveniet[6] proximo autumno falce deputari superiorem partem quam aestivo tempore pampinari, quoniam ex eo loco, unde nepotem ademeris, confestim alterum fundit; quo enato, nullus relinquitur oculus in ipsa materia qui sequenti anno cum fructu germinet.

VII. Omnis autem pampinationis ea[7] est tempestivitas, dum adeo teneri palmites sunt, ut levi tactu digiti decutiantur. Nam si vehementius induru-

[1] efficiemus *SAa*.
[2] eligere debebimus (debemus *a*) *SAacM, Ald.*: elicere debemus *Schn.*
[3] ab imo . . . pampinabimus *om. SA*.
[4] discerpemus (des- *a*) *SAa*.
[5] intractu relicto portavit *SA*.
[6] conveniet *acM* . convenit *Gesn., Schn.* : *om. SA*.
[7] ea *om. S, add. man. alt. A*.

---

[a] Columella appears to use *nepos* to mean both "water-sprouts" or "stock-shoots," sprouting from unfruitful

cutting—and we advise the pruning of this also—at any rate it must be brought about without fail in the case of vines planted in rows that they are not sapped of their strength by too many shoots, unless we are looking forward to future propagation by layers; but that they devote themselves each to one cane, whose growth we should encourage by applying a prop of greater length, along which they may creep up to such a height as to rise above the frame of the following year and to be bent over for bearing. When they have grown up to this 4
height, their tops should be broken off, so that they may rather grow in thickness and strength than make a slender growth of useless length. However, we will leaf-prune this same stem, which we let grow into firm wood, up to three and one-half feet from the bottom, and will frequently pull off all the stock-shoots that sprout from it within this space. Anything that sprouts forth then 5
above that point shall be left untouched. For it will be better that the upper part be cut away with the pruning-knife the following autumn than that superfluous shoots be removed in summer time, since from that spot from which you have taken the secondary shoot [a] it immediately puts forth a second; and when this has sprouted, there remains in the firm wood no eye to sprout and produce fruit the following year.

VII. But the proper time for removing all superfluous growth is while the shoots are so tender that they may be struck off by a light touch of the finger. For if they have hardened to a greater degree, they

wood, and "secondary shoots" or "laterals" growing out of fruiting canes.

erunt,[1] aut maiore nisu convellendi sunt aut falce deputandi, quod utrumque vitandum est: alterum, quia lacerat matrem, si revellere coneris; alterum, quia sauciat, quod in viridi et adhuc stirpe immatura
2 fieri noxium est. Neque enim eatenus plaga constitit[2] qua vestigium fecit acies; sed aestivis caloribus falce vulnus penitus impressum[3] latius inarescit ita ut[4] non minimam partem de ipso matris corpore necet.[5] Atque ideo si iam caulibus duris falcem adhiberi necesse est, paulum ab ipsa matre recidendum[6] est, et velut reseces relinquendi sunt, qui caloris excipiant iniuriam eatenus qua nascuntur a latere palmites; ultra enim non serpit vaporis vio-
3 lentia. In malleolo similis ratio est pampinandi et in longitudinem eliciendi[7] materiam, si eo velimus anniculo uti, quod ego saepe feci. Sed si propositum est utique recidere, ut bimo potius utamur, cum ad unum pampinum iam redegeris et is ipse excesserit pedalem longitudinem, decacuminare conveniet, ut in cervicem[8] potius confirmetur et sit robustior. Atque haec positorum seminum prima cultura est.

VIII. Sequens deinde tempus, ut prodidit Celsus, et Atticus, quos iure maxime nostra aetas probavit, ampliorem curam deposcit. Nam post Idus Octobris,

[1] *sic SAaM*: induruerint *c, et vulgo.*

[2] constitit *SAacM, vett. edd.*: consistit *vulgo.*

[3] impressum et latius *SAac*: i. in latum *M.*

[4] ita ut] aut *SA*. ut *om. a.* [5] enecet *M, et vulgo.*

[6] id paulum . . . recidendum *ac, vett. edd.*; ii paulum . . . recidendi (est *om.*) *Ald., Gesn.*: [ii] paulum . . . edendum (recedendum *in Corrig.*) *Schn.*: id (ii) paulum . . . resices *om. SA.*

[7] eligendi *AacM, vett. edd.*

[8] inter vitem *SAac*: in cervice *M.*

[a] See IV. 21. 3.

must either be pulled off with a greater effort or cut away with the pruning-knife, both of which are to be avoided: the one, because it tears the parent vine if you try to pull them off; the other, because it wounds the vine, which is a harmful thing to do in a stem that is green and not yet mature. For the injury does 2
not stop at the exact spot where the edge of the knife made its mark; but in the heat of summer a wound deeply imprinted by the knife dries up to a greater breadth, with the result that it kills more than a small part of the very body of the mother. And for this reason, if it is necessary that the knife be applied to stems that have already hardened, the cut must be made at a little distance from the mother vine, and spur-like ends [a] must be left to take upon themselves the injury of the heat up to the place where the shoots sprout from her side; for the heat's energy creeps no farther. In the case of the cutting there 3
is a similar method of pruning and of encouraging length of wood, if we wish to use a cutting of one year, which I have often done. But if it is your fixed intention to cut it off, so as to use it rather when it is two years old, when you have now reduced it to one shoot and that shoot has exceeded one foot in length, it will be proper to lop off its head, that it may be strengthened rather up to the neck and have more vigour. And this is the first step in the cultivation of plants after they are set.

VIII. The period next following, as Celsus has recorded, and Atticus too—men whom our age has especially and rightfully approved—demands greater care. For after the Ides of October,[b] before the

[b] Oct. 15th. Compare with this chapter Palladius, XI (Oct.). 5.

prius quam frigora invadant,[1] vitis ablaqueanda est. Quod opus adapertas ostendit aestivas radiculas, easque prudens[2] agricola ferro decidit.[3] Nam si passus est convalescere, inferiores deficiunt, atque evenit ut vinea summa parte terreni radices agat, quae et frigore infestentur et caloribus maiorem in modum aestuent ac vehementer sitire matrem Cani-
2 culae ortu[4] cogant. Quare quicquid intra sesquipedem natum est, cum ablaqueaveris, recidendum est. Sed huius non eadem ratio est amputandi quae traditur in superiore parte vitis. Nam minime adlevanda[5] plaga est, minimeque applicandum[6] ferramentum ipsi matri; quoniam si iuxta truncum radicem praecideris, aut ex cicatrice plures enascentur, aut[7] hiemalis, quae consistit in lacusculis[8] ablaqueationis aqua, brumae congelationibus nova vulnera peruret et ad medullam penetrabit. Quod[9] ne fiat, recedere[10] ab ipso codice instar unius digiti spatio conveniet, atque ita[11] radiculas praecidere; quae sic ademptae non amplius pullulant, et a cetera noxa truncum defendunt. Hoc opere consummato, si est hiems in ea regione placida, patens vitis relinquenda est; sin violentior hoc[12] facere nos pro-

[1] invadunt *M*, *Schn.*

[2] aesque frondes (frundens *A*) *SA*.

[3] cecidit *SAa* : excidit *M*.

[4] Caniculae ortu *Sobel* : ac niculae ortũ *S* : agniculae ortũ *A* : canicule in ortu *M* : canicule vehementer ortu *c* : in ortu caniculae *a*, *edd.*

[5] adlevanda *edd.* : ablaqueanda *SA* : allaqueanda *a* : oblaqueanda *cM*.

[6] adlevandum *S* : ad levandum *A*.

[7] pube nascentur ut *SA*.

[8] quae . . . lacusculis *om.* *SAac* : ex pluviis *post* quae *add.* *edd.*

[9] penetrabit, quod *cdd.*

coming of cold weather, the vine must be ablaqueated.[a] This operation lays bare the summer rootlets, and the wise husbandman cuts these off with a knife. For if he allows them to grow strong, the lower roots waste away; and the result is that the vine puts out its roots at the very surface of the earth, to be injured by the cold and burned to a greater degree by the heat, and to force a violent thirst upon the mother vine at the rising of the Dog Star. For 2
this reason, when you ablaqueate the vine, anything that has sprouted out of it within a foot and a half must be cut off. But the method of this root-pruning is not the same as that proposed for the upper part of the vine. For the wound is not to be smoothed off, and by no means is the knife to be applied to the mother herself; because, if you cut away a root close to the stock, either more roots will spring from the scar, or the rains of winter which stand in hollows in the loosened soil will gall the fresh wounds by freezing in midwinter and will penetrate to the very pith.[b] That this may not happen, it will be proper to keep a distance of about one finger's breadth from the stock itself, and so to trim off the small roots; when they are removed in this manner, they sprout out no more and protect the stem from further injury. When this 3
work is finished, the vine should be left exposed if the winter is mild in that region; but if a more severe

[a] *Cf.* IV. 4. 2, note. [b] *Cf. De Arb.* 5. 3.

---

[10] recidere *Aac, edd ante Gesn.*: reciderere *M.*
[11] ita *om. SAcM.*
[12] hoc *M* : hic *SAac* : id *edd.*

hibet, ante Idus Decembris praedicti lacusculi coaequandi sunt. Si vero etiam praegelida frigora regionis eius suspecta erunt, aliquid fimi, vel, si [1] est commodius, columbini stercoris, aut in hunc usum praeparatae veteris urinae senos sextarios, antequam vitem adobruas, radicibus [2] superfundes.
4 Sed ablaqueare omnibus autumnis oportebit primo quinquennio, dum vitis convalescat: ubi vero truncus adoleverit, fere triennio intermittendus est eius operis labor. Nam et minus ferro crura vitium laeduntur,[3] nec tam celeriter radiculae inveterato iam codice enascuntur.[4]

IX. Ablaqueationem deinde sequitur talis putatio, ut ex praecepto veterum auctorum vitis ad unam virgulam revocetur, duabus gemmis iuxta terram relictis. Quae putatio non debet secundum articulum fieri, ne reformidet oculus; sed medio fere internodio ea plaga obliqua falce fit, ne, si transversa fuerit cicatrix, caelestem superincidentem [5] aquam
2 contineat. Sed nec ad eam partem, qua est gemma, verum ad posteriorem declinatur, ut in terram [6] potius devexa quam in germen delacrimet. Namque defluens [7] umor caecat oculum nec patitur crescere.[8]

X. Putandi autem duo sunt tempora: [9] melius autem, ut ait Mago, vernum, antequam surculus progerminet, quoniam umoris plenus facilem plagam

[1] quod *cM*, *Schn.*
[2] radicis *SA*.
[3] laedantur *SA*.
[4] enascantur *A*.
[5] supercidentem *SAacM*.
[6] interdum *SAacM*.
[7] depluens *SA*, *Schn.*
[8] crescere *SAaM*: frondescere *c*, *edd.*
[9] genera *S*.

winter prevents our doing this, the above-mentioned hollows must be levelled off before the Ides of December.[a] In fact, if there is a suspicion of extremely cold weather for that region, you will spread some stable-dung or, if more convenient, some pigeon dung over the roots before you bury the vine; or you will pour over them six *sextarii* of stale urine previously made ready for such use. But it will be necessary to 4
ablaqueate the vine every autumn for the first five years, until it grows strong. However, when the main stem has come to maturity, this task may be omitted for about three-year intervals; for the lower parts[b] of the vine receive less injury from the iron, and small roots do not shoot out so rapidly, now that the stock has become old.

IX. Ablaqueation is then followed by pruning, in such a manner that the vine is reduced to one small rod, according to the directions of ancient authorities, leaving two eyes close to the ground. This pruning should not be done next to the joint, lest the eye be checked in its growth; but an oblique cut is made with the knife about midway between the joints, lest, if it be crosswise, the scar may hold the rain that falls upon it. But the slope is made, not toward the 2
side where the bud is, but to the opposite side, so that it may shed its tears upon the ground rather than upon the bud. For the sap that flows down from it blinds the eye and does not allow it to grow.[c]

X. There are two seasons for pruning; but the better time, as Mago says, is in the spring, before the shoot puts forth its buds, because, being full of

[a] Dec. 13th. [b] Lit. the legs.
[c] *Cf.* Pliny, *N.H.* XVII. 192.

et levem et aequalem accipit, nec falci repugnat. Hunc autem secuti sunt Celsus et Atticus. Nobis neque angusta putatione coercenda semina videntur, nisi si admodum invalida sunt; neque utique verno
2 recidenda. Sed primo quidem anno, quo sunt posita, frequentibus[1] fossionibus omnibus mensibus dum frondent ac pampinationibus adiuvanda sunt, ut robur accipiant, nec plus quam uni materiae serviant. Quam ut educaverint, autumno vel vere, si magis competit,[2] adradenda, et nepotibus, quos pampinator[3] in superiore parte omiserat, liberanda censemus, atque ita in iugum imponenda. Ea enim levis et recta sine cicatrice vinea est quae se primi anni flagello supra iugum extulit, quod tamen apud paucos agricolas et raro contingit; ideoque praedicti auctores primitias vitis resecare cen-
3 suerunt.[4] Sed nec utique verna omnibus regionibus melior putatio est: nam ubi caelum frigidum est, ea sine dubio eligenda est; ubi vero aprica loca sunt, mollesque hiemes, optima et maxime naturalis est autumnalis, quo tempore divina quadam lege et aeterna fructum cum fronde stirpes deponunt.

XI. Hoc facere, sive viviradicem sive malleolum conseveris, censeo. Nam illam veterem opinionem damnavit usus non esse ferro tangendos[5] anniculos malleolos quoniam reformident. Quod frustra Vergilius et Saserna Stolonesque et Catones timuerunt; qui non solum in eo errabant, quod primi anni capil-

[1] frequentius *SA*.
[2] competit *edd.*: competent (con- *SA*) *SAacM*.
[3] pampinatione *SAa, vett. edd.*
[4] consuerunt *A*: consueverunt *ac*.
[5] tangendos *vulgo*: frangendos *SAacM*.

[a] *Georg.* II. 362–370. [b] Cato, 33. 2.

sap, it allows an easy, smooth, and even cut, and does not resist the knife. Celsus and Atticus, moreover, have followed his method. To us it seems that plants should not be held back by close pruning unless they are very weak, and that at least they should not be cut in the spring. But, to be sure, in the first year 2
that they are set out they should be aided, every month while they are in leaf, by frequent digging and by leaf-pruning, so that they may gain strength and support not more than one branch of firm wood. And when they have reared this they should be trimmed clean, in our opinion, in the autumn, or in the spring if it is more convenient, and freed from secondary shoots which the leaf-pruner had left on the upper part; and so they should be placed upon the frame. For it is the smooth and straight vine, without a scar, that overtops the frame with a rod of the first year. This happens, however, with few farmers, and seldom; and for that reason the aforementioned authors thought it best to cut off the first shoots of the vine. But in any case, spring prun- 3
ing is not preferable in all regions: for where the climate is cold, that time of pruning is doubtless to be chosen; but in regions that are sunny, where winters are mild, the best and most natural pruning is that of autumn, at which season, by some divine and eternal law, plants drop both fruit and foliage.

XI. This, I believe, is the thing to do, whether you have planted a quickset or a cutting. For experience has condemned that long-standing belief that year-old cuttings should not be touched with the knife because they have a dread of it. This was a matter on which Vergil [a] and Saserna and the Stolos and the Catos [b] had groundless fears; and they were mistaken, not

lamenta seminum intacta patiebantur, sed et post biennium cum viviradix recidenda erat, omnem superficiem amputabant solo tenus iuxta ipsum
2 articulum, ut e duro pullularet. Nos autem magister artium docuit usus, primi anni malleolorum formare incrementa, nec pati vitem supervacuis frondibus luxuriantem silvescere; nec rursus in tantum coercere, quantum antiqui praecipiebant,[1] ut totam super-
3 ficiem amputemus. Nam id quidem [2] maxime contrarium est: primum quod cum ad terram decideris, semina, velut intolerabili adfecta vulnere, pleraque intereunt; nonnulla etiam, quae pertinaciter vixerunt, minus fecundas materias adferunt, siquidem e duro quae pullulant omnium confessione pampinaria
4 saepissime fructu carent. Media igitur ratio sequenda est, ut neque solo tenus malleolum recidamus, nec rursus in longiorem materiam provocemus; sed adnodato superioris anni pollice, iuxta [3] ipsam commissuram veteris sarmenti unam vel duas gemmas relinquemus ex quibus germinet.

XII. Putationem sequitur iam pedandae vineae cura. Verum hic annus nondum vehementem palum aut ridicam [4] desiderat; notatum est enim a me plerumque teneram vineam melius adminiculo modico quam vehementi palo adquiescere. Itaque aut

[1] praecipiendo *Sobel*: praecipienda *SA*.
[2] rationi *post* quidem *add. Schn.*; *om. SAacM.*
[3] iuxta *SAa, vett. edd.*: supra *c, Ald., Gesn., Schn.*: super *M.*
[4] rigidam *S.*

merely on this point, in that they allowed the first year's foliage of plants to go untouched, but also after two years, when the quickset was to be cut back, they lopped off all the upper part right down to the ground, close to the very joint, so that it might make new growth from the hard wood. But experience, the 2
master of arts, has taught us to regulate the growth of first-year cuttings and not to allow a vine to run wild with a rank growth of useless leafage; and, on the other hand, not to hold it back to the extent that the ancients directed, to the point of lopping off all the upper part. In fact, this method is most harmful; 3
in the first place because, when you cut to the ground, most plants die, being visited, as it were, by an unbearable wound; while some of them also, which have a more stubborn hold on life, produce less fruitful wood—seeing that, by the admission of everyone, shoots which sprout from the hard wood are very often destitute of fruit. Therefore a middle course is 4
to be followed; namely, that we neither cut back a cutting to the ground nor, on the other hand, draw it out into a woody branch of excessive length; but, trimming off the sprouts from the spur [a] of the year before, we shall leave, close to the crotch where the old branches were joined, one or two buds from which it may send out shoots.

XII. Attention to the propping of the vine follows the pruning. But the present, or first, year does not yet require a strong prop or stake; for it has been my observation that, for the most part, a young vine is better satisfied with a support of moderate size than with a stout prop. And so we shall attach each young

[a] Lit. "thumb," from the resemblance of the stub to that member.

veteres, ne novae radicem agant, harundines binas singulis vitibus applicabimus,[1] aut si regionis conditio permittit, de vepribus hastilia, quibus adnectantur singulae transversae perticae in unam partem
2 ordinis—quod genus iugi cantherium vocant rustici. Plurimum id refert esse quod paulum infra curvationem vitis prorepens pampinus statim apprehendat, et in transversa potius se fundat quam in edita, ventosque facilius sustineat subnixus[2] cantherio. Idque iugum intra quartum pedem convenit adlevari, dum se vinea corroboret.

XIII. Impedationem deinde sequitur alligator, cuius officium est ut rectam vitem producat in iugum. Quae sive iuxta palum est posita, ut quibusdam placuit auctoribus,[3] observare debebit, qui adnectit, ne in alliganda materia flexum pali, si forte curvus est, sequendum putet; nam ea res uncam vitem facit: sive, ut Attico et nonnullis aliis agricolis visum est, inter vitem et palum spatium relinquitur,[4] quod nec mihi displicet, recta harundo adiungenda stirpi est, et ita per crebra retinacula in iugum perducenda. Vinculi genus quale sit, quo religantur
2 semina, plurimum[5] refert. Nam dum novella vinea est, quam mollissimo nectenda est; quia si viminibus salicis aut ulmi ligaveris, increscens vitis se ipsa praecidit.[6] Optima est ergo genista, vel paludibus desectus iuncus, aut ulva; non pessime tamen in

[1] *sic acM, edd. ante Schn.*: harum singulis binas (vinas *A*) adplicavimus singulis viticulis (vitulicus *A*) *SA*: arundines singulis viticulis applicabimus *Schn.*

[2] subnexus *SA*.

[3] ut . . . auctoribus *om. SAa, vett. edd.*

[4] relinquendum est *a*.

[5] plurima seminum *SA*: plurimum semina *a*.

[6] procidit *SAa*.

vine either to two old reeds, lest new ones strike root; or, if local conditions allow it, to brier canes, to which single cross-bars may be tied along one side of the row—a kind of frame which farmers call a *can-* 2
terius or "horse."[a] It is of the greatest importance that this be such that the young vine-shoot, as it creeps forth, shall immediately grasp it a little below the point of its bending and spread out on the cross-bars rather than on the uprights, and so, resting upon the "horse," may more easily bear up against the winds. And it is proper that this frame should be raised up to less than four feet, until the vine becomes strong.

XIII. Then, after the propping, comes the binder, whose task it is to train the vine upright to the frame. And if the vine is set close to the stake, as has pleased some authorities, the man who ties it will have to guard against the notion that, in fastening the firm wood, he must follow the curve in the stake if it happens to be bent, for that makes a crooked vine; or, if space is left between the vines and the stake, as has seemed best to Atticus and some other husbandmen and is not displeasing to me, a straight reed must be joined to the stock, and so by numerous bindings the vine is to be guided up to the frame. What sort of bands they are with which the plants are tied, is of the greatest importance. For while the vine is young, it must 2
be tied with the very softest kind; because, if you bind with withes of willow or elm, the growing vine cuts itself. The best, then, is broom, or the rush that is cut in marshy places, or sedge; and yet the leaves

[a] *Cf.* Pliny, *N.H.* XVII. 165, *Simplici iugo constat porrecto ordine quem canterium appellant.*

umbra siccata faciunt in hunc usum harundinum quoque folia.

XIV. Sed et malleolorum similis cura agenda est, ut ad unam aut duas gemmas deputati autumno vel vere, prius quam germinent, iugentur.[1] Iis, ut dixi, cantherius propius[2] a terra quam vitibus ordinariis summittendus est; neque enim editior esse debet pedali altitudine, ut sit quem teneri adhuc pampini capreolis suis illigent nec[3] ventis explantentur. Insequitur deinde fossor, qui crebris bidentibus
2 aequaliter et minute[4] soli terga comminuat.[5] Hanc planam fossuram maxime nos probamus. Nam illa, quam in Hispania hibernam appellant, cum terra vitibus detrahitur, et in media spatia interordiniorum confertur, supervacua nobis videtur, quia iam praecessit autumnalis ablaqueatio, quae et[6] nudavit summas et ad inferiores radiculas[7] transmisit hibernos imbres. Numerus autem fossionis aut idem debet esse[8] qui primi anni, aut una minus; nam[9] utique frequenter solum exercendum est, dum id incremento suo vites inumbrent, nec patiantur her-
3 bam subcrescere. Pampinationis eadem debet esse ratio huius anni atque prioris. Adhuc enim compescenda quasi pueritia seminum est, nec plus quam in unum flagellum est summittenda; tanto quidem

[1] vincientur *cM*.
[2] proprius *SAa*.
[3] nec *SAa* . ne *cM*, *edd.*
[4] minute *cM* : minuti *SAa* : minutim *edd.*
[5] convertat *a* : convertit *M* : convertant *c*.
[6] et *SAacM* ; *om. Schn.*
[7] ad inferioris pervenit radiculas *SAacM* ; *et deinde* transmisit . . . imbres *om. SAa* : ad inferiores pervenit radiculas, et hibernos transmisit imbres *vulgo ante Schn.*
[8] debet esse *SAacM* : esse debet *edd.*

of reeds also, when dried in the shade, do not serve badly for this purpose.

XIV. But like attention should be given to cuttings, that after being cut back to one or two eyes in the autumn or in spring, before the time of budding, they shall be fastened to the frame. For these, as I have said, the "horse" must be placed closer to the ground than for mature vines in rows; for it should be not more than one foot in height, so as to be of such a sort that the still tender shoots may grasp it with their tendrils [a] and not be rooted out by the winds. Then follows the digger, to break up the surface soil evenly and finely with many strokes of the two-pronged hoe. This level digging we especially favour. For what they call the 2
"winter digging" in Spain—when earth is removed from the vines and brought into the space between the rows—seems to us unnecessary, because it has been already preceded by the autumn ablaqueation, which has exposed the upper rootlets and carried the winter rains to the roots below. Again, the number of diggings should be the same as of the first year, or less by one; for the ground is in special need of frequent working until the vines shade it with their growth and do not allow weeds to grow beneath them.
The same method of leaf-pruning should hold for this 3
year as for the year before. For the childhood of the plants, so to speak, must still be held in check and the plant allowed to grow to not more than one shoot;

[a] *Capreoli. Cf.* Varro, *R.R.* I. 31. 4, where the word is derived from *capio* (grasp); also Isidore, *Orig.* XVII. 5. 11, *Capreoli dicti quod capiant arbores.*

---

[9] minus nam *om. SAa, vett. edd.*

magis, quod tenera aetas eius non sustinet et fetu et materiis onerari.

XV. Sed cum annicula mensiumque sex ad vindemiam perducta est, sublato fructu protinus frequentanda est, et praesidiarii malleoli propagandi sunt, qui in hunc usum fuerant depositi; vel, si ne hi quidem sunt, ex ordinaria vite in alterum palum mergus est attrahendus. Nam plurimum interest adhuc nova consitione pedamen omne vestiri; nec mox vineam tum subseri, cum fructus capiendus est.
2 Mergi genus est, ubi supra terram iuxta suum adminiculum vitis curvatur, atque ex alto scrobe submersa perducitur ad vacantem palum: tum ex arcu vehementer citat materiam, quae protinus applicata
3 suo pedamento ad iugum evocatur. Sequente deinde anno insecatur superior pars curvaturae usque ad medullam, ne totas vires matris propagatum flagellum in se trahat, et ut paulatim condiscat suis radicibus ali. Bima deinde praeciditur proxime palmam quae ex arcu summissa est. Et id quod a matre abscisum recessit, confestim alte circumfoditur, et scrobiculo facto ad imum solum praeciditur,[1] adobruiturque, ut et radices deorsum agat, nec ex propinquo neglegenter in summa terra resectum[2]
4 progerminet. Tempus autem non aliud magis

[1] praeducitur *c.* [2] resecta *SAacM, vett. edd.*

---

[a] *I.e.* missing vines must be replaced.

[b] The *mergus*, "layer," was so called because, without being separated from the nurse vine, it "dives" (*mergit*) into the ground and then reappears, like a diving bird (*mergus*). *Cf.* Palladius, III. 16. 1, *Mergum dicimus, quoties velut arcus supra terram relinquitur, alia parte vitis infossa.*

[c] *I.e.* the bend under ground.

[d] Closer to the parent vine.

the more so, in fact, because its tender age does not endure the burden of both offspring and woody branches.

XV. But when the vineyard, at the age of one year and six months, is brought to the vintage, it must be recruited to full strength [a] immediately after the fruit has been removed, and reserve cuttings which were planted for this purpose must be set in the gaps; or, if these also are wanting, a layer [b] must be led from a vine in the row to another stake. For it is of the utmost importance up to this time that every prop be clothed with a new planting, and that the vineyard shall not be in a state of replanting later, when it is time to be taking its fruits. There is one kind of layer where the 2
vine is bent above ground close to its support, and so, being carried underground by a deep trench, is brought out beside a vacant stake; then from the "bow" [c] it puts forth a vigorous shoot of firm wood, which is immediately attached to its prop and brought up to the cross-bar. Then in the following year a cut is made 3
in the upper part of the bend,[d] as far as the pith, that the rod under propagation may not draw into itself all the strength of the mother vine, and that it may learn little by little to take its nourishment from its own roots. Next, when two years old, it is chopped off close to the branch which has been caused to spring up from the bow. And what is cut away and separated from the mother vine, immediately has the ground dug deep about it; then a small hole is made, and it is cut off at the very lowest point and covered with earth, so that it may drive its roots downwards and not sprout out near the top of the ground by being carelessly cut at the surface. Moreover, there is no time better 4

idoneum est hunc mergum amputandi quam ab Idib. Octob. in Idus Novemb., ut hibernis mensibus suas radices confirmet. Nam si vere id fecerimus, quo gemmare palmites incipiunt, matris alimentis subito destitutus [1] languescit.

XVI. Eadem ratio est in transferendo malleolo. Nam secundo autumno, si caeli et loci qualitas patitur, commodissime post Idus Octobris exemptus conseritur: [2] sin autem aliqua terrae vel aeris repugnat iniuria, tempestivitas eius in proximum ver differtur. Neque diutius in vineis relinquendus est, ne soli [3] vires absumat et ordinaria semina infestet: quae quanto celerius liberata sunt consortio viviradicum, tanto facilius convalescunt. At in seminario licet trimam atque etiam quadrimam vitem resectam vel anguste putatam custodire, quia non consulitur
2 vindemiae. Cum mensem tricesimum excessit posita vinea, id est tertio autumno, vehementioribus statuminibus statim impedanda [4] est, idque [5] non ut libet aut fortuito faciendum. Nam sive prope truncum deponitur [6] palus, pedali tamen spatio recedendum [7] est, ne aut premat aut radicem vulneret, et ut fossor tamen ab omni parte semina circumfodiat.
3 Isque palus sic ponendus est, ut frigorum et Aquilonum excipiat violentiam, vitemque protegat; sive medio interordinio pangetur, vel deponendus [8] est vel, prius paxillo perforato solo, altius adigendus,[9]

[1] destituta *SAac, vett. edd.*
[2] consequetur *SA, vett. edd.* [3] nec socii *SA.*
[4] impedienda *SA* : impedienda *M* : impendanda *c.*
[5] ita *SA* : itaque *ac.*
[6] deponitur *SAa, vett. edd.* : defigitur *cM, et vulgo.*
[7] recedendum *Ald., Gesn., Schn.* : recidendus *SAacM, vett. edd.*
[8] deponendus *SAaM, vett. edd.* : defodiendus *c, et vulgo.*
[9] adfrigendus (fr *expunct.*) *A* : adfigendus *S* : affigendus *a.*

suited for the amputation of this layer than from the Ides of October to the Ides of November,[a] so that it may strengthen its roots during the winter months. For, if we do this in the spring, when the branches are beginning to bud, it droops as a result of being suddenly robbed of its mother's nourishment.

XVI. The same method holds in transplanting the cutting. For in the second autumn, if conditions of weather and situation permit, it is taken up and planted to best advantage after the Ides of October; but if some harmful quality of soil or of air opposes this, the time of its planting is postponed to the next spring. And it should be left no longer in the vineyards, lest it use up the strength of the soil and impair the plants in the rows; the sooner they are relieved of the partnership of quicksets, the more readily do they gain strength. But in a nursery one may keep a vine for three or even four years, if it is cut back or closely pruned, because no thought is taken of a vintage. When the planted vineyard has passed its 2
thirtieth month, that is in the third autumn, it must be propped at once with stronger supports; and this is not to be done just as you please or in haphazard fashion. For if the stake is set near the vine stock, still it must be left one foot away so that it will not press upon or injure the root, yet so that the digger may work around the plants on every side. And this 3
stake must be so placed as to receive the fury of the colds and of the north winds and so protect the vine; or if it is placed midway between the rows, it must be either pushed well down or driven to a greater depth by first making a hole in the ground with a small stake, so that it may more easily support both the

[a] Oct. 15th to Nov. 13th.

quo facilius et iugum et fructum sustineat. Nam quanto propius truncum ridica statuitur, etiam leviter defixa stabilior est; quoniam contingens[1] vitem mutua
4 vice sustinetur et sustinet. Statuminibus deinde firmiora iuga sunt illiganda,[2] eaque vel saligneis perticis vel compluribus quasi fasciculis harundinum conectuntur, ut rigorem habeant nec pandentur[3] onere fructuum. Nam binae iam materiae singulis seminibus summittendae erunt; nisi si tamen gracilitas vitis alicuius angustiorem putationem desiderabit cuius unus palmes atque idem paucorum oculorum erit relinquendus.

XVII. Perticarum iugum fortius minusque operosum est.[4] Harundines pluribus operis iugantur, quoniam et pluribus locis nectuntur. Eaeque inter se conversis cacuminibus vinciendae sunt, ut aequalis crassitudo totius iugi sit; nam si cacumina in unum competunt, imbecillitas eius partis gravata pondere iam maturum fructum prosternit, et canibus ferisque
2 reddit obnoxium. At cum iugum in fascem pluribus harundinibus alterna cacuminum vice ordinatum est, fere quinquennii praebet usum.

Neque enim alia est[5] ratio putationis aut ceterae culturae quam quae primi biennii. Nam et autumnalis ablaqueatio sedulo facienda, nec minus vacantibus palis propagines applicandae; hoc enim opus numquam intermittendum est, quin omnibus in-

[1] constringens *SAa, vett. edd.*

[2] illiganda *acM, vett. edd.*: inligamenda *S*: inligamenta *A*: alliganda *vulgo.*

[3] pandantur *SAacM, edd. ante Gesn.*

[4] *Sic ex variis scripsi*: perticarum *Warmington*; perticum *SA*; perticae *acM*: fortius *SAa*; firmius *cM*: operosum est *acM*; onerosũ est *S*; oneum sum est *A*: Perticae iugum firmius faciunt (*deest SAacM*) minusque operosum *vulgo.*

trellis and the fruit. For the closer a prop is set to the stock, even when lightly fixed in the ground, the steadier it is; since, by standing close to the vine, it both supports and is supported in turn. Then stronger 4
cross-bars are to be bound to the standards; and these are made either of willow rods or of several reeds tied in some sort of bundles to give them stiffness, so that they may not be bent by the weight of the fruit. For now two firm wood branches must be allowed to grow on each plant; unless, however, the slenderness of some vine requires a closer pruning, in which case only one branch is to be left and that containing few eyes.

XVII. A frame of rods is stronger and requires less work. Reeds are put together with greater labour, because they are tied in several places. And these must be bound with their tops turned, one opposite to another, so that the whole frame may be of equal thickness; for if the tops come together, the weakness of that part, when burdened with weight, throws the fruit to the ground just as it ripens and exposes it to dogs and wild animals. But when a frame is duly 2
constructed of several reeds tied in bundles, with their tops in alternating order, it gives about five years of service.

Nor, indeed, is the method of pruning or other culture different from that of the first two years. For ablaqueation [a] must be carefully done in the autumn, and new layers must be applied to the vacant props none the less; for this work must never be discontinued but should be renewed every year.

[a] *Cf.* IV. 4. 2, note.

---

[5] alia est *acM*, *om. SA* : est alia *vulgo*.

3 stauretur[1] annis. Neque enim ea quae seruntur a nobis, immortalia esse possunt; ac tamen aeternitati eorum sic consulimus ut demortuis seminibus alia substituamus, nec ad occidionem universum genus perduci patiamur[2] complurium annorum neglegentia. Quin etiam crebrae fossiones dandae, quamvis possit una[3] detrahi culturae prioris anni. Pampinationes quoque saepe adhibendae; neque enim satis est semel aut iterum tota aestate viti detrahere frondem
4 supervacuam. Praecipue autem decutienda sunt omnia quae infra trunci caput egerminaverunt. Item si oculi singuli sub iugo binos pampinos emiserint, quamvis largum fructum[4] ostendant, detrahendi sunt singuli palmites, quo laetior, quae superest materia, consurgat et reliquum melius educet fructum.

Post quadragesimum et alterum mensem percepta[5] vindemia sic instituenda est putatio ut summissis
5 pluribus flagellis vitis in stellam dividatur. Sed putatoris officium est pedali fere spatio citra[6] iugum vitem compescere, ut e capite, quicquid teneri est, per bracchia emissum provocetur, et per iugum inflexum praecipitetur ad eam mensuram quae terram non possit[7] contingere. Sed modus pro viribus trunci servandus est, ne plures palmites summittantur quam quibus vitis sufficere queat. Fere autem praedicta aetas laeto solo truncoque tres

[1] insaturetur *SAa*.
[2] patiamur *acM* : patimur *SA*, *edd*
[3] possit una *SAacM* : una possit *edd.*
[4] largum fructum (fructus *SA*) *SAacM* : largos fructus *edd.*
[5] perfecta *acM*, *edd. ante Schn.*
[6] contra *SAaM* : circa *edd. ante Schn.*
[7] possint *SA*.

Surely those things that are planted by our hands 3
cannot be immortal; and yet we take such thought for their permanence that we set other plants in place of those that have died, and do not allow the whole genus to be brought to destruction through many years of neglect. Moreover, frequent diggings [a] must be given, although one may be subtracted from the number of the first year's cultivation. Leaf-pruning also must be practised often; for it does not suffice to remove excess leafage from the vine only once or
twice in a whole summer. And especially must 4
everything be broken off which has sprouted out below the head of the main stem. Likewise if any single eyes just below the frame should put out two shoots, even though they give evidence of an abundance of fruit, one branch must be pulled off from each, so that the remaining branch of strong wood may make more vigorous growth and better nourish the fruit that is left.

After the forty-second month, when the vintage has been gathered, the pruning must be so managed, by allowing the growth of more shoots, that the vine
may be spread out in the form of a star.[b] But it is 5
the duty of the pruner to check the vine at a distance of about one foot short of the cross-bar, so that any tender growth that is sent out from the head may be drawn out in the form of arms and that, after being bent over the frame, it may be dropped down to a length which cannot reach the ground. But a limit must be observed in proportion to the strength of the stock, that no more branches may be allowed to grow than the vine is able to support. And in general, when the soil is fertile and the stock thrifty, the afore-

[a] *Cf.* IV. 28. 2. [b] See IV. 26. 3.

materias, raro quattuor desiderat, quae per totidem
6 partes ab alligatore dividi debent. Nihil enim refert iugum in stellam decussari atque diduci,[1] nisi et palmites adiunguntur.[2] Quam tamen formam non omnes agricolae probaverunt; nam multi simplici ordine fuere contenti. Verum stabilior est vinea, et oneri sarmentorum et fructui ferendo, quae ex utraque parte iugo divincta pari libramento velut ancoris quibusdam distenditur.[3] Tum etiam per plura bracchia materias diffundit, et facilius eas explicat undique subnixa,[4] quam quae in simplici
7 cantherio frequentibus palmitibus stipatur. Potest tamen, si vel parum late disposita vinea [5] vel parum fructuosa caelumque non turbidum nec procellosum habeat, uno iugo contenta [6] esse. Nam ubi magna vis et incursus est pluviarum procellarumque, ubi frequentibus aquis vitis labefactatur, ubi praecipitibus clivis velut pendens plura [7] praesidia desiderat; ibi
8 quasi quadrato firmanda [8] est agmine. Calidis vero et siccioribus locis in omnem partem iugum porrigendum est, ut prorepentes undique pampini iungantur, et condensati camerae [9] more, terram sitientem obumbrent. Contra pluviis et frigidis et pruinosis regionibus simplices ordines instituendi; nam et sic facilius insolatur humus, et fructus percoquitur, perflatumque salubriorem habet; fossores quoque

[1] deduci *acM* : dici *SA*.
[2] adiunguntur *SAacM* : adiugentur *vulgo*.
[3] distenditur *SAacM, vett. edd.* : distinetur *vulgo*.
[4] vindemia quae subnexa *SA*.
[5] vineta *SAac, vett. edd.* [6] contentus *SAac, vett. edd.*
[7] plura *SAa, vett. edd.* : plurima *cM, et vulgo*.
[8] firmanda *SAa* : circumfirmanda *vulgo* : est agmine firmanda *cM*.
[9] camare *SAc*.

said age requires three firm wood branches, rarely four, which should be separated by the binder into as many different parts. For it is of no use that the 6
frame is given cross-pieces and made in the shape of a star unless fruit-bearing branches are joined to it. This arrangement, however, has not met the approval of all husbandmen; for many have been satisfied with a plain straight line. But that vine is more stable, both for supporting the burden of young branches and for bearing its fruit, which, being bound to the frame on both sides, is spread out in even balance as if with a kind of anchors. Then too a vine that is supported on every side spreads its woody branches over more arms and extends them more easily than one which is crowded with many fruiting canes on a simple "horse." However, if a vine is 7
not of wide spread or not very fruitful, and if it is in a climate that is not turbulent and stormy, it may be satisfied with a single frame. For where there is great violence and onslaught of rains and storms, where the vine is loosened by frequent downpours, where it hangs, as it were, on steep hillsides and requires a great many reinforcements, there it must be supported on every side, so to speak, by troops in square formation. But in warm and drier places the frame 8
must be extended in every direction, so that the shoots, as they creep forth on every side, may be joined and, being matted together in the fashion of an arched roof, may shade the thirsty earth. On the contrary, in rainy and cold and frosty districts plain straight rows are to be put up; for in that way the ground is more readily warmed by the sun, and the fruit is thoroughly ripened and has a more wholesome ventilation; also the diggers ply their hoes with

liberius et aptius iactant bidentes, meliusque perspicitur a custodibus fructus et commodius legitur a vindemiatore.[1]

XVIII. Sed quoquo modo[2] vineta placuerit ordinare, centenae stirpes per singulos hortos semitis distinguantur: vel, ut quibusdam placet, in semiiugera omnis modus dirimatur. Quae distinctio[3] praeter illud commodum, quod plus solis et venti vitibus praebet, tum etiam oculos et vestigia domini, res agro saluberrimas, facilius admittit, certamque aestimationem in exigendis operibus praebet; neque enim falli possumus per paria intervalla[4] iugeribus
2 divisis. Quin etiam ipsa hortulorum descriptio quanto est minoribus modulis concisa, fatigationem veluti minuit, exstimulatque[5] eos qui opera moliuntur, et ad festinandum invitat; nam fere vastitas instantis laboris animos debilitat. Non nihil etiam prodest vires et proventum cuiusque partis vinearum nosse, ut aestimemus quae magis aut minus colenda sit.[6] Vindemiatoribus[7] quoque hae semitae et iugum pedamentaque sarcientibus opportunam laxitatem praebent, per quam vel fructus vel statumina portentur.

XIX. De positione iugi, quatenus a terra levandum sit, hoc dixisse abunde est: humillimam esse quattuor pedum, celsissimam septem. Quae tamen in novellis seminibus vitanda est; neque enim haec prima constitutio vinearum esse debet, sed per

[1] vindemitore *SA*.

[2] quoquo modo *S*: quomodo *Aa*, *in abbr. cM*: quoquo *Schn.*: quando *alii*.

[3] distinctior *SAac*.

[4] inter bella *SA*.

[5] exstimulatque *Schn.*: extimulque *SA*; et simulat *c*: et simul *a*, *plerique edd.*: et *M*.

[6] sit *SAacM*: sint *Gesn.*, *Schn.*

greater freedom and precision, and the fruit is better examined by the overseer and more easily gathered by the vintager.

XVIII. But in whatever way it pleases you to arrange your vineyards, let them be set off by footpaths into individual plots of one hundred vines each; or, as pleases some, have the whole extent of the vineyard broken up into divisions of half a *jugerum*. This separation, apart from the advantage that it affords more sun and wind for the vines, also allows easier access for the eyes and feet of the proprietor—things most beneficial to the vines—and it provides a definite gauge in the exaction of labour; for we cannot be deceived when the *jugera* are divided at equal intervals. Furthermore, the marking out 2
of small plots in itself lessens the fatigue, as it were, in proportion to the smallness of the sections into which it is cut, and it goads on those who are performing the work and encourages them to hasten the task; for as a rule the immensity of impending work weakens their spirit. Also it is of some advantage to know the strength and the yield of each part of the vineyards, so that we may judge what part is in need of more or of less cultivation. These footpaths also provide for the vintagers and for those who repair the frames and props convenient room for the carrying of fruit or supports.

XIX. As for the placing of the frame, how far it should be raised above the ground, it is sufficient to say that the lowest is four feet and the highest seven. This last, however, is to be avoided in the case of young plants; for this regulation should not apply

---

[7] vindemitoribus *SAa*.

annorum longam seriem ad hanc altitudinem vitis
2 perducenda est. Ceterum quanto est umidius solum et caelum, placidioresque[1] venti, tanto est altius attollendum iugum. Nam laetitia vitium patitur se celsius evagari,[2] fructusque summotus a terra minus putrescit: et hoc uno modo perflatur ventis, qui nebulam et rorem pestiferum celeriter adsiccant, multumque ad deflorescendum et ad
3 bonitatem vini conferunt. Rursus exilis terra et acclivis torrensque aestu, vel quae vehementibus procellis obnoxia est, humilius iugum poscit. At si cuncta competunt voto, iusta est altitudo vineae pedum quinque; nec tamen dubium, quin tanto melioris saporis praebeat mustum, quanto in editiora iuga consurgat.[3]

XX. Pedatam vineam iugatamque sequitur alligatoris cura, cui antiquissimum esse debet, ut supra dixi, rectam conservare stirpem nec flexum[4] ridicae persequi, ne pravitas statuminis[5] ad similitudinem
2 sui vitem configuret. Id non solum ad speciem plurimum refert, sed ad firmitatem et ubertatem,[6] perpetuitatemque. Nam rectus truncus similem sui medullam gerit, per quam velut quodam itinere sine flexu atque impedimento facilius terrae matris alimenta meant[7] et ad summum perveniunt; at

[1] placidioresque *Gesn.*, *Schn.*: humidioresque *acM, edd. ante Gesn.*: umidiores quae *SA*.

[2] partitur se (sae *S*) celsius evaciri *SA*: patitur celsius evocari *Schn.*

[3] quin vites . . . praebeant . . . consurgunt *vulgo*: vites *deest SAacM*: prebeat *acM*; praebeant *SA*: consurgat *cM*; consurgant *SA*.

[4] plexum *SA*, *et deinde* radice *ScM*.

[5] statuminis *scripsi*: statuminis nisi *M*: statum nisi *a*: statū insidii *SA*: statumĩs insidi *c*: statuminum *edd.*

to vineyards at the start, but the vine must be carried to this height after a long succession of years. But the moister the soil and climate, and the gentler 2
the winds, the higher must the frames be raised. For the luxuriance of the vines allows them to spread themselves at a greater height, and the fruit is less inclined to rot when well removed from the earth; and by this method alone there is thorough ventilation by the winds, which quickly dry up the fog and pestilential dew, and contribute much to the casting of the flowers and the goodness of the wine. On the other 3
hand, land that is poor and sloping and parched with heat, or that is subject to violent storms, calls for a lower frame. But if all circumstances answer to your desire, the proper height for a vine is five feet; and yet there is no doubt that the vine yields wine of better flavour in proportion to the height of the frames to which it raises itself.

XX. After the vineyard is staked and yoked, there follows the work of the binder, whose first concern should be, as I remarked above, to keep the vine-stock straight and not to let it follow the curve of the prop, lest the crookedness of the support form a vine after its own likeness. This is of the greatest importance, not only to its appearance, but also to its strength, productiveness, and durability. For a 2
straight stem bears pith like itself, through which, as by a sort of road without a turn or obstruction, the nourishment of mother earth more easily makes its way and arrives at the very top; but vines that are

[6] libertatem *SA.*

[7] manant *c*: manant *SAa.*

quae curvae[1] sunt et[2] distortae, non aequaliter
alliduntur[3] inhibentibus nodis, et ipso flexu cursum
3 terreni umoris veluti salebris[4] retardante. Quare
cum ad summum palum recta vitis extenta est,
capistro constringitur, ne fetu gravata subsidat
curveturque. Tum ex eo loco quod proximum iugo
ligatum est, bracchia disponuntur in diversas partes,[5]
palmaeque superpositae deorsum versus circulo
curvantur, atque[6] id quod iugo dependet, fructu
impletur; rursus[7] curvatura iuxta[8] vinculum mater-
4 iam exprimit. Quidam eam partem, quam nos
praecipitamus, supra iugum porrigunt et crebris
viminibus innexis continent; quos ego minime pro-
bandos puto. Nam dependentibus palmitibus neque
pluviae neque pruinae[9] grandinesve tantum nocent
quantum religatis et quasi tempestatibus oppositis.
Idem tamen palmites priusquam fructus mitescant,
variantibus adhuc et acerbis uvis, religari debent,
quo minus roribus queant putrescere aut ventis
5 ferisve vastentur. Iuxta decumanum atque semitas
palmites intrinsecus flectendi sunt, ne praetereuntium
incursu laedantur. Et hac quidem ratione tempestiva
vitis perducitur ad iugum. Nam quae vel infirma
vel brevis est, ad duas gemmas recidenda est, quo

[1] curvae *om. SAa.*

[2] et *om. SAa*

[3] alligantur *acM, edd. ante Gesn.*: *num* alliciunt (eliciunt)?

[4] salubris *Sc* : salubus *A.*

[5] diversis partibus (partis *Aa*) *AacM.*

[6] *sic S* : circuatur atque *A* : curvantur atque *acM* : curvantur vinculo (*deest codd.*) itaque *vulgo.*

[7] rursusque *cM, et vulgo.*

[8] iuncta *SAc*

[9] neque ruinae (pluviae neque *om.*) *SA* : palmitibus . . . pruinae *om. a.*

bent and misshapen do not offer equally smooth paths,[a] because knots obstruct, and the bend itself, like rough places in a road, checks the passage of moisture from the earth. Therefore when the vine is drawn 3 straight up to the top of the stake, it is fastened with a band so that, when weighed down with its offspring, it may not sag and become bent. Then from that point where that which is nearest to the frame is tied, its arms are arranged in different directions, and the branches which are placed upon the frame are bent downward in a curve, and what hangs from the frame is filled with fruit; on the other hand, the bend puts forth firm wood next to the band. Some 4 spread out upon the frame that part which we bend down, and hold it fast by tying it with withes closely set; but I consider these not at all worthy of approval. For rains and frosts and hail do not harm hanging branches as much as those which are bound and, so to speak, exposed to stormy weather. Still, those same branches should be tied before the fruit mellows, while the grapes are still of different colours and sour, so that they may be less likely to rot with the dews or to be pillaged by winds or wild beasts. Along the main path and the bypaths the branches 5 should be bent inward, that they may not be injured by brushing against those who pass by. And by this method certainly the vine is brought to the frame at the proper time. For a vine that is weak or short must be cut back to two eyes, so that it may put

[a] The translation attempts to preserve the figure in some measure; but the text (*alliduntur*) seems doubtful. Gesner's interpretation, accepted by Schneider and perhaps correct, is that the flow of sap in the vine is compared, in *alliduntur*, to the beating of waves on a shore.

vehementiorem fundat materiam quae[1] protinus emicet in iugum.

XXI. Quinquennis vineae non alia est putatio quam ut figuretur quemadmodum supra institui dicere, neve supervagetur; sed ut caput trunci pedali fere spatio sit inferius iugo, quaternisque bracchiis, quae duramenta quidam vocant, dividatur in totidem partes. Haec bracchia sat erit interim[2] singulis palmitibus in fructum summitti, donec vineae iusti sint roboris. Cum aliquot deinde annis quasi iuvenilem aetatem ceperint, quot palmites relinqui
2 debeant incertum est. Nam loci laetitia plures, exilitas pauciores desiderat; siquidem luxuriosa vitis, nisi fructu compescitur, male deflorescit et in materiam frondemque effunditur; infirma rursus, cum onerata est, affligitur.[3] Itaque pingui terra singulis bracchiis licebit bina iniungere flagella, nec tamen numerosius[4] onerare, quam ut una vitis octo serviat palmitibus, nisi si admodum nimia ubertas plures postulabit; illa enim pergulae magis quam vineae figuram obtinet quae supra hunc modum
3 materiis distenditur. Nec debemus committere, ut bracchia pleniora trunco sint; verum adsidue, cum modo a lateribus eorum flagella licuerit summittere, amputanda erunt superiora duramenta, ne iugum excedant; sed novellis palmis semper vitis renovetur. Quae si satis excreverint, iugo superponantur; sin aliqua earum vel perfracta[5] vel parum procera

[1] quo *SA*. [2] interius *SAaM*. [3] adfligatur *SA*. [4] numerius *SA*. [5] praefracta *Schn.*

forth more vigorous wood which may immediately shoot up to the frame.

XXI. There is no other pruning for a vine five years old than that it shall be shaped as I have undertaken to describe above, and that it shall not spread too far; but that the head of the stock shall be about one foot below the frame and that, with its four arms, which some call *duramenta*, or "hardened branches," it shall be spread out into a corresponding number of spaces. It will suffice for a time that these arms be reduced to one fruiting branch each, until the vines are of proper strength. Then, some years later, when they have entered the juvenile stage, so to speak, it is uncertain how many branches should be left. For 2
richness of situation requires more, and leanness fewer; since, indeed, a vine of rank growth, unless it is checked by bearing, casts its blossoms badly and runs to wood and foliage; while a weak vine, on the contrary, is impaired when burdened with fruit. And so in rich ground it will be permissible to impose two rods upon each arm, but not to burden them with a number beyond the point where one vine supports eight rods, unless its very excessive fruitfulness shall demand more; for the vine which is extended with firm wood beyond this limit has the appearance of an arbour rather than of a vine. And 3
we should not allow the arms to be larger than the stock; but when presently the growth of lateral shoots from them is permitted, the upper hard canes must be constantly cut away so that they may not go beyond the frame; but the vine should always be renewed with young branches. These laterals, if they have made sufficient growth, should be placed upon the frame; but if one of them is broken or not

fuerit, locumque idoneum obtinebit unde vitis anno sequenti revocari[1] debeat, in pollicem tondeatur, quem quidam custodem, alii resecem, nonnulli praesidiarium appellant, id est, sarmentum gemmarum duarum vel trium, ex quo cum processere frugiferae[2] materiae, quicquid est supra vetusti bracchii amputatur, et ita ex novello palmite vitis pullulascit.[3] Atque haec ratio bene institutarum vinearum in perpetuum custodienda erit.

XXII. Si vero aliter formatas acceperimus,[4] et iam[5] multorum annorum neglegentia supervenerit[6] iugum, considerandum erit cuius longitudinis sint duramina quae excedant[7] praedictam mensuram. Nam si duorum pedum aut paulo amplius fuerint, poterit adhuc universa vinea sub iugum mitti, si tamen palus
2 trunco est applicitus; is enim a vite summovetur et in medio spatio duorum ordinum ad lineam pangitur; transversa deinde vitis ad statumen perducitur, atque ita iugo subicitur. At si duramenta eius longius excesserunt,[8] ut in quartum aut etiam in quintum statumen prorepserint, maiore sumptu restituitur;[9] mergis namque, qui[10] nobis maxime
3 placent, propagata celerrime provenit. Hoc tamen si vetus et exesa est superficies trunci; at si robusta et

[1] revocari *SAaM*, *vett. edd.*: renovari *c*, *et vulgo*.

[2] fructiferae *cM*, *Ald.*, *Gesn.*

[3] pullulascit *vulgo*: pullescit *SAa*, *vett. edd.*: pululescit *c*: *om. M.*

[4] vineas *post* acceperimus *suppl. Gesn.*, *Schn.*; *deest codd.*, *vett. edd.*, *Ald.*

[5] et iam *S*, *Sobel*. et *AacM*, *et vulgo*.

[6] supervenerit *codd.*, *vett. edd.*, *Ald.*: supervenerint *Gesn.*, *Schn.*

[7] excedant *SAacM*, *vett. edd.*: excedunt *vulgo*. *Deinde* supra dictum *acM*.

[8] excesserunt *SAc*, *vett. edd.*: excesserint *alii*.

of sufficient length, and if it occupies a suitable place from which the vine should be renewed[a] the following year, let it be cut down to a thumb (*pollex*), which some call *custos* or "keeper," others *resex* or "cut-back," and several *praesidiarium* or "reserve"—that is, a stub of two or three eyes, from which all of the old arm above is cut off after the fruit-bearing wood has come forth; and so the vine sprouts out again from the young branch. And this management of well-established vineyards must be constantly observed.

XXII. If, however, we have taken vineyards trained by another system, and if many years of neglect have now covered the frames, we shall have to consider the length of the old hardened branches that exceed the aforesaid measure. For if they are two feet long or a trifle more, the entire vine may still be put under the frame, provided that the supporting stake is close to the trunk; for it is moved away from 2
the vine and set exactly in the centre of the space between the two rows, and then the vine is carried across to the prop and so brought under the frame. But if its hardened branches have grown to a greater length, so that they have crept out to the fourth or even to the fifth prop, it is restored at greater expense; for when propagated by layers—a method which pleases us most—it comes forward very quickly. This, however, if the surface of the trunk is old and 3
decayed;[b] but if it is strong and sound, it requires

[a] *revocari*, in a technical sense. *Cf.* Palladius, III. 12. 4.
[b] *Cf.* Palladius, III. 16.

[9] restituitur *SA, vett. edd.*: restituentur *acM, Ald., Gesn.*: restituetur *Schn.*
[10] mergis. his namque, quod *vulgo ante Schn.*

integra, minorem operam desiderat. Quippe hiberno tempore ablaqueata fimo satiatur angusteque deputatur, et inter quartum ac tertium pedem a terra viridissima parte corticis acuto mucrone ferramenti vulneratur. Frequentibus deinde fossuris terra permiscetur, ut incitari vitis possit, et ab ea maxime parte, quae vulnerata est, pampinum fundere.
4 Plerumque autem germen de cicatrice procedit, quod sive longius prosiluerit,[1] in flagellum summittitur: sive brevius, in pollicem: sive admodum exiguum, in furunculum. Is ex quolibet vel minimo capillamento fieri potest. Nam ubi unius aut alterius folii pampinus prorepsit e duro, dummodo ad maturitatem perveniat, sequente vere si non adnodatus neque adrasus est, vehementem fundit materiam; quae cum convaluit et quasi bracchium fecit, licet tum supervagatam partem duramenti recidere, et ita reliquam
5 iugo subicere. Multi sequentes compendium temporis, tales vineas supra quartum pedem detruncant, nihil reformidantes eiusmodi resectionem; quoniam fere plurimarum stirpium natura sic se commodat ut iuxta cicatricem novellis frondibus repullescant. Sed haec quidem ratio minime nobis placet, siquidem vastior plaga nisi habeat superpositam valentem materiam, quae[2] possit inolescere, solis halitu torretur; mox deinde roribus et imbribus putrescit.
6 Ac tamen[3] cum est utique vinea recidenda, prius ablaqueare, deinde paulum infra terram convenit amputare, ut superiecta humus vim solis arceat et e

[1] prosiluit *SAacM*.
[2] quae *vel* que *codd.*: qua *vulgo*.
[3] ac tamen *codd.*: Hac tamen *vett. edd.*: attamen *vulgo*.

[a] *Cf.* Palladius, XII. 3.

less labour; for, having the soil loosened about its roots in the winter time, it is satiated with dung and closely pruned, and between the third and fourth foot from the ground it is wounded with the sharp point of an iron implement in the greenest part of the bark. Then the earth is thoroughly mixed by frequent digging, that the vine may be stimulated and that it may have the strength to put out a shoot especially from that place where it was wounded.[a] Generally, 4
moreover, a bud grows from the scar, and if it shoots out to considerable length it is allowed to grow for a cane; if rather short, for a thumb; and if very small, for a knurl. This last may be formed from any fibrous growth, even the smallest. For when a twig of one or two leaves has come out of the hard wood, provided only it comes to maturity, it puts forth a vigorous branch of firm wood the following spring, if it is not trimmed away or rubbed off; and when this has grown strong and has formed a sort of arm, you may then cut back that part of the old branch that has spread too far, and so bring under the frame that part which is left. Many, aiming at the saving of 5
time, chop off such vines above the fourth foot, having no fear of cutting them back in this way; since, as a rule, the nature of most stocks is so adapted that they sprout out with new leaves close to the scar. But this method is not at all pleasing to us, because a larger wound, unless it has vigorous wood above which may close in, is parched by the heat of the sun; and then presently it rots with the dews and the rains. Never- 6
theless, when a vine must in any case be cut down, it is best first to loosen the dirt about it and then to make the amputation a little below ground, so that the soil above may ward off the violence of the sun and

radicibus novellos prorumpentes caules transmittat, qui possint vel sua maritare statumina, vel siqua sunt
7 vidua in propinquo, propaginibus vestire. Haec autem ita fieri debebunt, si vineae altius positae nec in summo labantes radices habebunt, et si boni generis erunt. Namque aliter incassum dependitur [1] opera, quoniam degeneres etiam renovatae pristinum servabunt ingenium; at quae [2] summa parte terrae vix adhaerebunt, deficient [3] ante quam convalescant.
8 Altera ergo vinea fructuosis potius surculis inserenda erit, altera funditus exstirpanda et reserenda, si modo soli bonitas suadebit. Cuius cum vitio consenuit, nullo modo restituendam censemus. Loci porro vitia sunt, quae fere ad internecionem vineta perducunt, macies et sterilitas terrae, salsa vel amara uligo, praeceps et praerupta positio, nimium opaca et soli aversa vallis, harenosus etiam tofus, vel plus iusto ieiunus sabulo, nec minus terreno carens ac nuda glarea, et siqua est proprietas similis quae vitem
9 non alit. Ceterum si vacat his et horum similibus incommodis, potest ea ratione fieri restibilis vinea, quam priore libro praecepimus. Illa rursus mali generis vineta, quae quamvis robusta sint,[4] propter sterilitatem fructu carent, ut diximus, emendantur insitione facta, de qua suo loco disseremus [5] cum ad eam disputationem pervenerimus.

[1] dependitur *M, edd.*: dependetur *ac* · dependentē *SA*.
[2] atque *codd., edd. ante Pontedera*.
[3] et (eac *Gesn.*) *ante* deficient *add. omnes*; *deest SAacM*.
[4] sunt *SA*.
[5] emendantur . . . disseremus *om. SA*.

---

[a] Chap 29, below.

give passage to the young stems that spring from the roots, that they may be able either to wed their own props or to bedeck with their offspring any mateless props that are near by. However, this should be 7
done in this way on condition that the vines are rather deeply planted and do not have roots gliding along on the surface, and if they are of good stock. For otherwise the labour is spent to no purpose, because low-grade vines, even when renewed, will retain their former character; while those that barely cling to the surface of the earth will fail before they can recover strength. The one vine, then, will have to be grafted 8
rather with fruitful shoots, and the other completely rooted out and replanted, provided the goodness of the soil makes it advisable. When a vineyard has wasted away because of the bad quality of soil, we believe that it is in no way worthy of being restored. Furthermore, the bad qualities of a place which usually bring vineyards to destruction are meanness and barrenness of soil, salty or sour marshland, a steep and rugged situation, a valley that is too dark and not exposed to the sun, also sandy tufa, or gravel that is unduly hungry, and also gravel that is bare and destitute of earthy matter, and anything of like nature which does not nourish the vine. But if it is 9
free from these disadvantages and their like, a vineyard may be restored by the method which we advised in the preceding book. On the other hand, those vineyards of bad stock which, even though of vigorous growth, are destitute of fruit because of barrenness, are improved, as we have stated, by grafting; and we shall treat of this in its proper place [a] when we have come to that subject of discussion.

XXIII. Nunc quia[1] parum videmur de putatione vinearum locuti, maxime necessariam partem propositi operis diligentius persequemur. Placet ergo,[2] si mitis ac temperata permittit in ea regione, quam colimus, caeli clementia facta vindemia secundum Idus Octobris auspicari putationem: cum tamen aequinoctiales pluviae praecesserint et sarmenta iustam maturitatem ceperint; nam siccitas seriorem
2 putationem facit. Sin autem caeli status frigidus et pruinosus hiemis violentiam denuntiat, in Idus Febr. hanc curam differemus. Atque id licebit facere si erit exiguus possessionis modus. Nam ubi ruris vastitas electionem nobis temporis negat, valentissimam quamque partem vineti frigoribus, macerrimam vere vel autumno; quin etiam per brumam meridiano axi oppositas vites, aquiloni per
3 ver et[3] autumnum deputari conveniet. Nec dubium quin sit horum virgultorum natura talis[4] ut quanto maturius detonsa sint, plus materiae, quanto serius, plus fructus adferant.

XXIV. Quandoque igitur vinitor hoc opus obibit, tria praecipue custodiat: primum ut quam maxime fructui consulat; deinde ut in annum sequentem quam laetissimas iam hinc eligat[5] materias; tum etiam, ut quam longissimam perennitatem stirpi adquirat. Nam quicquid ex his omittitur, magnum adfert
2 domino dispendium. Vitis autem cum sit[6] per quattuor divisa partes, totidem caeli regiones aspicit.

[1] quia *SAac, vett. edd.*: quoniam *M, et vulgo.*
[2] igitur *cM.*
[3] ververet *A*: verberat *a*: aquilonibus vere vel autumno *M.*
[4] naturalis *SA.* [5] eligat *om. SAa.*
[6] sint *SAa.*

[a] Oct. 15th. [b] Feb. 13th.

XXIII. Now, since we seem not to have said enough about the pruning of vineyards, we shall set forth with greater care that most necessary part of the work proposed. It is proper, if a gentle and temperate mildness of climate permits it in that region which we are cultivating, to begin the pruning after the Ides of October,[a] when the vintage is finished: on condition, however, that the equinoctial rains have come before and that the branches have arrived at their proper maturity; for dry weather makes the 2
pruning later. If, however, the cold and frosty state of the weather gives notice of a severe winter, we shall postpone this matter to the Ides of February.[b] And it will be permissible to do this if the measure of our holding is small. For where a vast extent of land denies us the choice of time, it will be proper that the strongest part of the vineyard be pruned in cold weather, and the weakest part in spring or autumn; indeed vines with a southern exposure may be pruned even during the winter solstice, and those exposed to the north wind during spring and autumn. And there is no doubt that the nature of these plants 3
is such that the earlier they are trimmed, the more wood they produce, and the later, the more fruit.

XXIV. Therefore, at whatever time the vine-dresser shall enter upon this work, he should especially observe three things: first, to make fruit his chief consideration; next, to choose from the very start the most fruitful wood for the following year; and then, also, to make the vine-stock survive through as many years as possible. For any one of these that is neglected brings great loss to the owner. Moreover, when the vine is trained out into 2
four parts, it faces the same number of quarters of

Quae declinationes cum contrarias inter se qualitates habeant, variam quoque postulant ordinationem pro conditione suae positionis[1] in partibus vitium. Igitur ea bracchia, quae septentrionibus obiecta sunt, paucissimas plagas accipere debent, et magis si putabuntur[2] ingruentibus[3] iam frigoribus, quibus
3 cicatrices inuruntur. Itaque una tantummodo materia iugo proxima, et unus infra eam custos erit summittendus qui vitem mox in annum renovet. At e contrario per meridiem plures palmites summittantur, qui laborantem matrem fervoribus aestivis opacent nec patiantur ante maturitatem fructum inarescere.[4] Orientis atque occidentis haud sane magna est in putatione differentia, quoniam solem pari horarum numero sub utroque axe vitis[5] accipit.
4 Modus itaque materiarum is erit quem dictabit humi atque ipsius stirpis laetitia.

Haec in universum; illa per partes custodienda sunt. Nam ut ab ima vite quasi a quibusdam fundamentis incipiam, semper circa crus dolabella dimovenda[6] terra est. Et si suboles, quam rustici suffraginem vocant, radicibus adhaeret, diligenter explantanda ferroque adlevanda est, ut hibernas aquas respuat; nam praestat ex vulnere postea subolem[7] repullescentem vellere quam nodosam et

[1] positionis *S, Schn.* : compositionis *Aa, vett. edd.* : constitutionis *cM, alii*; *et deinde* a parte.

[2] putabantur *SA* : putantur *vett. edd.*

[3] ingredientibus *SA, vett. edd., Sobel.*

[4] fructum humū (humu *A*) legere *SA* : fructum humore legere *a* : humorem inarescere *M* : humor urescere *c*.

[5] axe vitis *M* : axi vitis *ac* : exivit is *S* : exiutas *A*.

[6] dimovenda *M, et vulgo* : demovenda *SAac, vett. edd.*

[7] vulnere postea subolem *a* : Postea sobolem (ut hibernas

the heavens. And since these different directions possess qualities that are contrary to one another, they also require a different arrangement in the parts of the vine according to the circumstances of their situation. Therefore those arms which are exposed to the north should receive the fewest wounds, and the more so if they are pruned at the onset of cold weather, by which the scars are blasted. And so only one firm wood branch next to the frame 3
is to be allowed to grow, and one reserve branch below it to renew the vine presently for a year. But, conversely, more rods should be set apart for growth toward the south, to shade their mother as she suffers from the summer heat and not allow the fruit to wither before it comes to maturity. In the pruning of the east and west sides there is no very great difference, because the vines receive the sun for an equal number of hours in each quarter. The 4
limit, therefore, of firm wood branches will be that which the fertility of the ground and of the stem itself shall prescribe.

The above must be observed in general, and the following in particular. For, to begin at the lowest part of the vine, as at the foundation, so to speak, the earth around the shank should always be laid open with a small mattock. And if any offspring which country people call a *suffrago* or "sucker," clings to the roots, it must be carefully pulled up and cut off smoothly with the knife, so that it may repel the rains of winter; for it is better to tear off a shoot that sprouts forth afterward from the

. . . ex vulnere *om. et post* vellere *insert.*) *cM* postea . . . vellere *om. SA* : vulnere sobolem (postea *om.*) *edd.*

scabram plagam relinquere. Hoc enim modo celeriter cicatricem ducit, illo cavatur atque putrescit.
5 Percuratis deinde quasi pedibus crura ipsa truncique circumspiciendi sunt, ne aut pampinarius palmes innatus [1] aut verrucae similis furunculus relinquatur: nisi si iugum [2] super secta [3] vitis desiderabit ab inferiore parte revocari. Si vero trunci pars senecta [4] solis adflatu peraruit, aut aquis noxiisque [5] animalibus, quae per medullas inrepunt, cavata vitis est, dolabella conveniet expurgare quicquid emortuum est; deinde falce radi [6] vivo tenus, ut a viridi cortice
6 ducat cicatricem. Neque est difficile mox adlevatas plagas terra, quam prius amurca madefeceris, linere. Nam et teredinem formicamque prohibet, solem etiam et pluvias arcet eiusmodi litura; propter quae celerius coalescit et fructum viridem conservat. Cortex quoque aridus fissusque per summa trunci dependens, corpore tenus delibrandus est; quod et melius vitis quasi sordibus liberata convalescit et minus vino faecis adfert. Iam vero muscus, qui more compedis crura [7] vitium devincta comprimit, situque et [8] veterno macerat, ferro destringendus et era-
7 dendus est. Atque haec in ima parte [9] vitis. Nec minus ea, quae in capite servanda sint, deinceps praecipiantur.

[1] innatus *Aa, Sobel*: inantus *S*: intus natus *c*: internatus *M*, *edd.*

[2] iugum *SAacM*, *vett. edd.*, *Sobel*: iugo *vulgo*

[3] super secta *vett. edd.*, *Sobel*: supersecta *SAa*: super recta *M*: superiecta *c*, *et vulgo*.

[4] senecta *SAc*: senectia *a*: pars (*in abbr.*) enecta *M*: secta *edd*

[5] noxiisque *SAacM*: noxiisve *edd.*

[6] radi *SAM*, *vett. edd.*: radici *c*: tradi *a*: cradi *vulgo*.

[7] umore (humorem *a*) consedit cura (crura *a*) *SAa*.

[8] et *om. SA*. [9] crate *SA*.

wound than to leave a cut that is knotty and rough.
For by the one method it quickly forms a callus,
and by the other it becomes hollow and rots.
Then, after care has been taken of the feet, so to 5
speak, the legs themselves and the trunks must be
examined to see that no sprouting leafy shoot or
wart-like knob is left; unless the vine, being cut
off above the frame, shall require renewal from the
lower part. But if the old part of the trunk is
dried out by the sun's blast, or if the vine is
hollowed out by rains and by harmful animals which
creep in through the pith, it will be proper to clear
away with the mattock any part of it that is dead;
and then that it be pared down to the quick with
the pruning-knife, so that it may form a callus from
the green bark. And it is not a difficult matter, 6
soon after the wounds are smoothed off, to daub them
with earth which you have first moistened with oil
lees. For a daubing of this sort keeps out the wood-
borer and the ant, and also keeps off the sun and the
rains; and because of this the wound grows together
more quickly and keeps the fruit green. Also the
dry and shaggy bark hanging along the upper parts
of the trunk must be peeled off down to the body;[a]
because a vine, when rid of its rags, so to speak,
thrives better and imparts less of dregs to the wine.
Moreover, the moss which binds and compresses the
legs of the vines in the manner of shackles, and
softens them with its mouldiness and old dirt, must
be stripped off and scraped away with the iron.
This, then, for the lower part of the vine. And 7
likewise those directions must next be given which
are to be observed with reference to the head.

[a] *I.e.* the sound bark.

Plagae, quas in duro vitis accipit, obliquae rotundaeque fieri debent, nam citius coalescunt,[1] et quamdiu cicatricem non obduxerunt,[2] commodius aquam fundunt;[3] transversae plus umoris et recipiunt et continent. Eam culpam maxime vinitor fugito. Sarmenta lata, vetera, male nata, contorta, deorsum spectantia decidito;[4] novella et fructuaria recta summittito. Bracchia tenera et viridia servato; arida et vetera falce amputato. Ungues custodum
8 annotinos resecato. In quattuor ferme pedes supra terram vitem elatam totidem bracchiis componito, quorum singula spectent[5] decussati iugi partes. Tum[6] vel unum flagellum si macrior vitis erit, vel duo si plenior,[7] bracchio cuique summittito, eaque
9 iugo superposita praecipitato. Sed meminisse oportebit ne in eadem linea unoque latere bracchii duas materias pluresve patiamur. Namque id maxime vitem infestat, ubi non omnis pars bracchii pari vice laborat, neque[8] aequa portione sucum proli suae dispensat sed ab uno latere exsugitur; quo fit ut ea vena, cuius omnis umor absumitur, velut icta fulgure arescat.

10 Vocatur[9] etiam focaneus palmes, qui solet in

[1] convalescunt *a*, *Ald.*, *Gesn.*: convalescent *cM*.
[2] obduxerint *aM*.
[3] fundent *M*.
[4] decidito *SA*, *vett. edd*: recidito *acM*, *et vulgo*.
[5] spectent *vulgo*: spectant *ScM*, *vett. edd.*. *om. Aa*.
[6] singulis *post* tum *add. Schn.*: *om. SAacM*.
[7] plenior *SAacM*, *et vulgo*: pinguior *Schn.*
[8] neque *Schn.*: atque (at *expunct. a*) *acM*, *et vulgo*. quae *SA*.

The wounds which a vine receives in its hard wood
should be made slantwise and rounded, for they grow
together more quickly and, as long as they have not
formed a scar, they shed water to better advantage;
while crosswise cuts receive and hold more moisture.
Let the vine-dresser especially avoid this fault.
Let him cut off branches that are far extended, old,
badly formed, crooked, and turning downward; and
let him permit the growth of those that are young
and fruitful and straight. Let him preserve the young
and tender arms, and remove the old and withered
with the pruning-hook. Let him trim off the tips [a] of
the reserve stubs when they are one year old. When 8
the vine has been raised to about four feet above
the ground, let him arrange it in the same number of
arms, each facing in the direction of one cross-piece
of the frame. Then let him allow the growth of
one rod to each arm if the vine is rather slender, or two
if it is more stocky; and, having placed them upon
the frame, let him cause them to hang down. But 9
we must bear it in mind not to allow two or more
branches of firm wood to be in the same line and on
one side of the arm. For it is especially injurious to
the vine when every part of the arm does not exert
itself equally, and when it does not dispense its
juice to its offspring in equal portions, but is drained
on one side only; whereby it comes about that that
vein whose moisture is entirely taken away withers
as though struck by lightning.

There is also a shoot, called the " throat-shoot " 10

[a] Lit. the nails (of the " thumbs "), for the stubs have been cut slantwise (Chap. 9, above).

---

[9] vocatur *M* : ocatur *a* : videtur *SAc*.

bifurco medius[1] prorepere; et idcirco eum praedicto vocabulo rustici appellant, quod inter duo bracchia, qua se dividit vitis, enatus velut fauces obsidet, atque utriusque duramenti trahens alimenta praeripit. Hunc ergo tamquam aemulum diligenter idem amputant et adnodant priusquam corroboretur. Si tamen ita praevaluit ut alterutrum bracchium adflixerit,[2] id quod imbecillius est tollitur et ipse
11 focaneus summittitur. Reciso enim bracchio, aequaliter utrique parti vires mater sumministrat. Igitur caput vitis pede[3] infra iugum constituito, unde[4] se pandant quattuor, ut dixi, bracchia, in quibus quotannis vitis renovetur, amputatis veteribus et summissis novis palmis, quarum dilectus[5] scite faciendus est. Nam ubi magna materiarum facultas est, putator custodire debet ne aut proximas duro, id est a trunco et capite vitis, relinquat, aut rursus extremas. Nam illae minimum vindemiae conferunt, quoniam exiguum fructum praebent, similes scilicet pampinariis; hae vitem exhauriunt, quia nimio fetu onerant et usque in alterum ac tertium palum, quod
12 vitiosum esse diximus, se extendunt.[6] Quare medio in bracchio commodissime palmae summittentur,

[1] melius *SAa*. [2] adfixerit *SA*.
[3] pedes *acM* : pedum *SA* : pendens *Ald.*
[4] constet retunde *SA*.
[5] dilectus *SAac* : delectus *M*, *et vulgo*.
[6] se extendunt *vulgo* : extendunt (se *om.*) *cM*, *vett. edd.* : ostendunt (se *om.*) *SAa*.

---

[a] Rustic dialect for *faucaneus*. *Cf.* Palladius, III. 12. 2, *Focaneus etiam, qui inter duo bracchia medius nascitur, debet*

(*focaneus*),[a] which usually comes out at the centre of the fork; and farmers call it by the aforesaid name because, sprouting out between the two arms where the vine divides itself, it obstructs the *fauces* or throat, so to speak, and forestalls both of the hardened branches by drawing off their nourishment. Therefore these same farmers are careful to cut off and trim away this rival, as it were, before it gains strength. If, however, it has already become so strong as to have impaired one arm or the other, the weaker arm is removed and the throat-shoot is allowed to grow. For when the arm is cut off, the mother 11 vine bestows her strength equally upon both parts. Therefore let the pruner establish the head of the vine one foot below the frame, from which, as I have said, there may extend the four arms by which the vine is renewed yearly by cutting away the old branches and allowing the growth of new ones, the choice of which must be made with skill. For where there is a great abundance of woody branches, the pruner should guard against leaving either those that are next to the hard wood (that is, from the stock and head of the vine), or on the other hand, those at the ends. For the former contribute very little to the vintage, since they yield scanty fruit, being, in fact, like leaf-branches; while the latter exhaust the vine, because they burden it with too much fruit and extend themselves as far as the second or third stake, which we have declared to be wrong. Therefore branches 12 will be let grow to best advantage on the middle

abradi ; qui si pinguitudine sua bracchium quodcumque proximum debilitaverit, illi deciso ipse succedat.

quae nec spem vidcmiae destituant nec emacient stirpem suam. Non nulli fructus avidius eliciunt, extrema et media flagella summittendo, nec minus proximum duro sarmentum in custodem resecando; quod faciendum, nisi permittentibus soli et trunci viribus, minime censeo. Nam ita se induunt uvis ut nequeant maturitatem capere [1] si benignitas
13 terrae atque ipsius trunci laetitia non adsit. Subsidiarius idemque custos in pollicem resecari non debet,[2] cum palmae, ex quibus proximi fructus sperantur, idoneo loco sitae sunt; nam ubi ligaveris eas, et in terram spectantes deflexeris, infra vinculum
14 materias exprimes. At si longius, quam ritus agricolarum permittit, a capite vitis emicuerit, et bracchiis in aliena iugorum compluvia perrepserit, custodem validum et quam maximum [3] iuxta truncum duorum articulorum [4] vel trium relinquemus, ex quo quasi pollice proximo anno citata materia formetur in bracchium; ut [5] sic recisa vitis ac revocata intra [6] iugum contineatur.

15 Sed in summittendo custode haec maxime sunt observanda. Primum ne resupina [7] caelum sed prona potius plaga terram spectet; sic enim et

[1] facere *SAa* : de curere *c*.
[2] debent *SAacM*.
[3] maxime *SAa*.
[4] particulorum *SAa*.
[5] ut *om. SA* : et *acM*.
[6] revocata in *SAa*, *vett. edd.*: renovata intra *vulgo*: renovata sed in *c* : renovata secundum (*in abbr.*) *M*.
[7] pro munere supina *SA* : primum supina *a*.

[a] So called from the resemblance of the cross-bars of the trellis, with their four-sided opening, to the square opening of the *compluvium* in the Roman house roof. *Cf.* Pliny, *N.H.* XVII.

of the arm, that they may neither disappoint the hope of a vintage nor cause the wasting of their own stem. Some men are more greedy in enticing the fruit by allowing the growth of terminal and medial shoots, and also by cutting the sprig next to the hard wood into a reserve stub; a thing which I believe should not be done in any circumstances unless strength of soil and stock permit it. For they cover themselves with grapes to such an extent that they cannot reach maturity if friendliness of the land and a thrifty condition of the stock itself are not present. The subsidiary branch, which is the 13
same as the reserve stub, should not be cut back into a spur when the rods from which the next fruits are expected are situated in a suitable place; for when you have bound them and bent them to look downward towards the earth, you will force the growth of hard wood below the binding. But if the vine has 14
sprung out from the head to a greater length than the practice of husbandmen allows, and has crept out with its arms to the roof-like [a] trellises that belong to other vines, we shall leave close to the main stem a strong reserve rod, and the largest possible, of two or three joints, from which, as from a spur, firm wood may be quickly fashioned into an arm the following year; so that the vine, cut back and restored in this way, may be kept within the frame.

But in setting aside a reserve stub for growth the 15
following points must be especially observed. First, that the wound shall not face upward toward the heavens, but rather that it slope downward toward the earth; for in this way it is both protected from the

[a] 166, *Compluviata copiosior vino est, dicta a cavis aedium compluviis.*

gelicidiis ipsa se protegit, et ab sole obumbratur. Deinde ne sagittae sed ungulae similis [1] fiat resectio; nam illa celerius et latius emoritur, haec tardius et angustius reformidat. Quodque etiam usurpari vitiosissime animadverto, maxime vitandum est; nam dum serviunt decori, quo sit brevior custos et similis
16 pollici, iuxta articulum sarmentum recidunt. Id autem plurimum officit, quoniam secundum plagam posita gemma pruinis et frigore tum deinde aestu laborat. Optimum est igitur medio fere internodio subsidiarium tondere [2] palmitem, devexamque resectionem facere post gemmam, ne, ut antea [3] diximus, superlacrimet [4] et gemmantem caecet
17 oculum. Si resecis facultas non erit, circumspiciendus est furunculus, qui, quamvis angustissime praecisus in modum verrucae, proximo vere materiam exigat, quam vel in bracchium vel in fructum [5] remittamus. Si neque is reperitur,[6] saucianda ferro est atque exulceranda vitis in ea parte qua pampinum studemus elicere.[7]

Iam vero ipsos palmites, quos vindemiae praeparamus, claviculis ac nepotibus liberandos magno-
18 pere censeo. Sed in iis recidendis alia conditio est, atque alia in iis quae procedunt e trunco. Nam

[1] sed ungulae similis *SA* : sed nec (seu *a* : sed ne *cM*) ungulae (*cM* : ungules *a*) quidem (*deest SAacM*) similis *Schn.* : sed ungulis quidem similis *Ald.*, *Gesn.* : sed nec (*vel* ne) ungulae similis *vett. edd.*

[2] tendere *SAa* : contendere *c*.

[3] antea *SA* : ante iam *acM* . iam (*inclusit Schn.*) antea (ante *Ald.*) *Ald.*, *Gesn.*, *Schn.* : ante *vett. edd.*

[4] super lacrimam *Aa*.

[5] fructum *SAac* : fructu *M* : fructuarium *edd.*

[6] reperitur *ScM* : repperitur *Aa* : reperiatur *edd.*

[7] eligere *Aac*.

frosts and shaded from the sun. Secondly, that the cut shall not be made like an arrow-point but hoof-shaped [a] rather; for the former dies more quickly and over a wider area, while the latter is checked more slowly and within narrower limits. There is also a practice which I observe to be employed, and very wrongly, which should be especially avoided; for in their attention to graceful appearance, so that the reserve stub may be shorter and like a thumb,
they cut the branch close to the joint. But this is 16
very detrimental, because the bud, being placed next to the wound, suffers from frost and cold, and afterwards from heat also. The best plan, then, is to clip the subsidiary branch about midway between the joints and to make a sloping cut behind the bud, so that, as I have already said,[b] its tears may not
drop upon the budding eye and blind it. If there is 17
no opportunity for a cut branch, we must look about for a knob which, even though cut very close in the manner of a wart, may put forth a firm wood branch the following spring, which we may leave either for an arm or for fruit. If such a knob is not to be found, the vine must be wounded with the knife and caused to form a "sore" in that place where we wish to draw out a shoot.

Now I strongly believe that those branches which we are making ready for bearing should be freed
of tendrils and secondary shoots. But one method 18
is employed in cutting these away, and another in removing those that come out of the main stem. For

[a] An oblique cut is to be made clear through, thus giving the stub the appearance of a horse's hoof, with its flat surface not round but of oblong shape.

[b] *Cf.* IV. 9. 2.

quicquid est, quod e duro prominet, vehementius
applicata falce adnodatur et eraditur, quo celerius
obducat[1] cicatricem; rursus quicquid e tenero
processit, sicut nepos, parcius detondetur, quoniam
fere coniunctam gerit ab latere gemmam, cui consulendum est ne falce destringatur. Pressius enim
si adnodes applicato ferro, aut tota tollitur aut
convulneratur; propter quod palmes, quem mox in
germinatione citaverit, imbecillus ac minus fructuosus
erit, tum etiam magis obnoxius ventis, scilicet quia[2]
19 infirmus de cicatrice prorepserit. Ipsius autem
materiae, quam summittimus, longitudini modum
difficile est imponere. Plerique tamen in tantum
provocant ut curvata et praecipitata per iugum nequeat terram contingere. Nos subtilius dispicienda
illa censemus: primum vitis habitum, nam si robusta
est ampliores materias sustinet;[3] deinde soli quoque
pinguitudinem, quae nisi adest, quamvis validissimam
vitem celeriter necabimus[4] procerioribus emaciatam
20 flagellis. Sed longi palmites non mensura verum
gemmarum numero aestimantur. Nam ubi maiora
sunt spatia inter articulos, licet eo usque materiam
producere dum paene terram contingat; nihilo
minus enim paucis frondescet pampinis. At ubi
spissa internodia frequentesque oculi sunt, quamvis
breve sarmentum multis palmitibus virescit, ac[5]

[1] obdurat *SA*. [2] quia *SAacM* : qui *Schn.*
[3] sustineat *SA*.
[4] necavimus *S* : negavimus *A* : notabimus *M*.
[5] ac *SAacM* : et *edd.*

anything that sprouts from mature wood is cut away and trimmed close by a more vigorous application of the pruning-hook, so that it may form a scar more quickly; while, on the contrary, anything that comes from young wood, such as the secondary shoot, is cut away with greater caution because it usually has a bud close beside it, and care must be taken that this is not grazed with the knife. For if, in applying the knife, you trim too closely, the bud is either taken away altogether or wounded severely; and because of this the branch which it presently puts forth in sprouting will be feeble and less fruitful and also more liable to injury by the winds, obviously because it will be weak when it comes forth from
the scar. Furthermore, it is difficult to set a limit to 19
the length of the woody branch which we allow to grow; yet most people draw it out to a length such that, when bent and falling down over the frame, it cannot touch the ground. We believe that the following points should be investigated more closely: first, the condition of the vine, for if it is strong it sustains a greater number of woody branches; and next, the richness of the soil, for if this quality is not present we shall quickly kill even the strongest vine if it is wasted away by rods that are
too long. But long branches are valued, not for 20
their length, but for the number of their eyes. For where there are rather considerable spaces between the joints, it is permissible to extend the wood to the point where it almost touches the ground, for nevertheless it will put forth but few leaves and shoots; but where the segments are short and eyes are found at close intervals, the branch, though short, is green with many sprouts and luxuriant with numerous off-

numeroso fetu exuberat. Quare modus talis generis necessario maxime est adhibendus, ne procerioribus fructuariis oneretur et ut consideret vinitor proximi
21 anni magna necne fuerit vindemia. Nam post largos fructus parcendum est vitibus, et ideo anguste putandum; post exiguos, imperandum. Super cetera illud etiam censemus, ut duris tenuissimisque et acutissimis ferramentis totum istud opus exsequamur. Obtusa enim et hebes et mollis falx putatorem moratur, eoque minus operis efficit et plus laboris adfert vinitori; nam sive curvatur acies, quod accidit molli, sive tardius penetrat, quod evenit in retuso et crasso ferramento, maiore nisu est opus. Tum etiam plagae asperae atque inaequales vites lacerant; neque enim
22 uno sed saepius repetito ictu res transigitur. Quo plerumque fit ut quod praecidi debeat praefringatur,[1] et sic vitis laniata scabrataque putrescat umoribus, nec plagae consanentur. Quare magnopere monendus putator est, ut prolixet aciem ferramenti, et quantum possit novaculae similem reddat. Nec ignoret in quaque re, qua parte falcis utendum sit; nam plurimos per hanc inscitiam vastare vineta comperi.

XXV. Est autem sic disposita vinitoriae falcis figura, ut capulo pars proxima, quae rectam gerit aciem, culter ob similitudinem nominetur; quae

[1] praefingatur *SAc*: perfringatur *aM*.

spring. Therefore it is necessary that a limit be set to such a sort especially, that it may not be burdened by fruiting branches of excessive length, and that the vine-dresser may take into account whether or not the vintage of the previous year was abundant.
For after a large yield the vines must be spared, and 21
for that reason they should be closely pruned; but after a scanty yield they must be urged. In addition to the other directions we are of this opinion also, that we should carry out the entire operation with the thinnest and sharpest of hard iron tools. For a knife that is blunt and dull and soft delays the pruner, and for that reason he accomplishes less work and causes more labour for the vine-dresser; for if the edge is curled over, which happens to soft iron, or if it penetrates too slowly, as is the case with a blunted and thick tool, greater effort is needed. Then, too, ragged and uneven wounds tear the vines; for the matter is not finished with a single stroke but by strokes
often repeated. And so the usual result is that what 22
should be cut off is broken off, and that in this way the vine, being mangled and jagged, is rotted with moisture and its wounds do not heal. Therefore the pruner should be expressly reminded to draw out the edge of his implement and to make it as razor-like as possible. And he should not be ignorant as to what part of the pruning-hook should be used in each operation; for I have learned that a great many men make havoc of vineyards through lack of knowledge on this point.

XXV. Now the shape of the vine-dresser's knife is so designed that the part next to the haft, which has a straight edge, is called the *culter* or " knife " because of the similarity. The part that is curved is

flectitur, sinus; quae a flexu procurrit, scalprum; quae deinde adunca est, rostrum appellatur; cui superposita semiformis lunae species securis dicitur; eiusque velut apex pronus imminens mucro vocatur. Harum partium quaeque suis muneribus fungitur, si
2 modo vinitor gnarus est iis utendi. Nam cum in adversum pressa manu desecare quid debet, cultro utitur; cum retrahere, sinu; cum adlevare, scalpro; cum incavare,[1] rostro; cum ictu caedere, securi; cum in angusto aliquid expurgare, mucrone. Maior autem pars operis in vinea ductim[2] potius quam caesim[3] facienda est; nam ea plaga quae sic efficitur, uno vestigio adlevatur, prius enim putator applicat
3 ferrum, atque ita quae destinavit praecidit. Qui caesim vitem petit, si frustratus est, quod saepe evenit, pluribus ictibus stirpem vulnerat. Tutior igitur et utilior putatio est, quae, ut rettuli, ductu falcis non ictu conficitur.

XXVI. Hac peracta, sequitur, ut ante iam diximus, adminiculandae iugandaeque vineae cura, cui stabiliendae melior est ridica palo, neque ea quaelibet; nam est praecipua cuneis fissa olea,[4] quercus et suber, ac si qua sunt similia robora. Tertium obtinet locum

[1] incavare *edd.*: incuuarre *a*: incure *SAc*: incidere *in marg. M*.
[2] duc *A* : ducit *cM* : in duo *a*.
[3] cresin *S* : chres in (chrea *suprascr. man. alt.*) *A* : cresim *c* : diresin *M* : in tres *a*.
[4] olea gotum *S* : oleam gotum *A* : oleam totum *a* : oleangotum *c* : oleragotum *M*.

[a] *Cf.* IV. 12. 1.
[b] With this chapter *cf.* Varro, *R.R.* I. 8; Pliny, *N.H.* XVII. 164–166, 174.

called the *sinus* or "bend"; that which runs on from the curve is the *scalprum* or "paring-edge"; the hook which comes next is called the *rostrum* or "beak," and the figure of the half-moon above it is called the *securis* or "hatchet"; and the spike-like part which projects straight forward from it is called the *mucro* or "point." Each of these parts performs its own peculiar tasks, if only the vine-dresser is skilful in using them. For when he is to cut something 2
with a thrust of the hand away from him, he uses the *culter*; when he is to draw it toward him, he uses the *sinus*; when he wishes to smoothe something, he uses the *scalprum*, or, to hollow it out, the *rostrum*; when he is to cut something with a blow, he uses the *securis*; and when he wants to clear away something in a narrow place, he makes use of the *mucro*. But the greater part of the work in a vineyard must be done by drawing the knife toward you rather than by hacking; for the wound which is made in this way is smoothed with one impression, since the pruner first puts the knife in place and so cuts off what he has intended to cut. One who attacks the vine by 3
chopping, if he misses his aim, as often happens, wounds the stock with many blows. Therefore that pruning is safer and more advantageous which, as I have said, is accomplished by the drawing of the knife and not by striking.

XXVI. When this is finished there follows, as I have said before,[a] the matter of propping and trellising the vineyard.[b] And for giving firmness to this the stake is better than the pole, and that not any stake you please; for chief of all is the olive tree split with wedges, the oak and the cork tree, and any other wood of like strength. The round prop holds third

pedamen teres, idque maxime probatur ex iunipiro, tum ex lauru et cupressu. Recte etiam faciunt ad rem silvestres pinus,[1] atque et sabuci[2] probabiles[3] usu statuminis.[4] Haec eorumque similia pedamenta post putationem retractanda sunt, partesque eorum
2 putres dedolandae acuendaeque;[5] atque alia convertenda, quae sinceritatem[6] habent; alia summovenda, quae vel cariosa vel iusto breviora sunt, eorumque in vicem idonea reponenda, iacentia statuenda, declinata corrigenda. Iugo, si non erit opus novo, sarturae recentia vincula inserantur. Si restituendum videbitur, antequam vitis palo applicetur, perticis vel harundinibus conectatur, ac tum demum, sicut in novella praecepimus, vitem iuxta caput infraque bracchia colligemus[7] cum ridica; idque facere non oportebit omnibus annis eodem loco, ne vinculum incidat et truncum strangulet.
3 Bracchia deinde sub stella quadripartito[8] locabimus, tenerosque palmites super iugum ligabimus nihil repugnantes naturae, sed ut quisquis obsequetur, leviter curvabitur, ne deflexus frangatur neve iam tumentes gemmae detergeantur. Atque ubi duae materiae per unam partem iugi mittentur, media pertica interveniat, diremptaeque palmae per iugorum

[1] pinus *edd.*: abuius *S*: ab huius *AacM*: sabinas *Sobel.*

[2] sambuci *cM*, *edd.*

[3] probabilis *SAac.*

[4] usu statum in his *A*: usu tantum in his *acM*, probabilis usus. Tamen in his haec *vulgo ante Schn.*

[5] acuendaeque *om. AacM*, *edd. ante Schn.*

[6] sinceritatem *cM*, *edd. ante Schn.*. ceritatem *SAa*: proceritatem *Schn.*

[7] infraque . . . colligemus *om. c*, *vett. edd.*: colligemus vitem cum ridica *aM*: vitem iuxta caput *post* colligemus *repet. SA*.

[8] quadripertito *SAa.*

place; and that is most approved which is made of juniper, and also of laurel and cypress. Also forest pines do well for this purpose, and elders too are acceptable in the capacity of supports. These props and their like must be gone over again after the pruning, and the decayed parts must be hewn away and sharpened; and some, if they are sound, 2
are to be reversed, while others, which are either rotten or shorter than is proper, must be removed and replaced with suitable props; those that are lying flat must be set up, and those that lean are to be straightened. As for the frame, if there is no need of a new one, have fresh bindings worked into the mending of it. If it seems to need rebuilding, let it be tied together with poles or reeds before the vine is attached to its prop, and then, as I have directed in the case of a newly planted vine,[a] we should bind the vine to the stake, close to the head and below the arms; and this tying should not be done every year in the same place, lest the band cut into the stock and choke it. Then we will arrange 3
the arms in four directions, below the star,[b] and bind the tender fruiting branches upon the frame, not forcing them contrary to their nature; but according as each branch will submit, it will be bent slightly, so as not to be broken in the bending and that the buds already swelling may not be rubbed off. And when two mature branches are extended along one part of the frame, let a bar come between them; and let the separated vine-shoots run out over the quadrangular openings[c] of the frames, and, as if plunging

[a] *Cf.* IV. 12–13.

[b] Of the frame, *i.e.* the X formed by the intersecting cross-bars (IV. 17. 6).

[c] See IV. 24. 14, with note.

compluvia decurrant, et velut mersae cacuminibus
4 in terram despiciant. Id ut scite fiat, meminerit alligator ne torqueat sarmentum sed tantum inflexum devinciat; et ut omnis materia, quae nondum[1] potest praecipitari, iugo superponatur, ut potius innixa perticae, quam e vinculo dependeat. Saepe enim notavi per imprudentiam rusticos subicere iugo palmam, et ita colligare ut solo vimine suspendant;[2] quae vinea cum accipit pampini et uvarum pondus, infringitur.

XXVII. Sic deinde ordinata vineta festinabimus emundare, sarmentisque et calamentis[3] liberare. Quae sicco tamen solo[4] legenda sunt, ne lutosa humus inculcata maiorem fossori laborem praebeat, qui protinus adhuc[5] silentibus vineis inducendus[6] est. Nam si palmis incientibus[7] progemmantibusque fossorem immiseris, magnam partem vindemiae decusserit. Igitur antequam germinent, per divortium veris et[8] hiemis quam altissime fodiendae vineae sunt, quo laetius atque hilarius pullulent; eaeque ubi se frondibus[9] vestierint, teneris caulibus
2 necdum adultis modus adhibendus[10] est. Idemque vinitor, qui ante ferro, nunc manu deputet,[11] umbras-

[1] nondum *Schn.*: mundo *SA*: modo *aM*, *Pontedera*, *Gesn.*: mihi *c*: nihil *edd. ante Gesn.*

[2] suspendant *Schn*: suspendeat *SacM vett. edd.*: suspendae at *A*: suppendeat *Ald.*, *Gesn.*

[3] calametis *S*, *et vulgo ante Schn.*: calamitis *A*.

[4] loco *SAcM*.

[5] ad huc id *cM*: ad id ut *SA*: ad id *a*.

[6] indicendus *SA*; indulgendus *acM*.

[7] incientibus *Schn. cum Pontedera*: initientibus *S*: inicientibus *A*: incipientibus *acM*, *et plerique*.

[8] et *SAa*: ac *M*: *om.* c: atque *vulgo*.

[9] *sic codd.*: et uvis *post* frondibus *add. edd.*

downward, let them look upon the ground with their tips. That this may be done skilfully, the binder must 4
remember not to twist the young branch but merely to bend it down and tie it; and he must bear in mind that every mature branch which cannot yet be bent down to earth is to be placed upon the frame, so that it may rather rest upon a bar than hang from its binding. For I have often observed that farmers, through want of foresight, place a fruiting branch under the frame and tie it in such a way as to let it hang merely by a withe; and when this vine receives the weight of its shoots and grapes, it is broken down.

XXVII. When our vineyards are so put in order, we shall next hasten to clean them and to rid them of the pruned twigs and deadwood. However, these must be gathered when the ground is dry, lest the earth, being trampled when muddy, make the task harder for the digger, who is to be brought in immediately while the vines are still dormant. For if you send the digger in when the fruiting branches are swelling and putting forth buds, he will knock off a large part of the vintage. Therefore vineyards are to be dug as deep as possible during the time when spring begins and winter ends, before the buds come, that they may sprout out more luxuriantly and joyfully; and when they have bedecked themselves with leaves, a limit must be set to the young shoots before they are full grown. And let 2
the same vine-dresser who made use of the knife before, now prune with his hand, and let him hold the

[10] habendus *SA*, *vett. edd.*
[11] deputet *acM* : decutet *SA* : decutiet *edd.*

que compescat, ac supervacuos pampinos deturbet;[1]
nam id plurimum refert non inscite facere, siquidem
vel magis pampinatio quam putatio vitibus consulit.
Nam illa quamvis multum iuvat, sauciat tamen et
resecat; haec clementius sine vulnere medetur, et
3 anni sequentis expeditiorem putationem facit. Tum
etiam vitem minus cicatricosam reddit, quoniam id
ex quo viride et tenerum decerptum[2] est, celeriter
consanescit. Super haec materiae, quae fructum
habent, melius convalescunt, et uvae commodius
insolatae percoquuntur.

4 Quare prudentis est ac maxime callentis vinitoris
aestimare ac dispicere quibus locis in annum debeat
materias summittere; nec orbos tantum detrahere
palmites, verum etiam frugiferos, si supra modum se
numerus eorum profuderit; siquidem evenit ut
quidam oculi trigeminis palmis egerminent, quibus
binos detrahere oportet, quo commodius singulos
5 alumnos educent. Est enim sapientis rustici repu-
tare, num maiore fructu vitis se induerit, quam ut
perferre eum possit. Itaque non solum frondem
supervacuam volet[3] decerpere, quod semper faciendum est, verum interdum partem aliquam fetus
decutere, ut ubere suo gravatam vitem levet. Idque
faciet variis de causis pampinator industrius, etiam
si non erit maior fructus, quam ut maturescere queat;
6 si aut[4] continuis superioribus annis dapsili pro-

[1] compescat . . . deturbet *SAacM*, *vett. edd.*: compescet . . . deturbabit *vulgo*.
[2] deceptum *SAM* : decertum *a*.
[3] volet *SAacM* : debet *vulgo*.
[4] si aut *SA* (= aut si) *Sobel*: si autem *acM*, *edd.*

[a] *Cf. De Arb.* 11.

shade in check and pull off superfluous foliage; and it is of the utmost importance not to do this unskilfully, since the removal of excess leafage is even more beneficial to vines than is pruning. For though the one is of great advantage, still it wounds and checks the vines; while the other heals them more gently, without a wound, and makes the next year's
pruning easier. Then too it produces a vine that is 3
freer from scars, because that from which a green and tender thing is plucked soon heals over. In addition, the mature branches which have fruit make a better recovery, and the grapes, being more completely exposed to the sun, are thoroughly ripened.[a]

Therefore it is the part of an intelligent vine- 4
dresser, and one especially expert, to take stock and consider in what places he should allow the growth of firm wood for the year, and to remove not only the branches that are destitute of buds, but fruitful branches as well, if their number has gone beyond proper bounds; since it happens that some eyes put forth three shoots, of which you must remove two, that
the eyes may better rear one nursling apiece. For 5
it is the business of a wise husbandman to consider whether the vine has bedecked itself with a greater quantity of fruit than it can carry to maturity. Accordingly he will wish, not only to pick off superfluous foliage, which should always be done, but sometimes to shake off a part of the fruit so as to lighten a vine that is overburdened by its own productiveness. And a diligent vine-trimmer will do this for various reasons, even if there is no more
fruit than is able to ripen; or if it is right that 6
a vine, fettered by heavy bearing in previous years

ventu religatam vitem requiescere[1] ac refici par erit,[2] si[3] futurae materiae consulendum. Nam cacumina flagellorum confringere[4] luxuriae comprimendae causa, vel dura parte trunci sitos[5] pampinos summovere, nisi ad renovandam vitem unus atque alter servandus est, tum e capite quicquid inter bracchia viret explantare, atque eos qui per ipsa duramenta steriles[6] nequiquam matrem opacant, palmites detergere, cuiuslibet vel pueri est officium.

XXVIII. Tempus autem pampinationis antequam florem vitis ostendat, maxime est eligendum, sed et postea licet eandem repetere. Medium igitur eorum dierum spatium, quo acini formantur, vinearum nobis aditum negat, quippe florentem fructum movere non expedit. Pubescentem vero, et quasi adolescentem convenit religare, foliisque omnibus nudare, tum et crebris fossionibus implere; nam fit uberior pulvera-
2 tionibus.[7] Nec infitior plerosque ante me rusticarum rerum magistros tribus fossuris contentos

[1] dapsili (dapsilis *aM*, dacili *SA*) proventu (probentur *SAM*, probantur *a*) religatam vitem requiescero *SAacM*, *Sobel*: d. p. fatigata (fatigatam *Cod. Laurent.* 53. 27, *teste Sobel*) vitis fuerit, requiescere *vulgo*.

[2] paruerit *SA* : par fuerit *Sobel* : patitur *a*.

[3] si *SAacM*, *vett. edd.*, *Sobel* : et sic *vulgo*.

[4] definge *SA* : defringe *a*.

[5] satos *c* : si post *SAa* : siccos *M*.

[6] steriles *M*, *edd.* : similes *SAac*.

[7] pulverationi *c*: pulveratione *M* : nudare . . . pulverationibus *om. SA*.

---

[a] *I.e.* the stripping off by hand of useless leaves and twigs (*pampini*), an operation described just above and frequently mentioned (*e.g.* Chap. 6, above; *De Arb.* 11. 2), and called *pampinatio*, as distinguished from *putatio* or pruning with

without interruption, should now rest and recover itself, if provision is to be made for the mature wood of the future. For to break off the tips of the rods for the purpose of checking rank growth, or to remove twigs that are situated on the hard part of the stock, unless it is necessary to preserve one or two for renewing the vine; as also to pull off every green shoot that comes out of the head and between the arms, and to strip away those sterile shoots which all along the mature wood shade the mother vine to no purpose, is a proper task for anyone at all, even for a child.

XXVIII. But the time for vine-trimming [a] must be chosen, preferably, before the vine shows its flower, though it is permissible to repeat the operation afterwards. Therefore the intervening period of days, when the berries are being formed, refuses us entrance to the vineyard, because it is not expedient to disturb the fruit when it is in the blossom. But when the fruit is passing from childhood and is in the adolescent stage, so to speak, it is proper to bind it and strip it of all leaves, and also to make it plump by frequent diggings; for fruit is made more plentiful by pulverizing the soil.[b] And I do not deny 2
that most teachers of husbandry before me were

a knife. With this sentence compare Pliny, *N.H.* XVII. 190, *Pampinatio verna in confesso est ab Idibus Maiis, intra dies x, utique antequam florere incipiat. . . . De sequente variant sententiae. Cum defloruit aliqui pampinandum putant, alii sub ipsa maturitate.*

[b] *Pulveratio* meant the working of the ground about the vine when it was dry, reducing it to powder, and raising clouds of dust to settle on the leaves and fruit as a protection against sun and fog; *cf.* XI. 2. 60; *De Arb* 12. 1; Pliny, *N.H.* XVII. 49.

fuisse; ex quibus Graecinus, qui sic refert: potest videri satis esse constitutam vineam ter fodere. Celsus quoque et Atticus consentiunt tres esse motus in vite seu potius in omni surculo naturales: unum, quo germinet; alterum, quo floreat;[1] tertium, quo maturescat. Hos ergo motus censent fossionibus concitari. Non enim natura quod vult satis efficit, nisi eam labore[2] cum studio iuveris. Atque haec colendarum vinearum cura finitur vindemia.

XXIX. Redeo nunc ad eam partem disputationis, qua sum professus vitium inserendarum tuendarumque insitionum praecepta. Tempus inserendi Iulius Atticus tradidit ex Kalendis Novembribus in Kalendas Iunias, quoad posse custodiri surculum sine germine adfirmat. Eoque debemus intellegere nullam partem anni excipi, si sit sarmenti silentis facultas. Id porro in aliis stirpium generibus, quae firmioris et sucosioris libri sunt, posse fieri sane
2 concesserim. In vitibus nimis temere tot mensium[3] rusticis insitionem permissam dissimulare non est fidei meae: nec quia ignorem[4] brumae temporibus aliquando insitam vitem comprehendere. Sed non quid in uno vel altero experimento casu fiat, verum quid certa ratione plerumque proveniat, discentibus praecipere debemus.[5] Etenim si exiguo numero periclitandum sit, in quo maior cura temeritati

[1] confloreat *SA*.
[2] laborem *SA*.
[3] mensum *SA*.
[4] nec quia ignorem *a*: nec qui nigriorem *SAc*: licet quidem ignorem (*ex* igriorem *ut vid.*) *M*: non quod ignorem *vulgo*.
[5] permiscere (permittere *a*) debeamus *SAac*, *Sobel*.

Cf. Pliny, *N.H.* XVII. 188–189.

content with three diggings;[a] among whom is Graecinus, who speaks as follows: "It may seem sufficient to dig an established vineyard three times." Celsus, too, and Atticus agree that there are three natural impulses in a vine, or rather in every branch: one which makes it sprout, another which makes it bloom, and the third which makes it ripen. These impulses, then, they think are stimulated by diggings: for nature does not sufficiently accomplish her purpose unless you diligently give her the benefit of your efforts. And this attention to the cultivating of vineyards comes to an end with the vintage.

XXIX. I return now to that part of my discussion in which I promised directions for the grafting of vines and protecting the grafts. Julius Atticus has said that the time for grafting is from the Calends of November to the Calends of June, up to which time he asserts that a scion can be kept without sprouting. And by that we should understand that no part of the year is excepted if we have a supply of dormant twigs. Furthermore, I would freely grant that this could be done in other kinds of stock that have stronger and sappier bark. In the case of 2
vines, one thing it is not in keeping with my honesty to conceal—that it is exceedingly rash to allow husbandmen to graft during so many months; not that I am unaware that a vine grafted in the dead of winter sometimes takes hold. But we should instruct learners, not what may come about by chance in one or two experiments, but what commonly occurs under a definite system. For if the risk is to be taken with a small number, in whose case greater care makes amends for rashness, I can

3 medetur, possum aliquatenus conivere;[1] cum vero
vastitas operis etiam diligentissimi agricolae curam
distendit,[2] omnem scrupulum summovere debemus.
Est enim contrarium, quod Atticus praecipit. Nam
idem per brumam negat recte putari vineam; quae
res quamvis minus laedat vitem, merito tamen fieri
prohibetur, quod frigoribus omnis surculus rigore
torpet, nec propter gelicidia corticem movet, ut
4 cicatricem consanet. Atque idem Atticus non
prohibet eodem ipso tempore inserere, quod tum et
totius obtruncatione vitis et cum eiusdem resec-
tionis fissura praecipit fieri. Verior itaque ratio est
inserendi tepentibus iam diebus post hiemem, cum
et gemma se et [3] cortex naturaliter movet, nec frigus
ingruit, quod possit aut surculum insitum aut fissurae
5 plagam inurere. Permiserim [4] tamen festinantibus
autumno vitem inserere, quia non dissimilis est eius
aeris qualitas vernae. Sed quocumque quis tempore
destinaverit inserere, non aliam sciat esse curam
surculis explorandis, quam quae tradita est priore
libro, cum de malleolis eligendis praecepimus.
Quos ubi generosos et fecundos et quam maturissimos
viti detraxerit, diem quoque tepidum silentemque
6 a ventis eligat. Tum consideret surculum teretem
solidique corporis, nec fungosae medullae, crebris
etiam gemmis et brevibus internodiis. Nam pluri-

[1] conivere *c*: convenire *a, et vulgo ante Schn.*: meri contueri *SA* : *om. M* : connivere *Schn.*

[2] distendit (discendit *a*, discendi *c*) atque impedit (impendit *c*) *acM*.

[3] gemmas et *AacM, et vulgo ante Schn.*; *et deinde* corticem *M, ante Schn.*

[4] permiserit *SA* : permisceri *cM*.

---

[a] III. 6. [b] cambium-layer.

wink at it to a certain extent; but when the extensiveness of the operation divides the attention of even the most careful husbandman, we ought to remove every uncertainty. There is, indeed, a contradiction in what Atticus directs. For he says that it is not right to prune a vineyard during the middle of winter; and although this does less injury to the vine, still it is forbidden to be done, with good reason, because in cold weather every branch is numb with the cold, and because in its frozen condition it produces no impulse in the bark to heal the scar. And 4 yet this same Atticus does not forbid grafting at the very same time, and he directs that it should then be done by cutting off the head of the whole vine and making a cleft at the point of this cutting. Therefore the more proper way of grafting is at the end of winter, when the days are now growing warm, when both bud and bark are stirred by nature, and when there is no attack of cold weather that may sear either the grafted scion or the wound made by the cleft. Nevertheless I would allow those 5 who are in haste, to graft the vine in the autumn, because the temperature of the air at that season is not unlike that of spring. But at whatever time one intends to graft, let him know that attention to the choosing of scions is not different from that which was prescribed in the preceding book when we gave directions for the selection of cuttings.[a] When he has pulled from the vine scions which are of good stock, fruitful, and as well ripened as possible, let him also choose a day that is warm and free from winds. Then let him look for a scion that is round and of 6 firm body, not of spongy pith,[b] and also with numerous eyes and short joints. For it is of the greatest

mum interest non esse longum sarmentum, quod inseratur; et rursus plures oculos, quibus egerminet, inesse. Itaque si sunt longa internodia, necesse erit [1] ad unam vel summum duas gemmas recidere surculum, ne proceriorem faciamus quam [2] ut tempestates et [3] ventos et imbres [4] immobilis pati possit.

7 Inseritur autem vitis vel recisa vel integra perforata terebra; sed illa frequentior et paene omnibus agricolis cognita insitio; haec rarior et paucis usurpata. De ea igitur prius disseram, quae magis in
8 consuetudine est. Reciditur vitis plerumque supra terram, nonnumquam tamen et infra, quo loco maxime [5] solida est atque enodis. Cum iuxta [6] terram insita est, surculus adobruitur cacumine tenus; at cum editior a terra est, fissura diligenter subacto luto linitur et [7] superposito musco ligatur, quod et calores et pluvias arceat. Temperatur ita surculus, ut calamo non absimilis sit. Purgamentum habeas ad fissuram,[8] sub qua nodus in vite desideratur, qui quasi alliget eam fissuram, nec rimam patiatur
9 ultra procedere. Is nodus etiam si quattuor digitis a resectione abfuerit,[9] inligari tamen eum, priusquam vitis findatur, conveniet, ne, cum scalpro factum

[1] erit *SAa*: esse *c*: est *M*, *edd.*
[2] ne . . . quam *om. SA.*
[3] et *om. SAa.*
[4] et imbres *om. SA.*
[5] maxime *SAac, vett. edd.*: magis *M*, *et vulgo.*
[6] iuxta *codd., et plerique*: supra *Schn.*
[7] et *codd.*: atque *vulgo.*
[8] u. c. n. a. sit. Purgamentum habeas a. f. *Sobel*: u. c. n. a. est purgamentum habens ad fissuram (affisuram *a*) *SAa*: u. c. non ut coagmentum fissuram (fixuram *c*) *cM*: u. c. non absimilis coagmentet fissuram *edd.*
[9] resectionibus fuerit *SAac.*

importance that the twig which is ingrafted be not long; and also that there be many eyes on it, from which it may put forth shoots. And so, if the joints are long, it will be necessary to shorten the scion to one or at most two eyes, lest we make it so long that it cannot endure the storms and winds and rains without being disturbed.

Now when a vine is grafted it is either cut off or left 7
whole and bored through with an auger; [a] but the former is the more usual graft and is known to almost all farmers, while the latter is less common and is employed by few. Therefore I shall discuss first the method which is more in use. The vine is gener- 8
ally cut above ground, though sometimes below, in the place where it is most solid and free from knots. When it is grafted close to the ground, the graft is covered with earth to its very top; but when the graft is higher above ground, the cleft is carefully daubed with kneaded clay and bound with an overlaying of moss to ward off heat and rains. The scion is so shaped as to be not unlike a reed pen. The piece that is pared off you should hold against the cleft; [b] and under this cleft there is need of a node in the vine, to bind it together, as it were, and not allow the crack to advance beyond that point. Even 9
if this node is four finger-breadths distant from the point of cutting, still it will be proper that it be bound before the vine is split, lest the wound spread wider

[a] With the instructions that follow compare Cato's chapter (41) on vine-grafting; also Pliny, *N.H.* XVII. 115–117, and Palladius, IV. 1.

[b] Sobel (*Stud. Colum.*, pp. 77–78) explains that the paring is to be used as a wedge to hold the cleft open while the scion is being inserted.

fuerit iter surculo, plus iusto plaga hiet. Calamus autem[1] non amplius tribus digitis debet allevari, atque[2] is ex ea parte, qua raditur, ut sit levis. Eaque rasura ita deducitur, ut medullam contingat uno latere, atque altero paulo ultra corticem destringatur, figureturque in speciem cunei, sic ut ab ima parte acutus[3] surculus, latere altero sit tenuior, atque altero plenior; perque tenuiorem partem insertus eo latere artetur quo est plenior, et utrimque contingat fissuram. Nam nisi cortex cortici sic applicatur,[4] ut nullo loco transluceat, nequit coalescere.[5]

10 Vinculi genus ad insitionem non unum est. Alii viminibus obstringunt; nonnulli circumdant libro fissuram; plurimi ligant iunco, quod est aptissimum. Nam vimen, cum inaruit, penetrat et insecat corticem. Propter quod molliora vincula magis probamus, quae cum circumvenere truncum, adactis harundineis cuneolis artantur. Sed antiquissimum est, et ante haec ablaqueari vitem, radicesque summas vel suboles amputari; et post haec adobrui truncum. Isque cum comprehendit, aliam rursus
11 exigit curam: nam saepius pampinandus est, cum germinat, frequentiusque detrahendae suboles quae a lateribus radicibusque prorepunt. Tum quod ex insito profundit[6] subligandum, ne vento surculus

[1] autem] ut rarior (non *om.*) *SA* : adradi *Schn.*
[2] aequaliter *vulgo ante Schn.*
[3] artus *SA*.
[4] applicetur *M, et vulgo* : appellatur *A*.
[5] nequid patiatur coalescere *SA* : nequid coalescere patiatur *a* : nequid coalescere *c*.
[6] profudit *SA*.

[a] Thus forming an unsymmetrical wedge. By *medulla* is meant the cambium-layer.

than it should when a way is made for the graft with the knife. Moreover, the pen-shaped scion should be tapered not more than three fingers, and so that it may be smooth on the side where it is shaved. And this shaving is carried so far as to reach the pith on one side, and on the other side to be pared down a little farther than the bark;[a] and to be fashioned in the form of a wedge, so that the scion may be sharp at its lowest point, thinner on one side and thicker on the other, and that, when inserted by the thinner side, it may be pressed close on that side which is thicker and may touch the cleft on both sides. For, unless bark is fitted to bark in such a way that the light shows through at no point, it cannot grow together.

There is more than one kind of band for grafting. 10
Some bind the cleft with willow withes; some wrap it with inner bark; very many tie it with rush, which is most suitable. For the willow withe, when it has dried, penetrates and cuts into the bark. For this reason we give higher approval to softer bindings which, after being wrapped around the stock, are drawn tight by forcing in small wedges of reed. But it is of very first importance that the ground be loosened around the vine beforehand, and that the surface roots and suckers be cut away; and afterwards that the stock be covered with earth. And when the stock has taken hold of the graft, it again requires
care of a different sort: for, when it buds, it must 11
be stripped oftener of superfluous growth, and the suckers which sprout from the sides and roots must be pulled off more frequently. Furthermore, anything that it puts forth from the place of ingraftment must be tied up, lest the scion should be

motus[1] labefactetur aut explantetur tener pampinus. Qui cum excrevit, nepotibus orbandus[2] est, nisi si propter penuriam et calvitium loci summittuntur[3] in propagines. Autumnus deinde falcem maturis palmitibus admovet. Sed putationis insitis[4] custoditur ea ratio, ut ubi nulla desideratur propago unus surculus evocetur in iugum; alter ita recidatur ut adaequetur plaga trunco, sic tamen ne quid radatur
12 e duro. Pampinandum non aliter est quam in novella viviradice; putandum vero sic ut usque in quartum annum parcius imperetur, dum plaga trunci ducat[5] cicatricem. Atque haec per fissuram insitarum est ordinatio.

13 Illa sic[6] per terebrationem: primum ex vicino fructuosissimam[7] considerare vitem, ex qua velut traducem inhaerentem matri palmitem attrahas, et per foramen transmittas. Haec enim tutior[8] et certior est insitio, quoniam, etsi proximo vere non comprehendit, sequente certe, cum increvit, coniungi cogitur; et mox a matre reciditur, atque ipsa superficies insitae vitis usque ad receptum surculum ob-
14 truncatur. Huius traducis si non est facultas, tum detractum viti quam recentissimum eligitur sarmentum, et leviter circumrasum, ut cortex tantum detrahatur, aptatur[9] foramini, atque ita luto circumlinitur

[1] motus *om. SA, vett. edd.* [2] ordinandus *SA.*
[3] summittuntur *S* : summittur *A* : summitur *a* : sumitur *c, edd. ante Gesn.* : submittitur *M, Gesn., Schn.*
[4] insitis *om. vett. edd., Schn.*
[5] ducit *S* : duci *A.*
[6] Ita *SAacM, Sobel* : In illa autem, quae fit *vulgo.*
[7] oportet *post* fruct. *add. vulgo*; *om. SAacM.*
[8] putatior *SA, Sobel.* [9] artatur *SA.*

[a] *Cf.* Pliny, *N.H.* XVII. 116; Palladius, III. 17. 7.

loosened when moved by the wind, or the tender shoot be pulled out. And when this shoot has increased in size it must be deprived of its secondary shoots, unless because of the poverty or baldness of the place they are reserved for layers. Then autumn applies the pruning-knife to the matured branches. But the following method of pruning is observed in grafted vines—that, where there is no desire for a layer, one shoot is brought up to the frame; and a second is cut back to such an extent that the wound is flush with the stock, though in such a way that nothing is pared from the hard wood. Excess foliage 12 must be removed just as in the case of the young quickset; but the pruning is to be done in such a way that demands are put upon it very sparingly up to the fourth year, until the wound of the trunk forms a scar. This, then, is the method of procedure in cleft-grafting.

The procedure by terebration or boring is as fol- 13 lows: [a] first, to take note of the most fruitful vine in the vicinity, from which you may draw over a traverse branch, so to speak, still clinging to its parent vine, and pass it through the hole. For this is a safer and surer way of grafting because, even though it does not take hold the next spring, at any rate it is forced to be united in the spring following, when it has grown larger; and presently it is cut loose from its mother, and the upper part of the grafted vine is lopped off close to the place where the scion was admitted. If 14 there is no opportunity for such a traverse branch, then a twig is selected—one taken as fresh as possible from the vine—and, being lightly pared all around in such a way that the bark alone is removed, it is fitted to the hole; and then the vine is cut back and daubed over with clay, that the whole stock

resecta vitis, ut totus truncus alieni generis viti[1] serviat. Quod quidem non[2] fit in traduce, qui a[3] materno sustinetur ubere dum inolescat.

15 Sed aliud est ferramentum quo priores vitem perforabant, aliud quod ipse usu nunc magis aptum comperi. Nam antiqua terebra, quam solam veteres agricolae noverant, scobem faciebat perurebatque eam partem quam perforaverat. Deusta porro raro revirescebat, vel cum priore coalescebat,[4] et insitus[5] surculus comprehendebat. Tum etiam scobis numquam sic eximebatur ut non inhaereret foramini; ea porro interventu suo prohibebat corpus surculi
16 corpori vitis applicari. Nos terebram, quam Gallicam dicimus, ad hanc insitionem commenti longe habiliorem utilioremque comperimus. Nam sic excavat truncum ne foramen inurat, quippe non scobem sed ramenta[6] facit; quibus exemptis plaga levis relinquitur, quae facilius omni parte sedentem surculum contingat, nulla interveniente lanugine
17 quam excitabat antiqua terebra. [Igitur secundum vernum aequinoctium perfectam vitium insitionem habeto, locisque aridis et siccis nigram vitem inserito, humidis albam.] Neque est ulla eius propagandi

[1] alieni generis viti (vitis *c*) *cM*, *Ald.*, *Gesn.*: alie in genere vitis *a*: alienigenis surculis *Schn.*: vitis ut . . . viti] vitis ultratus surculus *SA*.

[2] non *om. SA*.

[3] qua *SAa*: qui (a *om.*) *cM*.

[4] Deusta . . . coalescebat] *sic edd.*: deusta (devineta *S*, de vineta *A*) porro cum prore (rore *S*, parte *a*) convalescebat *SAa*. *Post* scobem *habent* faciebat raro revirescebat et perurebat eam partem quam perforaverat deusta. Porro et insitus surculus comprehendebat *cM*.

[5] coalesc., in eaque (*duo verba om. codd.*) nec (et *codd.*) insitus *vulgo*.

[6] ramenta *edd.*: rasamenta *acM*: tramenta *SA*.

may devote itself to a vine of different origin. However, this is not done in the case of a traverse shoot, which is nourished at its mother's breast until it grows into the other vine.

But there is one type of iron tool with which our ancestors used to bore through the vine,[a] and a different sort which I myself have now found by experience to be more suitable. For the ancient gimlet—the only kind that old-time farmers knew—would make sawdust and would burn the place which it perforated. Moreover, it was seldom that the burned part would revive or unite with the former and that the grafted scion would take hold. Then, too, the sawdust was never so completely removed that some did not remain in the hole; and this, by its intervention, kept the body of the scion from being closely joined to the body of the vine. We, having devised what we call the "Gallic auger"[b] for this kind of grafting, have found it far more suitable and practical. For it hollows out the stock in such a way as not to burn the hole, because it does not make dust but shavings; and when these are removed a smooth wound is left, which can more easily touch the seated scion on every side, since there is no interference of that woolly matter which the ancient gimlet produced. [Therefore see to it that the grafting of your vines is finished immediately after the vernal equinox; and graft the black vine in places that are parched and dry, the white vine in wet places.][c] [And there is no

[a] *Cf.* Cato, 41. 3–4.

[b] *Cf. De Arb.* 8. 4; Pliny, *loc. cit.*; Palladius, *loc. cit.*

[c] The passage is bracketed by Schneider as irrelevant at this point, perhaps having crept in from *De Arb.* (*loc. cit.*), where an almost identical statement follows the description of the Gallic wimble.

necessitas, si modo tam mediocris est crassitudo trunci ut incrementum insiti[1] plagam possit contingere;[2] nisi tamen vacuus locus demortui capitis vitem reposcit. Quod cum ita est, alter ex duobus surculis mergitur, alter eductus ad iugum in fructum summittitur. Neque inutile est ex ea vite, quam merseris, enascentes in arcu propaginis pampinos educare, quos possis mox, si ita competet,[3] vel propagare vel ad fructum relinquere.

XXX. Quoniam constituendis[4] colendisque vineis, quae videbantur utiliter praecipi posse, disseruimus, pedaminum iugorumque et viminum prospiciendorum tradenda ratio est. Haec enim quasi quaedam dotes vineis ante praeparantur. Quibus si deficitur agricola, causam faciendi vineta non habet, cum omnia, quae sunt necessaria, extra fundum quaerenda sint; nec emptionis tantum, sicut ait Atticus, pretium onerat vilici[5] rationem, sed est etiam comparatio
2 molestissima. Convehenda sunt enim tempore iniquissimo hiberno.[6] Quare salices viminales atque harundineta vulgaresque silvae, vel consulto consitae castaneis, prius faciendae[7] sunt. Salicum viminalium[8] Atticus putat singula iugera sufficere posse[9] quinis et vicenis iugeribus ligandae vineae,

[1] insita *SAa*.
[2] contegere *M*, *edd. ante Schn.*
[3] competit *cM*.
[4] constituendisque, *deinde* colendisque *om. SAa*.
[5] vilici *Sobel*: vitici *S*: vici *Aa*: rustici *cM*: vitis *edd.*
[6] hiberni *SAacM*.
[7] facienda *Ac*, *edd.*
[8] Salicum viminalium *Schn.*: licet viminalibus *S*, *vett. edd.*: licet ut (in *M*, ut in *c*) viminalibus *Aa*: Viminalium (Salicum *om.*) ut (*om. codd.*) Atticus *vulgo*.
[9] posse *SAacM*, *vett. edd.*: possunt *vulgo*.

need of propagating this if only the stock is of so moderate a thickness that the growth of a grafted scion can cover the wound on all sides; unless, however, the place left vacant in a vine whose head is dead demands a replacement. When this is the case, one of the two shoots is turned down for a layer, and the other is carried up to the frame and set apart for fruit. And it is not without advantage to rear shoots from the vine which you have layered, as they sprout from the arched part of the layer, which, if it so happens, you may either use for further layers or leave for fruit.][a]

XXX. Inasmuch as we have discussed those matters which it seemed could be taught to advantage for the establishing and cultivating of vineyards, a method must be set down for the provision of props, frames, and withes. For these are prepared beforehand, as dowries, so to speak, for the vineyards. And if the farmer is destitute of these, he has no reason for making vineyards, since everything that is needed will have to be sought outside the farm; and, just as Atticus says, not only does the cost of purchase put a burden upon the accounts of the overseer, but also the procuring of them is a very great annoyance. For 2
they must be brought together at a most inconvenient season—in winter. Therefore osier-willows and reed thickets must be provided beforehand, and also ordinary woods or woods purposely planted with chestnut trees. Atticus thinks that one *iugerum* of osier-willows may suffice for binding twenty-five *iugera*

[a] This passage, printed as it stands in the manuscripts and editions, is obviously out of place. It appears to belong, as Schneider points out, at the beginning of Sec. 12 of this chapter, after the words *radatur e duro*.

harundineti singula iugera vicenis iugandis; castaneti iugerum totidem palandis, quot harundineti iugandis.
3 Salicem vel riguus ager vel uliginis abundans[1] optime, nec incommode tamen alit planus et pinguis. Atque is debet converti bipalio; ita enim praecipiunt veteres, in duos pedes[2] et semissem pastinare salicto destinatum solum. Nec refert cuius generis vimen
4 seras, dum sit lentissimum. Putant tamen tria esse genera praecipue Graecae, Gallicae, Sabinae salicis,[3] quam plurimi vocant Amerinam. Graeca flavi coloris est; Gallica obsoleti purpurei, et tenuissimi viminis;[4] Amerina salix gracilem virgam et rutilam gerit. Atque hae vel cacuminibus vel taleis deponuntur. Perticae cacuminum modicae plenitudinis,[5] quae tamen dupondiarii orbiculi crassitudinem non excedat,[6] optime panguntur eousque dum ad
5 solidum demittantur. Taleae sesquipedales terreno immersae paulum obruuntur. Riguus locus spatia laxiora desiderat, eaque senum pedum per quincuncem recte faciunt; siccaneus spissiora, sic ut sit facilis accessus colentibus ea. Quinum pedum interordinia esse abunde est, ut tamen in ipsa linea consitionis alterna vacuis intermissis bipedaneis spatiis
6 consistant semina. Satio est eorum priusquam

[1] uliginis abundans (habundans *a*) *SAacM* : uliginosus *edd.*
[2] pedes *vulgo* : *om. SAacM.*
[3] salicis *post* praecipue *ponunt edd.*
[4] viminis *codd., plerique edd.* : *om. Schn.*
[5] plenitudinis *edd.* : planitudinis *SAacM.*
[6] excedat *a, Schn.* : exedat *SA* : excedant *cM, et plerique.*

---

[a] So Pliny, *N.H.* XVII. 143.
[b] *Cf.* Pliny, *N.H.* XVI. 177.

of vineyard,[a] and one *iugerum* of reed thicket for framing twenty; and that a *iugerum* planted with chestnut trees is enough to provide as many props as a *iugerum* of reeds can furnish with cross-rails. Ground 3
that is either well watered or abounding in marshland is best for nourishing the willow, and yet level and rich ground is not unsuitable. And this ground should be turned with the double spade; for the ancients direct us to trench ground intended for a willow-bed to a depth of two and one-half feet. And it makes no difference what kind of osier you plant, if only it is very pliant. Still they think that there 4
are chiefly three kinds of willows:[b] the Greek, the Gallic, and the Sabine, which most people call the Amerine. The Greek is of a yellow colour; the Gallic of a dingy purple, and with very slender switches; and the Amerine has a slim and reddish rod. And either top-shoots or truncheons of these are planted. Top rods of moderate stoutness, which, however, should not exceed the thickness of a circular two-pound weight,[c] are best planted if they are put down as far as solid ground. Truncheons of one and 5
one-half feet are stuck into the earth and covered over with a little of it. A well-watered spot requires wider spaces, and spaces of six feet in the quincunx arrangement do very well; a place that is normally dry needs closer planting, but in such a way as to give easy access to those who cultivate it. In this case it is satisfactory that the distance between rows be five feet, yet so that the plants may stand at two-foot intervals in the line of planting, alternating with empty spaces between. The time for planting them is before they 6

[c] Probably in the form of a rod or bar, an old Roman unit of weight.

germinent, dum silent virgae, quas arboribus detrahi[1] siccas convenit. Nam[2] roscidas si recideris, parum commode[3] proveniunt; ideoque[4] pluvii dies in exputanda salice vitantur. Fodienda[5] sunt primo triennio salicta crebrius, ut novella vineta. Cum deinde convaluerint, tribus fossuris contenta sunt;
7 aliter culta celeriter deficiunt. Nam quamvis adhibeatur cura, plurimae salices intereunt. Quarum in locum[6] ex propinquo mergi[7] propagari debent, curvatis et defossis cacuminibus,[8] quibus restituatur quicquid intercidit. Anniculus deinde mergus decidatur a stirpe, ut suis radicibus tamquam vitis ali possit.

XXXI. Perarida loca, quae genus id virgultorum non recipiunt, genistam postulant. Eius cum sit satis firmum tum etiam lentissimum est vinculum. Seritur autem semine, quod cum est natum, vel defertur bima viviradix, vel relicta cum id tempus excessit, omnibus annis more segetis iuxta terram dēmeti potest. Cetera vincula, qualia sunt ex rubo, maiorem operam sed in egeno tamen necessariam
2 exigunt. Perticalis fere salix eundem agrum, quem viminalis, desiderat; melior tamen riguo provenit. Atque ea taleis conseritur, et cum germinavit, ad unam perticam summittitur, crebroque foditur atque exherbatur nec minus quam vinea pampinatur, ut in longitudinem ramorum[9] potius quam in lati-

[1] detrahit *SAa*.
[2] Nam *cM*, *edd.*: At *a*: ab *SA*, *Sobel*.
[3] commode *SAa*, *Sobel*: prospere commode (commodeque *M*)*cM*: prospere *vulgo*.
[4] ideoque *SAa*: itaque *vett. edd.*: ideo *vulgo*.
[5] facienda *SAa*, *vett. edd.*
[6] loco *Aac*, *edd. ante Schn.*
[7] mergis *SAacM*, *Ald.*, *Gesn.*
[8] *sic vulgo*: curvata et defossa cacumina *SAacM*, *vett. edd.*

bud, while the slips are dormant, and it is best that they be taken from the trees when they are dry. For if you cut them off when they are wet with dew, they do not grow properly; and for this reason rainy days are avoided in lopping off the willows. Willow copses are to be dug more frequently during the first three years, as are new vineyards. Later, when they have gained strength, they are satisfied with three diggings; under any other cultivation they quickly run out. For, even though care is taken, very many willows 7
die. In their place layers should be propagated from a near-by plant, by bending down and burying its leaders, so that anything that has died may be replaced with these. Then when the layer is a year old, let it be cut loose from its stock, that it may be fed by its own roots just like a vine.

XXXI. Very dry places, which do not admit copses of this sort, require broom. A band of this material not only has sufficient strength, but also it is very pliant. The plant is raised from seed, and when it has sprouted, it is either transplanted as a quickset when two years old; or, if left where sown after that time has passed, it may be cut close to the ground every year in the manner of standing grain. Other bindings, such as those made of bramble, require greater labour, but still a necessary labour in poor soil. Willow for 2
poles requires about the same land as that for withes; nevertheless it thrives better in well-watered ground. And it is planted in the form of truncheons; and when it has sprouted it is made to grow as a single shaft, and is frequently cultivated and weeded; and excess foliage is removed no less than in the vine, that it may be encouraged to length rather than spread of branches.

[9] ramorum *om. SA.*

tudinem evocetur. Sic culta quarto demum anno
3 caeditur. Nam quae vinculis praeparatur, potest annicula praecidi ad semissem supra[1] duos pedes, ut e trunco fruticet et in bracchia velut humilis vinea disponatur; si tamen siccior fuerit ager, bima potius resecabitur.

XXXII. Harundo minus alto[2] pastinato, melius tamen bipalio seritur. Ea cum sit vivacissima nec recuset ullum locum, prosperius resoluto quam denso; umido, quam sicco; vallibus, quam clivis;[3] fluminum ripis, et limitibus ac vepribus[4] commodius quam
2 mediis agris deponitur. Seritur bulbus radicis, et talea calami; nec minus toto prosternitur corpore. Bulbus tripedaneis intervacantibus spatiis obrutus anno celerius maturam perticam praebet. Talea et tota harundo serius praedicto tempore evenit. Sed sive recisa in dupondium et semissem talea, sive totae harundines prostratae deponentur,[5] exstent earum cacumina;[6] quod si obruta sunt, totae
3 putrescunt. Sed cultus harundineti[7] primo triennio non alius est quam ceteris. Cum deinde consenuit, repastinandum est. Ea est autem senectus, cum vel exaruit situ et inertia plurium annorum, vel ita densatum est, ut gracilis et cannae similis harundo
4 prodeat. Sed illud de integro refodi debet; hoc

[1] super *SAa*.
[2] alto *SAacM* : alte *edd.*, *deinde* pastinatur *Ald.*, *Gesn.*
[3] clivis *edd.*, : dumis *SAacM*.
[4] vepribus *ScM*, *vett. edd.*: veperibus *a* : veribus *A* : vepretis *vulgo*.
[5] deponentur *cM*, *vett. edd.*: deponeretur *SAa* : deponantur *vulgo*.
[6] oportet *post* cacumina *add. vulgo*.
[7] harundineti *scripsi* : harundinetis *vel* arundinetis *codd.*, *edd.*

When so cared for it is cut finally in its fourth year. For the willow which is prepared for bindings may 3
be cut off when it is one year old, at about two and a half feet above ground, so that it may send out branches from the trunk and be arranged in arms like a low vine; but if the ground has been rather dry, it will be cut back preferably at the age of two years.

XXXII. The reed [a] is planted in ground that is not worked so deep, though it is better to plant it with the two-foot spade. Although it is very hardy and does not refuse any situation, it succeeds better when put in loose soil than in compact; better in a damp place than in a dry one; better in valleys than on hillsides; and on river banks and in borders and thickets better than in midfield. Its bulbous root 2
is planted, as also truncheons of the cane; and again the whole reed is laid flat in the ground. The bulb, when buried with three-foot spaces between, yields a full-grown stalk in less than a year. The truncheon and the whole reed are longer than the aforementioned time in coming to maturity. But whether truncheons of two and one-half feet are planted, or entire reeds laid flat, their tops should extend above ground; because, if they are entirely buried, they rot completely. But the culture 3
of the reed thicket, for the first three years, is not different from that of the other thickets. Later, when it has become old, the ground must be trenched again. And this is its old age, when it has either dried up completely because of many years of decadence and sloth, or has become so crowded that the reeds grow up slender and cane-like. But in 4
the former case it should be dug up again from the

[a] *Cf.* Pliny, *N H.* XVII. 144–146.

potest intercidi et dirarari,[1] quod opus rustici castrationem [2] vocant. Quae tamen refectio [3] harundineti caeca est, quia non apparet in terra quid aut tollendum sit aut relinquendum; tolerabilius tamen harundo castratur antequam caeditur, quatenus velut indices calami [4] demonstrant quid eruendum sit.
5 Tempus repastinandi et conserendi est priusquam oculi harundinum egerminent. Caeditur deinde post brumam; nam usque in id tempus incrementum capit, ac tum compescitur,[5] cum obriguit hiberno frigore. Fodiendum quotiens et vineta; sed macies eius cinere vel alio stercore iuvanda est, propter quod caesum plerique incendunt harundinetum.

XXXIII. Castanea roboribus proxima est, et ideo stabiliendis vineis habilis. Tum in repastinato nux posita celeriter emicat, et post quinquennium caesa more salicis [6] recreatur, atque [7] in palum formata fere usque in alteram caesionem perennat. Ea pullam terram et resolutam desiderat; sabulonem umidum vel refractum tofum non respuit; opaco et septentrionali clivo laetatur; spissum solum et
2 rubricosum [8] reformidat. Seritur ab Novembri mense per totam hiemem sicca terra et repastinata in altitudinem dupondii et semissis. Nuces [9] in ordinem semipedalibus; ordines autem quinum pedum spatiis

[1] dirarari *SA*, *Sobel*: disrarari *aM*, *et vulgo*: disrari *c*.

[2] castrationem *M*, *Ald.*, *Gesn.*: stipationem *SAac*, *vett. edd.*, *Schn*, *Sobel*.

[3] refectio *SAaM*, *Sobel*: refodio *c*: resectio *edd.*

[4] velut indices calami *SAac*: indices velut calami *M*: calami velut indices *vulgo*.

[5] conficitur *Aac*: conficitur compescitur *M*.

[6] salicis *SAa*: salicti *cM*, *edd.*

[7] neque *SA*, *Schn.*

[8] solum et rubricosum *om.* *SA*: et rubricosum *om.* *a*.

beginning; in the latter it may be cut out and thinned—an operation which farmers call *castratio.*[a] However, this repairing of a reed thicket is done blindly, because it is not apparent on the surface what should be removed or what should be left; still the reed suffers castration better before the time of cutting, since the small canes, like pointers, show what
is to be plucked out. The time for redigging and 5
planting is before the eyes of the reed sprout. Then the time for cutting is after the winter solstice; for it makes growth up to that time, and is then checked when stiffened by the winter cold. The reed plot must be dug as often as the vineyard; but its leanness must be relieved with ashes or other fertilizer, and for this reason most people burn it over after it is cut.

XXXIII. The chestnut tree[b] is next best to the oaks, and for this reason it is suitable for supporting vines. Its nut, too, when planted in prepared ground, quickly springs up; and when cut down, after five years, it renews itself in the manner of the willow, and when made into a stake it lasts usually to the next cutting. It likes a black and loose soil; does not refuse a damp, gravelly soil or crumbling tufa; delights in a shady slope with a northern exposure; and fears a
heavy soil that is full of red ochre. It is planted from 2
the month of November throughout the whole winter, in ground that is dry and worked to a depth of two feet and a half. The nuts are placed in a row, half a foot apart; and the rows are separated by five-foot inter-

[a] *Cf.* Cato, 33. 2; Pliny, *N.H.* XVI. 206, XVII. 144, *et al.*
[b] *Cf.* Pliny XVII 147–150.

[9] nucē *SA* : nucem *cM* : crucem *a.*

dirimuntur. In altitudinem dodrantis castanea depressis sulcis committitur. Qui ubi nucibus sunt consiti, priusquam complanentur, breves harundines ab latere castanearum panguntur, ut per hos sationis
3 indices tutius fodi et runcari possint. Simul atque semina stilaverint,[1] etiam bima transferri queunt, intervelluntur, ac bini pedes arbusculis vacui relinquuntur, ne densitas plantas emaciet. Spissius[2] autem propter varios casus deponitur: nam interdum priusquam enascatur, aut siccitatibus nux inarescit, aut aquarum abundantia putrescit; interdum subterraneis animalibus sicuti muribus[3] et talpis infestatur. Propter quae saepe novella castaneta[4] calvescunt; atque ubi frequentanda sunt, melius ex vicino, si competit, mergi more pertica declinata
4 propagatur, quam exempta reseritur. Haec enim velut immota sua sede vehementer germinat; at quae radicibus exempta et deposita est, biennio reformidat. Propter quod compertum est commodius nucibus quam viviradicibus eiusmodi silvas institui. Spatia huiusce sationis, quae supra scripta sunt, capita castanearum recipiunt MMDCCCLXXX, cuius summae, sicut ait Atticus, ex facili iugera singula praebebunt statuminum duodena milia. Etenim taleae propius stirpem recisae quadrifidas[5] plerumque, ac deinde secundae taleae eiusdem arboris bifidas[6] ridicas sumministrant; quod genus fissilis adminiculi

[1] stilaverint *Schn.*: stillaverint *SAa, et plerique*: distillaverit *c*: destilaverunt *M*.

[2] ipsius *SAa*: spissus c. *Deinde* semen *post* autem *add. vulgo, om. codd.*

[3] sicuti muribus *om. SA*.

[4] castanieta *SAac*.

[5] quadripedas *SAc*.

vals. The chestnut is committed to furrows sunk to a depth of three-fourths of a foot; and when these furrows are planted with nuts, and before they are levelled off, short reeds are set beside the chestnuts, so that, with these markers of the planting, they may be dug and weeded with greater safety. As soon as 3
the plants have formed a stem—and they may be transplanted when two years old—they are thinned out; and two feet of room is left free for the young saplings, lest crowding weaken the plants. The planting is closer, moreover, because of various mishaps: for the nut is sometimes dried up by droughts before it springs forth, or it decays from excessive wetness; and sometimes it is destroyed by underground animals, such as mice and moles. For these reasons young plantations of chestnut often 4
grow up in thin numbers; and when it is necessary to increase them, it is better that a near-by sapling, if such a one is suitable, be bent over and propagated in the manner of a layer, than that it be taken up and replanted. For such a sapling, being undisturbed at its base, sends out shoots vigorously; but one that is torn out by the roots and transplanted is retarded for two years thereafter. On this account it has been found more advantageous to start trees of this sort from nuts rather than from quicksets. The spaces allotted to this planting, as described above, admit 2880 chestnut trees; of which total, as Atticus says, every *iugerum* of land will easily yield 12000 props. For the lengths cut closest to the stump generally supply four stakes when split, and then the second cuts of the same tree yield two; and this sort of split

---

[6] vi fluvias *SA*. bifluvias *a*.

5 manet diutius quam teres palus. Cultus idem est positionis fossionisque [1] qui vineae. Supputari debet bima, quin etiam trima; nam bis ferro repetenda est veris [2] principio, ut incitetur eius proceritas. Potest etiam quercus simili ratione seri; verum biennio tardius quam castanea deciditur. Propter quod ratio postulat tempus potius lucrari, nisi si dumosi glareosique montes, atque ea genera terrae, quae supra diximus, glandem magis quam castaneam postulabunt.

6 Haec de vineis Italicis vinearumque instrumentis, quantum reor, non inutiliter et abunde disserui: mox agricolarum provincialium vineaticos nec minus nostratis et Gallici arbusti cultus traditurus.

[1] fossionis positionisque *vulgo, sed inclusit Schn.* · positionis qui *SAc* : positionis fossionis qui *a* : fossionis qui *M*.

[2] verni *SAacM*.

prop lasts longer than the round pole. The management of setting and digging is the same as that of the vineyard. It should be pruned lightly when two years old, and again when three; for twice in early spring it must be attacked with the knife, that its upward growth may be hastened. The oak also may be planted in like manner; but it is cut down two years later than the chestnut. For this reason common sense requires that we profit rather by the gain in time, unless it happens that brush-covered and stony mountains, and the kinds of soil which we mentioned above, demand the acorn rather than the chestnut. 5

These matters concerning Italian vineyards and vineyard equipment I have discussed, so I believe, fully and not without profit. I intend presently to give an account of viticulture among our provincial farmers, also of the management of the *arbustum* both in our own country and in Gaul. 6

NOTE

Triticum is wheat in general; often common wheat and two other varieties; *siligo* is usually common wheat, but sometimes club-wheat; *far* and *adoreum* are both emmer-wheat (two-grained wheat).

PRINTED IN GREAT BRITAIN BY
RICHARD CLAY AND COMPANY, LTD.
BUNGAY, SUFFOLK.

THE LOEB CLASSICAL LIBRARY

VOLUMES ALREADY PUBLISHED

Latin Authors

Ammianus Marcellinus. Translated by J. C. Rolfe. 3 Vols.

Apuleius: The Golden Ass (Metamorphoses). W. Adlington (1566). Revised by S. Gaselee.

St. Augustine: City of God. 7 Vols. Vol. I. G. H. McCracken. Vol. VI. W. C. Greene.

St. Augustine, Confessions of. W. Watts (1631). 2 Vols.

St. Augustine, Select Letters. J. H. Baxter.

Ausonius. H. G. Evelyn White. 2 Vols.

Bede. J. E. King. 2 Vols.

Boethius: Tracts and De Consolatione Philosophiae. Rev. H. F. Stewart and E. K. Rand.

Caesar: Alexandrian, African and Spanish Wars. A. G. Way.

Caesar: Civil Wars. A. G. Peskett.

Caesar: Gallic War. H. J. Edwards.

Cato: De Re Rustica; Varro: De Re Rustica. H. B. Ash and W. D. Hooper.

Catullus. F. W. Cornish; Tibullus. J. B. Postgate; Pervigilium Veneris. J. W. Mackail.

Celsus: De Medicina. W. G. Spencer. 3 Vols.

Cicero: Brutus, and Orator. G. L. Hendrickson and H. M. Hubbell.

[Cicero]: Ad Herennium. H. Caplan.

Cicero: De Oratore, etc. 2 Vols. Vol. I. De Oratore, Books I. and II. E. W. Sutton and H. Rackham. Vol. II. De Oratore, Book III. De Fato; Paradoxa Stoicorum; De Partitione Oratoria. H. Rackham.

Cicero: De Finibus. H. Rackham.

Cicero: De Inventione, etc. H. M. Hubbell.

Cicero: De Natura Deorum and Academica. H. Rackham.

Cicero: De Officiis. Walter Miller.

Cicero: De Republica and De Legibus; Somnium Scipionis. Clinton W. Keyes.

Cicero: De Senectute, De Amicitia, De Divinatione. W. A. Falconer.

Cicero In Catilinam, Pro Flacco, Pro Murena, Pro Sulla. Louis E. Lord.

Cicero. Letters to Atticus. E. O. Winstedt. 3 Vols.

Cicero: Letters to His Friends. W. Glynn Williams. 3 Vols.

Cicero: Philippics. W. C. A. Ker.

Cicero: Pro Archia Post Reditum, De Domo, De Haruspicum Responsis, Pro Plancio. N. H. Watts.

Cicero: Pro Caecina, Pro Lege Manilia, Pro Cluentio, Pro Rabirio. H. Grose Hodge.

Cicero: Pro Caelio, De Provinciis Consularibus, Pro Balbo. R. Gardner.

Cicero· Pro Milone, In Pisonem, Pro Scauro, Pro Fonteio, Pro Rabirio Postumo, Pro Marcello, Pro Ligario, Pro Rege Deiotaro. N. H. Watts.

Cicero· Pro Quinctio, Pro Roscio Amerino, Pro Roscio Comoedo, Contra Rullum. J. H. Freese.

Cicero: Pro Sestio, In Vatinium. R Gardner.

Cicero: Tusculan Disputations. J. E. King.

Cicero: Verrine Orations. L. H. G. Greenwood. 2 Vols.

Claudian. M. Platnauer. 2 Vols.

Columella: De Re Rustica. De Arboribus. H B Ash, E. S. Forster and E Heffner 3 Vols

Curtius, Q.: History of Alexander. J. C. Rolfe. 2 Vols.

Florus. E. S. Forster; and Cornelius Nepos. J. C. Rolfe.

Frontinus: Stratagems and Aqueducts. C. E. Bennett and M. B. McElwain.

Fronto: Correspondence C R Haines. 2 Vols.

Gellius, J. C. Rolfe. 3 Vols.

Horace: Odes and Epodes. C. E. Bennett.

Horace: Satires, Epistles, Ars Poetica. H. R Fairclough.

Jerome: Selected Letters. F. A. Wright.

Juvenal and Persius. G. G. Ramsay.

Livy. B. O. Foster, F G. Moore, Evan T Sage, and A. C. Schlesinger and R. M. Geer (General Index). 14 Vols.

Lucan. J. D. Duff.

Lucretius. W. H. D. Rouse.

Martial. W. C. A. Ker. 2 Vols.

Minor Latin Poets: from Publilius Syrus to Rutilius Namatianus, including Grattius, Calpurnius Siculus, Nemesianus, Avianus, and others with "Aetna" and the "Phoenix." J. Wight Duff and Arnold M. Duff.

Ovid: The Art of Love and Other Poems. J. H. Mozley.

OVID. FASTI. Sir James G. Frazer.

OVID: HEROIDES and AMORES. Grant Showerman.

OVID: METAMORPHOSES. F. J. Miller. 2 Vols.

OVID: TRISTIA and EX PONTO. A L. Wheeler.

PERSIUS. Cf. JUVENAL.

PETRONIUS. M. Heseltine; SENECA: APOCOLOCYNTOSIS. W. H. D. Rouse.

PLAUTUS. Paul Nixon. 5 Vols.

PLINY LETTERS. Melmoth's Translation revised by W. M L. Hutchinson. 2 Vols.

PLINY: NATURAL HISTORY. H. Rackham and W H. S. Jones. 10 Vols. Vols. I.–V. and IX. H. Rackham. Vols. VI. and VII. W. H. S. Jones.

PROPERTIUS. H. E. Butler.

PRUDENTIUS. H. J. Thomson. 2 Vols.

QUINTILIAN. H. E. Butler. 4 Vols.

REMAINS OF OLD LATIN. E. H. Warmington. 4 Vols. Vol I. (ENNIUS AND CAECILIUS.) Vol. II. (LIVIUS, NAEVIUS, PACUVIUS, ACCIUS) Vol. III. (LUCILIUS and LAWS OF XII TABLES.) (ARCHAIC INSCRIPTIONS.)

SALLUST. J. C. Rolfe.

SCRIPTORES HISTORIAE AUGUSTAE. D. Magie 3 Vols.

SENECA: APOCOLOCYNTOSIS. Cf. PETRONIUS.

SENECA: EPISTULAE MORALES. R. M. Gummere. 3 Vols.

SENECA: MORAL ESSAYS. J. W. Basore. 3 Vols.

SENECA. TRAGEDIES. F. J. Miller. 2 Vols.

SIDONIUS: POEMS and LETTERS. W. B. Anderson. 2 Vols.

SILIUS ITALICUS. J. D. Duff. 2 Vols.

STATIUS. J. H. Mozley. 2 Vols.

SUETONIUS. J. C Rolfe 2 Vols.

TACITUS: DIALOGUES. Sir Wm. Peterson. AGRICOLA and GERMANIA. Maurice Hutton.

TACITUS: HISTORIES AND ANNALS C. H. Moore and J. Jackson. 4 Vols.

TERENCE John Sargeaunt. 2 Vols.

TERTULLIAN: APOLOGIA and DE SPECTACULIS. T. R. Glover. MINUCIUS FELIX. G. H. Rendall.

VALERIUS FLACCUS. J. H. Mozley.

VARRO: DE LINGUA LATINA. R. G. Kent. 2 Vols.

VELLEIUS PATERCULUS and RES GESTAE DIVI AUGUSTI. F. W. Shipley.

VIRGIL. H. R. Fairclough. 2 Vols

VITRUVIUS: DE ARCHITECTURA. F. Granger. 2 Vols.

Greek Authors

Achilles Tatius. S. Gaselee.

Aelian: On the Nature of Animals. A. F. Scholfield 3 Vols.

Aeneas Tacticus, Asclepiodotus and Onasander. The Illinois Greek Club.

Aeschines. C. D. Adams.

Aeschylus. H. Weir Smyth. 2 Vols.

Alciphron, Aelian, Philostratus. Letters. A. R. Benner and F. H. Fobes.

Andocides, Antiphon, Cf. Minor Attic Orators.

Apollodorus. Sir James G. Frazer. 2 Vols.

Apollonius Rhodius. R. C. Seaton.

The Apostolic Fathers. Kirsopp Lake. 2 Vols.

Appian: Roman History. Horace White. 4 Vols.

Aratus. Cf. Callimachus.

Aristophanes. Benjamin Bickley Rogers. 3 Vols. Verse trans.

Aristotle: Art of Rhetoric. J. H. Freese.

Aristotle: Athenian Constitution, Eudemian Ethics, Vices and Virtues. H. Rackham.

Aristotle: Generation of Animals. A. L. Peck.

Aristotle: Metaphysics. H. Tredennick. 2 Vols.

Aristotle: Meterologica. H. D. P. Lee.

Aristotle: Minor Works. W. S. Hett. On Colours, On Things Heard, On Physiognomies, On Plants, On Marvellous Things Heard, Mechanical Problems, On Indivisible Lines, On Situations and Names of Winds, On Melissus, Xenophanes, and Gorgias.

Aristotle: Nicomachean Ethics. H. Rackham.

Aristotle: Oeconomica and Magna Moralia. G. C. Armstrong; (with Metaphysics, Vol. II.).

Aristotle: On the Heavens. W. K. C. Guthrie.

Aristotle: On the Soul. Parva Naturalia. On Breath. W. S. Hett.

Aristotle: Organon—Categories, On Interpretation, Prior Analytics. H. P. Cooke and H. Tredennick.

Aristotle. Organon—Posterior Analytics, Topics. H. Tredennick and E. S. Forster.

Aristotle. Organon—On Sophistical Refutations.
On Coming to be and Passing Away, On the Cosmos. E. S. Forster and D. J. Furley.

Aristotle: Parts of Animals. A. L. Peck; Motion and Progression of Animals. E. S. Forster.

Aristotle Physics. Rev. P. Wicksteed and F. M Cornford. 2 Vols.

Aristotle: Poetics and Longinus W. Hamilton Fyfe; Demetrius on Style. W. Rhys Roberts.

Aristotle: Politics. H. Rackham.

Aristotle: Problems. W. S. Hett. 2 Vols.

Aristotle: Rhetorica Ad Alexandrum (with Problems Vol. II.). H. Rackham.

Arrian: History of Alexander and Indica. Rev. E. Iliffe Robson. 2 Vols.

Athenaeus: Deipnosophistae. C. B. Gulick. 7 Vols.

St. Basil: Letters. R. J. Deferrari. 4 Vols.

Callimachus: Fragments. C. A. Trypanis

Callimachus, Hymns and Epigrams, and Lycophron. A. W. Mair; Aratus. G. R. Mair.

Clement of Alexandria. Rev. G. W. Butterworth

Colluthus. Cf. Oppian.

Daphnis and Chloe. Thornley's Translation revised by J. M. Edmonds; and Parthenius. S. Gaselee.

Demosthenes I: Olynthiacs, Philippics and Minor Orations. I.–XVII. and XX. J. H. Vince.

Demosthenes II.: De Corona and De Falsa Legatione C. A. Vince and J. H. Vince.

Demosthenes III: Meidias, Androtion, Aristocrates, Timocrates and Aristogeiton, I. and II. J. H. Vince.

Demosthenes IV.–VI.: Private Orations and In Neaeram. A T. Murray.

Demosthenes VII: Funeral Speech, Erotic Essay, Exordia and Letters. N. W. and N. J. DeWitt.

Dio Cassius: Roman History. E. Cary. 9 Vols.

Dio Chrysostom. J. W. Cohoon and H. Lamar Crosby. 5 Vols.

Diodorus Siculus. 12 Vols. Vols. I.–VI. C. H. Oldfather. Vol. VII. C. L. Sherman, Vols IX. and X. R. M. Geer. Vol. XI. F. Walton

Diogenes Laeritius. R. D. Hicks. 2 Vols.

Dionysius of Halicarnassus: Roman Antiquities. Spelman's translation revised by E Cary. 7 Vols

Epictetus. W. A. Oldfather. 2 Vols.

Euripides. A. S. Way. 4 Vols. Verse trans.

Eusebius· Ecclesiastical History. Kirsopp Lake and J. E. L. Oulton. 2 Vols.

Galen. On the Natural Faculties. A. J. Brock.

The Greek Anthology W R. Paton. 5 Vols.

Greek Elegy and Iambus with the Anacreontea. J. M. Edmonds. 2 Vols.

The Greek Bucolic Poets (Theocritus, Bion, Moschus) J. M. Edmonds.

Greek Mathematical Works. Ivor Thomas. 2 Vols.

Herodes. Cf. Theophrastus: Characters.

Herodotus. A. D. Godley. 4 Vols.

Hesiod and The Homeric Hymns. H. G. Evelyn White.

Hippocrates and the Fragments of Heracleitus. W. H. S. Jones and E. T. Withington. 4 Vols.

Homer: Iliad. A. T. Murray. 2 Vols.

Homer: Odyssey. A. T. Murray. 2 Vols.

Isaeus. E. W. Forster.

Isocrates. George Norlin and LaRue Van Hook. 3 Vols.

St. John Damascene: Barlaam and Ioasaph. Rev. G. R. Woodward and Harold Mattingly.

Josephus. H. St. J. Thackeray and Ralph Marcus. 9 Vols. Vols. I.–VII.

Julian. Wilmer Cave Wright. 3 Vols.

Lucian. 8 Vols. Vols. I.–V. A. M. Harmon Vol. VI. K. Kilburn.

Lycophron. Cf. Callimachus.

Lyra Graeca. J. M. Edmonds. 3 Vols.

Lysias. W. R. M. Lamb.

Manetho. W. G. Waddell: Ptolemy: Tetrabiblos. F. E. Robbins.

Marcus Aurelius. C R Haines

Menander. F. G. Allinson.

Minor Attic Orators (Antiphon, Andocides, Lycurgus, Demades, Dinarchus, Hypereides). K. J. Maidment and J. O. Burtt. 2 Vols.

Nonnos: Dionysiaca. W. H. D. Rouse. 3 Vols

Oppian, Colluthus, Tryphiodorus. A. W. Mair.

Papyri. Non-Literary Selections. A. S. Hunt and C. C. Edgar. 2 Vols. Literary Selections (Poetry). D. L. Page

Parthenius. Cf. Daphnis and Chloe.

Pausanias: Description of Greece. W. H S Jones 4 Vols. and Companion Vol. arranged by R. E. Wycherley.

Philo. 10 Vols. Vols. I.–V.; F. H Colson and Rev. G H. Whitaker. Vols VI.–IX.; F. H. Colson.

Philo: two supplementary Vols. (*Translation only.*) Ralph Marcus.

Philostratus: The Life of Apollonius of Tyana. F. C. Conybeare. 2 Vols.

Philostratus: Imagines; Callistratus: Descriptions. A. Fairbanks.

PHILOSTRATUS and EUNAPIUS. LIVES OF THE SOPHISTS. Wilmer Cave Wright.

PINDAR. Sir J. E. Sandys.

PLATO CHARMIDES, ALCIBIADES, HIPPARCHUS, THE LOVERS, THEAGES, MINOS and EPINOMIS. W R. M. Lamb.

PLATO: CRATYLUS, PARMENIDES, GREATER HIPPIAS, LESSER HIPPIAS. H. N. Fowler.

PLATO: EUTHYPHRO, APOLOGY, CRITO, PHAEDO, PHAEDRUS. H. N. Fowler.

PLATO· LACHES, PROTAGORAS, MENO, EUTHYDEMUS. W. R. M. Lamb.

PLATO. LAWS. Rev. R G. Bury. 2 Vols.

PLATO· LYSIS, SYMPOSIUM, GORGIAS. W. R. M. Lamb

PLATO: REPUBLIC. Paul Shorey. 2 Vols.

PLATO: STATESMAN, PHILEBUS. H. N. Fowler; ION. W. R. M. Lamb.

PLATO: THEAETETUS and SOPHIST. H. N Fowler.

PLATO: TIMAEUS, CRITIAS, CLITOPHO, MENEXENUS, EPISTULAE. Rev. R. G. Bury.

PLUTARCH: MORALIA. 15 Vols. Vols. I.–V. F. C. Babbitt. Vol. VI. W. C. Helmbold. Vol VII. P. H. De Lacy and B. Einarson. Vol. IX. E. L. Minar, Jr., F. H. Sandbach, W. C. Helmbold. Vol. X. H. N. Fowler. Vol. XII. H. Cherniss and W. C. Helmbold.

PLUTARCH: THE PARALLEL LIVES. B. Perrin. 11 Vols.

POLYBIUS. W. R. Paton. 6 Vols.

PROCOPIUS: HISTORY OF THE WARS. H. B. Dewing. 7 Vols.

PTOLEMY: TETRABIBLOS Cf. MANETHO.

QUINTUS SMYRNAEUS. A S. Way. Verse trans

SEXTUS EMPIRICUS. Rev. R. G. Bury. 4 Vols.

SOPHOCLES. F. Storr. 2 Vols. Verse trans.

STRABO: GEOGRAPHY. Horace L. Jones. 8 Vols.

THEOPHRASTUS: CHARACTERS. J. M. Edmonds. HERODES, etc. A. D. Knox.

THEOPHRASTUS: ENQUIRY INTO PLANTS. Sir Arthur Hort, Bart. 2 Vols.

THUCYDIDES. C. F. Smith. 4 Vols.

TRYPHIODORUS. Cf. OPPIAN.

XENOPHON: CYROPAEDIA. Walter Miller. 2 Vols.

XENOPHON: HELLENICA, ANABASIS, APOLOGY, and SYMPOSIUM. C. L. Brownson and O J. Todd. 3 Vols.

XENOPHON: MEMORABILIA and OECONOMICUS. E. C. Marchant.

XENOPHON: SCRIPTA MINORA. E. C. Marchant.

IN PREPARATION

Greek Authors

ARISTOTLE: HISTORY OF ANIMALS. A. L. Peck.

PLOTINUS: A. H. Armstrong.

Latin Authors

BABRIUS AND PHAEDRUS. Ben E. Perry.

DESCRIPTIVE PROSPECTUS ON APPLICATION

London WILLIAM HEINEMANN LTD
Cambridge, Mass. HARVARD UNIVERSITY PRESS

CPSIA information can be obtained at www.ICGtesting.com
Printed in the USA
BVOW01s1329171014

371243BV00014B/283/P

9 781293 458570